# THE COMPLETE KETO COOKBOOK WITH EASY RECIPES FOR BEGINNERS

## 600 Ketogenic Diet Recipes To Lose Weight Quick and Easy 2019-2020

Written by: Amanda Klein

# CONTENTS

# INTRODUCTION

Doubtless, every person must eat in order to exist. However, eating simply to keep life in the body is not enough for the human race. Our body must be supplied with an adequate amount of essential nutrients that are needed for its growth, cell regeneration, and working power. What kind of food should we eat to supply our cells with the necessary building material? There is a jungle of information out there, so knowing what constitutes a healthy diet can be a tricky part of your food intake. Almost everyone agrees that a well-balanced diet is the key factor that contributes to a healthy and productive lifestyle. In other words, you should eat all major types of nutrients: protein, carbohydrates, and fats.

Furthermore, the cooking of food is another important factor in creating a well-balanced and healthy diet. Many studies have shown that people who regularly cook at home are more likely to meet dietary guidelines. When you follow a special dietary regimen and you have to track your nutrient intake, cooking at home is the best choice. If you follow a ketogenic diet, the right cookbook is exactly what you need.

# Basic Keto Diet Rules

A ketogenic diet is a low-carb, adequate-protein, and high-fat eating plan. The main goal of a ketogenic diet is to get into a state of ketosis. If you want to reach ketosis, you should avoid eating carbs; just keep your carb intake between 20 to 50 grams of net carbs per day. It means the fewer carbs you eat, the more effective results you get. When your body is in a fat-burning mode, it makes ketones to provide energy. In this way, your body burns fats rather than carbs and you will stay healthy and lose weight naturally. Foods recommended on a ketogenic diet include:

- **Meat (preferably grass fed)** – pastured poultry, pork, beef, goat, and veal.
- **Fish & Seafood** – catfish, tuna, haddock, salmon, shrimp, crab, etc.
- **Non-starchy vegetables** – broccoli, greens, celery, onions, leeks, cauliflower, cabbage, green beans, peppers, tomato, mushrooms, asparagus, and Brussels sprouts.
- **Dairy products** – whole milk, sour cream, heavy cream, unsweetened yogurt, cheese, kefir, and butter.
- **Eggs**
- **Fats & Oils** – olive oil, flaxseed oil, coconut oil peanut butter, and sesame oil.
- **Sweeteners** – Splenda, monk fruit powder, xylitol, erythritol, stevia, and yacon sweetener.
- **Nuts and seeds** – walnuts, almonds, macadamia nuts, sesame, sunflower, and pumpkin.
- **Fruits** – berries, apples, watermelon, peaches and avocado.
- **Condiments** – soy sauce, coconut aminos, mustard, pickles, fermented foods, vinegar, mayonnaise, and homemade sauces.
- **Fermented soy products**
- **All kinds of spices and herbs**
- **Beverages** – coffee, tea, lemonade

Foods to avoid on a ketogenic diet include rice, grains, beans, starchy fruits, root vegetables processed food, and sugar. There are foods that are strictly off-limits and food that you can eat in moderation. With this in mind, you can easily start the ketogenic diet and achieve great results. "When a person goes on a keto diet, they lose a lot of weight. That's just what happens," says the New York City–based dietitian Kristen Mancinelli, RD.

Many surprising benefits come from a diet that focuses on a variety of wholesome, all-natural Ingredients and low-carb foods. Healthy food choices lead to a healthy lifestyle that is free of stress, obesity and diseases. Certain studies tend to show that you can lose your weight and significantly improve the quality of your life on a keto diet. A ketogenic diet helps in treating and controlling diabetes, hyperglycemia, and Alzheimer's disease. It can also boost your mood naturally and improves your heart health.

This dietary regimen may help reduce the risk of cancer as a suitable complementary treatment to chemotherapy and radiation.

A well-balanced diet and healthy food choices are key factors that contribute to your health and overall well-being. Ketogenic diet and meal prep go hand in hand because cooking homemade meals helps you limit processed foods and refined carbs. It is more about good eating habits rather than following strict dietary rules.

# Top Five Benefits of a Keto Diet

**1) A genius way to regulate hunger and satiety while losing weight in the process** – When you avoid carbs, your body start burning stored fat as the primary energy source. It will automatically cause weight loss.

**2) Increased energy** – You will also have more energy because your body

breaks down fat instead of carbs. If you observe an energy content of nutrients, you can see that carbohydrates contain 4 calories in each gram. A gram of protein provides 4 calories too, but a gram of fat contains even 9 calories.

**3) Mental clarity** – Due to the reduction of glucose, your brain starts using ketones as fuel, and the level of toxins decreases. It will improve your concentration and increase your productivity.

**4) A natural way to lower your triglycerides** – As you probably already know, your body converts excess calories into triglycerides and they are stored in your fat cells.

Increasing an intake of unsaturated fats automatically leads to a reduction in blood triglyceride levels. Unsaturated fat-packed foods are nuts, seeds, avocado, vegetable oils, and peanut butter.

Fatty fish such as salmon, mackerel, tuna, herring, and sardines are well known for their ability to lower triglycerides. Experts recommend eating fatty fish once or twice a week because it can reduce the risk of stroke.

**5) Reduced insulin levels** – When you eat carbohydrates, they are broken down into glucose (a type of blood sugar). High blood sugars are toxic and your body starts producing insulin as a response; it actually elevates your blood sugar levels. Insulin is responsible for bringing the glucose into your cells so your body will use it as energy. When there's too much glucose, insulin stimulates your liver to store excess glucose for later use. From the above, it is clear that cutting out carbs can lower blood sugar and insulin levels.

# A Few Tips and Tricks for Success with a Ketogenic Diet

**1) Keep it simple** – If you have little time but you want to prepare keto meals for you and your family, you can still succeed. This recipe collection is chock-full of recipes that take 15 minutes or less to prepare. In addition, you can watch your carbohydrate intake because every recipe includes nutritional information. As a matter of fact, the ketogenic diet requires a little pre-planning to ensure you're making healthy choices during your diet. Stock your pantry with products that will help you stay on track with your weight loss goals. Don't be confused by all these fancy-schmancy products. Simply purchase real foods which are listed in the table below. A well-stocked pantry is a must while reducing your favorite carbohydrates, especially sugars.

**2) Go at your own pace** – If you are feeling a little overwhelmed, stop, take a deep breath, and learn to listen to your body. Make your own meal plan and set your own weight loss goals. Everyone is different, even people of the same weight can have very different Basal Metabolic Rate (BMR). Stop comparing yourself to others.

Do you have a few excess pounds? Who cares? You are beautiful just the way you are. Always be yourself, be unique and watch what happens. Consequently, from a "big picture" standpoint, you will start losing your weight.

When it comes to the ketogenic diet, bear in mind that it is a journey, not a final destination, it should be an enjoyable lifestyle, not struggling and starving.

**3) Get regular exercise** – Many studies have shown that there is a link between regular exercise and happiness! Doubtless, exercise burns calories, boosts your metabolism and helps release toxins. Find an activity that fits into your lifestyle, whatever it is – running, jogging, walking, stair climbing or something else.

**4) Stay hydrated** – Drinking enough water will speed up your metabolism. It may sound cliché but it is an undeniable fact. Moreover, you should be drinking more water on a keto diet so those eight glasses of water are not enough. When you are in ketosis, your body loses more water in the form of urine. Therefore, reach for soups, full-fat yogurt and smoothies. If you have a hard time drinking water, add a few drops of lemon to it. Besides that, you should replenish your electrolytes by consuming homemade bone broth.

# Easy Ketogenic Cooking

"The only real stumbling block is fear of failure. In cooking, you've got to have a what-the-hell attitude."
— Julia Child

Food and cooking are extremely important parts of different cultures all over the world. Although people have been cooking from ancient time, a modern cooking is a form of art that is constantly revamping itself with new techniques and diet regimens.

Cooking at home requires skills, willingness and confidence, but this is one of the most important things you can do for your health. Starting is the hardest part of anything, but it's easy to turn cooking at home into a habit. These recipes contain the Ingredients that are available everywhere and are quick to prepare. You will explore 100 of the best keto recipes ever! Once you get the hang of it, you can experiment and come up with your own flavors.

The recipes presented in this cookbook are diverse, starting from traditional, classic dishes, to contemporary innovations. Hence, here you would be having simple soups and dipping sauce, along with more complicated casseroles and desserts. This recipe collection is comprehensive enough to teach anyone about keto diet. Regardless of whether you are a newbie or not, these recipes will make their way to your table with results that satisfy. Do not forget to add a heaping spoonful of love to every recipe!

# VEGETABLES & SIDE DISHES

## 1.Broccoli and Baby Bella Mushrooms Delight

**(Ready in about 20 minutes | Servings 4)**

**Per serving: 235 Calories; 20.9g Fat; 4.5g Carbs; 4.8g Protein;**

### INGREDIENTS

1/2 stick butter, room temperature
1/2 head broccoli, cut into small florets
10 ounces baby Bella mushrooms
1 teaspoon garlic, minced
1/3 cup chicken broth
1/3 cup whipping cream

1 teaspoon tarragon
1/2 teaspoon kosher salt, or more to taste
1/4 teaspoon crushed red pepper flakes
2 tablespoons Parmesan cheese
1/4 cup mayonnaise, preferably homemade

### DIRECTIONS

Melt the butter in a skillet that is preheated over a moderate flame. Now, add the broccoli and mushrooms and cook until the mushrooms are slightly shriveled.
Add the garlic and continue cooking until fragrant, stirring constantly.
Add the broth, whipping cream and seasonings; cover with the lid and reduce the heat to medium-low. Cook an additional 10 minutes, stirring occasionally, until most of the liquid has evaporated.
Stir the Parmesan cheese into the mushroom mixture until everything comes together. Plate and serve with mayo. Enjoy!

## 2. Roasted Turnips and Bell Peppers

**(Ready in about 35 minutes | Servings 6)**

**Per serving: 137 Calories; 11.1g Fat; 3.1g Carbs; 1.2g Protein;**

### INGREDIENTS

1 ½ pounds turnips, cut into wedges
1 bell pepper, sliced
1 fresh jalapeño, minced
3 tablespoons ghee, cubed
1 teaspoon dried marjoram
1 onion, thinly sliced

1 garlic clove, minced
2 tablespoons olive oil
1 teaspoon salt
1/2 teaspoon freshly ground black pepper
1/2 teaspoon cayenne pepper

### DIRECTIONS

Begin by preheating an oven to 425 degrees F. Lightly grease a baking dish with a nonstick cooking spray.
Toss the turnips and bell peppers with the remaining ingredients.
Roast the turnips and peppers for 25 to 35 or until they're softened. Taste, adjust the seasoning and serve warm. Bon appétit!

## 3. Paprika Mushrooms with Coconut Flour Naan

**(Ready in about 20 minutes | Servings 6)**

**Per serving: 281 Calories; 21.4g Fat; 6.1g Carbs; 6.4g Protein;**

### INGREDIENTS

3/4 cup coconut flour
1/2 teaspoon baking powder
2 tablespoons psyllium powder
A pinch of salt
8 tablespoons coconut oil, melted

1 egg plus 1 egg yolk, beaten
1 pound cremini mushrooms, thinly sliced
1 teaspoon kosher salt
1 teaspoon smoked paprika

### DIRECTIONS

In a mixing bowl, combine the coconut flour with the baking powder, psyllium and salt; mix to combine well.
Add 6 tablespoons of coconut oil, egg and egg yolk; add the hot water to form a dough; let it rest for 10 minutes at room temperature.
Now, divide the dough into 6 balls; flatten the balls on a working surface.
Heat up a pan with 1 tablespoon of coconut oil over a medium-high flame. Fry the naan breads until they are golden.
Then, heat the remaining 1 tablespoon of coconut oil in a nonstick skillet. Sauté the mushrooms until tender and fragrant; season with kosher salt and paprika.
Serve with the naan and enjoy!

# 4. Zoodles with Mushroom Sauce

**(Ready in about 15 minutes | Servings 4)**

**Per serving: 85 Calories; 3.5g Fat; 6.4g Carbs; 5.8g Protein;**

## INGREDIENTS

2 zucchinis
2 tablespoons avocado oil
1 tablespoon shallots, minced
1 teaspoon garlic, minced
1 pound mushrooms, chopped

2 ripe tomatoes, chopped
1 cup chicken stock
1 teaspoon dried basil
1/2 teaspoon dried oregano
1/4 teaspoon chili powder

## DIRECTIONS

Firstly, cut off the ends of each zucchini. Make the zucchini noodles by using your spiralizer, a julienne peeler or mandoline.
Now, bring a pot of lightly salted water to a boil; cook your zucchini noodles for one minute. Reserve.
In the meantime, heat the avocado oil in a large-sized pan over a moderate flame. Cook the shallot and garlic for 2 minutes. Add the mushrooms and cook an additional 3 minutes.
Now, stir in the remaining ingredients; cover the pot and bring the mixture to a simmer over a medium-low heat. Cook until everything is warmed through.
Top your zoodles with the prepared mushroom sauce and serve immediately. Enjoy!

# 5. Kohlrabi with Thick Mushroom Sauce

**(Ready in about 25 minutes | Servings 4)**

**Per serving: 220 Calories; 20g Fat; 5.3g Carbs; 4g Protein;**

## INGREDIENTS

3/4 pound kohlrabi, trimmed and thinly sliced
3 tablespoons butter
1/2 pound mushrooms, sliced
1/2 cup scallions, chopped
1 garlic clove, minced

1 teaspoon sea salt
1/2 teaspoon ground black pepper
1/4 teaspoon red pepper flakes
1 ½ cups double cream

## DIRECTIONS

Parboil the kohlrabi in a large pot of salted water for 7 to 9 minutes. Drain and set aside.
Warm the butter over medium-high heat. Sauté the mushrooms, scallions, and garlic until tender and fragrant.
Season with salt, black pepper, and red pepper flakes.
Slowly stir in the double cream, whisking continuously until the sauce has thickened, about 8 to 12 minutes.
Pour the mushroom sauce over the kohlrabi and serve warm.

# 6. Spinach and Strawberry Salad

**(Ready in about 10 minutes | Servings 4)**

**Per serving: 190 Calories; 17.6g Fat; 4.6g Carbs; 4.3g Protein;**

## INGREDIENTS

4 cups baby spinach
1/2 cup strawberries, hulled and sliced
1 cup avocado, pitted, peeled and sliced
2 tablespoons olive oil
1/2 lime, freshly squeezed

1/2 teaspoon kosher salt
White pepper, to taste
1/3 cup brie cheese, crumbled
2 tablespoons fresh basil leaves, chopped

## DIRECTIONS

Pat the spinach leaves dry and transfer them to a salad bowl.
Add the slices of strawberries and avocado.
Now, make the dressing by whisking the olive oil, lime juice, salt and white pepper. Dress the salad and top with the crumbled cheese.
Serve garnished with fresh basil leaves. Bon appétit!

# 7. The Best Family Squash Stew

**(Ready in about 35 minutes | Servings 6)**

**Per serving: 113 Calories; 7.9g Fat; 3.7g Carbs; 2.8g Protein;**

## INGREDIENTS

1/2 stick butter
2 shallots, chopped
1 teaspoon garlic, finely chopped
6 ounces butternut squash, chopped
1 celery, chopped
2 tablespoons fresh cilantro, roughly chopped
1/2 teaspoon sea salt

1/4 teaspoon ground black pepper, or more to the taste
1/4 teaspoon smoked paprika, or more to the taste
1/2 teaspoon chili powder
1 pound ripe tomatoes, chopped
2 tablespoons red wine
1 bay leaf

## DIRECTIONS

Melt the butter in a stock pot over a moderate heat. Now, sauté the shallots and garlic until fragrant, about 4 minutes.
Add the eggplant, celery and cilantro; cook an additional 5 minutes.
Stir in the remaining ingredients; reduce the heat to a medium-low and let it simmer, covered, for 20 to 25 minutes.
Serve with cauliflower mash. Bon appétit!

# 8. Japanese-Style Enoki Mushrooms with Sesame Seeds

**(Ready in about 15 minutes | Servings 3)**

**Per serving: 103 Calories; 6.7g Fat; 5.9g Carbs; 2.7g Protein;**

## INGREDIENTS

1 ½ tablespoons ghee, room temperature
1 cup scallions
2 cloves garlic, smashed
1 (7-ounce) package Enoki mushrooms, trim away about
1-inch of the root section

1/2 teaspoon salt
1/2 teaspoon Sansho Japanese pepper
1/2 teaspoon wasabi powder
2 teaspoons oyster sauce
1 tablespoon black sesame seeds

## DIRECTIONS

Melt the ghee in a wok over a moderately high heat. Now, sauté the scallions and garlic for 5 minutes, until they are softened.
Stir in the mushrooms and cook an additional 4 minutes. Remove from the heat. Season with salt, Japanese pepper, and wasabi powder.
Afterwards, add the oyster sauce and stir to combine well. Garnish with toasted sesame seed and eat warm.

# 9. Classic Creamy Cauliflower Soup

**(Ready in about 20 minutes | Servings 4)**

**Per serving: 260 Calories; 22.5g Fat; 4.1g Carbs; 7.2g Protein;**

## INGREDIENTS

3 cups chicken broth
3 cups cauliflower, cut into florets
1 cup almond milk, unsweetened
1 cup avocado, pitted and chopped

1/4 teaspoon Himalayan rock salt
1/4 teaspoon freshly cracked mixed peppercorns
1 bay leaf

## DIRECTIONS

Simmer the chicken broth over a moderate flame. Add the cauliflower and cook for 10 minutes.
Turn the heat to low. Add the remaining ingredients and cook for a further 5 minutes.
Puree the mixture using an immersion blender. Bon appétit!

# 10. Grilled Zucchini with Herbed Sauce

**(Ready in about 15 minutes | Servings 4)**

**Per serving: 132 Calories; 11.1g Fat; 4.1g Carbs; 3.1g Protein;**

## INGREDIENTS

1 pound zucchini, cut lengthwise into quarters
1/4 cup avocado oil
1 teaspoon granulated garlic
1/2 teaspoon cayenne pepper
Salt, to taste

**For the Sauce:**
3/4 cup sour cream
1 tablespoon fresh cilantro, chopped
1 teaspoon fresh rosemary, finely chopped

## DIRECTIONS

Start by preheating your grill to a medium-low heat.
Drizzle the zucchini slices with the avocado oil. Sprinkle with garlic, cayenne pepper and salt.
Place your zucchini on a lightly-greased grill. Grill your zucchini about 5 minutes per side or until they are tender and slightly browned.
Meanwhile, make the sauce by mixing all of the sauce ingredients. Serve warm with the sauce on the side.

# 11. Buttery Mixed Greens with Cheese

**(Ready in about 25 minutes | Servings 5)**

**Per serving: 160 Calories; 10g Fat; 5.1g Carbs; 11g Protein;**

## INGREDIENTS

1 tablespoon butter
2 garlic cloves, chopped
1 bunch of scallions
2 pounds mixed greens, trimmed and torn into pieces
1/4 cup chicken broth

1 tablespoon apple cider vinegar
1 teaspoon cayenne pepper
1/2 teaspoon salt
1/4 teaspoon black pepper
1 cup Colby cheese, shredded

## DIRECTIONS

Melt the butter in a large pan over a moderately high heat. Sauté the garlic and scallions about 2 minutes or until tender and aromatic.
Stir in the mixed greens and chicken broth; continue to cook until the leaves are wilted and all the liquid has evaporated, about 13 minutes.
Now, add the apple cider vinegar, cayenne pepper, salt and black pepper. Remove from the heat.
Sprinkle with the shredded cheese and serve immediately. Bon appétit!

# 12. Cheesy Broccoli Casserole

**(Ready in about 25 minutes | Servings 3)**

**Per serving: 195 Calories; 12.7g Fat; 6.7g Carbs; 11.6g Protein;**

## INGREDIENTS

3 tablespoons avocado oil
1 shallot, minced
1/2 teaspoon garlic, minced
1 head broccoli, cut into small florets
3 eggs, well-beaten

1/2 cup half-and-half
1/2 teaspoon dried basil
1/2 teaspoon turmeric powder
Kosher salt and cayenne pepper, to taste
2 ounces Monterey Jack cheese, shredded

## DIRECTIONS

Preheat your oven to 310 degrees F.
Melt the avocado oil in a pan over a moderate heat. Now, sauté the shallots and garlic for a few minutes. Stir in the broccoli florets and cook until they're tender. Transfer the mixture to a lightly greased casserole dish.
In a separate mixing bowl, combine the eggs with the half-and-half, basil, turmeric, salt and cayenne pepper.
Pour the egg mixture over the broccoli mixture. Bake for 20 minutes or until set. Check the temperature with an instant-read food thermometer. Serve warm topped with cheese.

# 13. Family Vegetable Bake

**(Ready in about 1 hour | Servings 4)**

**Per serving: 159 Calories; 10.4g Fat; 5.7g Carbs; 6.4g Protein;**

## INGREDIENTS

1 large eggplant, cut into thick slices
1 tomato, diced
1/2 garlic head, crushed
1 medium-sized leek, sliced
1 celery, peeled and diced

1 Habanero pepper, minced
1 teaspoon Taco seasoning mix
2 tablespoons extra-virgin olive oil
1 tablespoon fresh sage leaves, chopped
1/3 cup Parmigiano-Reggiano cheese, shredded

## DIRECTIONS

Place the eggplant in a medium-sized bowl; sprinkle with salt and let it stand for 30 minutes; now, drain and rinse the eggplant slices.
Meanwhile, preheat your oven to 345 degrees F. Spritz a casserole dish with a nonstick cooking spray.
Mix the vegetables along with the seasoning, olive oil, and sage in the prepared casserole dish.
Roast the vegetables approximately 20 minutes. Scatter shredded cheese over the top and bake an additional 10 minutes. Serve right away!

# 14. Easy and Yummy Cabbage with Bacon

**(Ready in about 20 minutes | Servings 6)**

**Per serving: 259 Calories; 18.1g Fat; 3.6g Carbs; 15.5g Protein;**

## INGREDIENTS

1 tablespoon lard
1 large-sized head of red cabbage, shredded
1 carrot, finely chopped
1/2 pound bacon, chopped

1 bouillon cube
1/2 cup water
1/2 teaspoon cayenne pepper

## DIRECTIONS

Melt the lard in a pan that is preheated over a moderate heat. Now, cook the cabbage and carrot until they are tender,
Add the remaining ingredients, reduce the heat to a medium-low and cover the pan. Let it simmer for 10 minutes more.
Taste, adjust the seasonings, and serve right away!

# 15. Ground Turkey and Cheese Stuffed Tomatoes

**(Ready in about 25 minutes | Servings 4)**

**Per serving: 413 Calories; 28.2g Fat; 2.8g Carbs; 35.2g Protein;**

## INGREDIENTS

4 tomatoes
1 tablespoon olive oil
1/2 pound ground turkey
1/2 cup scallions, chopped
1 garlic clove, smashed
1 tablespoon fresh parsley, chopped

1 teaspoon fresh rosemary, chopped
Seasoned salt and ground black pepper, to taste
1 cup Monterey Jack cheese, shredded
1 cup Romano cheese, freshly grated
1/2 cup chicken stock

## DIRECTIONS

Slice the top off of each tomato. Discard the hard cores and scoop out the pulp from the tomatoes with a small metal spoon.
Now, heat the oil in a cast-iron skillet that is preheated over a moderately high heat. Brown the turkey meat for 3 to 4 minutes; reserve.
In the same skillet, sauté the scallions and garlic until they are just tender, about 4 minutes. Add the reserved beef and tomato pulp; sprinkle with fresh parsley, rosemary, salt, and pepper.
Arrange the tomatoes in a casserole dish. Divide the stuffing among the tomatoes and top with cheese.
Pour the chicken stock around the tomatoes and bake in the middle of the preheated oven at 360 degrees F, approximately 18 minutes. Bon appétit!

# 16. Refreshing and Nutty Spring Salad

**(Ready in about 5 minutes | Servings 4)**

**Per serving: 184 Calories; 16.8g Fat; 4g Carbs; 2.1g Protein;**

## INGREDIENTS

1 medium-sized head lettuce, torn into bite-sized pieces
1/2 pound cucumber, thinly sliced
1 large-sized carrot, grated
1 cup radishes, thinly sliced
2 spring onions, sliced
1 ounce macadamia nuts, chopped

1/2 lime, freshly squeezed
3 tablespoons peanut oil
1 teaspoon chili sauce, sugar-free
1/2 teaspoon red pepper flakes, crushed
Coarse salt, to taste
1 tablespoon sesame seeds, lightly toasted

## DIRECTIONS

Add the vegetables along with the macadamia nuts to a large salad bowl. Toss to combine.
In a small mixing dish, thoroughly whisk the lime juice, peanut oil, chili sauce, red pepper and salt.
Dress the salad and serve sprinkled with toasted sesame seeds.

# 17. Spicy Cremini Mushroom Stew

**(Ready in about 30 minutes | Servings 4)**

**Per serving: 133 Calories; 3.7g Fat; 5.7g Carbs; 14g Protein;**

## INGREDIENTS

1 tablespoon olive oil
1 cup shallots, chopped
1 teaspoon chili pepper, finely minced
1 teaspoon garlic, minced
1 celery, chopped
2 carrots, chopped
1/2 pound Cremini mushrooms, chopped
2 ½ cups bone broth, low-sodium
1/4 cup dry white wine

1/2 cup water
2 ripe tomatoes, crushed
Salt and ground black pepper, to taste
1/4 teaspoon ground ginger
1/2 teaspoon ground allspice
1/4 teaspoon ground cinnamon
2 bay leaves
1/2 cup fresh basil, chopped

## DIRECTIONS

Heat the oil in a large heavy pot that is preheated over a moderate flame. Now, sweat the shallots, peppers, garlic, celery, carrots, and mushrooms approximately 8 minutes.
Add the broth, tomatoes, and seasonings, except for the basil; bring to a boil. Now, turn the heat to medium and let it simmer for 18 minutes, stirring periodically.
Serve in individual bowls, garnished with fresh basil leaves. Bon appétit!

# 18. Sour Cream Cabbage Soup

**(Ready in about 25 minutes | Servings 4)**

**Per serving: 185 Calories; 16.6g Fat; 2.4g Carbs; 2.9g Protein;**

## INGREDIENTS

1 ½ tablespoons butter, melted
1 leek, chopped
2 garlic cloves, minced
2 carrots, chopped
1 cup cabbage, shredded

1 green pepper, chopped
4 cups water
2 bouillon cubes
1 cup sour cream
Fresh tarragon sprigs, for garnish

## DIRECTIONS

Warm the butter in a large pot over a medium flame. Sauté the leeks until just tender and fragrant. Now, add the remaining vegetables and cook for 5 to 7 minutes, stirring periodically.
Add the water and bouillon cubes; cover partially and cook an additional 13 minutes.
Blend the mixture until creamy, uniform and smooth. Stir in the sour cream; gently heat, stirring continuously, until your soup is hot.
Ladle into individual bowls and serve garnished with fresh tarragon. Bon appétit!

# 19. Vegetables à la Grecque

**(Ready in about 15 minutes | Servings 4)**

**Per serving: 318 Calories; 24.3g Fat; 5.1g Carbs; 15.4g Protein;**

## INGREDIENTS

2 tablespoons olive oil
2 garlic cloves, minced
1/2 cup red onion, chopped
1/2 pound button mushrooms, chopped
1 cup cauliflower, cut into small florets
1 medium-sized eggplant, chopped
1 teaspoon dried basil

1 teaspoon dried oregano
1 rosemary sprig, leaves picked
1 thyme sprig, leaves picked
1/2 cup tomato sauce
1/4 cup dry white wine
8 ounces Halloumi cheese, cubed

## DIRECTIONS

Heat the olive oil in a saucepan over a moderately high heat. Now, sauté the garlic for 1 to 1½ minutes.

Now, stir in the onion, mushrooms, cauliflower, and eggplant; cook an additional 5 minutes, stirring periodically.

Add the seasonings, tomato sauce, and wine; continue to cook for 4 more minutes. Remove from the heat and divide among individual plates.

Serve topped with Halloumi cheese and enjoy!

# 20. Roasted Asparagus with Feta Cheese

**(Ready in about 15 minutes | Servings 6)**

**Per serving: 128 Calories; 9.4g Fat; 2.9g Carbs; 6.4g Protein;**

## INGREDIENTS

1 ½ pounds asparagus spears
2 tablespoons butter, melted
2 green onions, chopped
2 garlic cloves, minced

Salt and black pepper, to the taste
1 cup feta cheese, crumbled
1/2 cup fresh parsley, roughly chopped

## DIRECTIONS

Preheat an oven to 420 degrees F.

Drizzle the asparagus with the melted butter. Toss with the green onions, garlic, salt, and black pepper.

Place the asparagus on a lightly-greased baking pan in a single layer. Roast for about 14 minutes.

Scatter the crumbled feta over the warm asparagus spears. Serve garnished with fresh parsley.

# 21. Chinese Cabbage Stir-Fry

**(Ready in about 15 minutes | Servings 4)**

**Per serving: 53 Calories; 3.7g Fat; 3.2g Carbs; 1.7g Protein;**

## INGREDIENTS

1 tablespoon sesame oil
2 spring onions, sliced
3/4 pound Chinese cabbage, cored and cut into chunks
1/2 teaspoon ground cumin
Salt, to taste
1/4 teaspoon rougui (Chinese cinnamon)

1/2 teaspoon fennel seeds
1/2 teaspoon Sichuan peppercorns, crushed
1 tablespoon tamari sauce
1/2 teaspoon chili sauce, sugar-free
2 tablespoons Chardonnay
1 tablespoon oyster sauce

## DIRECTIONS

Heat the oil in a pan over a medium-high heat. Now, sauté the spring onions until translucent. Now, add the Chinese cabbage and seasonings.

Cook about 3 minutes or until the cabbage leaves are wilted. Add the tamari sauce, chili sauce, and Chardonnay; cook for a further 4 minutes, stirring often.

Stir in the oyster sauce and cook an additional minute. Serve warm in individual serving bowls.

# 22. Creamy and Easy Greek-Style Salad

**(Ready in about 15 minutes + chilling time | Servings 4)**

**Per serving: 318 Calories; 24.3g Fat; 4.1g Carbs; 15.4g Protein;**

## INGREDIENTS

1 cup Greek-style yogurt
1 teaspoon garlic, minced
1 tablespoon fresh lime juice
1 teaspoon fresh or dried rosemary, minced
2 green onions, thinly sliced

4 cucumbers, sliced
6 radishes, sliced
Sea salt and ground black pepper, to taste
4 Boston lettuce leaves

## DIRECTIONS

In a mixing bowl, thoroughly whisk the Greek-style yogurt, garlic, lime juice and rosemary.
Toss the green onions, cucumbers, and radishes with prepared yogurt dressing; season with salt and pepper to taste and toss to coat well.
Divide the Boston lettuce leaves among four serving plates. Mound well-chilled salad onto each lettuce leaf and serve. Bon appétit!

# 23. Coleslaw with Sunflower Seeds

**(Ready in about 10 minutes + chilling time | Servings 4)**

**Per serving: 242 Calories; 20.5g Fat; 6.2g Carbs; 1g Protein;**

## INGREDIENTS

3/4 pound Napa cabbage, cored and shredded
1 large-sized carrot, shredded
1 cup mayonnaise
1 teaspoon coarse ground mustard
1/2 cup fresh parsley leaves, loosely packed and coarsely

chopped
1 teaspoon celery seeds
Salt and ground pepper, to taste
2 tablespoons sunflower seeds

## DIRECTIONS

Add the cabbage and carrots to your salad bowl. Now, stir in the mayonnaise, mustard, parsley, celery seeds, salt, and pepper.
Gently stir to combine all ingredients. Allow it to sit for 3 hours in the refrigerator. Serve sprinkled with sunflower seeds.

# 24. Spicy Vegetarian Delight

**(Ready in about 15 minutes | Servings 4)**

**Per serving: 290 Calories; 21.7g Fat; 6.5g Carbs; 10.6g Protein;**

## INGREDIENTS

2 tablespoons olive oil
2 small-sized shallots, chopped
1 garlic clove, minced
1 pound cremini mushroom, sliced
1/2 teaspoon salt

1/2 teaspoon ground black pepper
1 cup tomatillo, chopped
4 eggs
1/4 cup enchilada sauce
1 medium-sized avocado, pitted and mashed

## DIRECTIONS

Heat the olive oil in a saucepan over a moderate flame. Now, cook the shallot and garlic until just tender and fragrant.
Now, add the mushrooms and stir until they're tender. Season with salt and pepper; stir in the chopped tomatillo.
Stir in the eggs and scramble them well. Top with the enchilada sauce; serve warm with avocado slices.

# 25. Cucumber and Cheese Balls

**(Ready in about 25 minutes | Servings 2)**

**Per serving: 133 Calories; 9.9g Fat; 6.8g Carbs; 6g Protein;**

## INGREDIENTS

1 ounce blue cheese
1 ounce Neufchatel
1 medium-sized cucumber, chopped

1 tablespoon fresh parsley, chopped
2 tablespoons walnuts, chopped

## DIRECTIONS

Drop the chopped cucumbers into a colander; sprinkle with a pinch of salt. Let it stand for 20 minutes in the sink; press your cucumber firmly to drain away the excess liquid.
Thoroughly mix the cheese, cucumber, and parsley in a bowl.
Shape into 4 balls and roll them in chopped walnuts. Refrigerate until ready to serve.

# 26. Yummy Oven-Roasted Asparagus

**(Ready in about 20 minutes | Servings 4)**

**Per serving: 48 Calories; 1.6g Fat; 4.4g Carbs; 5.5g Protein;**

## INGREDIENTS

1 pound asparagus spears
Salt and freshly ground black pepper, to your liking
1 teaspoon onion powder

1/4 teaspoon cumin powder
1/2 teaspoon dried thyme
4 tablespoons bacon bits

## DIRECTIONS

Start by preheating your oven to 460 degrees F.
Toss the asparagus spears with the salt, black pepper, onion powder, cumin powder, and thyme. Arrange them on a baking sheet.
Spritz with a nonstick cooking spray. Bake for 8 to 10 minutes; turn them over and bake an additional 8 minutes.
Serve garnished with bacon bits and enjoy!

# 27. Roasted Vegetables with Spicy Sour Cream Dip

**(Ready in about 45 minutes | Servings 4)**

**Per serving: 357 Calories; 35.8g Fat; 5.2g Carbs; 3.4g Protein;**

## INGREDIENTS

2 carrots, cut into sticks
1 celery stalk, cut into sticks
1 red bell pepper, sliced
1 green bell pepper, sliced
1 red onion, sliced into rings
1/4 cup olive oil
1 garlic clove, minced
1 tablespoon fresh parsley, minced
1/2 teaspoon paprika

For the Spicy Sour Cream Dip:
1 ½ cups sour cream
2 tablespoons mayonnaise
3/4 teaspoon Dijon mustard
1 jalapeño pepper, finely minced
1 tablespoon lime juice
Salt and black pepper, to taste
2 tablespoons sage leaves, chopped

## DIRECTIONS

Preheat your oven to 390 degrees F. Line a baking sheet with parchment paper.
In a mixing dish, toss the carrots, celery, bell pepper, onion, olive oil, garlic, parsley, and paprika.
Arrange the vegetables on the baking sheet and roast about 40 minutes; be sure to stir halfway through.
Combine all ingredients for the sour cream dip; whisk until everything is well incorporated. Serve with the roasted vegetables and enjoy!

## 28. Stuffed Chanterelles with Prosciutto

**(Ready in about 25 minutes | Servings 6)**

**Per serving: 98 Calories; 5.8g Fat; 3.9g Carbs; 8.4g Protein;**

### INGREDIENTS

6 medium-sized Chanterelles, stems removed
3 teaspoons sesame oil
1 tablespoon Worcestershire sauce
Coarse salt and ground black pepper, to your liking

3 slices of prosciutto, finely chopped
2 tablespoons fresh cilantro, minced
1 teaspoon fresh rosemary, minced
2 ounces Asiago cheese, grated

### DIRECTIONS

Start by preheating your oven to 355 degrees F. Line a baking sheet with a piece of parchment paper.
Rub the sesame oil and Worcestershire sauce on the mushroom caps. Season them with salt and pepper.
Now, combine the prosciutto, cilantro, rosemary and cheese; mix well. Stuff the mushroom caps and bake for 18 to 22 minutes.
Adjust the seasonings and serve immediately. Bon appétit!

## 29. Bell Pepper Casserole with Appenzeller

**(Ready in about 1 hour | Servings 4)**

**Per serving: 408 Calories; 28.9g Fat; 4.6g Carbs; 24.9g Protein;**

### INGREDIENTS

8 bell peppers
3/4 pound Appenzeller, shredded
2 red onions, thinly sliced
1 garlic clove, crushed

6 whole eggs
1/3 cup sour cream
Sea salt and ground black pepper, to taste
1 teaspoon smoked paprika

### DIRECTIONS

Preheat an oven to 470 degrees F. Arrange the peppers on a baking sheet in a single layer.
Bake the peppers in the preheated oven until the skins are browned and blackened, about 20 minutes.
Turn them over and bake another 10 to 15 minutes. Remove your peppers from the oven; cover with a plastic wrap and allow them to steam for 1 hour.
Then, remove the skins, stems, and seeds. Place 4 peppers in a lightly oiled casserole dish.
Top with half of the shredded Appenzeller; add a layer of sliced onions and crushed garlic. Place another layer of roasted peppers, followed by the remaining Appenzeller.
In a mixing dish, whisk the eggs with the sour cream, salt, pepper, and paprika. Pour the mixture over the peppers. Cover tightly with a piece of foil and bake about 20 minutes.
Next, remove the foil and bake another 20 minutes. Serve warm.

## 30. Sautéed Green Beans with Tapenade

**(Ready in about 15 minutes | Servings 4)**

**Per serving: 183 Calories; 16.1g Fat; 4.4g Carbs; 3.2g Protein;**

### INGREDIENTS

1 pound green beans
1 tablespoon sesame oil
1 celery stalk, shredded
1 garlic clove, smashed
1/2 teaspoon smoked paprika
Flaky sea salt and ground black pepper, to taste

**For Tapenade:**
1/2 cup Kalamata olives
1 ½ tablespoons capers
2 anchovy fillets
1 tablespoon fresh lemon juice
3 tablespoons extra-virgin olive oil

### DIRECTIONS

Put the green beans in a steamer basket over boiling water; steam approximately 4 minutes or until crisp-tender.
Heat the sesame oil in a sauté pan over a moderate flame. Add the celery and garlic; sauté an additional 4 minutes, stirring periodically.
Season with paprika, salt, and black pepper.
Puree all the ingredients for the tapenade in your food processor. Serve immediately with the sautéed green beans. Bon appétit!

# 31. Sautéed Spinach with Cottage Cheese

**(Ready in about 10 minutes | Servings 4)**

**Per serving: 208 Calories; 13.5g Fat; 6g Carbs; 14.5g Protein;**

## INGREDIENTS

1/2 stick butter
2 garlic cloves, minced
2 pounds spinach leaves, rinsed and torn into pieces
1 teaspoon salt

1/2 teaspoon cayenne pepper
1/4 teaspoon turmeric powder
1 cup cottage cheese

## DIRECTIONS

Melt the butter in a Dutch oven and sauté the garlic until it's just browned.
Add the spinach leaves, salt, cayenne pepper, and turmeric powder; cook another 2 to 3 minutes over a moderate heat, adding a splash of warm water if needed.
Next, turn the heat on high, and cook for 1 to 2 minutes more, stirring often. Taste and adjust the seasonings.
Serve topped with cottage cheese.

# 32. Sunday Vegetable Patties

**(Ready in about 15 minutes | Servings 6)**

**Per serving: 153 Calories; 11.8g Fat; 6.6g Carbs; 6.4g Protein;**

## INGREDIENTS

2 medium-sized zucchinis, shredded
2 carrots, shredded
1 small-sized celery stalk, shredded
2 tablespoons parsley, chopped

1 white onion, finely chopped
1 garlic clove, finely minced
1 cup cheddar cheese, grated
2 tablespoons olive oil

1 egg yolk
Salt and black pepper, to taste
Lemon wedges, to serve

## DIRECTIONS

Start by preheating your oven to 360 degrees F. Line a baking sheet with parchment paper.
Now, press the shredded vegetables firmly to drain away the excess liquid. Then, thoroughly combine all ingredients, except for the lemon wedges, in a mixing bowl.
Shape the mixture into 12 patties and bake for 5 minutes per side. Serve with fresh lemon wedges and enjoy!

# 33. Sautéed Broccoflower with Blue Cheese Sauce

**(Ready in about 30 minutes | Servings 6)**

**Per serving: 159 Calories; 12.3g Fat; 7.2g Carbs; 5.7g Protein;**

## INGREDIENTS

2 pounds broccoflower, trimmed and broken into small florets
1 ½ tablespoons sesame oil
2 green onions, chopped
2 garlic cloves, smashed
1/4 teaspoon curry powder

Flaky sea salt and freshly ground black pepper, to taste
1/2 teaspoon fresh ginger root, minced
1 tablespoon fresh cilantro, chopped

**For the Blue Cheese Sauce:**
1 ½ tablespoons ghee
1/3 cup double cream
1/2 cup blue cheese, crumbled
1/4 teaspoon freshly cracked mixed peppercorns

## DIRECTIONS

Place the broccoflower in a large pot of boiling water; parboil for 2 to 3 minutes. Drain well.
Heat the sesame oil in a sauté pan over a moderately high flame. Sweat the green onions for 2 minutes. Stir in the garlic and cook until fragrant, about 1 to 2 minutes.
Now, stir in the broccoflower along with the curry powder, salt, pepper, and ginger. Continue to sauté, stirring constantly, for 2 to 3 minutes.
Add a splash of water, cover and cook 6 minutes longer, or until it has softened.
Next, warm the ghee in a pan over a moderate heat. Add the cream and stir until thoroughly heated; now, fold in the blue cheese and freshly cracked peppercorns.
Stir until your cheese is completely melted. If it is too thick, pour in 1 to 2 tablespoons of water and stir to combine.
Serve garnished with fresh cilantro and the blue cheese sauce on the side. Bon appétit!

## 34. Slow-Roasted Cherry Tomatoes with Parmesan

**(Ready in about 25 minutes | Servings 4)**

**Per serving: 247 Calories; 19.8g Fat; 5.3g Carbs; 11g Protein;**

### INGREDIENTS

1 ½ pounds cherry tomatoes, halved
1/4 cup olive oil
1 tablespoon Worcestershire sauce
1 tablespoon white wine vinegar
1 teaspoon garlic, minced

Sea salt and freshly ground black pepper, to taste
1 spring of fresh rosemary, chopped
2 sprigs of fresh thyme, chopped
1 cup Parmesan cheese, freshly grated

### DIRECTIONS

Preheat the oven to 400 degrees F.
Place the tomatoes in a broiler-proof ceramic baking dish. Drizzle the tomatoes with olive oil Worcestershire sauce, and vinegar. Sprinkle with the garlic, salt, pepper, rosemary and thyme. Top with Parmesan cheese.
Roast for 20 to 22 minutes, until the tomatoes begin to caramelize but not split. Bon appétit!

## 35. Buttered Savoy Cabbage with Scallions

**(Ready in about 20 minutes | Servings 4)**

**Per serving: 142 Calories; 11.6g Fat; 5.7g Carbs; 2g Protein;**

### INGREDIENTS

1/2 stick butter, melted
1 bunch scallions, chopped
1 garlic clove, minced
1 pound Savoy cabbage, outer leaves discarded, cored and shredded
1 large-sized carrot, thinly sliced
1/4 teaspoon fresh ginger root, grated

1/2 teaspoon sea salt
1/2 teaspoon mixed peppercorns, freshly cracked
1/4 cup chicken stock
1 tablespoon dry white wine
1/3 teaspoon mustard seeds
A pinch of nutmeg

### DIRECTIONS

Melt the butter in a pan over a medium-high flame. Now, sauté the scallions and garlic until they're just tender and fragrant.
Stir in the cabbage, carrots, and ginger; cook for 10 minutes, stirring occasionally.
Add the remaining ingredients and cook an additional 5 minutes. Test to check if the Savoy cabbage is done to your liking. Enjoy!

## 36. Cabbage with Ham and Fried Eggs

**(Ready in about 15 minutes | Servings 4)**

**Per serving: 173 Calories; 10.6g Fat; 5.6g Carbs; 14.2g Protein;**

### INGREDIENTS

2 tablespoons bacon fat
1 cup spring onions, minced
1 garlic clove, minced
2 cups red cabbage, shredded
1 bay leaf

1/2 teaspoon salt
1/2 teaspoon ground black pepper
4 rashers of ham, chopped
2 teaspoons dry red wine
4 eggs

### DIRECTIONS

Heat 1 tablespoon of the bacon fat in a nonstick skillet over a moderate flame. Now, sauté the onions and garlic until just tender.
Then, add the cabbage and cook, stirring continuously, until tender or about 5 minutes. Add the bay leaf, salt, pepper and chopped ham.
Add the wine and cook an additional 3 minutes.
Heat the remaining 1 tablespoon of bacon fat in another skillet. Crack the eggs into another skillet and cook to the desired doneness.
Divide the prepared cabbage among four serving plates; top with the fried egg and serve immediately.

# 37. Colorful Vegetable and Broccoli Rice

**(Ready in about 20 minutes | Servings 4)**

**Per serving: 126 Calories; 11.6g Fat; 5.4g Carbs; 1.3g Protein;**

## INGREDIENTS

1 head broccoli, broken into florets
1/2 stick butter
1/2 yellow onion, chopped

1 garlic clove, minced
1 red bell pepper, chopped
1 Aji Fantasy chili pepper, minced

1/2 celery stalk, chopped
Salt and ground black pepper, to taste

## DIRECTIONS

Blitz the broccoli in your food processor until it has reached a rice-like texture.

Now, melt the butter in a sauté pan over a moderate heat. Sweat the yellow onion for 2 to 3 minutes; stir in the garlic and cook until slightly browned and fragrant.

After that, add the peppers and celery; cook an additional 4 minutes or until they're just tender. Add the broccoli "rice" and season with salt and pepper.

Cook for a further 5 minutes, stirring periodically. Serve warm and enjoy!

# 38. Bok Choy with Shrimp

**(Ready in about 15 minutes | Servings 4)**

**Per serving: 171 Calories; 8.4g Fat; 5.8g Carbs; 18.9g Protein;**

## INGREDIENTS

2 tablespoons sesame oil
2 garlic cloves, crushed
1 ½ pounds Bok choy, trimmed and thinly sliced
1 (1/2-inch) piece ginger, freshly grated

1 tablespoon oyster sauce
Salt and ground black pepper, to taste
1 teaspoon cayenne pepper
10 ounces shrimp, peeled and deveined

## DIRECTIONS

Heat 1 tablespoon of the sesame oil in a sauté pan over a moderate heat. Now, cook the garlic until it is just browned.

Stir in the Bok choy and ginger. Add the oyster sauce, salt, black pepper and cayenne pepper. Cook for 5 minutes, gently stirring. Transfer to a serving platter and reserve.

Now, heat the remaining tablespoon of sesame oil in a clean sauté pan. Cook the shrimp, stirring periodically, until they are just pink and opaque, about 3 minutes.

Serve with the reserved Bok choy, garnished with lemon wedges.

# 39. Spring Artichoke Salad with Feta Cheese

**(Ready in about 25 minutes | Servings 6)**

**Per serving: 146 Calories; 9.4g Fat; 6.1g Carbs; 5.8g Protein;**

## INGREDIENTS

2 tablespoons extra-virgin olive oil
3 artichoke hearts, defrosted
1 teaspoon coarse salt
1/2 teaspoon freshly ground black pepper
1 cup white onions, peeled and finely chopped

2 tablespoons lime juice, freshly squeezed
1 ½ teaspoons brown mustard
3 tablespoons champagne vinegar
1/2 pint grape tomatoes
1/3 cup baby green oak lettuce
1/3 cup red Swiss chard
1/3 cup arugula

1/3 cup butter lettuce
3 tablespoons capers, drained
1 roasted poblano pepper, sliced thin
1/2 teaspoon dried basil
2 ounces Kalamata olives, pitted and sliced
4 ounces feta cheese, crumbled

## DIRECTIONS

Start by preheating your oven to 350 degrees F. Line a baking sheet with parchment paper or a silicone mat.

Arrange the artichoke hearts on the prepared sheet pan and drizzle with olive oil. Season your artichokes with the salt and pepper and roast for 18 to 23 minutes.

In the meantime, thoroughly combine the onions, lime juice, mustard and vinegar in a mixing dish; mix to combine well.

Transfer the cooled artichoke hearts to a serving bowl; dress with the prepared vinaigrette.

Toss with the remaining ingredients, except for the feta cheese. Serve well chilled, garnished with crumbled feta. Enjoy!

# 40. Sautéed Chicory with Pistachios

**(Ready in about 10 minutes | Servings 4)**

**Per serving: 65 Calories; 4.7g Fat; 5.7g Carbs; 2.1g Protein;**

## INGREDIENTS

2 heads chicory greens, outer ribs discarded and cut into pieces
3 teaspoons olive oil
1 teaspoon garlic cloves, minced
2 green onions, chopped

Salt and pepper, to taste
1/2 teaspoon hot red pepper flakes
1/4 cup shelled pistachios

## DIRECTIONS

Cook the chicory in a pot of boiling salted water about 5 minutes. Drain well.
Dry the pot and heat the olive oil over moderately high heat until it simmers. Add the chicory, garlic and green onions.
Season with salt, black pepper and red pepper flakes; sauté until the leaves are wilted.
Serve garnished with pistachios. Bon appétit!

# 41. Two-Cheese, Mushroom and Cauliflower Casserole

**(Ready in about 35 minutes | Servings 4)**

**Per serving: 275 Calories; 21.3g Fat; 5.3g Carbs; 14g Protein;**

## INGREDIENTS

2 tablespoons lard
1 cup chicken stock
4 eggs, lightly beaten
1/2 cup sour cream
1 cup chive & onion cream cheese
1 cup aged goat cheese
1 tablespoon Piri piri sauce

1 teaspoon yellow mustard
1/2 pound brown cremini mushrooms, thinly sliced
1 teaspoon fresh or dry rosemary, minced
1/2 teaspoon coarse salt
1/3 teaspoon freshly ground black pepper
1 large head cauliflower, cut into florets

## DIRECTIONS

Start by preheating your oven to 360 degrees F. Then, spritz a casserole dish with a nonstick cooking spray.
Next step, melt the lard in a pan that is preheated over a moderate heat. Cook the stock, eggs, sour cream, cheese, Piri piri sauce and mustard in the pan until heated through.
Layer the cremini mushrooms and cauliflower on the bottom of your baking dish. Season with rosemary, salt, and black pepper.
Pour the saucepan mixture over the top. Bake for 25 to 35 minutes and serve warm. Bon appétit!

# 42. Spinach and Cheddar Breakfast Muffins

**(Ready in about 30 minutes | Servings 6)**

**Per serving: 252 Calories; 19.7g Fat; 3g Carbs; 16.1g Protein;**

## INGREDIENTS

1 cup full-fat milk
8 eggs
2 tablespoons vegetable oil
1/3 teaspoon salt

1/4 teaspoon ground black pepper, or more to the taste
1 cup spinach, chopped
1 ½ cups cheddar cheese, grated

## DIRECTIONS

Preheat your oven to 350 degrees F.
In a bowl, mix the milk, with the eggs and oil. Add the remaining ingredients. Mix well to combine.
Add the mixture to a lightly greased muffin tin.
Bake for 25 minutes or until your muffins spring back when lightly pressed.

# 43. Gruyère Cheese and Kale Muffins

**(Ready in about 25 minutes | Servings 6)**

**Per serving: 275 Calories; 15.8g Fat; 2.2g Carbs; 21.6g Protein;**

## INGREDIENTS

5 eggs
1/2 cup full-fat milk
Sea salt, to taste
1/2 teaspoon dried basil

1 ½ cups Gruyère cheese, grated
10 ounces kale, cooked and drained
1/2 pound prosciutto, chopped

## DIRECTIONS

Start by preheating your oven to 360 degrees F. Spritz a muffin tin with cooking spray.
Whisk the milk, salt, basil and cheese in a mixing bowl. Toss in the kale and prosciutto. Spoon the batter into each muffin cup (3/4 full).
Bake for 20 to 25 minutes and serve with sour cream.

# 44. Family Pizza with Spring Vegetables

**(Ready in about 25 minutes | Servings 4)**

**Per serving: 234 Calories; 16.1g Fat; 6.3g Carbs; 13.6g Protein;**

## INGREDIENTS

**For the Crust:**
A spray coating
1 pound cauliflower
1/2 cup Edam cheese
4 medium-sized eggs
1/4 cup heavy cream
1 tablespoon basil-infused oil
Salt, to taste

**For the Topping:**
1 cup spring mix
3/4 cup tomato sauce, sugar-free
2 tablespoons chives, finely chopped
1 tablespoon fresh sage
1/4 cup Kalamata olives, pitted and sliced
1 cup mozzarella cheese

## DIRECTIONS

Cook the cauliflower in a large pot of salted water until it is just tender; cut into florets and add the remaining ingredients for the crust.
Then, preheat your oven to 380 degrees F; add an oven rack to the middle of the oven. Lightly grease a baking pan with a thin layer of spray coating.
Spread the crust mixture onto the bottom of the prepared baking pan. Bake for 15 minutes or until the crust is firm and golden.
Remove from the oven and add the remaining ingredients, ending with the mozzarella cheese; bake until the cheese has completely melted.
Add a few grinds of black pepper if desired and serve immediately.

# 45. Roasted Carrots with Green Peppercorn Sauce

**(Ready in about 40 minutes | Servings 6)**

**Per serving: 183 Calories; 14.2g Fat; 6.5g Carbs; 2.6g Protein;**

## INGREDIENTS

1 ½ pounds carrots, trimmed and halved lengthwise
2 tablespoons butter, melted
1/4 teaspoon freshly grated nutmeg
1/2 teaspoon celery salt

1/4 teaspoon freshly ground black pepper
2 tablespoons apple cider vinegar
1 tablespoon green garlic, minced
For the Sauce:
2 tablespoons butter

1/2 cup green onions, minced
3 tablespoons Cognac
1 ½ cups beef broth
1 cup whipping cream
2 tablespoons green peppercorns in brine, drained and crushed slightly

## DIRECTIONS

Preheat your oven to 425 degrees F.
Toss the carrots with the butter, nutmeg, celery salt, black pepper, vinegar and green garlic.
Roast, stirring once or twice, until the carrots have softened, about 35 minutes.
Meanwhile, melt the 2 tablespoons of butter in a pan over a moderately high flame. Sweat the onions for 2 minutes.
Add the Cognac and bring it to a boil for 2 minutes. Pour in the beef broth and let it boil another 4 minutes.
Lastly, stir in the cream and peppercorns; turn the heat to medium. Continue to simmer until the sauce is thickened and thoroughly warmed.
Serve with roasted carrots and enjoy!

# 46. Mushroom and Caciocavallo Stuffed Peppers

**(Ready in about 30 minutes | Servings 6)**

**Per serving: 319 Calories; 18.8g Fat; 5.6g Carbs; 10.3g Protein;**

## INGREDIENTS

2 tablespoons avocado oil
1 shallot, chopped
1 teaspoon garlic, minced
3/4 pound button mushrooms, chopped
1 teaspoon Pimento
2 tablespoons fresh chives, chopped

1 teaspoon caraway seeds
Salt to taste
6 bell peppers, seeds and tops removed
1/2 cup Caciocavallo cheese, grated
1/2 cup tomato sauce

## DIRECTIONS

Preheat your oven to 380 degrees F. Heat the oil in a pan that is preheated over moderately high heat.
Sauté the shallots and garlic until the shallot softens. Stir in the mushrooms and cook an additional 4 minutes or until the mushrooms are fragrant.
Add the pimento, chives, caraway seeds and salt; stir until everything is heated through.
Place the peppers in a foil-lined roasting pan; fill them with the mushroom stuffing. Top each pepper with the Caciocavallo cheese.
Afterwards, pour the tomato sauce over everything. Bake for 18 to 23 minutes or until the cheese is lightly browned. Enjoy!

# 47. Baked Avocado with Bacon and Cottage Cheese

**(Ready in about 25 minutes | Servings 6)**

**Per serving: 255 Calories; 21g Fat; 3.3g Carbs; 10.8g Protein;**

## INGREDIENTS

3 medium-sized ripe avocados, halved and pitted, skin on
2 eggs, beaten
3 ounces Cottage cheese
2 tablespoons fresh chives, chopped

3 ounce cooked bacon, crumbled
Salt and pepper, to taste
1/4 teaspoon smoked paprika

## DIRECTIONS

Preheat your oven to 390 degrees F. Place the avocado halves in shallow ramekins.
In a mixing bowl, thoroughly combine the other ingredients. Divide the mixture among he avocado halves.
Bake for about 20 minutes and serve right away!

# 48. Cabbage "Noodles" with Turkey Sauce

**(Ready in about 20 minutes | Servings 4)**

**Per serving: 236 Calories; 8.3g Fat; 5.1g Carbs; 29.9g Protein;**

## INGREDIENTS

1 pound white cabbage
2 slices bacon
1 yellow onion, chopped
1 garlic clove, minced
3/4 pound turkey meat, ground
1 Aleppo chili pepper, minced

Sea salt and ground black pepper, to taste
1/2 teaspoon cayenne pepper
1/2 teaspoon dried oregano
1/2 teaspoon dried basil
1/4 teaspoon bay leaf, ground

## DIRECTIONS

Remove any loose outer leaves of your cabbage. Now, spiralize your cabbage and reserve.
Bring a pot of lightly salted water to a rolling boil; parboil the cabbage for 3 minutes, until crisp-tender; drain.
Heat a nonstick skillet over a moderately high heat. Now, cook the bacon for 3 to 4 minutes, crumbling with a fork; reserve.
Now, cook the onion and garlic in pan drippings until tender. Add the turkey meat and chili pepper; cook until the meat is browned.
Sprinkle with seasonings and stir to combine.
Then, add the cabbage and bacon back to the skillet. Serve warm and enjoy!

# 49. Keto Pasta with Alfredo Sauce

**(Ready in about 30 minutes | Servings 4)**

**Per serving: 614 Calories; 55.9g Fat; 3.6g Carbs; 25.6g Protein;**

## INGREDIENTS

2 ounces cream cheese, room temperature

3 eggs, room temperature

1/2 teaspoon wheat gluten

1 stick butter

1 cup heavy cream

1 garlic clove, minced

2 cups Parmesan cheese, grated

1 teaspoon Italian seasoning

## DIRECTIONS

Start by preheating your oven to 320 degrees F. Line a baking sheet with a Silpat mat.

Blend the cream cheese, eggs, and gluten until uniform and creamy.

Press the batter into the pan, keeping it nice and thin. Bake in the preheated oven for 5 to 6 minutes.

Allow it to rest for 5 to 10 minutes before cutting into strips. Now, simmer the pasta in a lightly salted water for a couple of minutes or until it's done.

Then, melt the butter in a skillet. Now, add the cream and garlic, and cook over a moderate heat, stirring with wire whisk.

Stir in the parmesan cheese and Italian seasonings; remove from heat. The sauce will thicken as it cools. Add the warm pasta and serve immediately.

# POULTRY

## 50. Creamy and Cheesy Chicken Salad

**(Ready in about 20 minutes | Servings 6)**

**Per serving: 183 Calories; 12.5g Fat; 1.7g Carbs; 16.3g Protein;**

### INGREDIENTS

2 chicken breasts
2 medium-sized cucumbers, sliced
1/2 teaspoon coarse salt
1/4 teaspoon ground black pepper
1/4 teaspoon chili pepper flakes

1/2 teaspoon dried oregano
1/3 teaspoon dried basil
2 romaine hearts, leaves separated
1/4 cup Parmesan, finely grated

**For the dressing:**
2 garlic cloves, minced
2 large egg yolks
1 tablespoon fresh lime juice
1 teaspoon mustard
1/4 cup olive oil

### DIRECTIONS

Firstly, grill the chicken breast until done; cut them into cubes.
Toss the cucumbers and chicken with the salt, black pepper, chili pepper, oregano, and basil. Place the romaine leaves in a salad bowl.
Now, add the cucumber and chicken mixture. Prepare the dressing by whisking all the dressing ingredients.
Dress the salad; scatter parmesan over the top, serve and enjoy!

## 51. The Best Ever Chicken Stew

**(Ready in about 1 hour | Servings 6)**

**Per serving: 239 Calories; 14.7g Fat; 2.5g Carbs; 25.6g Protein;**

### INGREDIENTS

2 tablespoons tallow, room temperature
2 medium-sized shallots, finely chopped
2 garlic cloves, sliced
1 quart chicken broth
1 sprig rosemary

1 teaspoon dried marjoram
1 pound chicken drumsticks
1 celery, chopped
1/2 pound carrots, chopped
1 bell pepper, chopped

1 poblano pepper, chopped
2 ripe tomatoes, chopped
1 teaspoon salt
1/2 teaspoon ground black pepper
1/2 teaspoon smoked paprika

### DIRECTIONS

Melt the tallow in a large heavy pot that is preheated over a moderate flame. Sweat the shallots and garlic until aromatic and just tender.
Now, turn the heat to medium-high. Stir in the chicken broth, rosemary, marjoram, and chicken drumsticks; bring to a boil.
Add the remaining ingredients and reduce the heat to medium-low. Simmer, covered, for 50 minutes.
Discard the bones and chop the chicken into small chunks. Serve hot!

## 52. Rutabaga, Taro Leaf and Chicken Soup

**(Ready in about 45 minutes | Servings 4)**

**Per serving: 256 Calories; 12.9g Fat; 3.2g Carbs; 35.1g Protein;**

### INGREDIENTS

1 pound chicken thighs
1/2 cup rutabaga, cubed
2 carrots, peeled
2 celery stalks
1/2 cup leek, chopped
1/4 teaspoon garlic, granulated
1/4 teaspoon ground cloves

1/2 cup taro leaves, roughly chopped
1 tablespoon fresh parsley, chopped
Salt and black pepper, to taste
1 cup chicken consommé, canned
3 cups water
1 teaspoon cayenne pepper

### DIRECTIONS

Add all of the above ingredients, except for the cayenne pepper, to a large-sized stock pot. Bring to a rapid boil over high heat.
Now, turn the heat to medium-low. Let it simmer, partially covered, an additional 35 minutes or until the chicken is pinkish-brown.
Next, discard the chicken and vegetables. Add the cayenne pepper to the broth; allow it to simmer an additional 8 minutes.
When the chicken thighs are cool enough to handle, cut off the meat from the bones. Afterwards, add the meat back to the soup and serve warm.

# 53. Chicken Liver Pâté with Keto Flatbread

**(Ready in about 2 hours | Servings 4)**

**Per serving: 395 Calories; 30.2g Fat; 3.6g Carbs; 17.9g Protein;**

## INGREDIENTS

10 ounces chicken livers
1/2 teaspoon Italian seasoning blend
4 tablespoons olive oil
1 white onion, finely chopped
1 teaspoon granulated garlic

**For Flatbread:**
1/2 cup flax meal
1 ¼ cups almond flour
1 ½ tablespoons psyllium husks
Salt, to taste

1 cup lukewarm water
1/2 stick butter
1/2 teaspoon turmeric powder
1/2 teaspoon fresh ginger, minced

## DIRECTIONS

Blend the chicken livers, Italian seasoning, olive oil, onion and granulated garlic. Mix until everything is well combined and reserve.
Then, prepare the flatbread by mixing all dry ingredients in a bowl. Then, mix all wet ingredients. After that, add the wet ingredients to the dry mixture. Mix well.
Allow the dough to rest at room temperature for 1 to 2 hours. Now, divide the dough into 8 balls. Roll out each dough ball until it is very thin. Cook in a lightly greased skillet that is preheated over medium-high heat. Cook for 1 minute per side. Serve with the chicken liver pâté. Enjoy!

# 54. Chinese-Style Turkey Meatballs

**(Ready in about 20 minutes | Servings 4)**

**Per serving: 244 Calories; 13.7g Fat; 5g Carbs; 27.6g Protein;**

## INGREDIENTS

**For the Meatballs:**
3/4 pound ground turkey
1 egg
1/3 cup cheddar cheese, freshly grated
1/3 teaspoon black pepper

1/3 teaspoon Five-spice powder
For the Sauce:
1 1/3 cups water
1/3 cup red wine vinegar
2 tablespoons Worcestershire sauce

1/2 cup tomato puree, sugar-free
1/2 teaspoon cayenne pepper
3/4 cup erythritol
1/3 teaspoon guar gum

## DIRECTIONS

Thoroughly combine the ground turkey, egg, cheese, black pepper and Five-spice powder in a mixing bowl. Now, form the mixture into balls (about 28 meatballs).
Preheat a nonstick skillet over a medium heat. Brown your meatballs on all sides for 3 to 4 minutes; set them aside.
Next, add the water, vinegar, Worcestershire sauce, tomato puree, cayenne pepper and erythritol to the skillet. Whisk until well mixed.
After that, gradually add the guar gum. Whisk until the sauce has thickened. Decrease the temperature and bring the sauce to a simmer; make sure to stir periodically.
Add the meatballs to the sauce; continue to simmer for 8 to 12 minutes on low or until your meatballs are thoroughly cooked. Serve with lettuce and enjoy!

# 55. Kid-Friendly Parmesan Chicken Meatballs

**(Ready in about 20 minutes | Servings 6)**

**Per serving: 252 Calories; 9.7g Fat; 5.3g Carbs; 34.2g Protein;**

## INGREDIENTS

**For the Meatballs:**
3/4 cup Parmesan cheese, grated
2 eggs, lightly beaten
1 tablespoon fresh parsley leaves, chopped
1 tablespoon sage leaves, chopped
1 teaspoon onion powder

2 garlic cloves, finely minced
1/3 teaspoon dried rosemary
Salt and ground black pepper, to your liking
1/2 teaspoon red pepper flakes, crushed
1 ¼ pounds chicken, ground

**For the sauce:**
2 ½ tablespoons bacon fat
1 white onion, peeled and finely chopped
3 ripe tomatoes, chopped
1 cup chicken stock

## DIRECTIONS

Thoroughly combine all ingredients for the meatballs. Now, shape your meatballs to the desired size.
Warm 1 tablespoon of the bacon fat in a nonstick skillet over a moderate heat. Now, cook the meatballs for 2 to 4 minutes or until they are cooked through; reserve, keeping them warm.
Next, heat the remaining fat in the same skillet. Sauté the onions until translucent. Stir in the tomatoes and chicken stock; cook 3 to 4 minutes more.
Fold in the reserved meatballs, reduce the heat to medium-low and let it simmer approximately 6 minutes. Enjoy!

# 56. Tomato, Yogurt and Chicken Chowder

**(Ready in about 35 minutes | Servings 6)**

**Per serving: 238 Calories; 15.5g Fat; 6.1g Carbs; 36g Protein;**

## INGREDIENTS

2 tablespoons coconut oil

3 chicken drumsticks, deboned and chopped

1/2 teaspoon sea salt

1/2 teaspoon mixed peppercorns, freshly ground

2 shallots, chopped

1/2 cup celery, thinly sliced

1 fresh jalapeño, deveined and minced

2 cloves garlic, roughly chopped

2 cups tomato bisque, preferably homemade, sugar-free

2 cups water

1 bay leaf

1 tablespoon flax seed meal

1/2 cup Greek-style yogurt

## DIRECTIONS

Melt the coconut oil in a large pot over a moderately high heat. Sear the meat, stirring periodically, for 6 minutes or until it is browned. Season with salt and peppercorns; then, reserve, keeping warm.

Now, sauté the shallots, celery, jalapeño and garlic in pan drippings until they are tender and aromatic.

Add a splash of the tomato bisque to scrape and stir the browned bits from the pot. Next, pour in the remaining tomato bisque along with 2 cups of water.

Throw in the bay leaf and let it simmer for 25 minutes over medium-low heat.

Afterwards, add the flax seed meal and yogurt; continue to cook over low heat until it is thoroughly heated. Serve in individual bowls garnished with fresh garden chervil. Bon appétit!

# 57. Country Chicken Soup with Root Vegetables

**(Ready in about 25 minutes | Servings 4)**

**Per serving: 342 Calories; 22.4g Fat; 6.3g Carbs; 25.2g Protein;**

## INGREDIENTS

1 tablespoon olive oil

1 teaspoon garlic, finely minced

1 parsnip, chopped

1/2 cup turnip, chopped

1 carrot, chopped

2 chicken breasts, boneless and cut into chunks

Salt and pepper, to taste

4 cups water

1 cup full-fat milk

1 cup heavy cream

2 bouillon cubes

1 whole egg

4 tablespoons fresh chives, roughly chopped

## DIRECTIONS

Heat the oil in a heavy pot over a moderate heat; now, cook the garlic until aromatic. Add the parsnip, turnip and carrot. Cook until your vegetables are softened.

Stir in the chicken; cook until it is no longer pink, for 3 to 4 minutes, stirring periodically. Season with salt and pepper.

Pour in the water, milk, and heavy cream. Add the bouillon cubes and bring it to a boil.

Reduce the heat to medium-low; let it simmer for 20 minutes longer. Add the beaten egg and stir an additional minute.

Remove from the heat. Serve in individual bowls, garnished with chopped chives. Bon appétit!

# 58. Chicken Drumsticks with Tangy Cauliflower Salad

**(Ready in about 20 minutes | Servings 2)**

**Per serving: 444 Calories; 36g Fat; 5.7g Carbs; 20.6g Protein;**

## INGREDIENTS

1/2 head of cauliflower

2 teaspoons butter

2 chicken drumsticks

1 teaspoon Hungarian paprika

Sea salt and ground black pepper, to

taste

1/2 cup mayonnaise

1 teaspoon Dijon mustard

2 tablespoons dry white wine

1 red onion, finely minced

1/2 cup Colby cheese grated

2 tablespoons fresh Italian parsley, to serve

## DIRECTIONS

Cook the cauliflower in a large pot of salted water until tender; cut into small florets and transfer to a salad bowl.

Now, warm the butter in a pan over medium-high heat. Add the chicken, Hungarian paprika salt, and pepper.

Cook for 7 to 8 minutes, turning periodically.

Meanwhile, mix the mayonnaise with the mustard, wine, and minced red onion. Add to the bowl with the cauliflower. Top with grated cheese.

Serve with the warm chicken drumsticks, garnished with Italian parsley. Bon appétit!

# 59. Parmesan Breaded Chicken Breasts with Peppers

**(Ready in about 30 minutes | Servings 4)**

**Per serving: 367 Calories; 16.9g Fat; 6g Carbs; 43g Protein;**

## INGREDIENTS

1 pound chicken breasts, butterflied
1 teaspoon salt
1/4 teaspoon ground black pepper, or more to taste
1 teaspoon fresh or dried dill, chopped
1/3 cup crushed pork rinds

1/3 cup Parmigiano-Reggiano, freshly grated
2 teaspoons vegetable oil
1 garlic clove, minced
3 bell peppers, quartered lengthwise

## DIRECTIONS

Begin by preheating your oven to 420 degrees F. Cover the sides and bottom of a baking pan with a sheet of foil.
Place the butterflied chicken breast on the baking pan. Season with salt and pepper.
Now, combine the dill, pork rinds, Parmigiano-Reggiano, vegetable oil and garlic clove. Dip each chicken breast into this mixture.
Arrange the bell peppers around the prepared chicken breasts. Bake for 20 minutes or until the juices run clear. Serve immediately and enjoy!

# 60. Chicken Sausage with Spaghetti Squash

**(Ready in about 15 minutes | Servings 4)**

**Per serving: 447 Calories; 37.3g Fat; 2.8g Carbs; 21.3g Protein;**

## INGREDIENTS

2 teaspoons tallow
1 ½ pounds cheddar & bacon chicken sausages, sliced
1/2 cup yellow onions, finely chopped
1 banana pepper, deveined and finely minced
1 teaspoon garlic, minced

8 ounces spaghetti squash
1 teaspoon kosher salt
1/4 teaspoon black pepper, freshly ground
1 ¼ cups chicken broth
2/3 cup whipped cream

## DIRECTIONS

Melt the tallow in a pan over a moderate heat. Then, cook the sausages about 8 minutes. Reserve.
Cook the onions, pepper and garlic in pan drippings.
Add the squash, salt, black pepper and chicken broth; bring to a boil until the sauce has thickened.
Stir in the whipped cream and cook until thoroughly heated. Serve with reserved sausages. Bon appétit!

# 61. Prosciutto-Wrapped Chicken with Cottage Cheese

**(Ready in about 35 minutes | Servings 2)**

**Per serving: 499 Calories; 18.9g Fat; 5.7g Carbs; 41.6g Protein;**

## INGREDIENTS

1 chicken breasts, boneless, skinless and flattened
1 teaspoon smoked paprika
Salt and ground black pepper, to taste pepper

1/2 cup Cottage cheese
1 tablespoon fresh cilantro, chopped
4 slices of prosciutto

## DIRECTIONS

Start by preheating your oven to 390 degrees F. Line a baking pan with parchment paper.
Season the chicken breasts with smoked paprika, salt and pepper. Spread the Cottage cheese over the chicken breasts; scatter fresh cilantro over the top.
Roll up and cut into 4 pieces. Now, wrap each piece with one slice of prosciutto; secure with a toothpick.
Place the wrapped chicken in the baking pan; bake for 25 to 35 minutes. Serve warm.

# 62. Sensational Chicken Wings with Broccoli

**(Ready in about 50 minutes | Servings 4)**

**Per serving: 450 Calories; 35.5g Fat; 4.6g Carbs; 25.1g Protein;**

## INGREDIENTS

1 pound chicken wings
1 pound broccoli, broken into florets
1 carrot, sliced
1 cup scallions, chopped

1 teaspoon garlic paste
1 teaspoon Italian seasoning mix (such as Old Sub Sailor)
3 tablespoons olive oil
2 cups Colby cheese, shredded

## DIRECTIONS

Preheat your oven to 390 degrees F. Lightly grease a rimmed baking sheet.
Roast the wings until cooked through and the skin is crispy, about 35 minutes. Add the broccoli, carrots, scallions, and garlic paste.
Season the chicken and broccoli with the Italian seasoning mix; drizzle them with olive oil.
Roast an additional 13 to 15 minutes. Scatter the shredded cheese over the top and serve warm. Bon appétit!

# 63. Zesty Chicken with Mayo-Avocado Sauce

**(Ready in about 20 minutes | Servings 4)**

**Per serving: 370 Calories; 25g Fat; 4.1g Carbs; 31.4g Protein;**

## INGREDIENTS

1/3 cup almond meal
Sea salt and pepper, to your liking
1 teaspoon shallot powder
1 teaspoon lime zest
1 teaspoon cayenne pepper
1/3 teaspoon ground cumin
1/4 teaspoon chili flakes
2 eggs

8 chicken thighs, cut into bite-size chunks
2 tablespoons olive oil
For the Sauce:
1/2 cup mayonnaise
1/2 medium Hass avocado
1/2 teaspoon coarse salt
1 teaspoon garlic paste

## DIRECTIONS

In a food processor, thoroughly combine the meal, salt, pepper, shallot powder, lime zest, cayenne pepper, cumin and chili flakes.
Whisk the eggs in a separate shallow dish.
Dry the chicken thighs off with a paper towel. Dip the chicken chunks in the whisked eggs, then in the almond meal mixture.
Heat the oil in a skillet over medium heat; fry the chicken for 4 to 6 minutes; turn over and cook on the other side until thoroughly cooked.
Place on paper towels to soak up the excess oil.
In the meantime, make the sauce by mixing all of the sauce ingredients. Serve the warm chicken with the sauce and enjoy!

# 64. Eggplant and Duck Quiche

**(Ready in about 45 minutes | Servings 4)**

**Per serving: 562 Calories; 49.5g Fat; 6.7g Carbs; 22.5g Protein;**

## INGREDIENTS

1 ½ cups almond flour
1/2 teaspoon kosher salt
8 eggs
1 ½ tablespoons butter, melted
1 pound ground duck meat

1/4 teaspoon ground black pepper
1/2 teaspoon celery seeds
1/2 teaspoon basil, dried
1/3 cup whipping cream
1/2 pound eggplant, peeled and sliced

## DIRECTIONS

Preheat your oven to 350 degrees F
Mix the almond flour with kosher salt. Fold in one egg and the melted butter; mix to combine well.
Now, press the crust into the bottom of a lightly-greased baking dish.
Then, heat up a skillet and brown ground duck meat for 2 to 3 minutes, stirring continuously.
In a mixing bowl, combine the remaining eggs with the black pepper, celery seeds, basil, and whipping cream.
Stir in the browned meat; stir until everything is thoroughly combined. Pour the mixture into the prepared crust. Add the eggplant slices.
Bake your quiche for 37 to 42 minutes. Transfer to a wire rack to cool slightly before slicing and serving.

# 65. Hungarian-Style Chicken Fillets

**(Ready in about 30 minutes | Servings 6)**

**Per serving: 239 Calories; 8.6g Fat; 5.5g Carbs; 34.3g Protein;**

## INGREDIENTS

1 ½ pounds chicken fillets
1 teaspoon garlic paste
1 teaspoon Hungarian paprika
1/2 teaspoon marjoram
1 teaspoon dry thyme
1 teaspoon coarse salt

1/2 teaspoon freshly ground black pepper
1/2 cup tomato sauce, preferably homemade
1/4 cup low-sodium soy sauce
1 bell pepper, deveined and chopped
1 large-sized red onion, chopped
2 tablespoons curly parsley, for garnish

## DIRECTIONS

Rub each chicken fillet with the garlic paste and seasonings. Place in a heavy pot that is preheated over medium flame.
Cook for 4 to 5 minutes on each side.
Pour in the tomato sauce and soy sauce; bring it to a boil. Add the bell pepper and onion.
Reduce the heat to medium-low. Cook, partially covered, for 25 minutes more. Serve warm, garnished with fresh parsley. Bon appétit!

# 66. Roasted Chicken Wings with Cashew-Basil Pesto

**(Ready in about 35 minutes | Servings 4)**

**Per serving: 580 Calories; 44.8g Fat; 5g Carbs; 38.7g Protein;**

## INGREDIENTS

1 pound chicken wings, skinless
Salt and ground black pepper, to taste
1 teaspoon cayenne pepper
1 cup scallions
For the Cashew-Basil Pesto:

1/2 cup fresh basil leaves
2 garlic cloves, minced
1/2 cup cashews
1/2 cup Romano cheese
1/2 cup olive oil

## DIRECTIONS

Begin by preheating your oven to 392 degrees F. Rub the chicken wings with the salt, black pepper, and cayenne pepper.
Arrange the chicken wings in a lightly greased baking dish; scatter the scallions around the chicken.
Roast for 30 minutes, turning the baking dish once.
In a food processor, pulse the basil, garlic, cashews and Romano cheese. Add the oil in a constant tiny stream. Season with sea salt to taste.
Serve the chicken wings on a platter, garnished with the roasted scallions and cashew-basil pesto. Bon appétit!

# 67. Mediterranean Chicken Breasts

**(Ready in about 40 minutes | Servings 8)**

**Per serving: 306 Calories; 17.8g Fat; 3.1g Carbs; 31.7g Protein;**

## INGREDIENTS

4 chicken breasts, skinless and boneless
2 garlic cloves, pressed
1 teaspoon dried oregano
1/2 teaspoon dried basil
2 sprigs thyme
1 sprig rosemary

Salt and ground black pepper, to taste
2 tablespoons peanut oil
1 bell pepper, deveined and thinly sliced
10 Kalamata olives, pitted
1 ½ cups chicken stock

## DIRECTIONS

Rub the chicken breast with the garlic and seasonings. Heat the peanut oil in a pan that is preheated over a moderately high heat.
Now, fry the chicken until it is browned on all sides, for 4 to 6 minutes.
Add the remaining ingredients; bring it to boil. Reduce the heat to medium-low. Continue cooking, partially covered, for 30 minutes.
Enjoy!

# 68. Roasted Turkey Legs with Avocado Sauce

**(Ready in about 1 hour 40 minutes | Servings 4)**

**Per serving: 362 Calories; 22.3g Fat; 5.6g Carbs; 34.9g Protein;**

## INGREDIENTS

2 fat turkey legs
1 tablespoon poultry seasoning
1 ½ tablespoons olive oil

**For the Sauce:**
1 small-sized avocado, pitted and mashed
1 ounce full-fat sour cream
1 ounce mascarpone cheese
1 teaspoon fresh lemon juice
2 tablespoons fresh cilantro, finely chopped
1/3 teaspoon sea salt

## DIRECTIONS

Preheat your oven to 345 degrees F. Sprinkle the turkey legs with the poultry seasoning. Drizzle them with olive oil and lay on a baking sheet. Roast the turkey for about 45 minutes; turn over and roast another 50 minutes.
Meanwhile, make the sauce by whisking all the sauce ingredients; keep in the refrigerator until ready to serve.
To serve, slice the meat off the bones and serve with your avocado sauce.

# 69. Chicken with Gorgonzola Panna Cotta

**(Ready in about 20 minutes + chilling time | Servings 4)**

**Per serving: 483 Calories; 35.2g Fat; 1.5g Carbs; 38.5g Protein;**

## INGREDIENTS

1 tablespoon olive oil
2 chicken breasts, boneless and skinless
2 gelatin sheets
3/4 cup heavy cream
2 teaspoons granular Swerve

3 tablespoons water
1 cup gorgonzola dolce, crumbled
1/2 teaspoon ground bay leaf
1/2 teaspoon black peppercorns, whole
Salt and cayenne pepper, to your liking

## DIRECTIONS

Heat the olive oil in a heavy-bottomed skillet over moderately high heat; now, fry the chicken breasts for 5 to 6 minutes per side.
Soak the gelatin sheets in cold water for a few minutes to soften. Place in a pan; add the cream, Swerve, water and cheese.
Add the spices. Simmer over a low flame, stirring for 2 to 4 minutes. Evenly divide the mixture between 4 ramekins.
Place in your refrigerator overnight. To serve, run a thin knife around the edge of the panna cotta; now, flip the ramekin onto a serving plate.
Serve with the fried chicken breasts. Bon appétit!

# 70. Mediterranean Chicken Legs in Sauce

**(Ready in about 50 minutes | Servings 6)**

**Per serving: 333 Calories; 20.2g Fat; 2g Carbs; 33.5g Protein;**

## INGREDIENTS

2 tablespoons ghee
1 ½ pounds chicken legs, skinless
1/2 cup scallions, chopped
2 garlic cloves, minced
1/2 cup dry sherry
1 rosemary sprig, chopped

2 thyme sprigs, chopped
1 tablespoon fresh oregano, chopped
1 tablespoon fresh basil, chopped
1 cup heavy cream
1/2 teaspoon salt
1/2 teaspoon mixed peppercorns, freshly crushed

## DIRECTIONS

Preheat your oven to 400 degrees F.
Melt the ghee in a pan that is preheated over a moderate flame; now, brown the chicken legs for 6 to 8 minutes.
After that, stir in the scallions, garlic, sherry, and herbs. Transfer to a lightly greased casserole dish and cover it.
Bake for 35 minutes or until a meat thermometer registers 165 degrees F; reserve.
Mix the cooking juices with the heavy cream, salt and crushed peppercorns; simmer for a couple of minutes or until it is thickened and cooked through. Serve with the reserved chicken. Bon appétit!

# 71. Fried Chinese Cabbage with Ground Turkey

**(Ready in about 45 minutes | Servings 4)**

**Per serving: 263 Calories; 22.8g Fat; 5.2g Carbs; 9.8g Protein;**

## INGREDIENTS

1 tablespoon canola oil
1/2 cup shallots, chopped
1 teaspoon fresh garlic, minced
1 pound Chinese cabbage, finely chopped
2 ripe tomatoes, chopped
1/2 teaspoon dried basil

1/2 teaspoon dried marjoram
1/2 teaspoon mustard seeds
1/3 teaspoon fennel seeds
Coarse salt and ground black pepper, to taste
1/2 pound turkey ground
2 slices smoked bacon, chopped

## DIRECTIONS

Heat the canola oil in a pan over a moderate flame. Now, cook the shallots and garlic until aromatic.

Now, add the cabbage along with the tomatoes and all seasonings. Cook an additional 5 minutes or until the leaves are wilted.

Stir in the ground turkey and chopped bacon. Turn the heat to medium-low and cook an additional 35 minutes, crumbling the meat with a wooden spatula.

Serve warm in individual bowls. Bon appétit!

# 72. Smoked Turkey and Goat Cheese Spread

**(Ready in about 10 minutes | Servings 6)**

**Per serving: 212 Calories; 18.8g Fat; 2g Carbs; 10.6g Protein;**

## INGREDIENTS

4 ounces smoked turkey ham, chopped
4 ounces goat cheese, crumbled
2 tablespoons fresh cilantro, roughly chopped

2 tablespoons flaxseed meal
2 tablespoons sunflower seeds

## DIRECTIONS

Combine all ingredients in your food processor until everything is well incorporated.

Place in a serving bowl and scatter sunflower seeds over the top. Serve with veggie sticks and enjoy!

# 73. Chicken Fillets with Herby Sauce

**(Ready in about 15 minutes | Servings 6)**

**Per serving: 357 Calories; 26.2g Fat; 0.6g Carbs; 29.2g Protein;**

## INGREDIENTS

1 ½ tablespoons olive oil
1 ½ pounds chicken fillets
1 teaspoon kosher salt
1/2 teaspoon ground black pepper
1 stick butter

1 teaspoon garlic, finely minced
2 tablespoons shallots, finely minced
1/3 cup fresh cilantro, chopped
2 teaspoons apple cider vinegar

## DIRECTIONS

Heat the olive oil in a nonstick skillet that is preheated over a medium heat. Now, fry the chicken fillets on both sides for 10 minutes or until they're browned.

In a mixing dish, thoroughly combine the remaining ingredients.

Serve with the fried chicken fillets and enjoy!

# 74. Cheesy Turkey Meatballs with Basil Chutney

**(Ready in about 30 minutes | Servings 6)**

**Per serving: 390 Calories; 27.2g Fat; 1.8g Carbs; 37.4g Protein;**

## INGREDIENTS

2 tablespoons olive oil

**For the Meatballs:**
1 ½ pounds ground turkey
1/2 teaspoon sea salt
1/4 teaspoon ground black pepper, or more to taste
3 tablespoons flax seed meal

1/2 cup Parmesan cheese, grated
1/2 teaspoon paprika
1/2 teaspoon garlic powder
1/2 teaspoon onion powder
1/4 teaspoon dried thyme
1/2 teaspoon celery seeds
2 small-sized eggs, lightly beaten

**For the Basil Chutney:**
2 tablespoons fresh lemon juice
1/2 cup fresh basil leaves
1/2 cup coriander leaves
1 teaspoon fresh ginger root, grated
2 tablespoons olive oil
2 tablespoons water
Salt and pepper, to taste
1 tablespoon green chili, minced

## DIRECTIONS

Thoroughly combine all ingredients for the meatballs. Divide the mixture into 16 meatballs and reserve.

Heat 2 tablespoons of olive oil in a cast-iron skillet that is preheated over a moderate heat. Brown the meatballs for 7 to 8 minutes on all sides.

Then, prepare the chutney by mixing all the chutney ingredients in your food processor. Make sure to blend very well.

Serve the warm meatballs with the basil chutney on the side.

# 75. Crock Pot Turkey Legs

**(Ready in about 6 hours | Servings 6)**

**Per serving: 280 Calories; 22.2g Fat; 4.3g Carbs; 15.8g Protein;**

## INGREDIENTS

2 turkey legs
1 tablespoon butter
1 tablespoon mustard
4 garlic cloves, sliced

1 leek, chopped
Salt and pepper, to taste
1 teaspoon dried rosemary
1/2 teaspoon smoked paprika

**For the Gravy:**
1/2 stick butter
1 cup heavy cream
3/4 teaspoon guar gum
Salt and pepper, to taste

## DIRECTIONS

Rub the turkey legs with 1 tablespoon of butter and mustard.

Add the turkey legs to a heavy-bottomed skillet that is preheated over moderately high heat. Brown the turkey legs for a couple of minutes on all sides.

Transfer the browned turkey to your crock pot; reserve the fat in the skillet. Now, add the garlic, leeks, salt, pepper, rosemary, and paprika. Cook on low for 6 hours; reserve.

Warm 1/2 stick of the butter in the skillet with the reserved fat over a moderate flame. Add the heavy cream and whisk until heated through. Next, stir in the guar gum, salt, and pepper. Allow the sauce to thicken, whisking continuously. Serve with the warm turkey drumsticks and enjoy!

# 76. Grandma's Cauliflower and Turkey Soup

**(Ready in about 35 minutes | Servings 4)**

**Per serving: 274 Calories; 14.4g Fat; 5.6g Carbs; 26.7g Protein;**

## INGREDIENTS

2 tablespoons sesame oil
2 shallots, chopped
2 garlic cloves, chopped
1 carrot, chopped
1 parsnip, chopped

4 ½ cups chicken stock
1/2 head cauliflower, broken into florets
1 pound turkey thighs
1 rosemary sprig
1/2 teaspoon celery seeds

2 bay leaves
Salt and ground black pepper, to your liking
1/2 teaspoon cayenne pepper
4 dollops of sour cream

## DIRECTIONS

Heat the sesame oil in a heavy pot that is preheated over a moderate flame. Now, sauté the shallots and garlic until they're aromatic.

After that, stir in the carrots and parsnip; cook until they are softened, stirring constantly. Pour in the chicken stock, bringing to a boil.

Add the cauliflower, turkey, rosemary, celery seeds, bay leaves, salt, black pepper and cayenne pepper.

Reduce the heat to medium-low; let it simmer for 25 to 30 minutes.

Lastly, ladle the soup into four individual bowls. Serve with sour cream and enjoy!

## 77. Leftover Chicken Chowder

**(Ready in about 35 minutes | Servings 4)**

**Per serving: 350 Calories; 25.8g Fat; 5.5g Carbs; 20g Protein;**

### INGREDIENTS

2 tablespoons coconut oil
A bunch of scallions, chopped
2 cloves garlic, roughly chopped
1/2 pound leftover roast chicken, shredded and skin removed
2 rosemary sprigs
1 thyme sprigs
1 bay leaves

1 tablespoon chicken bouillon granules
3 cups water
1 ½ cups milk
1/2 cup whipped cream
1 whole egg, lightly beaten
2 tablespoons dry sherry

### DIRECTIONS

Melt the coconut oil in a stockpot over a moderate flame. Now, sauté the scallions and garlic until they're just tender and aromatic.
Add the chicken, seasonings, chicken bouillon granules and water; bring to a boil. Cook your chowder, partially covered, for 20 minutes.
Lower the heat. Pour in the milk and whipped cream and cook until it has thickened. Add the egg and cook, stirring constantly, 1 to 2 minutes longer.
Taste and adjust the seasonings. Afterwards, drizzle each serving with dry sherry and serve right away!

## 78. Absolutely Incredible Turkey Kebabs

**(Ready in about 30 minutes | Servings 6)**

**Per serving: 293 Calories; 13.8g Fat; 3.7g Carbs; 34.5g Protein;**

### INGREDIENTS

1 ½ pounds British turkey diced thigh
2 tablespoons butter, at room temperature
1 tablespoon dry ranch seasoning
2 orange bell peppers, sliced

1 red bell peppers, sliced
1 green bell peppers, sliced
1 zucchini, cut into thick slices
1 red onion, cut into wedges
1 cucumber, sliced

1 cup radishes, sliced
2 tablespoons red wine vinegar
1 tablespoon fresh parsley, roughly chopped

### DIRECTIONS

Rub the turkey with the softened butter and toss with the dry ranch seasoning. Thread the turkey pieces onto skewers.
Alternate with bell peppers, zucchini, and onion until all the ingredients are used up. Now, place your skewers in the refrigerator while you're lighting the grill.
Grill your kebabs, turning periodically, for 9 minutes or until they are cooked through.
In the meantime, toss the cucumbers and radishes with red wine vinegar and fresh parsley.
Serve the kebabs immediately with the cucumber-radicchio salad on the side. Bon appétit!

## 79. Easy Grilled Chicken Salad

**(Ready in about 20 minutes | Servings 4)**

**Per serving: 408 Calories; 34.2g Fat; 4.8g Carbs; 22.7g Protein;**

### INGREDIENTS

2 chicken breasts
1/2 teaspoon sea salt
1/3 teaspoon red pepper flakes, crushed
1/4 teaspoon dried thyme, or more to taste

1 large-sized avocado, pitted and sliced
2 egg yolks
1 tablespoon lime juice
1/2 teaspoon mustard powder

1/3 teaspoon sea salt
1/3 cup olive oil
1 tablespoon Worcestershire sauce

### DIRECTIONS

Preheat your grill on high. Season the chicken breasts with salt, pepper and thyme. Now, grill the chicken for 3 to 5 minutes on each side.
Cut the grilled chicken into the strips.
Divide the avocado slices among four serving plates.
Then, prepare the dressing. In a mixing dish or a measuring cup, thoroughly combine the remaining ingredients.
Place the chicken strips on the serving plates and drizzle with the prepared dressing. Enjoy!

# 80. Spicy Chicken Strips with Hemp Seeds

**(Ready in about 55 minutes | Servings 6)**

**Per serving: 420 Calories; 28.2g Fat; 5g Carbs; 35.3g Protein;**

## INGREDIENTS

3 chicken breasts, cut into strips
1/2 stick butter
Salt and pepper, to taste
2 tablespoons soy sauce
3 teaspoons apple cider vinegar

1/2 teaspoon hot chili sauce, sugar-free
2 tablespoons tomato paste
2 cloves garlic, minced
2 eggs
1/4 cup hemp seeds

## DIRECTIONS

Preheat your oven to 410 degrees F. Lightly grease a baking dish with a nonstick cooking spray.
Now, rub the chicken wings with the butter, salt, and pepper.
Drizzle with soy sauce, vinegar, chili sauce, tomato sauce and garlic. Let it marinate at least 30 minutes in your refrigerator.
In a mixing dish, whisk the eggs with the hemp seeds. Dip each chicken strip in the hemp mixture. Transfer your chicken to the baking dish.
Bake for 20 to 25 minutes, turning once. You can broil these chicken strips to make them crispy, if desired.
Serve garnished with fresh chives.

# 81. Chicken Fillets with Cream-Mustard Sauce

**(Ready in about 25 minutes | Servings 4)**

**Per serving: 311 Calories; 16.9g Fat; 2.1g Carbs; 33.6g Protein;**

## INGREDIENTS

1 pound chicken fillets
Salt and pepper, to taste
1 tablespoon butter, melted
1/2 cup scallions, chopped
1 teaspoon garlic paste

1/4 cup dry white wine
1/4 cup low-sodium chicken broth
1/2 cup double cream
2 tablespoons whole grain mustard
1/2 cup fresh cilantro, roughly chopped

## DIRECTIONS

Rub the chicken fillets with salt and pepper to your liking.
Melt the butter in a saucepan that is preheated over a moderate flame. Now, cook the chicken fillets until they are just barely done. Transfer the chicken to a plate and set it aside.
Add the scallions and garlic paste to the saucepan; cook, stirring often, until it is aromatic or about 4 minutes.
Raise the heat to medium-high; pour in the wine and scrape the bits that may be stuck to the bottom of your saucepan.
Next, pour in the broth; allow the liquid to reduce by about half. Stir in the double cream and mustard.
Pour the sauce over the reserved chicken fillets and serve garnished with fresh cilantro. Enjoy!

# 82. Easy and Yummy Chicken Drumettes

**(Ready in about 30 minutes | Servings 4)**

**Per serving: 165 Calories; 9.8g Fat; 4.7g Carbs; 12.4g Protein;**

## INGREDIENTS

2 tablespoons tallow
4 chicken drumettes
Salt, to taste
1/2 cup leeks, chopped
1 carrot, sliced

2 cloves garlic, minced
1 teaspoon cayenne pepper
1 teaspoon dried marjoram
1/2 teaspoon mustard seeds
1 cup turkey stock

2 tomatoes, crushed
1 tablespoon Worcestershire sauce
1 teaspoon mixed peppercorns
1 thyme sprig
1 rosemary sprig

## DIRECTIONS

Melt the tallow in a saucepan over medium-high heat. Sprinkle the chicken drumettes with salt.
Then, fry the chicken drumettes until they are no longer pink and lightly browned on all sides; reserve.
Now, cook the leeks, carrots and garlic in pan drippings over medium heat for 4 to 6 minutes.
Reduce the heat to simmer, and add the remaining ingredients along with the reserved chicken. Simmer, partially covered, for 15 to 20 minutes. Serve warm.

# 83. Chicken Sausage with Salsa

**(Ready in about 15 minutes | Servings 4)**

**Per serving: 156 Calories; 4.2g Fat; 4.1g Carbs; 16.2g Protein;**

## INGREDIENTS

2 teaspoons lard, room temperature
4 chicken sausage, sliced
1/4 cup Sauvignon Blanc
1 cup pureed tomatoes
1 teaspoon granulated garlic

2 bell peppers, deveined and chopped
1 minced jalapeno, chopped
1 cup onion, diced
2 tablespoons fresh cilantro, minced
3 teaspoons lime juice

## DIRECTIONS

Warm the lard in a heavy-bottomed skillet over moderately high heat.
Sauté the sausage until well browned; pour in the wine and cook an additional 3 minutes. Reserve.
Then, make the salsa by mixing the pureed tomatoes, garlic, bell pepper, jalapeno pepper, onions, cilantro and lime juice.
Serve the sausage with the salsa on the side. Bon appétit!

# 84. Turkey Sausage with Bok Choy

**(Ready in about 50 minutes | Servings 4)**

**Per serving: 189 Calories; 12g Fat; 2.6g Carbs; 9.4g Protein;**

## INGREDIENTS

1 tablespoon butter
4 mild turkey sausages, breakfast links, sliced
2 shallots, chopped
Coarse salt and ground black pepper, to taste
1 pound Bok choy, tough stem ends trimmed

1 cup chicken stock
1/2 cup full-fat milk
1/8 teaspoon freshly grated nutmeg
6 ounces Gruyère, coarsely grated

## DIRECTIONS

Start by preheating an oven to 360 degrees F. Melt the butter in a pan; now, brown the sausage for a couple of minutes, stirring periodically; reserve.
Add the shallots, salt, pepper, and Bok choy. Add the chicken stock and cook until just tender, 2 to 3 minutes.
Spread the Bok choy mixture in a lightly greased baking dish. Top with the reserved sausage.
In a mixing bowl, thoroughly combine the chicken stock, milk, and nutmeg. Pour the mixture over the sausage.
Cover with a piece of foil and bake for 40 minutes. Remove the foil and scatter grated cheese over the top.
Bake in the upper third of oven an additional 4 minutes or until bubbly.

# 85. Easy Herby Turkey Drumsticks

**(Ready in about 1 hour | Servings 2)**

**Per serving: 488 Calories; 24.5g Fat; 2.1g Carbs; 33.6g Protein;**

## INGREDIENTS

2 tablespoons apple cider vinegar
2 thyme sprigs, chopped
2 rosemary sprigs, chopped
1 teaspoon dried marjoram
1 teaspoon dried basil

1 teaspoon granulated garlic
2 tablespoons olive oil
2 turkey drumsticks
Salt and black pepper, to taste
1/2 cup Taco bell sauce

## DIRECTIONS

To make the marinade, thoroughly combine the apple cider vinegar, thyme, rosemary, marjoram, basil, granulated garlic, and olive oil in a mixing bowl.
Now, marinate the turkey at least 3 hours in the refrigerator.
Cook the turkey drumsticks on a preheated grill for 45 minutes to 1 hour or until a meat thermometer has reached the temperature of 180 degrees F. Season with salt and pepper to taste.
Serve with Taco bell sauce on the side. Bon appétit!

## 86. Mediterranean Chicken Drumsticks with Aioli

**(Ready in about 35 minutes | Servings 4)**

**Per serving: 562 Calories; 43.8g Fat; 2.1g Carbs; 40.8g Protein;**

### INGREDIENTS

1 ½ tablespoons ghee
4 chicken drumsticks
Sea salt and crushed mixed peppercorns, to taste

1 tablespoon fresh parsley, chopped
6 Kalamata olives, pitted and halved
1 cup Halloumi cheese, cubed
1 hard-boiled egg yolk

1 tablespoon garlic, finely minced
1 tablespoon lemon juice
1/2 cup extra-virgin olive oil
1/4 teaspoon sea salt

### DIRECTIONS

Preheat your oven to 395 degrees F.

Melt the ghee in a nonstick skillet.

Season the chicken drumsticks with salt and crushed peppercorns; brown the chicken drumsticks in the hot skillet for 3 to 4 minutes.

Arrange the fried chicken on a baking sheet; scatter fresh parsley and olives over the top.

In the meantime, make the Aioli by mixing the remaining ingredients, except for the cheese, with an immersion blender. Mix until it comes together.

Now, spread the Aioli over the fried chicken. Bake in the preheated oven approximately 25 minutes. Add the Halloumi on top and bake an additional 3 to 4 minutes. Serve warm.

## 87. Ground Chicken with Peppers and Asiago Cheese

**(Ready in about 15 minutes | Servings 4)**

**Per serving: 301 Calories; 11.4g Fat; 5.2g Carbs; 37.9g Protein;**

### INGREDIENTS

1 tablespoon olive oil
1 teaspoon garlic, minced
1 cup shallots, chopped
1 chili pepper, deveined and chopped

4 bell peppers, deveined and chopped
1 pound chicken, ground
1/3 cup dry sherry
1 teaspoon Italian seasonings

Salt and black pepper, to taste
1/2 cup Asiago cheese, shredded

### DIRECTIONS

Heat the oil in a pan that is preheated over a moderate flame. Now, sauté the garlic and shallots until they are aromatic.

Now, stir in the peppers and ground chicken; cook until the chicken is no longer pink.

Add the sherry, Italian seasonings, salt and pepper. Cook an additional 5 minutes or until everything is thoroughly heated.

Scatter Asiago cheese over the top, remove from heat and serve immediately. Bon appétit!

## 88. The Best Chicken Tacos Ever

**(Ready in about 20 minutes | Servings 4)**

**Per serving: 535 Calories; 33.3g Fat; 4.8g Carbs; 47.9g Protein;**

### INGREDIENTS

2 teaspoons lard, room temperature
2 small-sized white onions, peeled and finely chopped
1 clove garlic, minced
1 pound ground chicken

2 slices bacon, chopped
1 tablespoon Mexican seasoning
Coarse salt and freshly ground black pepper
2 ripe tomatoes, pureed

1 ½ cups Cotija cheese
1/2 cup Pico de gallo
1/2 cup sour cream
1 head lettuce

### DIRECTIONS

Melt the lard in a pan over moderately high heat. Now, sweat the onions until translucent.

Add the garlic, chicken, and bacon; continue sautéing until the chicken is no longer pink. Add the Mexican seasoning, salt, and black pepper.

After that, stir in the tomatoes and cook for 5 minutes longer; reserve.

Then, preheat your oven to 360 degrees F. Line a baking sheet with parchment paper. Make 4 piles of shredded cheese and gently press them down.

Bake the cheese piles for 6 minutes in the middle of the preheated oven.

Let the tacos cool for 5 minutes and add the chicken mixture. Serve garnished with Pico de gallo, sour cream, and fresh lettuce leaves.

## 89. Turkey Soup with Baby Bok Choy

**(Ready in about 40 minutes | Servings 8)**

**Per serving: 211 Calories; 11.8g Fat; 3.1g Carbs; 23.7g Protein;**

### INGREDIENTS

1 tablespoon olive oil

2 stalks celery with leaves, chopped

2 carrots, sliced

1/2 cup onion, halved water to cover salt and pepper to taste

1/2 pound baby Bok choy, sliced into quarters lengthwise

2 pounds turkey carcass

2 teaspoons bouillon granules

1 tablespoon chili garlic sauce

6 cups water

### DIRECTIONS

Heat the oil in a large pot or Dutch oven over medium-high heat. Sauté the celery, carrots, onion and Bok choy until just tender, about 5 minutes.

Add the remaining ingredients and bring to a rolling boil.

Turn the heat to medium-low and cover the pot.

Cook an additional 30 minutes or until everything is cooked through. Bon appétit!

## 90. Mom's Turkey Soup

**(Ready in about 30 minutes | Servings 4)**

**Per serving: 256 Calories; 18.8g Fat; 5.4g Carbs; 15.8g Protein;**

### INGREDIENTS

1/2 cup full fat Greek-style yogurt

1/2 stick butter

1/2 cup yellow squash, diced

2 garlic cloves, minced

4 ½ cups chicken broth

1/2 teaspoon sea salt

1/4 teaspoon ground black pepper

1/3 cup heavy cream

1 ½ cups leftover turkey, shredded

### DIRECTIONS

Add the Greek-style yogurt, butter, squash, and garlic to a stock pot; bring to a simmer over a medium-low heat.

Cook until everything is thoroughly warmed. Add the remaining ingredients. Cook another 20 minutes, partially covered, and serve warm.

## 91. Vodka Duck Fillets

**(Ready in about 20 minutes | Servings 4)**

**Per serving: 351 Calories; 24.7g Fat; 6.6g Carbs; 22.1g Protein;**

### INGREDIENTS

1 tablespoon lard, room temperature

4 duck fillets

4 green onions, white and green parts, chopped

Salt and cayenne pepper, to taste

1 teaspoon mixed peppercorns

1 ½ cups turkey stock

3 tablespoons Worcestershire sauce

2 ounces vodka

1/2 teaspoon ground bay leaf

1/2 cup sour cream

### DIRECTIONS

Melt the lard in a skillet that is preheated over medium-high heat. Sear the duck fillets, turning once, for 4 to 6 minutes.

Now, add the remaining ingredients, except for the sour cream, to the skillet. Cook, partially covered, for a further 7 minutes.

Serve warm, garnished with sour cream. Bon appétit!

## 92. Spicy Chicken with Brussels Sprouts

**(Ready in about 20 minutes | Servings 4)**

**Per serving: 273 Calories; 15.4g Fat; 4.2g Carbs; 23g Protein;**

### INGREDIENTS

2 tablespoons sesame oil

1 ½ pounds Brussels sprouts, trimmed and cut into halves

1/4 teaspoon seasoned salt

2 cloves garlic, minced

3/4 pound chicken breasts, chopped into bite-sized pieces

1/2 cup white onions, chopped

1 cup bone broth, low-sodium

2 tablespoons Sauvignon wine

1/2 teaspoon chipotle chile powder

1/2 teaspoon whole black peppercorns

2 tablespoons fresh chives, chopped

### DIRECTIONS

Heat 1 tablespoon of the oil in a pan over moderate heat. Now, sauté the Brussels sprouts for 2 to 4 minutes or until golden brown. Season with salt; reserve.

Heat the remaining 1 tablespoon of oil in the same pan that is preheated over moderately high heat Add the garlic and chicken; cook about 3 minutes.

Add the onions, broth, wine, chipotle chile powder, and black peppercorns. Bring to a boil and reduce the heat to a simmer. Simmer for 4 minutes more.

Add the reserved Brussels sprouts to the pan and serve warm garnished with fresh chopped chives. Bon appétit!

## 93. Classic Tarragon Chicken Salad

**(Ready in about 20 minutes | Servings 4)**

**Per serving: 353 Calories; 23.5g Fat; 5.8g Carbs; 27.8g Protein;**

### INGREDIENTS

2 cups shredded skinless, boneless rotisserie chicken

2 avocados, pitted, peeled and diced

1 red onion, thinly sliced

1 tablespoon fresh tarragon, chopped

1/3 cup plain Greek yogurt

1/4 cup canola mayonnaise

1 tablespoon Dijon mustard

Salt and black pepper, to taste

3 hard-boiled eggs, cut into quarters

### DIRECTIONS

Add the shredded chicken and diced avocado to a mixing bowl. Toss with the onion and tarragon.

Stir in the Greek yogurt, mayonnaise, and mustard; season with salt and pepper to taste and gently stir to combine well.

Transfer to a nice salad bowl, garnish with hard-boiled eggs and serve well-chilled.

## 94. Chorizo with Asiago Cheese

**(Ready in about 20 minutes | Servings 4)**

**Per serving: 330 Calories; 17.2g Fat; 4.5g Carbs; 34.4g Protein;**

### INGREDIENTS

1 tablespoon extra-virgin olive oil

16 ounces smoked turkey and chicken chorizo, crumbled

4 spring onions, chopped

1 teaspoon garlic paste

Sea salt and ground black pepper, to taste

3/4 teaspoon ground ginger

1 teaspoon sage, dried

1 teaspoon basil

1 tomato, pureed

2 tablespoons ketchup

1 tablespoon dry sherry

1 teaspoon chili powder

2 tablespoons fresh parsley, roughly chopped

1 ½ cups Asiago cheese, grated

### DIRECTIONS

Start by preheating an oven to 370 degrees F.

Heat the oil in a heavy-bottomed over moderately high heat. Now, brown the ground turkey, along with the onion for 5 to 6 minutes. Make sure to stir continuously, crumbling the meat.

Add the garlic paste, salt, pepper, ginger, sage, basil, and tomato puree. Cook for a couple of minutes more or until everything is heated through.

Add the remaining ingredients, ending with the grated cheese; cook an additional 8 minutes or until the cheese has completely melted.

Garnish with avocado and cilantro. Serve with sour cream. Enjoy!

# 95. Creamy Cauliflower and Chicken Soup

**(Ready in about 30 minutes | Servings 6)**

**Per serving: 231 Calories; 18.2g Fat; 5.9g Carbs; 11.9g Protein;**

## INGREDIENTS

1/2 stick butter
1/2 cup shallot, finely chopped
1 spring garlic, finely minced
1 celery, chopped
1/2 teaspoon kosher salt
1/4 teaspoon ground white pepper

1/4 teaspoon ground black pepper, or more to the taste
2 ½ cups water
3 cups chicken stock
1 cup leftover roast chicken, shredded
1 ¼ cups heavy cream
1 head cauliflower, broken into small-sized florets

## DIRECTIONS

Melt the butter in a stock pot over a moderate heat. Now, sauté the shallot, spring garlic and celery for 4 minutes or until they're tender, stirring periodically.

Then, stir in the salt, white pepper and black pepper, bringing to a boil. Add the remaining ingredients and lower the temperature; continue to simmer for 25 minutes.

After that, blend the mixture with an immersion blender and serve immediately in individual bowls, garnished with dill pickles.

# 96. Cheesy Turkey Dip with Fresno Chiles

**(Ready in about 25 minutes | Servings 4)**

**Per serving: 284 Calories; 19g Fat; 3.2g Carbs; 26.7g Protein;**

## INGREDIENTS

Nonstick cooking spray
1 tablespoon olive oil
1 onion, chopped
1 garlic clove, minced
1 pound ground turkey
1 ½ cups Cottage cheese, creamed, 4% fat, softened

1/4 cup Greek-style yogurt
Salt and black pepper, to taste
1 Fresno chile, minced
1 teaspoon dried oregano
1/2 cup blue cheese, shredded
1 ½ cups Gruyère, shredded

## DIRECTIONS

Preheat an oven to 360 degrees F. Lightly grease a baking pan with a nonstick cooking spray.

Heat up a skillet over a moderately high flame. Heat the oil and sauté the onion and garlic until the onions are translucent.

Now, brown the turkey until it is no longer pink; reserve.

In a bowl, mix the Cottage cheese and Greek yogurt until creamy and uniform. Add the salt, pepper, Fresno chiles and oregano along with the reserved turkey/onion mixture.

Spoon into the prepared baking dish; scatter the shredded cheese on top. Bake approximately 18 minutes or until thoroughly heated. Serve with fresh veggie sticks.

# 97. Habanero and Turkey Bacon Balls

**(Ready in about 5 minutes | Servings 4)**

**Per serving: 195 Calories; 16.7g Fat; 2.2g Carbs; 8.8g Protein;**

## INGREDIENTS

4 ounces turkey bacon, chopped
4 ounces Cottage cheese
1 tablespoon butter, cold

1 habanero pepper, deveined and minced
1 teaspoon fresh sage, minced
2 tablespoons chives, finely chopped

## DIRECTIONS

Thoroughly combine the bacon, cheese, butter, habanero pepper and fresh sage.

Shape this mixture into 8 balls.

Place the finely chopped chives on a plate; roll your balls through to coat. Serve right away!

# 98. Oven Fried Crispy Chicken Legs

**(Ready in about 50 minutes | Servings 4)**

**Per serving: 345 Calories; 14.1g Fat; 0.4g Carbs; 50.8g Protein;**

## INGREDIENTS

4 chicken legs
1 tablespoon butter
1 teaspoon bouillon powder
1/4 teaspoon ground black pepper, or more to the taste

Salt, to your liking
1 teaspoon paprika
1 teaspoon dried basil
1 teaspoon dried rosemary

## DIRECTIONS

Start by preheating an oven to 420 degrees F. Line a rimmed baking sheet with a piece of parchment paper.
Next, air-dry the chicken legs and rub them with the butter. Then, sprinkle the chicken with all remaining ingredients.
Arrange the chicken legs out in a single layer on the prepared baking sheet.
Bake the chicken legs until the skin is crispy, about 45 minutes. Serve with your favorite hot sauce.

# 99. Holiday Turkey Wrapped in Prosciutto

**(Ready in about 30 minutes | Servings 6)**

**Per serving: 286 Calories; 9.7g Fat; 6.9g Carbs; 39.9g Protein;**

## INGREDIENTS

2 pounds turkey breasts, marinated
1 ½ tablespoons coconut butter, room temperature
1 teaspoon cayenne pepper
1/2 teaspoon chili powder
1 sprig rosemary, finely chopped
2 sprigs fresh thyme, finely chopped

2 tablespoons Cabernet Sauvignon
1 teaspoon garlic, finely minced
1 teaspoon sea salt
1/2 teaspoon freshly ground black pepper
10 strips prosciutto

## DIRECTIONS

Cut the turkey breasts into 10 even slices.
Melt the coconut butter in a nonstick skillet over a moderate heat. Sear the turkey breasts for 2 to 3 minutes on each side.
Sprinkle the turkey breasts with all seasonings and minced garlic; drizzle with wine. Now, wrap each turkey piece into one prosciutto strip.
Preheat your oven to 450 degrees F. Lay the wrapped turkey in a roasting pan; roast about 25 minutes.
Serve garnished with fresh cilantro. Bon appétit!

# 100. Tomato Rum-Glazed Chicken Thighs

**(Ready in about 1 hour + marinating time | Servings 4)**

**Per serving: 307 Calories; 12.1g Fat; 2.7g Carbs; 33.6g Protein;**

## INGREDIENTS

2 pounds chicken thighs
2 tablespoons olive oil
Sea salt and ground black pepper, to taste
1 teaspoon paprika
1 teaspoon dried oregano
1 teaspoon dried marjoram
2 ripe tomatoes, pureed

3/4 cup dark rum
3 tablespoons soy sauce
2 tablespoons Swerve
2 habanero chile peppers, minced
1 tablespoon minced fresh ginger
1 teaspoon ground allspice
2 tablespoons fresh lime juice, plus wedges for serving

## DIRECTIONS

Start by preheating your oven to 420 degrees F.
Now, toss the chicken thighs with the olive oil, salt, black pepper, paprika, oregano, and marjoram.
In a separate mixing bowl, thoroughly combine the pureed tomato puree, rum, soy sauce, Swerve, habanero peppers, ginger, allspice and fresh lime juice.
Pour the rum/tomato mixture over the chicken thighs and refrigerate, covered, for 2 hours.
Discard the marinade and arrange the chicken thighs on a rimmed baking pan. Bake for 50 minutes or until thoroughly cooked.
In the meantime, cook the reserved marinade in a pan over a moderate heat; continue to cook until the liquid has reduced by half.
Pour the sauce over the chicken thighs and place under the broiler for 4 minutes on high. Serve immediately.

# PORK

## 101. The Easiest Meatballs Ever

**(Ready in about 30 minutes | Servings 6)**

**Per serving: 284 Calories; 14.8g Fat; 1.3g Carbs; 34.4g Protein;**

### INGREDIENTS

**For the Meatballs:**
1 pound ground pork
1/2 pound ground beef
1 tablespoon beef bouillon granules
2 small-sized eggs
2 cloves garlic, minced
1 tablespoon Montreal steak seasoning

**For the Sauce:**
3 teaspoons butter
1/2 teaspoon dried thyme
Salt and pepper to taste
1 cup bone broth
1 cup heavy whipping cream
Salt and pepper, to taste

### DIRECTIONS

Begin by preheating an oven to 360 degrees F.
Thoroughly combine all ingredients for the meatballs in a mixing bowl. Shape into 20 balls with oiled hands.
Arrange the meatballs on a cookie sheet that is previously greased with a nonstick cooking spray.
Bake for 18 to 22 minutes or until the meatballs are thoroughly cooked. Now, place your meatballs under the broiler for a couple of minutes to achieve a browned, crispy crust.
Meanwhile, make the sauce in a pan. Firstly, melt the butter over a moderate heat. Slowly and gradually stir in the other ingredients for the sauce, whisking constantly.
Bring to a boil and cook until the sauce has thickened. Serve the meatballs with the sauce on the side.

## 102. Peppery Pork with Blue Cheese and Avocado

**(Ready in about 20 minutes | Servings 2)**

**Per serving: 431 Calories; 22.9g Fat; 5.2g Carbs; 42.2g Protein;**

### INGREDIENTS

1 tablespoon bacon grease
1/2 pound ground pork
1 bell pepper, deveined and chopped
1 jalapeno pepper, deveined and chopped
1/4 cup beef bone broth

Kosher salt and black pepper, to your liking
1/4 teaspoon marjoram
1 small head of Romaine lettuce, leaves separated
1/2 cup radicchio, trimmed and sliced

1 avocado, pitted, peeled and diced
2 teaspoons fresh lemon juice
2 shallots, chopped
2 tomatoes, diced
1/2 cup Greek yogurt
1/2 cup blue cheese, crumbled

### DIRECTIONS

Warm the bacon grease in a saucepan over medium heat; now, brown the ground pork for 8 minutes or so. Make sure to stir constantly, breaking the meat with a wooden spatula.
Add the peppers and cook until they are tender and aromatic, approximately 3 minutes. Pour in the bone broth; season with salt, pepper, and marjoram; cook an additional 4 to 5 minutes; reserve.
Create a bed of lettuce leaves on two serving plates. Mound the meat-pepper mixture onto the plate.
Arrange the radicchio and avocado around the meat mixture; drizzle the radicchio and avocado with fresh lemon juice.
Top with the shallots and tomatoes. Serve garnished with Greek yogurt and blue cheese. Bon appétit!

## 103. Pork Belly with Homey Barbecue Sauce

**(Ready in about 2 hours | Servings 8)**

**Per serving: 561 Calories; 34g Fat; 1.7g Carbs; 52.7g Protein;**

### INGREDIENTS

2 pounds pork belly
2 tablespoons vegetable oil
2 garlic cloves, halved
1 teaspoon salt
1/2 teaspoon freshly ground black pepper

**For the Barbecue Sauce:**
1/2 cup tomato puree
1 teaspoon hot sauce
1 teaspoon Dijon mustard

A few drops of liquid smoke
1/3 teaspoon ground cumin
1/3 teaspoon smoked paprika

### DIRECTIONS

Preheat your oven to 420 degrees F.
Now, rub the pork belly with the vegetable oil and garlic. Sprinkle with salt and pepper.
Roast the pork for 18 to 22 minutes. Now, decrease the heat to 330 degrees F. Roast for a further 1 hour 30 minutes.
Meanwhile, whisk all ingredients for the barbecue sauce until everything is well blended.
Remove the crackling and cut the pork belly into slices. Serve with the sauce on the side.

# 104. Oven-Roasted Pork Cutlets with Veggies

**(Ready in about 30 minutes + marinating time | Servings 4)**

**Per serving: 452 Calories; 34.8g Fat; 4.7g Carbs; 26.3g Protein;**

## INGREDIENTS

1 teaspoon garlic paste
1/2 teaspoon sea salt
1/2 teaspoon freshly ground black pepper
1 tablespoon yellow mustard
2 tablespoons cider vinegar

2 tablespoons lard, melted
4 pork cutlets
1 celery stalk, diced
2 carrots, sliced
1 cup leeks, sliced

## DIRECTIONS

In a mixing bowl, combine the garlic paste, salt, black pepper, mustard and cider vinegar until well mixed. Add the pork cutlets and let them marinate for 2 hours.

Now, melt the lard in an oven-safe pan over a moderate heat. Brown the pork cutlets for 5 minutes on each side. Add the celery, carrots, and leeks.

Cook an additional 5 minutes, stirring periodically.

Transfer the pan to the oven; roast the pork with the vegetables for about 13 minutes. Serve the meat and vegetables along with the pan juices. Bon appétit!

# 105. Juicy Pork Medallions with Scallions

**(Ready in about 20 minutes | Servings 4)**

**Per serving: 192 Calories; 6.9g Fat; 0.9g Carbs; 29.8g Protein;**

## INGREDIENTS

1 pound pork tenderloin, cut crosswise into 12 medallions
Coarse salt and ground black pepper, to taste
1/2 teaspoon garlic powder
1/2 teaspoon red pepper flakes, crushed
1 tablespoon butter

A bunch of scallions, roughly chopped
1 thyme sprig, minced
2 rosemary sprigs, minced
1 teaspoon dried sage, crushed

## DIRECTIONS

Season each pork medallion with salt, black pepper, garlic powder and red pepper flakes.

Then, melt the butter in a saucepan over medium-high heat. Cook the pork tenderloin about 3 minutes per side.

Add the scallions, thyme, and rosemary; cook until heated through, an additional 3 minutes. Serve sprinkled with dried sage. Bon appétit!

# 106. Crock Pot Peppery Pork Ribs

**(Ready in about 8 hours | Servings 4)**

**Per serving: 192 Calories; 6.9g Fat; 0.9g Carbs; 29.8g Protein;**

## INGREDIENTS

1 tablespoon lard
1 pound pork ribs
1 teaspoon Ancho chiles, minced
1 bell pepper, thinly sliced
1/4 cup Worcestershire sauce
1/4 cup dry red wine

1/2 teaspoon smoked cayenne pepper
1 garlic clove, crushed
1/2 teaspoon ground oregano
1/2 teaspoon ground cloves
1 teaspoon grated orange peel

## DIRECTIONS

Treat the sides and bottom of your Crock pot with melted lard. Arrange the pork chops and peppers on the bottom.

Drizzle the Worcestershire sauce and wine over everything. Sprinkle with cayenne pepper, garlic, oregano and ground cloves.

Slow cook on Low setting approximately 8 hours. Serve on individual plates garnished with grated orange peel.

# 107. Pork Stuffed Peppers with Yogurt-Chive Sauce

**(Ready in about 40 minutes | Servings 4)**

**Per serving: 330 Calories; 20.8g Fat; 3.6g Carbs; 27.1g Protein;**

## INGREDIENTS

6 bell peppers, deveined
1 tablespoon olive oil
1 small-sized yellow onion, chopped
1 garlic clove, minced
1/2 pound ground pork

1/3 pound ground veal
1 ripe tomato, chopped
1/2 teaspoon ground coriander
1/2 teaspoon sea salt

1/4 teaspoon ground black pepper, to taste
1 teaspoon paprika
1/2 cup Greek yogurt
2 tablespoon chives, chopped

## DIRECTIONS

Parboil the peppers in salted water for 4 to 6 minutes.

Heat the oil in a pan that is preheated over a moderate flame. Sauté the onions and garlic until tender and aromatic.

Add the ground meat and cook, crumbling it with a spatula, for 5 to 6 minutes. Add the chopped tomatoes and cook an additional 4 minutes or until thoroughly heated.

Season with the ground coriander, salt, black pepper, and paprika. Preheat the oven to 360 degrees F.

Stuff the peppers and transfer them to a baking dish. Bake approximately 22 minutes.

Meanwhile, combine the Greek yogurt with chopped chives. Divide the peppers among individual serving plates; serve with a dollop of prepared yogurt-chive sauce and enjoy!

# 108. Rolled Pork Loin with Leeks

**(Ready in about 1 hour + marinating time | Servings 6)**

**Per serving: 220 Calories; 6g Fat; 3g Carbs; 33.3g Protein;**

## INGREDIENTS

1 thyme sprig, chopped
1 rosemary sprig, chopped
1 teaspoon mustard seeds
1/2 teaspoon celery seeds

2 garlic cloves, pressed
1 tablespoon butter
1 ½ pounds boneless pork loin, butterflied

1/2 cup Burgundy wine
1 cup bone broth
1 leek, thinly sliced
1 teaspoon whole black peppercorns

## DIRECTIONS

Pour boiling water over your pork to ensure a crisp crackling; pat it dry. Spritz a roasting pan with a nonstick cooking spray.

In a mixing dish, combine the thyme, rosemary, mustard seeds, celery seeds, garlic and butter.

Unfold the pork loin; spread the herb/butter mixture all over the cut side; roll the pork loin. Secure with kitchen string and place in the roasting pan. Let it marinate at least 2 hours in the refrigerator.

Preheat your oven to 400 degrees F.

Add the wine, broth and leeks to the roasting pan; scatter whole peppercorns around the meat. Roast for 55 minutes to 1 hour, until juices run clear. Serve with fresh or pickled salad. Bon appétit!

# 109. Grandma's Famous Pork Stew

**(Ready in about 45 minutes | Servings 8)**

**Per serving: 390 Calories; 27.8g Fat; 4.7g Carbs; 28.3g Protein;**

## INGREDIENTS

2 tablespoons lard, at room temperature
2 pounds pork shoulder, cut into 3/4-inch cubes
1 teaspoon sea salt
1 teaspoon mixed peppercorns, freshly cracked
1 large-sized red onion, chopped

1 chili pepper, minced
2 garlic cloves, finely minced
2 carrots, peeled and chopped
1 celery stalk, chopped
2 tablespoons dry red wine
3 cups beef stock, preferably homemade

2 ripe tomatoes, chopped
1 bay leaf
1/2 teaspoon dried basil
1 ½ teaspoons dried sage
1 teaspoon dried marjoram
1 cup fresh button mushrooms, sliced
1/2 cup fresh cilantro, chopped

## DIRECTIONS

Melt the lard in a stockpot that is preheated over a moderate heat. Then, brown the meat for a few minutes; season with salt and peppercorns and reserve.

Then, cook the onions, chili pepper, garlic, carrots and celery until they are tender. Add the wine to deglaze the bottom of your pot.

Add the remaining ingredients, except for the fresh cilantro. Cook for 40 minutes, partially covered. Serve topped with the fresh cilantro.

## 110. Pork Chops with Ancho Chile Sauce

**(Ready in about 30 minutes | Servings 6)**

**Per serving: 347 Calories; 29.2g Fat; 0.2g Carbs; 20.2g Protein;**

### INGREDIENTS

1 tablespoon olive oil
6 pork chops
For the Sauce:
2 Ancho chiles, chopped
1/2 cup bone broth
2 garlic cloves, minced

1/2 teaspoon ground cumin
1 teaspoon dried basil
1/2 teaspoon red pepper flakes, crushed
Salt and ground black pepper, to taste
2 teaspoons olive oil

### DIRECTIONS

Heat 1 tablespoon of olive oil in a saucepan that is preheated over a moderately high flame. Sear the pork chops until they're well browned and their juices run clear.

To make the sauce, in a pot, boil the Ancho chiles and bone broth for a couple of minutes. Now, remove your pot from the heat; allow the chiles to stand in the hot water for 15 to 25 minutes.

Add the chiles along with the liquid to a blender or food processor; add the remaining ingredients for the sauce.

Puree until creamy, smooth and uniform. Serve with the warm pork chops and enjoy!

## 111. Crock Pot Spare Ribs

**(Ready in about 4 hours 30 minutes | Servings 4)**

**Per serving: 412 Calories; 22g Fat; 3g Carbs; 46.3g Protein;**

### INGREDIENTS

1 tablespoon lard, at room temperature
1 ½ pounds spare ribs
3/4 cup vegetable stock, preferably homemade
2 teaspoons Swerve
2 cloves garlic, chopped
1 Serrano pepper, chopped

A bunch of scallions, chopped
Salt, to taste
1/2 teaspoon ground cumin
1 teaspoon whole black peppercorns
2 bay leaves

### DIRECTIONS

Melt the lard in a pan over a moderately high heat. Cook the spare ribs for 8 minutes, turning occasionally.

In the meantime, whisk the stock, Swerve, garlic, Serrano pepper, scallions, salt and cumin in a mixing dish.

Transfer the browned spare ribs to your crock pot; pour in the stock mixture. Add the black peppercorns and bay leaves.

Cook for 4 hours 30 minutes on Low heat setting. Serve on a bed of cauliflower rice. Bon appétit!

## 112. Bacon and Blue Cheese Balls

**(Ready in about 5 minutes | Servings 4)**

**Per serving: 232 Calories; 17.6g Fat; 3.9g Carbs; 14.2g Protein;**

### INGREDIENTS

3 ounces blue cheese, crumbled
3 ounces Ricotta cheese
1 ½ tablespoons mayonnaise

2 teaspoons ketchup
1/2 cup bacon, chopped
2 tablespoons parsley, chopped

### DIRECTIONS

Thoroughly combine all ingredients in a mixing dish.
Shape the mixture into 8 equal balls. Serve well chilled.

# 113. Sage and Milk Pork Loin

**(Ready in about 1 hour 35 minutes | Servings 8)**

**Per serving: 293 Calories; 15.4g Fat; 5.4g Carbs; 31.4g Protein;**

## INGREDIENTS

3 teaspoons olive oil

2 pounds pork loin

Salt and cayenne pepper, to taste

1 teaspoon dried thyme

1/2 cup shallots, sliced

2 bell peppers, deveined and thinly sliced

2 cup full-fat milk

1 tablespoon dried sage, crushed

## DIRECTIONS

Start by preheating your oven to 330 degrees F.

Heat the oil in a pan over a moderate flame. Sear the pork loin in a pan until just browned.

Transfer the loin to a baking pan. Season with salt, pepper, and thyme. Scatter the sliced shallot and peppers around the meat.

Pour in the milk and cover the pan tightly with a piece of foil. Roast for 1 hour 30 minutes, turning the loin once or twice.

Carve the pork loin and transfer to a serving plate along with the roasted vegetables as well as the cooking liquid. Serve garnished with sage leaves. Bon appétit!

# 114. Fried Cabbage with Smoked Ham

**(Ready in about 45 minutes | Servings 4)**

**Per serving: 93 Calories; 2.6g Fat; 6.1g Carbs; 6.8g Protein;**

## INGREDIENTS

4 slices smoked ham, chopped

2 medium-sized shallots, diced

1 teaspoon garlic, minced

1 pound green cabbage, shredded

1/2 teaspoon kosher salt, or to taste

1/4 teaspoon cayenne pepper

1/2 teaspoon black peppercorns

1/4 teaspoon ground cumin

## DIRECTIONS

Cook the ham in a pot over medium-high heat for about 8 minutes.

Add the shallots and garlic; sauté them for 5 to 7 minutes more. Stir in the cabbage and continue stirring for a couple of minutes more, adding a splash of stock if needed.

Then, sprinkle with kosher salt, cayenne pepper, black peppercorns and ground cumin. Afterwards, turn the heat to low; let it simmer, covered, for 25 minutes longer. Enjoy!

# 115. Grilled Creole-Style Pork Shoulder

**(Ready in about 30 minutes + marinating time | Servings 6)**

**Per serving: 335 Calories; 24.3g Fat; 0.8g Carbs; 26.4g Protein;**

## INGREDIENTS

Salt and ground black pepper, to taste

1 teaspoon cayenne pepper

3 teaspoons extra-virgin olive oil

2 clove garlic, minced

A few drops of liquid smoke

1 tablespoon Creole seasoning

1 ½ tablespoons Worcestershire sauce

1 ½ pounds pork shoulder, cut into 6 serving portions

## DIRECTIONS

Mix the salt, black pepper, cayenne pepper, olive oil, garlic, liquid smoke Creole seasoning, and Worcestershire sauce until you get a thick, creamy mixture.

Rub the pork shoulder on all sides with the spice mixture, covering it completely. Allow it to stand for 1 hour 30 minutes at room temperature.

Now lightly grease your grill and preheat it. Grill the pork about 18 minutes, turning occasionally.

Serve with cauliflower mash and salad of choice. Bon appétit!

# 116. Pork and Mushroom Stuffed Zucchini

**(Ready in about 50 minutes | Servings 8)**

**Per serving: 230 Calories; 11.8g Fat; 5.5g Carbs; 23.2g Protein;**

## INGREDIENTS

4 medium-sized zucchinis, cut into halves

2 tablespoons canola oil

2 shallots, chopped

1 garlic clove, pressed

1 pound ground pork

1 cup button mushrooms, chopped

Salt and ground black pepper, to taste

2 tomatoes, pureed

1/2 cup chicken stock

1 cup Colby cheese, freshly grated

## DIRECTIONS

Scoop out the zucchini flesh to create indentations.

Preheat your oven to 360 degrees F. Then, spritz a baking pan with a nonstick cooking spray.

Heat the oil in a saucepan over a moderate flame, Now, sweat the shallots for 2 to 3 minutes, stirring continuously.

Now, add the garlic and cook an additional minute. Stir in the ground pork and mushrooms; cook for a further 5 minutes.

After that, add the pureed tomatoes and chicken stock. Season with salt and pepper.

Reduce the heat to medium-low; let it simmer, partially covered, for 10 minutes, stirring periodically.

Divide the mixture between the zucchini halves. Bake about 27 minutes in the preheated oven. Top with freshly grated cheese and serve immediately. Bon appétit!

# 117. Country Pork Goulash with Cauliflower Rice

**(Ready in about 25 minutes | Servings 6)**

**Per serving: 228 Calories; 8.7g Fat; 5.8g Carbs; 30.1g Protein;**

## INGREDIENTS

1 tablespoon lard, room temperature

2 white onions, chopped

1 heaping teaspoon garlic paste

1 ¼ pounds ground pork

2 slices bacon, chopped

Salt and red pepper, to taste

1 teaspoon capers

2 ripe Roma tomatoes, crushed

1 ½ cups bone broth

1/2 teaspoon fennel seeds

2 teaspoons smoked cayenne pepper

1 bay leaf

1/2 cup loosely packed fresh cilantro, roughly chopped

2 cups cauliflower rice, cooked

## DIRECTIONS

Melt the lard in a pan that is preheated over a moderately high heat. Sauté the onions and garlic until just tender and fragrant.

Stir in the ground pork, and cook for 7 minutes, crumbling with a fork or spatula. Add the bacon, salt, red pepper, and capers and cook for 2 minutes more.

Add the tomatoes, broth, fennel seeds, cayenne pepper, and bay leaf. Turn the heat to medium-low and simmer for 10 to 13 minutes or until everything is heated through.

Garnish with fresh cilantro and serve with hot cauliflower rice.

# 118. Timeless Pork Stew with Steamed Broccoli

**(Ready in about 2 hours | Servings 6)**

**Per serving: 336 Calories; 15.9g Fat; 6g Carbs; 35g Protein;**

## INGREDIENTS

1 ½ pounds pork stew meat, cubed

Ground black pepper to taste

1 teaspoon paprika

2 tablespoons lard, at room temperature

1 leek, chopped

1 teaspoon garlic, finely minced

1/4 cup dry red wine

2 bay leaves

1/2 teaspoon celery seeds

3 cups water

1 tablespoon beef bouillon granules

2 bell peppers, chopped

1 habanero pepper, chopped

1 stalk celery, chopped

1 tablespoon fresh coriander, chopped

1 tablespoon flax seed meal

1 cup broccoli, broken into florets

## DIRECTIONS

Rub the pork stew meat with the black pepper and paprika.

Melt the lard in a stockpot that is preheated over a high flame. Brown the pork about 8 minutes, stirring periodically. Reserve, keeping warm.

Now, sauté the leeks and garlic in the pan drippings for 8 to 9 minutes or until they're tender. Add a splash of dry red wine to scrape up any browned bits from the bottom of your stockpot.

Add the other ingredients, minus the flax seed meal and broccoli. Turn the heat to medium-low and cover the pot; allow it to simmer for 1 hour 45 minutes.

Now, stir in the flax seed meal and continue cooking for 4 minutes more, stirring constantly.

Meanwhile, fill a large pan with about 1-inch of water; bring to a rolling boil. Cook the broccoli in a steamer basket inside the pan. Steam about 9 minutes or until the broccoli is tender.

Season with salt to taste and serve with warm pork stew.

# 119. Mom's Signature Pork Stew

**(Ready in about 25 minutes | Servings 4)**

**Per serving: 295 Calories; 19.6g Fat; 4.7g Carbs; 20.3g Protein;**

## INGREDIENTS

1 tablespoon butter
2 shallots, chopped
1 carrot, chopped
1 teaspoon habanero pepper, deveined and minced

3/4 pound boneless pork shoulder, cubed
1/2 tablespoon garlic paste
1 ½ cups bone broth
1/2 teaspoon ground bay leaf
1/2 teaspoon ground cloves

Himalayan salt and ground black pepper, to taste
1 tablespoon fresh parsley, chopped
1 avocado, pitted, peeled and diced
1/2 cup sour cream, full-fat

## DIRECTIONS

Melt the butter in a heavy-bottomed pot that is preheated over a moderate heat.
Now, sauté the shallots, carrot, and habanero pepper for 3 minutes or until they are tender.
After that, add cubed pork; cook an additional 5 minutes, stirring frequently.
Then, add the garlic paste, broth, bay leaf powder ground cloves, salt, and pepper; turn the heat to a medium-high and bring it to a boil.
Next, decrease the heat to a simmer. Cook an additional 15 minutes or until thoroughly heated.
Serve in individual bowls, topped with fresh parsley and avocado and dolloped with well-chilled sour cream. Enjoy!

# 120. Pork Meatballs with Herby Tomato Sauce

**(Ready in about 50 minutes | Servings 6)**

**Per serving: 237 Calories; 12g Fat; 5.6g Carbs; 26.4g Protein;**

## INGREDIENTS

**For the Meatballs:**
1 pound beef, ground
1 egg, beaten
1/4 cup almond flour
3/4 cup grated parmesan cheese
2 ounces full-fat milk

Salt and ground black pepper, to taste
1 white onion, finely chopped
1 teaspoon garlic paste
1/2 tablespoon chili powder
1 teaspoon onion flakes
2 tablespoons fresh parsley, chopped

**For the Sauce:**
2 tablespoons olive oil
2 ripe tomatoes, chopped
Salt and ground black pepper, to taste
1 teaspoon red pepper flakes, crushed
1 teaspoon garlic powder
1 rosemary sprig
1 thyme sprig
1 tablespoon cider vinegar

## DIRECTIONS

Start by preheating your oven to 360 degrees F. Now, spritz an oven safe dish with a nonstick cooking spray.
In a mixing dish, thoroughly combine all ingredients for the meatballs. Next, shape the mixture into 2-inch balls; place them in a single layer in the greased baking dish. Spritz the meatballs with cooking spray.
In another mixing dish, thoroughly combine all ingredients for the sauce. Pour the sauce over the meatballs.
Bake for 45 minutes or until everything is heated through. Bon appétit!

# 121. Spicy Pork Soup

**(Ready in about 1 hour | Servings 4)**

**Per serving: 341 Calories; 12.9g Fat; 5.8g Carbs; 45.4g Protein;**

## INGREDIENTS

2 tablespoons olive oil
1 ½ pounds pork stew meat, cubed
Salt and black pepper, to taste
1 onion, chopped
2 garlic cloves, crushed
1/2 cup dry white wine

2 carrots, thinly sliced
2 parsnips, thinly sliced
4 cups beef bone broth
1 ripe Roma tomato, crushed
1 Anaheim chile, seeded and cut into very thin strips with scissors

1/2 teaspoon dried basil
2 thyme sprigs
2 rosemary sprigs
Fresh cilantro, for garnish

## DIRECTIONS

Heat the olive oil in a heavy-bottomed pot that is preheated over a moderately high flame. Now, sear the pork cubes until they are just browned; reserve.
Then, cook the onions and garlic in pan drippings for 3 to 4 minutes. Pour in wine to deglaze the bottom.
Add the carrots, parsnip, and beef bone broth, bringing to a boil. Turn the heat to medium-low and simmer 6 to 7 more minutes.
Add the tomato, chile, basil, thyme, and rosemary; let it simmer an additional 50 minutes, partially covered. Serve hot garnished with chopped cilantro.

## 122. Bacon and Sausage Kraut

**(Ready in about 35 minutes | Servings 6)**

**Per serving: 309 Calories; 20.6g Fat; 4.2g Carbs; 19.3g Protein;**

### INGREDIENTS

4 slices bacon, chopped
2 pork sausages, sliced
1 onion, chopped
1 jalapeno pepper, finely minced
1 teaspoon garlic, finely minced
1/2 teaspoon celery seeds, ground
1/2 teaspoon ground cumin

1/4 teaspoon ground bay leaf
1 cup chicken stock
1/3 cup dry white wine
1 ½ pounds prepared sauerkraut, drained
1 tablespoon fresh parsley, for garnish
1 tablespoon Dijon mustard, for garnish

### DIRECTIONS

Cook the bacon in a deep pan that is preheated over a moderate flame. Cook about 8 minutes, stirring periodically; reserve.
Leave 1 tablespoon of the bacon grease in the pan. Now, add the sausage and cook until browned on all sides, about 5 minutes.
Sauté the onions, jalapeno pepper and garlic in pan drippings until tender and aromatic, about 6 minutes.
Add the celery seeds, cumin, ground bay leaf, stock, wine and sauerkraut. Bring to a rolling boil and decrease the heat to low. Continue to cook an additional 15 minutes.
Serve on individual plates garnished with parsley and Dijon mustard. Bon appétit!

## 123. Three-Cheese and Pork Sausage Balls

**(Ready in about 15 minutes + chilling time | Servings 6)**

**Per serving: 353 Calories; 30.7g Fat; 3g Carbs; 16.1g Protein;**

### INGREDIENTS

1 tablespoon olive oil
1/2 pound pork sausage, ground
1 tomato, pureed
1 teaspoon garlic paste
2 tablespoons onion, minced
4 ounces Neufchatel cheese, room temperature

1/4 teaspoon kosher salt
1/4 teaspoon ground black pepper
4 ounces chive & onion cream cheese
4 ounces fontina cheese, crumbled
2 tablespoons flaxseed meal

### DIRECTIONS

Heat the oil in a skillet that is preheated over moderate heat. Now, brown the sausage for 3 to 4 minutes, stirring periodically.
Add the tomatoes, garlic paste, and onion; cook for a further 5 minutes. Add the other ingredients and mix well to combine.
Place the mixture in your refrigerator to harden. Shape the mixture into bite-sized balls. Serve well-chilled.

## 124. Country Brie-Stuffed Meatballs

**(Ready in about 25 minutes | Servings 5)**

**Per serving: 302 Calories; 17.3g Fat; 1.9g Carbs; 33.4g Protein;**

### INGREDIENTS

1 pound ground pork
1/3 cup heavy cream
2 eggs, beaten
1 tablespoon fresh cilantro
2 tablespoons shallots, minced

2 cloves garlic, minced
1 teaspoon kosher salt
1/2 teaspoon ground black pepper
1 teaspoon dried thyme
10 (1-inch) cubes of brie

### DIRECTIONS

Combine all ingredients, except for the cubes of brie, in a mixing bowl.
Then, shape the mixture into 10 patties by using oiled hands. Now, place a piece of brie in the center of each patty and roll into a ball.
Preheat your oven to 390 degrees F. Arrange the meatballs on a foil-lined baking pan. Bake for 20 to 22 minutes.
Serve with mustard or low-carb salsa. Enjoy!

# 125. North Carolina Pulled Pork

**(Ready in about 4 hours 30 minutes + marinating time | Servings 4)**

**Per serving: 350 Calories; 11g Fat; 5g Carbs; 53.6g Protein;**

## INGREDIENTS

1 teaspoon chipotle powder
1/2 tablespoon paprika
1 teaspoon garlic powder
1 teaspoon onion powder

Kosher salt and freshly ground black pepper, taste
1 teaspoon ground cumin
1 tablespoon liquid smoke sauce

1 ½ pounds pork butt
2 onions, cut into wedges
Water, enough to cover pork

## DIRECTIONS

In a mixing bowl, thoroughly combine the chipotle powder, paprika, garlic powder, onion powder, salt, black pepper, cumin and liquid smoke sauce.
Spread this rub all over the pork butt. Cover the pork butt with a plastic wrap; let it marinate in your refrigerator for 3 hours.
Then, preheat your oven to 325 degrees F. Wrap the pork tightly with aluminum foil. Roast the pork for 3 hours. Take the pork butt out of the oven; turn the oven up to 375 degrees F.
Unwrap the pork and bake for a further 90 minutes or until internal temperature reaches 190 degrees F.
Transfer the pork to a pot; add the onion wedges and water. Continue to cook over a moderately high heat until thoroughly cooked.
Afterwards, shred the pork with meat claws or two forks; taste and adjust the seasonings. Serve with your favorite ketogenic salad on the side.

# 126. Breakfast Muffins with Ground Pork

**(Ready in about 25 minutes | Servings 6)**

**Per serving: 479 Calories; 42g Fat; 5.8g Carbs; 17.9g Protein;**

## INGREDIENTS

1 tablespoon canola oil
1 ½ cups ground pork
Salt and cayenne pepper, to your liking
1 stick butter

3 ½ cups almond flour
1/2 teaspoon baking powder
1/2 teaspoon baking soda
3 large eggs, lightly beaten

2 tablespoons full-fat milk
1/2 teaspoon ground cloves
1/2 teaspoon dried oregano

## DIRECTIONS

Heat the oil in a frying pan over medium heat. Now, cook the ground pork until the juices run clear, about 4 to 5 minutes.
Then, preheat your oven to 360 degrees F.
Add the remaining ingredients to a mixing dish, in the order listed above. Thoroughly combine until everything is well incorporated.
Divide the mixture among 12 muffin cups. Bake in the preheated oven for 15 to 18 minutes.
Allow your muffins to cool down before removing from the baking tin. Serve with full-fat sour cream. Bon appétit!

# 127. Dinner Party Pork Gumbo

**(Ready in about 35 minutes | Servings 6)**

**Per serving: 427 Calories; 26.2g Fat; 3.6g Carbs; 35.2g Protein;**

## INGREDIENTS

2 tablespoons olive oil
1 pound pork shoulder, cubed
8 ounces pork sausage, sliced
2 shallots, toughly chopped
1 teaspoon beef bouillon granules

Sea salt and freshly cracked black pepper
1 teaspoon gumbo file
1 teaspoon crushed red pepper
1 tablespoon Cajun spice
4 cups bone broth

1 cup water
2 bell peppers, deveined and thinly sliced
2 celery stalks, chopped
1/4 cup flaxseed meal
3/4 pound okra

## DIRECTIONS

Heat the oil in a heavy-bottomed pot that is preheated over a moderately high flame. Now, cook the pork until it is just browned; reserve.
Add the sausage and cook in pan drippings approximately 5 minutes; reserve.
Stir in the shallots and cook until they soften. Add the beef bouillon granules, salt, pepper, gumbo file, red pepper, Cajun spice and bone broth. Bring it to a boil.
Add the water, bell pepper and celery, and reduce the heat to medium-low. Cook an additional 15 to 23 minutes.
Afterwards, stir in the flax seed meal and okra; cook for a further 5 minutes or until heated through.

# 128. Pork Meatloaf with Homemade Tomato Sauce

**(Ready in about 45 minutes | Servings 6)**

**Per serving: 251 Calories; 7.9g Fat; 4.5g Carbs; 34.6g Protein;**

## INGREDIENTS

Nonstick cooking spray
1 ½ pounds ground pork
1/4 cup pork rinds, crushed
1/3 cup flaxseed meal
2 shallots, chopped

3 cloves garlic, finely minced
1 large egg
Sea salt and ground black pepper
1 teaspoon mustard powder

**For the Sauce:**
2 ripe plum tomatoes, pureed
2 tablespoons ketchup
1 ½ tablespoons Swerve
1 tablespoon cider vinegar
1/2 teaspoon dried thyme
1 teaspoon fresh parsley

## DIRECTIONS

Start by preheating your oven to 360 degrees F. Lightly spray a loaf pan with a nonstick cooking oil or line with foil.

Add the pork mince, pork rinds, flaxseed meal, shallot, garlic, egg, salt, pepper, and mustard powder to a mixing dish. Thoroughly combine the ingredients until everything is well mixed.

Press the meatloaf mixture into the pan.

Next, cook the sauce ingredients over moderate heat. Pour the sauce evenly over the meatloaf. Bake for 40 minutes or until meat thermometer registers 165 degrees F.

Allow it to cool down for a couple of minutes before slicing. Cut into 3/4-inch thick slices and serve immediately.

# 129. Pork Shoulder with Blue Cheese Sauce

**(Ready in about 30 minutes | Servings 6)**

**Per serving: 495 Calories; 36.9g Fat; 3.6g Carbs; 33.4g Protein;**

## INGREDIENTS

1 ½ pounds pork shoulder, boneless
and cut into 6 pieces
Salt and freshly cracked black peppercorns, to taste
1 teaspoon dried thyme

1 tablespoon butter
1 onion, chopped
2 garlic cloves, chopped
1/3 cup dry sherry wine
1/3 cup broth, preferably homemade

1 teaspoon dried hot chile flakes
1 tablespoon soy sauce
6 ounces blue cheese
1/3 cup double cream

## DIRECTIONS

Rub each piece of the pork shoulder with salt, black peppercorns, and thyme.

Now, warn the butter in a sauté pan over a moderately high heat. Then, brown the pork on all sides about 18 minutes; reserve.

Next, sauté the onions and garlic until the onions are caramelized. Add the wine and broth and stir, scraping up any brown bits from the bottom.

Turn the heat to medium and add the other ingredients; continue to simmer until the desired thickness is reached by evaporation.

Serve the reserved pork with the sauce on the side. Bon appétit!

# 130. Carrot and Meat Loaf Muffins

**(Ready in about 35 minutes | Servings 6)**

**Per serving: 220 Calories; 6.3g Fat; 5.4g Carbs; 33.8g Protein;**

## INGREDIENTS

1 pound pork, ground
1/2 pound turkey, ground
1 cup carrots, shredded
2 ripe tomatoes, pureed
1 ounce envelope onion soup mix

1 tablespoon Worcestershire sauce
1 tablespoon Dijon mustard
1/2 teaspoon dry basil
1 teaspoon dry oregano

Kosher salt and ground black pepper,
to taste
2 cloves of garlic, minced
1 eggs, whisked
1 cup mozzarella cheese, shredded

## DIRECTIONS

Start by preheating your oven to 350 degrees F.

Then, thoroughly combine all ingredients until everything is blended.

Spoon the mixture into a muffin tin that is previously coated with a nonstick cooking spray.

Bake for 30 minutes; allow them to cool slightly before removing from the tin. Bon appétit!

# 131. Hearty Pork Soup with Avocado

**(Ready in about 20 minutes | Servings 6)**

**Per serving: 423 Calories; 31.8g Fat; 6g Carbs; 25.9g Protein;**

## INGREDIENTS

2 tablespoons lard
1 medium-sized yellow onion, peeled and chopped
2 cloves garlic, peeled and minced
1 teaspoon Mezzeta pepper, seeded and minced

1 celery, chopped
1 ¼ pounds pork shoulder, cut into chunks
3 cups beef broth, less-sodium
Sea salt and ground black pepper, to taste

A pinch of dried basil
2 ripe tomatoes, undrained
1/4 cup fresh parsley, roughly chopped
1 medium-sized avocado, pitted and sliced

## DIRECTIONS

Melt the lard in a large-sized stock pot over a moderate flame. Next, sauté the onion, garlic, Mezzeta pepper and celery for 2 to 3 minutes or until the onion is translucent.

Stir in the pork chunks and continue cooking for 4 minutes more, stirring continuously. Add the other ingredients.

Now, lower the heat and simmer for 10 minutes, partially covered; make sure to stir periodically.

Serve topped with fresh parsley leaves and sliced avocado.

# 132. Greek Souvlaki with Tzatziki Sauce

**(Ready in about 20 minutes + marinating time | Servings 6)**

**Per serving: 147 Calories; 4.8g Fat; 6.2g Carbs; 17.3g Protein;**

## INGREDIENTS

1/3 cup red wine vinegar
2 tablespoons cilantro, chopped
2 tablespoons fresh lemon juice
3 cloves garlic, smashed
Sea salt and ground black pepper, to taste

1 teaspoon Greek oregano
2 pounds pork loin, trimmed of silver skin and excess fat, cut into 1-inch cubes
Wooden skewers, soaked in cold water for 30 minutes before use

**For Tzatziki Sauce:**
1 small-sized cucumber, shredded and drained
1 cup full-fat Greek yogurt
1 teaspoon garlic, smashed
3 teaspoons olive oil
Sea salt, to taste
2 teaspoons fresh dill, finely minced

## DIRECTIONS

To make the marinade, thoroughly combine the vinegar, cilantro, lemon juice, garlic, salt, black pepper and Greek oregano.

Add the pork loin to the marinade. Let it marinate in your refrigerator for 3 hours. Now, thread the pork cubes onto the skewers.

Grill your souvlaki until they are browned on all sides, about 8 to 12 minutes in total.

Mix all ingredients for the Tzatziki sauce. Serve with the souvlaki skewers. Bon appétit!

# 133. Kansas City-Style Meatloaf

**(Ready in about 1 hour 10 minutes | Servings 8)**

**Per serving: 318 Calories; 14.7g Fat; 6.2g Carbs; 39.3g Protein;**

## INGREDIENTS

2 pounds ground pork
2 eggs, beaten
1/2 cup shallots, chopped
1/2 cup chipotle salsa, bottled
8 ounces sharp Cheddar cheese, shredded
1 teaspoon garlic powder

1 teaspoon paprika
Sea salt and freshly ground black pepper, to taste
1 teaspoon lime zest
1 tablespoon whole grain mustard
1/2 cup tomato paste
1 tablespoon Swerve

## DIRECTIONS

Start by preheating your oven to 360 degrees F.

In a mixing bowl, thoroughly combine the ground pork with the eggs, shallots, chipotle salsa, cheddar cheese, garlic powder, paprika, salt, pepper, lime zest, and mustard.

Mix until everything is well incorporated. Press the mixture into a loaf pan that is previously greased with a nonstick cooking spray.

Then, whisk the tomato paste with the Swerve; pour the mixture over the top of your meatloaf.

Bake about 65 minutes, rotating the pan once or twice. Place under the broiler during the last 5 minutes if desired.

Let your meatloaf stand 5 to 10 minutes before slicing and serving.

# 134. Indian-Style Saucy Pork

**(Ready in about 1 hour 15 minutes | Servings 8)**

**Per serving: 369 Calories; 20.2g Fat; 2.9g Carbs; 41.3g Protein;**

## INGREDIENTS

1 tablespoon olive oil
2 pounds pork belly, cubed
Salt and freshly ground pepper
1/2 teaspoon ground coriander
A bunch of scallions, chopped
2 garlic cloves, minced
1/2 tablespoon curry powder

1/2 tablespoon ground cloves
2 tomatoes, pureed
1 bell pepper, deveined and chopped
1 Thai chile, deveined and minced
1/2 teaspoon fennel seeds
1/2 cup unsweetened coconut milk
2 cups bone broth

## DIRECTIONS

Heat the oil in a saucepan over moderate heat. Sprinkle the pork belly with salt, pepper and ground coriander.
Cook the pork about 10 minutes, stirring frequently.
Next, cook the scallions, garlic, curry, and cloves in pan drippings. Scrape the mixture into the slow cooker. Add the remaining ingredients.
Cook, covered, for 1 hour over low heat. Serve warm.

# 135. Pork Rib Chops with Spinach

**(Ready in about 25 minutes + marinating time | Servings 6)**

**Per serving: 234 Calories; 11g Fat; 2g Carbs; 29.8g Protein;**

## INGREDIENTS

1 ½ pounds pork rib chops
Sea salt and ground black pepper, to taste
2 tablespoons oyster sauce
1 tablespoon cider vinegar
1 tablespoon fresh lime juice
1/4 cup Champagne wine

1 tablespoon garlic paste
2 teaspoons olive oil
1 red onion, sliced
1 celery stalk, sliced
1 bell pepper, chopped
2 cups spinach

## DIRECTIONS

Season the pork rib chops with salt and pepper. In another small dish, make the marinade by whisking the oyster sauce, vinegar, lime juice, Champagne and garlic paste.
Add the pork to the marinade; let it stand for at least 2 hours.
Next, heat 1 teaspoon of the olive oil in a large-sized pan that is preheated over a moderate flame; cook the onion, celery and bell pepper about 5 minutes, stirring frequently; reserve.
Heat another teaspoon of the olive oil in the same pan. Add the pork, along with the marinade, to the pan. Now, brown the pork for 3 to 5 minutes per side.
Add the reserved vegetables to the pan along with the spinach. Cook until the spinach leaves are wilted, about 6 minutes. Serve warm. Bon appétit!

# 136. Breakfast Pork in a Mug

**(Ready in about 10 minutes | Servings 2)**

**Per serving: 327 Calories; 16.6g Fat; 5.8g Carbs; 40g Protein;**

## INGREDIENTS

1/2 pound ground pork
1/2 cup Asiago cheese, shredded
1/2 cup tomato sauce
Salt and ground black pepper, to taste

1 teaspoon garlic paste
1/2 teaspoon onion powder
1/2 teaspoon cayenne pepper

## DIRECTIONS

Thoroughly combine all ingredients in a mixing bowl.
Divide the mixture among 2 microwave-safe mugs.
Microwave for 7 minutes and serve warm with pickles. Bon appétit!

# 137. Hot and Creamy Pork Chop Soup

**(Ready in about 25 minutes | Servings 4)**

**Per serving: 490 Calories; 44g Fat; 6.1g Carbs; 24.3g Protein;**

## INGREDIENTS

2 tablespoons olive oil
1 shallot, chopped
1 small-sized carrot, chopped
1 celery stalk, chopped
3/4 pound bone-in pork chops

3 cups water
1 tablespoon chicken bouillon granules
1/2 teaspoon red pepper flakes
Seasoned salt and freshly cracked
black pepper, to taste

2 tomatoes, pureed
1 cup double cream
1/2 teaspoon Tabasco sauce
1/2 cup avocado, pitted, peeled and
diced

## DIRECTIONS

Heat 1 tablespoon of the olive oil in a pot that is preheated over medium-high heat. Now, sauté the shallots until they have just softened. Then, stir in the carrots and celery. Cook until they are slightly softened; reserve.

Heat the remaining tablespoon of olive oil; brown the pork chops for 4 minutes, stirring periodically.

When the pork chops are cool enough to handle, discard any bones and chop them into bite-size chunks. Add to the pot along with the reserved vegetables.

Add the water, bouillon granules, red paper flakes, salt, pepper and pureed tomatoes. Continue to simmer, partially covered, for 10 minutes more. Stir in the double cream and cook until heated through, stirring continuously. Serve drizzled with Tabasco sauce and garnished with avocado. Bon appétit!

# 138. Pork Lettuce Wraps

**(Ready in about 15 minutes | Servings 4)**

**Per serving: 110 Calories; 2.7g Fat; 5.1g Carbs; 15.8g Protein;**

## INGREDIENTS

2 tablespoons apple cider vinegar
1/4 teaspoon kosher salt
1 celery, grated
2 spring onions, sliced
1 teaspoon capers
1/2 pound ground pork

2 garlic cloves, finely minced
1 jalapeno pepper, deveined and finely
minced
1 tablespoon Worcestershire sauce
1/2 teaspoon salt

1/3 teaspoon freshly cracked mixed
peppercorns
1 ½ teaspoons Dijon mustard
1 head lettuce
1 tablespoon sunflower seeds

## DIRECTIONS

In a mixing dish or a measuring cup, thoroughly whisk the vinegar with the kosher salt, celery, spring onions and capers.

In a pan, brown the ground pork with the garlic and jalapeno for 7 minutes over a moderate flame.

Now, add the Worcestershire sauce, salt, peppercorns, and mustard to the pan; stir to combine.

Then, assemble your wraps. Divide the pork mixture among lettuce leaves; top with the reserved celery mixture. Afterwards, sprinkle with raw sunflower seeds and serve.

# 139. Pan-Seared Pork Steaks

**(Ready in about 30 minutes | Servings 4)**

**Per serving: 305 Calories; 20.6g Fat; 3.7g Carbs; 22.5g Protein;**

## INGREDIENTS

2 tablespoons lard, room temperature
4 pork butt steaks
1/4 cup dry red wine
1 teaspoon celery seeds

1/2 teaspoon cayenne pepper
1/2 teaspoon salt
1/2 teaspoon freshly ground black
pepper

1 red onion, peeled and chopped
1 garlic clove, minced

## DIRECTIONS

Melt 1 tablespoon of the lard in a cast-iron skillet that is preheated over a moderate heat. Cover the skillet and sear the butt steaks for 10 minutes on each side.

Add a splash of red wine to deglaze the pot. Season with the celery seeds, cayenne pepper, salt and black pepper; cook an additional 8 to 12 minutes; reserve.

Warm the remaining 1 tablespoon of lard in the same skillet; cook the onions and garlic until tender and aromatic. Serve with the seared pork butt steaks. Bon appétit!

# 140. Grilled Pork and Vegetable Skewers

**(Ready in about 20 minutes + marinating time | Servings 6)**

**Per serving: 428 Calories; 31.6g Fat; 7.7g Carbs; 28.9g Protein;**

## INGREDIENTS

2 tablespoons fresh lime juice

3 tablespoons olive oil

3 tablespoons tamari sauce

1 tablespoon Italian spice mix

2 cloves garlic, crushed

1 ½ pounds pork shoulder, cubed

1 pound small button mushrooms

1 onion, cut into wedges

1 zucchini, cubed

1 green bell pepper, cut into thick slices

1 red bell pepper, cut into thick slices

Wooden skewers, soaked in cold water for 30 minutes

## DIRECTIONS

To make the marinade, thoroughly combine the fresh lime juice, olive oil, tamari sauce, Italian spice mix and crushed garlic.

Now, marinate the pork for a couple of hours. Thread the pork cubes, mushrooms, onion, zucchini and peppers onto skewers.

Cook on the preheated grill approximately 13 to minutes, or to the desired doneness, turning the skewers frequently for even cooking. Enjoy!

# 141. Pork Loin with Cauliflower and Bamboo Shoots

**(Ready in about 20 minutes | Servings 6)**

**Per serving: 356 Calories; 19.5g Fat; 6.4g Carbs; 33.1g Protein;**

## INGREDIENTS

1 ½ pounds pork loin, boneless

Celery salt and ground black pepper, to taste

1/4 teaspoon dried thyme

1/2 teaspoon dried marjoram

1/2 teaspoon garlic powder

2 tablespoons oyster sauce

1/4 cup vodka

1 ½ tablespoons olive oil

1 yellow onion, chopped

1 head cauliflower, broken into florets

1 (8-ounce) can bamboo shoots

## DIRECTIONS

Add the pork loin to a mixing dish. Add celery salt, black pepper, thyme, marjoram, garlic powder, oyster sauce, vodka and olive oil to the mixing dish; toss to combine well.

Now, heat 1 tablespoon of the olive oil in a nonstick skillet over medium-high heat; sauté the onions until translucent.

Add the cauliflower and cook an additional 3 to 4 minutes or until just tender; reserve.

Heat another tablespoon of olive oil in the same skillet over high heat. Discard the marinade and brown the pork for 3 minutes on each side.

Pour in the reserved marinade; add the reserved cauliflower mixture and canned bamboo shoots.

Continue to cook an additional 3 to 4 minutes or until the liquid has thickened. Serve immediately. Enjoy!

# 142. Easy Aromatic Pork Chops

**(Ready in about 30 minutes | Servings 4)**

**Per serving: 335 Calories; 26.3g Fat; 2.5g Carbs; 18.3g Protein;**

## INGREDIENTS

2 tablespoons lard, melted

1/2 cup red onion, thinly sliced

3 cloves garlic, minced

4 pork chops

1/4 cup dry white wine

2 tablespoons Worcestershire sauce

1 teaspoon dried thyme

4 allspice berries, lightly crushed

1/2 teaspoon fresh ginger root, grated

## DIRECTIONS

Melt the lard in a saucepan over medium heat. Sauté the onions and garlic until aromatic and just browned.

Add the pork and cook 15 to 20 minutes, turning once or twice. Add the dry white wine, Worcestershire sauce, thyme, crushed allspice berries and fresh ginger.

Cook an additional 8 minutes or until everything is thoroughly heated. Bon appétit!

# 143. Super Crispy Roasted Pork Shoulder

**(Ready in about 25 minutes | Servings 4)**

**Per serving: 476 Calories; 35.3g Fat; 6.2g Carbs; 31.1g Protein;**

## INGREDIENTS

1 pound pork shoulder, cut into 1-inch-thick pieces
Salt and cayenne pepper, to taste
2 tablespoons lard
2 shallots, sliced

2 cloves garlic, smashed
1 thyme sprig
1 rosemary sprig
1 tablespoon tamarind paste
1 tablespoon fish sauce

2 tablespoons Kalamata olives, pitted and sliced
2 tablespoons rice vinegar
1 cup bone broth
1/2 cup Asiago cheese, freshly grated

## DIRECTIONS

Start by preheating your broiler. Sprinkle your pork with salt and cayenne pepper on all sides.

Melt the lard in a pan that is preheated over a moderately high flame. Sweat the shallots and garlic for about 5 minutes; reserve.

Warm the remaining 1 tablespoon of lard. Sear the pork for 7 to 8 minutes, turning once; reserve.

Now, cook the garlic, thyme, rosemary, tamarind paste, fish sauce, olives, vinegar, and bone broth in pan drippings. Cook until the sauce is reduced by about half. Transfer to an oven-safe dish.

Add the reserved pork along with the shallot mixture; sprinkle with grated Asiago cheese. Lastly, broil until everything is thoroughly heated, about 5 minutes.

# 144. Spicy Pork Sausage Frittata

**(Ready in about 35 minutes | Servings 4)**

**Per serving: 423 Calories; 35.4g Fat; 4.1g Carbs; 22.6g Protein;**

## INGREDIENTS

3 tablespoons olive oil
1 cup onion, chopped
1 teaspoon jalapeno pepper, finely minced

2 garlic cloves, minced
1 teaspoon salt
1/2 teaspoon ground black pepper
1/4 teaspoon cayenne pepper

1/2 pound pork sausages, thinly sliced
8 eggs, beaten
1 teaspoon dried sage, crushed

## DIRECTIONS

Heat the oil in a nonstick skillet over a medium-high heat. Now, sauté the onions, peppers and garlic until the onion becomes translucent, about 4 minutes.

Season with salt, black pepper, and cayenne pepper. Then, stir in the sausage and cook, stirring often, until they're no longer pink.

Transfer the mixture to a lightly greased baking dish. Pour the eggs over the top and sprinkle with dried sage.

Bake in the preheated oven at 420 degrees F for 25 minutes. Bon appétit!

# 145. Chinese Pork Stir-Fry with Muenster Cheese

**(Ready in about 20 minutes | Servings 6)**

**Per serving: 320 Calories; 15.4g Fat; 2.7g Carbs; 39.8g Protein;**

## INGREDIENTS

1 tablespoon lard, softened
1 ½ pounds pork butt, cut into strips
Celery salt and freshly ground black pepper, to taste
1/2 teaspoon red pepper flakes

A bunch of scallions, roughly chopped
2 bell peppers, sliced
1/4 cup bone broth
1/2 teaspoon Chinese hot sauce
1 tablespoon peanut butter

1 tablespoon soy sauce
2 tablespoons Sauvignon
3 ounces Muenster cheese, cut into small pieces

## DIRECTIONS

Melt the lard in an oven-safe skillet that is preheated over a moderately high heat. Toss the pork strips with salt, black pepper, and red pepper flakes.

Stir-fry the pork strips approximately 4 minutes. Add the scallions and bell peppers; cook an additional 3 minutes.

Now, add the bone broth, hot sauce, peanut butter, soy sauce, and Sauvignon; stir-fry for a couple of minutes more.

Scatter small pieces of Muenster cheese on top of the pork mixture, cover and continue to cook until the cheese has just melted. Bon appétit!

# 146. Crock Pot Hungarian Goulash

**(Ready in about 10 hours | Servings 4)**

**Per serving: 517 Calories; 35.7g Fat; 5.7g Carbs; 38.2g Protein;**

## INGREDIENTS

1 ½ tablespoons butter
1 pound pork shoulder off the bone, chopped
1 cup yellow onions, chopped
3 garlic cloves, crushed
2 teaspoons cayenne pepper
1 teaspoon sweet Hungarian paprika
1 teaspoon caraway seeds, ground

4 cups chicken stock
2 ½ cups tomato puree
2 chili peppers, deveined and finely chopped
For the Sour Cream Sauce:
1 cup sour cream
1 bunch parsley, chopped
1 teaspoon lemon zest

## DIRECTIONS

Melt the butter in a sauté pan that is preheated over a moderate heat. Now, cook the pork until just browned; reserve.

Add the onions and garlic and continue to sauté until they are just tender and fragrant.

Transfer the reserved pork along with the onions and garlic to your crock pot. Add the cayenne pepper, paprika, caraway seeds, stock, tomato puree and chili peppers.

Cover and cook for 8 to 10 hours on low heat setting.

In the meantime, make the sour cream sauce by whisking all the sauce ingredients. Serve the warm goulash in individual bowls, dolloped with the sour cream sauce. Enjoy!

# 147. Pork Quiche with Bell Peppers

**(Ready in about 50 minutes | Servings 6)**

**Per serving: 478 Calories; 36g Fat; 4.9g Carbs; 33.5g Protein;**

## INGREDIENTS

6 eggs, lightly beaten
2 ½ cups almond flour
1 stick butter, melted
1 ¼ pounds ground pork
Salt and pepper, to the taste

1 green bell pepper, thinly sliced
1 red bell pepper, thinly sliced
1 cup heavy cream
1/2 teaspoon mustard seeds
1/2 teaspoon dried dill weed

## DIRECTIONS

Start by preheating your oven to 350 degrees F

Add the flour, butter and one egg to a mixing dish; mix to combine well.

Press the batter dough in a baking pan that is previously greased with a nonstick cooking spray.

Next, brown the ground pork for 3 to 5 minutes, crumbling with a wide spatula; season with salt and pepper.

In another mixing bowl, thoroughly combine the remaining ingredients; add the browned pork.

Spread this mixture over the crust and bake for 35 to 43 minutes in the preheated oven. Eat warm and enjoy!

# 148. Summer Baby Back Ribs

**(Ready in about 1 hour 40 minutes + marinating time | Servings 6)**

**Per serving: 255 Calories; 13.9g Fat; 0.8g Carbs; 29.9g Protein;**

## INGREDIENTS

1 ½ pounds baby back ribs
Salt and ground black pepper, to taste
1 teaspoon dried marjoram

1 lime, halved
1 garlic clove, minced

## DIRECTIONS

Season the baby back ribs with the salt, pepper and marjoram. Now, rub your ribs with the cut sides of lime.

Cover and transfer to your refrigerator for 6 hours. Place the minced garlic on top of the ribs.

Grill for about 1 hour 30 minutes, turning twice to ensure even cooking. Serve with mustard and salads on the side.

# 149. Ground Pork and Swiss Chard Skillet

**(Ready in about 25 minutes | Servings 4)**

**Per serving: 349 Calories; 13g Fat; 4.4g Carbs; 45.3g Protein;**

## INGREDIENTS

2 tablespoons vegetable oil

2 cloves garlic, pressed

1 cup leeks, sliced

1 Serrano pepper, sliced

1 bell pepper, chopped

1 ½ pounds ground pork

1 teaspoon sea salt

1/4 teaspoon lemon pepper, or more to taste

1/4 cup tomato puree

1/4 cup dry sherry wine

1 bunch Swiss chard, trimmed and roughly chopped

1 cup beef bone broth

## DIRECTIONS

Heat 1 tablespoon of vegetable oil in a pan over a moderately high heat. Now, sauté the garlic, leeks, and peppers until they are just softened; reserve.

Heat the remaining tablespoon of vegetable oil; add the ground pork and cook, stirring frequently, for 3 to 4 minutes more.

Add the remaining ingredients along with the sautéed vegetables. Cook, covered, an additional 10 minutes or until everything is thoroughly cooked.

Uncover and cook for a further 5 minutes or until the liquid has evaporated. Serve warm!

# 150. Pork Ribs with Roasted Peppers

**(Ready in about 2 hours | Servings 4)**

**Per serving: 370 Calories; 21.3g Fat; 4.3g Carbs; 33.7g Protein;**

## INGREDIENTS

2 tablespoons olive oil

1 pound baby back ribs

Salt and pepper, to your liking

1 tablespoon garlic paste

1 red onion, chopped

2 rosemary sprigs

1 tablespoon crushed sage

1 tablespoon tamarind paste

1 cup beef broth

1/2 cup dry sherry

1/2 cup soy sauce

2 roasted red bell peppers, chopped

2 roasted chile peppers, chopped

## DIRECTIONS

Start by preheating your oven to 340 degrees F. Spritz a roasting pan with a nonstick cooking spray.

Heat the oil in an ovenproof pan over a moderately high heat. Now, brown the meat on all sides for 10 minutes; sprinkle with salt and pepper.

Add the garlic paste, onion, rosemary and sage. Cook an additional 4 minutes or until heated through. Stir in the remaining ingredients.

Bake for 1 hour 30 minutes in the middle of the preheated oven and serve immediately.

# 151. Holiday Pork and Bacon Meatloaf

**(Ready in about 1 hour 10 minutes | Servings 6)**

**Per serving: 405 Calories; 24.6g Fat; 2.8g Carbs; 40.6g Protein;**

## INGREDIENTS

1 teaspoon lard, melted

1 yellow onion, chopped

1 teaspoon garlic, finely minced

1 ¼ pounds ground pork

1 egg, beaten

2 ounces half-and-half

1 teaspoon celery seeds

Salt and ground black pepper, to taste

1/4 teaspoon cayenne pepper

1/2 pound pork sausage, broken up

1 bunch cilantro, roughly chopped

6 strips bacon

## DIRECTIONS

Preheat your oven to 395 degrees F. Lightly grease a baking dish and set it aside.

Heat the lard in a cast-iron skillet over a medium heat. Next, sauté the onions and garlic until they are tender and fragrant, for 2 to 4 minutes. Stir in the pork and cook until it is no longer pink, about 2 minutes.

In a mixing bowl, thoroughly combine the egg, half-and-half, celery seeds, salt, black pepper, cayenne pepper, pork sausage and cilantro. Add the reserved pork mixture; stir to combine well. Lastly, shape the mixture into a loaf.

Place the bacon on top of your meatloaf. Bake about 1 hour. Allow it to cool on a wire rack before serving. Bon appétit!

# BEEF

## 152. Spicy Habanero and Ground Beef Dinner

**(Ready in about 40 minutes | Servings 6)**

**Per serving: 361 Calories; 21.9g Fat; 6.4g Carbs; 29g Protein;**

### INGREDIENTS

2 tablespoons tallow, at room temperature
1 ½ pounds ground chuck
1/4 teaspoon caraway seeds, ground
1/2 teaspoon dried basil
1/2 teaspoon dried thyme
1/2 teaspoon paprika
1/2 teaspoon ground bay leaf

1 teaspoon fennel seeds
1/2 teaspoon salt
1/2 teaspoon ground black pepper
2 shallots, chopped
2 garlic cloves, minced
1 teaspoon habanero pepper, minced
2 ripe Roma tomatoes, crushed
1/2 cup dry sherry wine

**For Ketogenic Tortillas:**
4 egg whites
1/4 cup coconut flour
1/3 teaspoon baking powder
6 tablespoons water
A pinch of table salt
A pinch of Swerve

### DIRECTIONS

Melt the tallow in a wok that is preheated over a moderately high heat.
Now, brown the ground chuck for 4 minutes, crumbling it with a fork. Add all seasonings along with the shallots, garlic, and habanero pepper. Continue to cook 9 minutes longer.
Now, stir in the tomatoes and sherry. Now, turn the heat to medium-low, cover, and let it simmer an additional 20 minutes.
Meanwhile, make the tortillas by mixing the eggs, coconut flour and baking powder in a bowl. Add the water, salt and Swerve and mix until everything is well incorporated.
Preheat a nonstick skillet over a moderate flame. Bake the tortillas for a couple of minutes on each side. Repeat until you run out of batter.
Serve the ground beef mixture with the warm tortillas. Enjoy!

## 153. Meatballs with Roasted Peppers and Manchego

**(Ready in about 1 hour | Servings 4)**

**Per serving: 348 Calories; 13.7g Fat; 5.9g Carbs; 42.8g Protein;**

### INGREDIENTS

4 bell peppers, deveined and chopped
2 chipotle peppers, deveined and minced
2 leeks, chopped
3 garlic cloves

3 tablespoons parmesan cheese, grated
1 egg
Salt and freshly ground black pepper
1 pound ground beef
2 ripe tomatoes, crushed

1 ½ cups chicken broth
1/2 teaspoon fresh ginger, ground
1 teaspoon lemon thyme
1/2 cup Manchego cheese, crumbled

### DIRECTIONS

Broil the peppers for approximately 20 minutes, turning once or twice. Allow them to stand at least 30 minutes to loosen the skin.
Peel the peppers; remove stems and seeds; slice the chipotle peppers into halves and reserve.
In a mixing dish, combine the leeks, garlic, parmesan, egg, salt, pepper, and ground beef. Heat a heavy-bottomed skillet over a moderately high heat.
Brown the meatballs on all sides about 10 minutes.
Now, make the tomato sauce. Heat the tomatoes, chicken broth, ginger and lemon thyme in a pan that is preheated over medium-high heat; season with salt and pepper to taste.
Bring to a boil and then, decrease the heat to medium. Add the meatballs and let them simmer until they are thoroughly cooked, gently stirring.
Serve the meatballs with the tomato sauce and roasted peppers. Garnish with crumbled Manchego and enjoy!

## 154. The Best Sloppy Joes Ever

**(Ready in about 30 minutes | Servings 6)**

**Per serving: 313 Calories; 20.6g Fat; 3.5g Carbs; 26.6g Protein;**

### INGREDIENTS

2 teaspoons tallow, room temperature
2 shallots, finely chopped
1 teaspoon garlic, minced
1 ½ pounds ground chuck

1/2 cup pureed tomatoes
1 teaspoon deli mustard
1 teaspoon celery seeds
1 tablespoon coconut vinegar

Salt and ground pepper, to taste
1 teaspoon cayenne pepper
1 teaspoon chipotle powder

### DIRECTIONS

Melt 1 tablespoons of tallow in a heavy-bottomed skillet over a moderately high flame.
Now, sauté the shallots and garlic until tender and aromatic; reserve.
In the same skillet, melt another tablespoon of tallow. Now, brown the ground chuck, crumbling with a spatula.
Add the vegetables back to the skillet; stir in the remaining ingredients. Turn the heat to medium-low; simmer for 20 minutes; stirring periodically.
Serve over keto buns. Bon appétit!

# 155. Grilled Rib Eye Steak

**(Ready in about 20 minutes | Servings 6)**

**Per serving: 314 Calories; 11.4g Fat; 1g Carbs; 48.2g Protein;**

## INGREDIENTS

1 tablespoon oyster sauce
1 tablespoon Worcestershire sauce
2 tablespoons Swerve sweetener
2 garlic cloves, smashed
1 thyme sprig, chopped
2 rosemary sprigs, chopped

1 teaspoon dried sage, crushed
1/2 teaspoon chipotle powder
Celery salt and ground black pepper, to taste
2 tablespoons dry red wine
2 tablespoons olive oil
2 pounds rib eye steaks

## DIRECTIONS

In a mixing bowl, thoroughly combine the oyster sauce, Worcestershire sauce, Swerve, garlic, thyme, rosemary, sage, chipotle powder, salt, pepper, wine and olive oil.
Now, marinate the rib eye steaks in your refrigerator overnight.
Preheat your grill that is previously lightly greased. Grill the rib eye steaks over direct heat for 4 to 5 minutes on each side for medium-rare.
Bon appétit!

# 156. Beef Sausage with Mayo Sauce

**(Ready in about 15 minutes | Servings 4)**

**Per serving: 549 Calories; 49.3g Fat; 4.7g Carbs; 16.2g Protein;**

## INGREDIENTS

1 tablespoon lard, at room temperature
1 red onion, chopped
1 garlic clove, finely minced
1 pound beef sausage, crumbled
1/2 teaspoon salt
1/3 teaspoon red pepper flakes
1/2 teaspoon dried marjoram

2 tablespoons cilantro, minced
For the Sauce:
1/4 cup mayonnaise
1 tablespoon tomato puree
1 ½ teaspoon mustard
1 teaspoon cayenne pepper
A pinch of salt

## DIRECTIONS

Melt the lard over medium-high heat. Add the onion and garlic and cook for 2 minutes or until tender and fragrant.
Stir in the beef and continue to cook for about 3 minutes more. Stir in the salt, red pepper, marjoram and cilantro; cook for 1 more minute.
Then, make the sauce by whisking all the sauce ingredients. Serve over low-carb flat bread. Enjoy!

# 157. Slow Cooker Beef Chuck Roast

**(Ready in about 6 hours | Servings 8)**

**Per serving: 519 Calories; 39.6g Fat; 2.7g Carbs; 34.4g Protein;**

## INGREDIENTS

2 pounds beef chuck roast
2 tablespoons olive oil
1 large-sized white onion, cut into wedges
3 garlic cloves, minced
2 rosemary springs
1 thyme sprig

1/3 cup dry red wine
Salt and pepper to taste
2 tablespoons Worcestershire sauce
1/2 cup beef broth
2 tablespoons fresh parsley, chopped
1 cup Provolone, sliced

## DIRECTIONS

Add the beef, olive oil, onion, garlic, rosemary and thyme to your Crock pot.
Now, add the dry red wine, salt, pepper, Worcestershire sauce, beef broth.
Cover and cook on High settings until the meat is tender, about 6 hours.
Serve garnished with fresh parsley and sliced Provolone cheese. Bon appétit!

## 158. Finger-Lickin' Good Beef Brisket

**(Ready in about 3 hours 30 minutes | Servings 8)**

**Per serving: 219 Calories; 7.2g Fat; 0.6g Carbs; 34.6g Protein;**

### INGREDIENTS

2 pounds beef brisket, trimmed
1 tablespoon Dijon mustard
2 garlic cloves, halved
1 teaspoon sea salt
1/2 teaspoon freshly ground black pepper

1 teaspoon shallot powder
1 teaspoon dried rosemary
1 teaspoon dried marjoram
1/4 cup dry red wine

### DIRECTIONS

Start by preheating an oven to 375 degrees F. Rub the raw brisket with garlic and Dijon mustard.
Then, make a dry rub by mixing the remaining ingredients. Season the brisket on both sides with the rub. Pour the wine into the pan.
Lay the beef brisket in a baking pan. Roast in the oven for 1 hour.
Decrease the oven temperature to 300 degrees F; roast an additional 2 hours 30 minutes.
Afterwards, slice the meat and serve with the juice from the baking pan. Bon appétit!

## 159. Winter Guinness Beef Stew

**(Ready in about 1 hour | Servings 6)**

**Per serving: 444 Calories; 14.2g Fat; 6.1g Carbs; 66.3g Protein;**

### INGREDIENTS

1 ½ tablespoons canola oil
1 ½ pounds chuck shoulder, cut into bite-size cubes
1 cup leeks, chopped
1 celery stalk, chopped
1 parsnip, chopped
2 carrots, chopped
1 ½ cups tomato puree

3 cups boiling water
1 cup Guinness beer
1 tablespoon beef bouillon granules
1 bay leaf
1/2 teaspoon caraway seeds
1/4 cup mint leaves, chopped, to serve

### DIRECTIONS

Heat the oil in a stockpot over medium-high heat. Now, sauté the chuck shoulder cubes until they are browned; reserve.
Then, sauté the vegetables in pan drippings for 8 minutes, stirring periodically.
Throw in the remaining ingredients, except for the mint leaves, and bring to a rapid boil. Now, turn the heat to medium-low; let it simmer about 50 minutes.
Ladle into individual serving bowls and serve garnished with mint leaves. Bon appétit!

## 160. Greek Prosciutto-Wrapped Meatloaf

**(Ready in about 55 minutes | Servings 8)**

**Per serving: 442 Calories; 20.6g Fat; 4.9g Carbs; 56.3g Protein;**

### INGREDIENTS

3 teaspoons sesame oil
2 shallots, finely chopped
2 pounds ground beef
1/2 pound ground lamb
1/4 cup half-and-half
6 ounces feta cheese, crumbled

2 eggs, beaten
2 teaspoons Greek seasoning blend
1 tablespoon brown mustard
1 tablespoon Worcester sauce
1/2 cup chopped Kalamata olives
8 slices of prosciutto

### DIRECTIONS

Preheat your oven to 390 degrees F.
Heat the oil in a cast-iron skillet that is preheated over a medium flame. Sauté the shallot until it becomes soft and lightly browned.
In a large mixing bowl, thoroughly combine the remaining ingredients, except for the prosciutto. Add the sautéed onion and mix well.
Shape the mixture into a meatloaf. Wrap the meatloaf in the slices of prosciutto and transfer it to a baking pan.
Cover with a piece of aluminum foil. Bake for 40 minutes. Remove the foil and bake an additional 10 to 13 minutes. Bon appétit!

# 161. Greek-Style Cold Beef Salad

**(Ready in about 20 minutes | Servings 6)**

**Per serving: 315 Calories; 13.8g Fat; 6.4g Carbs; 37.5g Protein;**

## INGREDIENTS

2 cucumbers, thinly sliced
1 orange bell pepper, thinly sliced
1 green bell pepper, thinly sliced
1 red onion, peeled and thinly sliced
1 cup grape tomatoes, halved

1 head of butter lettuce, leaves separated
1 ½ pounds beef rump steak
Salt and ground black pepper, to your liking

1/2 teaspoon dried oregano
1 tablespoon fresh lemon juice
1/4 cup extra-virgin olive oil
1 tablespoon soy sauce

## DIRECTIONS

In a salad bowl, toss the cucumbers, bell pepper, onions, tomato, and butter lettuce leaves.
Preheat a barbecue grill; cook the steak for 3 minutes per side. Then, thinly slice steak across the grain.
Add the slices of meat to the salad.
Make the dressing by whisking the salt, pepper, oregano, lemon juice, olive oil and soy sauce.
Dress the salad and serve well-chilled. Enjoy!

# 162. Slow Cooker Cajun Beef Brisket and Veggies

**(Ready in about 6 hours + marinating time | Servings 6)**

**Per serving: 296 Calories; 12g Fat; 5g Carbs; 35.2g Protein;**

## INGREDIENTS

1 ½ pounds beef brisket
1 teaspoon garlic, smashed
Ground black pepper, to taste
1 tablespoon Cajun seasonings

2 tablespoons dry red wine
2 tablespoons Worcestershire sauce
2 tablespoons vegetable oil
2 yellow onions, sliced into half moons

2 carrots, sliced
2 celery stalks, chopped
1 cup stock

## DIRECTIONS

Rub the beef brisket with the garlic, black pepper and Cajun seasonings. Add the wine, Worcestershire sauce and 1 tablespoon of vegetable oil.
Wrap with foil and place in the refrigerator for 3 hours.
Heat 1 tablespoon of vegetable oil in your slow cooker. Now, sauté the onions until just tender.
In a pan, sear the brisket until it has a golden brown crust. Transfer to your slow cooker. Add the carrots, celery and stock
Cover and cook on Low heat setting for 6 hours or until the beef brisket is as soft as you want it. Bon appétit!

# 163. Colorful Beef Skewers with Spicy Relish

**(Ready in about 20 minutes | Servings 6)**

**Per serving: 413 Calories; 21.1g Fat; 5.8g Carbs; 45.3g Protein;**

## INGREDIENTS

2 teaspoons yellow mustard
2 garlic cloves, minced
1 small red chile pepper, finely chopped
3 tablespoons olive oil
2 ½ tablespoons sherry vinegar

Salt and ground black pepper, to taste
2 pounds beef tenderloin, cut into cubes
1 cup onions, cut into wedges
2 zucchinis, cut into thick slices
1 green bell peppers, diced

1 red bell pepper, diced
1/2 medium-sized pineapple, peeled and diced
12 bamboo skewers, soaked in cold water (for 30 minutes)

## DIRECTIONS

Preheat your grill on medium-high.
Prepare the relish by mixing the yellow mustard, garlic, chile pepper, olive oil and sherry vinegar.
Season the meat and vegetables with the salt and pepper. Spritz the ingredients with a nonstick cooking spray.
Thread the meat cubes onto skewers, alternating with vegetables and pineapple. Season to taste and grill about 10 minutes, turning periodically. Serve with the relish.

# 164. Oven Roasted Rib-Eye Steak

**(Ready in about 25 minutes | Servings 6)**

**Per serving: 343 Calories; 27.3g Fat; 3g Carbs; 20.1g Protein;**

## INGREDIENTS

1 tablespoon vegetable oil
1 ½ pounds rib-eye steak
1 teaspoon sea salt
1/2 teaspoon ground black pepper

2 garlic cloves, minced
1/2 cup Worcester sauce
2 tablespoons apple cider vinegar

## DIRECTIONS

Preheat your oven to 350 degrees F. Grease a roasting pan with a nonstick cooking spray.

Heat the vegetable oil in a skillet that is preheated over a medium-high heat. Season the steak with salt and black pepper; sear the steak until just browned or about 3 minutes.

Place the steak in the prepared roasting pan. In a mixing bowl, combine the garlic, Worcester sauce and apple cider vinegar. Pour this mixture over the steak.

Afterwards, cover tightly with a piece of foil. Roast the steak about 20 minutes or until it is tender and well browned. Enjoy!

# 165. Stuffed Tomatoes with Cotija Cheese

**(Ready in about 35 minutes | Servings 4)**

**Per serving: 244 Calories; 9.6g Fat; 6g Carbs; 28.9g Protein;**

## INGREDIENTS

1 tablespoon olive oil
1 cup scallions, chopped
2 cloves garlic, minced
1 pound ground beef
2 tablespoons tomato paste, sugar-free
Salt and pepper, to your liking

1/2 teaspoon cumin seeds
8 tomatoes, scoop out the pulp and chop it
1 teaspoon mild paprika
1 teaspoon dried coriander leaves
1/2 cup beef broth
3/4 cup Cotija cheese, shredded

## DIRECTIONS

Start by preheating your oven to 350 degrees F. Lightly grease a casserole dish with cooking spray.

Heat the oil in a saucepan over a moderately high heat. Sauté the scallions and garlic until aromatic.

Stir in the ground meat; cook for 5 minutes, crumbling with a spatula. Add the tomato paste and cook until heated through. Season with salt, pepper and cumin seeds.

Fill the tomatoes with the beef mixture and transfer them to the prepared casserole dish.

In a mixing bowl, whisk the tomato pulp with the paprika, coriander and broth. Pour the mixture over the stuffed tomatoes.

Bake until the tomatoes are tender, about 20 minutes. Top with Cotija cheese and bake an additional 5 minutes. Bon appétit!

# 166. Juicy Grilled Steak Medallions

**(Ready in about 50 minutes | Servings 4)**

**Per serving: 326 Calories; 11.1g Fat; 1.6g Carbs; 52g Protein;**

## INGREDIENTS

4 steak medallions, 1 1/2 inches thick
1 teaspoon sea salt
1/2 teaspoon ground black pepper
1 tablespoon cayenne pepper
1 teaspoon fennel seeds

1 teaspoon celery seeds
1/2 teaspoon chipotle powder
2 tablespoons fresh lime juice
1 tablespoon ginger root, freshly grated

## DIRECTIONS

Place the steak medallions in a large-sized resealable bag. Then, thoroughly combine the remaining ingredients to make the marinade. Marinate the steak medallions for 40 minutes at room temperature.

Preheat your grill to medium-high. Remove the medallions from the marinade and grill on each side to the desired doneness, about 5 to 6 minutes. Serve warm.

# 167. Smoked Beef Sausage Bake with Broccoli

**(Ready in about 45 minutes | Servings 4)**

**Per serving: 289 Calories; 19.7g Fat; 6.3g Carbs; 19.8g Protein;**

## INGREDIENTS

4 smoked beef sausages, sliced
1 red bell pepper, thinly sliced
1 green bell pepper, thinly sliced
2 shallots, chopped

1 cup broccoli, broken into florets
2 garlic cloves, minced
Salt and black pepper, to taste
1 teaspoon marjoram

1/2 teaspoon ground bay leaf
6 eggs, whisked
2 tablespoons fresh parsley, roughly chopped

## DIRECTIONS

Start by preheating your oven to 370 degrees F.

Heat up a nonstick skillet over a moderate flame; now, cook the sausage for 3 minutes, stirring periodically.

Add the peppers, shallots, broccoli, and garlic; continue cooking for 5 minutes. Season with salt, pepper, marjoram, and ground bay leaf.

Transfer the sausage mixture to a previously greased baking dish. Pour the whisked eggs over it. Bake for 35 minutes. Serve garnished with fresh parsley.

# 168. Keto Tacos with Bacon Sauce

**(Ready in about 30 minutes | Servings 4)**

**Per serving: 258 Calories; 19.3g Fat; 5g Carbs; 16.3g Protein;**

## INGREDIENTS

1 ½ cups Cotija cheese, shredded
1 ½ cups ground beef
2 Campari tomatoes, crushed
Salt and ground black pepper, to taste

1/2 teaspoon onion powder
1/2 teaspoon celery salt
1/2 teaspoon ground cumin
6 slices bacon, chopped

1/2 cup bone broth
3 tablespoons tomato paste
2 teaspoon champagne vinegar
2 jalapeno peppers, minced

## DIRECTIONS

Start by preheating your oven to 390 degrees F. Spritz a baking pan with nonstick cooking spray.

Spread 6 piles of Cotija cheese on the baking pan; bake for 15 minutes; leave the taco shells to cool down for a couple of minutes.

In a nonstick skillet, brown the beef for 4 to 5 minutes, crumbling with a spatula. Add the crushed tomatoes, salt, pepper, onion powder, celery salt, and ground cumin.

Cook until everything is cooked through.

Then, make the sauce by cooking the bacon for 2 to 3 minutes, stirring constantly. Add the remaining ingredients and cook until everything comes together.

Afterwards, assemble your tacos. Divide the meat mixture among the 6 taco shells; top with the bacon sauce. Bon appétit!

# 169. Broccoli and Ground Beef Delight

**(Ready in about 20 minutes | Servings 4)**

**Per serving: 241 Calories; 7.6g Fat; 6g Carbs; 36g Protein;**

## INGREDIENTS

2 teaspoons avocado oil
1 head broccoli, cut into small florets
1 teaspoon garlic, minced
1 cup red onion, sliced

1 pound ground beef
1/2 teaspoon salt
1/2 ground black pepper
1/4 teaspoon cayenne pepper

1/2 cup beef bone broth
2 tablespoons Marsala wine
1/2 teaspoon dill weed
1/2 teaspoon turmeric

## DIRECTIONS

Heat 1 teaspoon of the avocado oil in a pan that is preheated over a moderate flame. Then, cook the broccoli for 3 to 4 minutes, stirring often.

Now, stir in the garlic and onion; cook until aromatic and just tender, or about 2 minutes. Reserve.

Heat another teaspoon of the avocado oil. Stir in the beef and cook until it is well browned.

Add the reserved broccoli mixture, lower the heat and add the remaining ingredients. Cook, covered, until everything is heated through, or about 10 minutes.

Serve with a dollop of sour cream. Enjoy!

# 170. Burgundy Beef Soup with Pancetta

**(Ready in about 2 hours 10 minutes | Servings 4)**

**Per serving: 340 Calories; 19.6g Fat; 6.5g Carbs; 30.2g Protein;**

## INGREDIENTS

2 tablespoons olive oil
4 ounces pancetta, chopped
1 shallot, chopped
2 cloves garlic, minced
1/2 cup carrots, thinly sliced
1 celery rib, chopped

1 pound beef, cubed
2 bay leaves
2 sprigs thyme
1 sprig rosemary
1 small-sized ripe tomato, crushed
1 tablespoon soy sauce

2 tablespoons dry red wine
1/2 tablespoon bouillon granules
4 cups water
1 tablespoon flaxseed meal
2 tablespoons fresh parsley, roughly chopped

## DIRECTIONS

Start by preheating your oven to 320 degrees F.

Heat 1 tablespoon of oil in a stock pot that is preheated over a moderate flame. Now, fry the pancetta for 3 to 4 minutes, crumbling it with a fork; reserve.

Now, heat another tablespoon of olive oil; sauté the shallots and garlic for 3 minutes or until they have softened. Stir in the beef and cook until it browns.

Add the remaining ingredients, except for the flaxseed and parsley, bringing to a rolling boil. Decrease the heat, cover the pot, and let your soup simmer for a further 2 hours.

Uncover and stir in 1 tablespoon of flax seed meal that has been dissolved in 2 tablespoons of cold water.

Stir to combine well and cook an additional 3 minutes or until thoroughly warmed. Serve garnished with fresh parsley and crumbled pancetta. Bon appétit!

# 171. Smoky and Yummy Beef Medley

**(Ready in about 1 hour 40 minutes | Servings 6)**

**Per serving: 375 Calories; 13.3g Fat; 5.6g Carbs; 55.1g Protein;**

## INGREDIENTS

3 teaspoons tallow, room temperature
2 pounds boneless beef sirloin steak, cubed
Seasoned salt and cayenne pepper, to taste
1/2 teaspoon black peppercorns, crushed

1 cup yellow onions, chopped
2 cloves garlic, minced
1 tablespoon smoked paprika
1 teaspoon caraway seeds, crushed
1/2 teaspoon mustard seeds
2 thyme sprigs

1 rosemary sprig
6 cups bone broth
1 tablespoon fish sauce
2 ripe Roma tomatoes, pureed
1 tablespoon dry white wine
2 bay leaves

## DIRECTIONS

Heat 1 teaspoon of tallow in a heavy-bottomed pot over a moderate heat. Now, brown the beef until it is no longer pink.

Season with salt, cayenne pepper, and black peppercorns; reserve.

In the same pot, heat remaining 2 teaspoons of tallow over a moderate heat. Cook the onions and garlic until they're softened, stirring continuously.

Now, add the paprika, caraway seeds, mustard seeds, thyme, and rosemary; cook an additional minute or until they are fragrant.

Add the remaining ingredients. Cook, partially covered, for 1 hour 30 minutes more. Discard bay leaves and serve in individual bowls. Bon appétit!

# 172. Beef Soup with Chili Drizzle

**(Ready in about 1 hour 10 minutes | Servings 6)**

**Per serving: 375 Calories; 14.4g Fat; 4.8g Carbs; 47.6g Protein;**

## INGREDIENTS

1 tablespoon canola oil
2 pounds beef chuck (well-marbled), boneless and cubed
2 onions, peeled and chopped
1 parsnip, chopped
1 celery with leaves, chopped
2 carrots, chopped

1/2 cup ripe olives, pitted and halved
1 ripe tomato, pureed
6 cups water
2 tablespoons instant bouillon granules
1/2 teaspoon ground bay leaf
1/2 teaspoon ground cumin
1/2 cup frozen green peas

**For the chili drizzle:**
2 red chilies
1 tablespoon extra-virgin olive oil
2 tablespoons lemon juice
Salt, to taste

## DIRECTIONS

Heat the oil in a stockpot over a moderately high heat. Now, brown the beef cubes for 3 to 5 minutes, stirring often; reserve.

Next, in the pan drippings, cook the onions, parsnip, celery and carrots until just tender. Add the olives, tomato, water, bouillon granules, ground bay leaf and cumin.

Stir in the reserved beef and bring the soup to a boil.

Turn the heat to medium-low; let it simmer, partially covered, about 50 minutes. Add the green peas and cook for a further 15 minutes.

Meanwhile, make the chili drizzle by blending all ingredients in your food processor.

Afterwards, top with the chili drizzle and serve.

# 173. Rich Beef Mishmash

**(Ready in about 2 hours | Servings 4)**

**Per serving: 467 Calories; 18.7g Fat; 3.7g Carbs; 58g Protein;**

## INGREDIENTS

2 tablespoons lard
1 ½ pounds ground beef
2 garlic cloves, minced
2 leeks, chopped
1 carrot, chopped
2 bell peppers, chopped
1 jalapeno, pepper, finely minced

1 celery with leaves, chopped
4 cups beef broth
Salt and pepper, to taste
1 teaspoon dried marjoram
1 teaspoon fennel seeds
1/4 teaspoon freshly grated nutmeg
1 tablespoon flaxseed meal

## DIRECTIONS

Melt 1 tablespoon of the lard in a pan (Dutch oven). Then, brown the beef, crumbling with a spatula; reserve.
In the same pan (Dutch oven), melt the remaining tablespoon of lard. Cook the vegetables until they have softened.
Add the beef back to the pan (Dutch oven) and pour in the beef broth. Add the seasonings and bring to a boil.
Reduce the heat to medium-low. Let it simmer approximately 1 hour 50 minutes.
Afterwards, stir in the flaxseed meal. Let it boil for 1 to 2 minutes, stirring frequently. Serve warm in individual bowls.

# 174. Cheeseburger Soup with Ume Plum Vinegar

**(Ready in about 30 minutes | Servings 6)**

Per serving: 238 Calories; 12.6g Fat; 5.6g Carbs; 25.1g Protein;

## INGREDIENTS

1 tablespoon olive oil
1 ½ pounds ground chuck
2 onions, chopped
2 garlic cloves, chopped
2 cups bone broth
1 cup ripe tomatoes, pureed

Salt and ground black peppercorns, to your liking
2 bay leaves
1 teaspoon dried oregano
1 cup Colby cheese, shredded
2 tablespoons ume plum vinegar

## DIRECTIONS

Heat the oil in a pot over a moderately high heat. Now, cook the beef until it is well browned, crumbling with a fork. Drain and reserve.
Cook the onion and garlic in pan drippings. Cook until they are tender, about 5 minutes.
Add the other ingredients, minus the cheese and ume plum vinegar, and bring to a rapid boiling. Cook an additional 20 minutes.
Stir in the Colby cheese and continue to cook until the cheese melts.
Ladle into individual soup bowls. Drizzle each serving with ume plum vinegar and serve right away. Bon appétit!

# 175. Marsala Beef Ribs

**(Ready in about 2 hours 30 minutes | Servings 8)**

**Per serving: 231 Calories; 8.9g Fat; 1.3g Carbs; 34.7g Protein;**

## INGREDIENTS

2 pounds beef ribs
1 teaspoon kosher salt
1/4 teaspoon ground black pepper, or more to taste
1/2 teaspoon chili powder

1 tablespoon coconut oil
1/2 cup Marsala wine
3/4 cup pureed fresh ripe tomatoes
2 garlic cloves, minced

## DIRECTIONS

Start by preheating your oven to 325 degrees F.
Season the beef ribs with salt, black pepper and chili powder on all sides.
Preheat the coconut oil in a large-sized skillet over a medium-high flame. Sear the ribs until browned on all sides.
Transfer the beef ribs to a baking dish. In a mixing bowl, combine the remaining ingredients; pour this mixture over the beef ribs.
Cover with a piece of foil. Let it roast for 2 hours in the preheated oven. Remove the foil and roast for a further 20 to 30 minutes.

# 176. Beef Sausage and Colby Dip

**(Ready in about 20 minutes | Servings 8)**

**Per serving: 333 Calories; 29.2g Fat; 2.9g Carbs; 14.7g Protein;**

## INGREDIENTS

1 tablespoon lard, at room temperature
1 onion, finely chopped
2 garlic cloves, minced
1 ½ cups smoked beef sausages, crumbled

1 cup cream cheese, at room temperature
1 ½ cups Colby cheese, shredded
2 tablespoons fresh chives, roughly chopped

## DIRECTIONS

Start by preheating an oven to 330 degrees F.

Melt the lard in a pan over a moderately high heat. Then, sweat the onion for 3 to 4 minutes. Stir in the garlic and continue sautéing until aromatic.

Add the sautéed onion and garlic to a mixing dish. Add the sausage, cream cheese, Colby cheese; mix to combine well.

Transfer the mixture to a baking dish; bake for 15 minutes. Garnish with fresh chives and serve with veggie sticks. Bon appétit!

# 177. Bacon-Wrapped Meatballs with Parsley Sauce

**(Ready in about 30 minutes | Servings 6)**

Per serving: 399 Calories; 27g Fat; 1.8g Carbs; 37.7g Protein;

## INGREDIENTS

1 pound ground beef
1 egg, beaten
1 ½ tablespoons olive oil
1/2 cup crushed pork rinds
1/4 cup fresh cilantro, chopped
2 cloves garlic, smashed
Sea salt and ground black pepper, to your liking
1/2 teaspoon cayenne pepper

1/2 pound bacon slices
Toothpicks
For the Parsley Sauce:
1 cup fresh parsley
1 tablespoon almonds, toasted
1 tablespoon sunflower seeds, soaked
1/2 tablespoon olive oil
Sea salt and black pepper, to taste

## DIRECTIONS

Preheat your oven to 390 degrees F.

Then, in a mixing bowl, thoroughly combine the ground beef, egg, olive oil, crushed pork rinds, cilantro, garlic, salt, black pepper, and cayenne pepper.

Shape the mixture into 1.5-inch meatballs. Wrap each ball with a slice of bacon; secure with a toothpick.

Arrange the meatballs on a baking sheet; bake in the preheated oven for 25 to 30 minutes.

In the meantime, make the parsley sauce. Pulse all ingredients in a food processor until uniform and smooth.

Serve the warm meatballs with the parsley sauce on the side and enjoy!

# 178. Sunday Flank Steak

**(Ready in about 20 minutes + marinating time | Servings 6)**

**Per serving: 350 Calories; 17.3g Fat; 2.1g Carbs; 42.7g Protein;**

## INGREDIENTS

2 tablespoons olive oil
2 tablespoons soy sauce
1 teaspoon garlic paste
A bunch of scallions, chopped
1 tablespoon lime lemon juice

1/4 cup dry red wine
2 pounds flank steak
Salt and cayenne pepper, to taste
1/2 teaspoon black peppercorns, crushed

## DIRECTIONS

In a mixing bowl, thoroughly combine the oil, soy sauce, garlic paste, scallions, lemon juice, and red wine.

Now, season the flank steak with salt, cayenne pepper and black peppercorns. Place the meat in the marinade; cover and refrigerate for 6 hours.

Preheat a nonstick skillet over a moderately high flame. Fry your steaks about 10 minutes, turning once. Bon appétit!

## 179. Father's Day Stuffed Avocado

**(Ready in about 20 minutes | Servings 6)**

**Per serving: 407 Calories; 28.8g Fat; 16.4g Carbs; 23.4g Protein;**

### INGREDIENTS

1 tablespoon avocado oil
3/4 pound beef, ground
1/3 cup beef broth
1/2 cup shallots, sliced
Salt and black pepper, to taste

3 ripe avocados, pitted and halved
2 small-sized tomatoes, chopped
3/4 cup Colby cheese, shredded
3 tablespoons Kalamata olives, pitted and sliced
1/2 cup mayonnaise

### DIRECTIONS

Preheat an oven to 340 degrees F.

Het the avocado oil in a pan over a moderate heat; now, brown the ground beef for 2 to 3 minutes, crumbling it with a wooden spatula. Add the broth and shallots. Cook until the shallots turn translucent. Season with salt and pepper.

Then, scoop out some of the middle of each avocado. Mash the avocado flash that you scooped out along with the chopped tomatoes. Add the reserved beef mixture and stuff your avocado. Afterward, top with the shredded cheese and sliced olives.

Place the stuffed avocado on a roasting pan. Bake for 8 to 10 minutes in the preheated oven. Serve with mayonnaise and enjoy!

## 180. Beef Sausage and Vegetable Skillet

**(Ready in about 40 minutes | Servings 4)**

**Per serving: 250 Calories; 17.5g Fat; 5.4g Carbs; 6.8g Protein;**

### INGREDIENTS

2 tablespoons canola oil
4 beef sausages, sliced
2 shallots, chopped
2 spring garlic, minced
2 bell peppers, deveined and chopped
1 parsnip, chopped
Salt and pepper, to taste

2 ripe tomatoes, pureed
2 tablespoons ketchup, sugar-free
1 ½ cups beef bone broth
1/4 cup dry red wine
2 thyme sprigs
2 rosemary sprigs

### DIRECTIONS

Heat the oil in a deep skillet over a moderate heat. Cook the sausage for 2 to 3 minutes, stirring periodically.

Stir in the shallots, garlic, bell peppers, and parsnip; season with salt and pepper. Cook approximately 7 minutes.

Add the remaining ingredients and bring it to a boil. Reduce the heat to medium-low. Let it simmer for 25 minutes. Serve warm.

## 181. Spicy Sausage and Vegetable Casserole

**(Ready in about 30 minutes | Servings 4)**

**Per serving: 424 Calories; 32.4g Fat; 6g Carbs; 23.7g Protein;**

### INGREDIENTS

1 tablespoon tallow, softened
4 beef sausages
1 banana shallot, sliced
1 cup broccoli, broken into small florets
1 carrot, sliced
1 celery stalk, chopped
1 bell pepper, sliced

1 dried Poblano pepper, crushed
2 garlic cloves, finely chopped
Salt, to taste
1 teaspoon black peppercorns, freshly crushed
1/2 teaspoon smoked cayenne pepper
1 ¼ cups beef stock, preferably homemade

### DIRECTIONS

Melt the tallow in a nonstick skillet over a moderately high heat. Cook the sausages until they are browned on all sides; reserve.

Now, cook the shallot, broccoli, carrots, celery, peppers, and garlic in the same skillet; cook for 6 to 9 minutes or until the vegetables are tender. Season with salt, peppercorns and smoked cayenne pepper. Transfer the sautéed vegetables to a lightly greased casserole dish. Nestle the reserved sausages within the sautéed vegetables.

Pour in the stock and bake in the preheated oven at 350 degrees F for about 10 minutes. Serve warm garnished with fresh chives if desired.

# 182. Hamburger Soup with Cabbage

**(Ready in about 35 minutes | Servings 4)**

**Per serving: 307 Calories; 23.6g Fat; 5.4g Carbs; 14.8g Protein;**

## INGREDIENTS

2 tablespoons lard, melted
3/4 pound ground chuck
1/2 cup scallions, chopped
2 cloves garlic, minced
1 carrot, diced

1 cup cabbage, shredded
1 celery with leaves, diced
1 tomato, pureed
6 cups chicken broth
1 bay leaf

Seasoned salt and ground black pepper, to taste
1 cup sour cream

## DIRECTIONS

Melt the lard in a stockpot. Cook the chuck until it is no longer pink; reserve.

Then, cook the scallions, garlic, carrot, cabbage, and celery in the pan drippings, stirring constantly.

Stir in the other ingredients along with the reserved chuck, bringing to a rapid boil. Turn the heat to a simmer. Cook another 27 minutes, partially covered.

Taste and adjust the seasonings. Ladle into individual bowls; serve dolloped with full-fat sour cream.

# 183. Ultimate Thai Beef Salad

**(Ready in about 15 minutes | Servings 4)**

**Per serving: 404 Calories; 32.9g Fat; 6.3g Carbs; 12.8g Protein;**

## INGREDIENTS

1/2 pound beef rump steak, cut into strips
1/2 teaspoon sea salt
1/3 teaspoon freshly cracked black pepper
1 teaspoon soy sauce

2 tablespoons sesame oil
1 red onion, peeled and sliced
1 garlic clove, minced
1 bunch fresh mint
2 avocados, pitted, peeled and sliced
2 cucumbers, sliced

1 bunch fresh Thai basil, leaves picked
1 teaspoon minced Thai chili
2 tablespoons rice vinegar
1 tablespoon fresh lime juice
1/4 cup pumpkin seeds

## DIRECTIONS

Combine the beef with the salt, pepper and soy sauce.

Preheat the oil in a nonstick skillet over medium-low heat. Then, sauté the onion and garlic until tender and aromatic, about 4 minutes.

Cook the beef on a grill pan for 5 minutes or until cooked to your liking.

Arrange the fresh mint, avocado slices, cucumber, Thai basil, and Thai chili in a nice salad bowl. Top with the beef slices. Add the onion-garlic mixture.

Drizzle with rice vinegar and lime juice. Sprinkle with pumpkin seeds and serve.

# 184. Hungarian Beef Stew

**(Ready in about 1 hour 25 minutes | Servings 4)**

**Per serving: 357 Calories; 15.8g Fat; 5g Carbs; 40.2g Protein;**

## INGREDIENTS

2 tablespoons olive oil
1 ¼ pounds chuck-eye roast, diced
Celery salt and ground black pepper, to taste
1 tablespoon Hungarian paprika

1 tablespoon pear cider vinegar
1/2 cup Cabernet Sauvignon
4 cups water
2 tablespoons beef bouillon granules
1/4 teaspoon ground bay leaf

2 onions, peeled and chopped
1 celery with leaves, chopped
2 carrots, peeled and cut into 1/4-inch rounds
1 tablespoon flaxseed meal

## DIRECTIONS

Heat the oil in a heavy-bottomed pot. Then, cook the meat until no longer pink, for 3 to 4 minutes; work in batches and set aside. Season with celery salt, pepper, and Hungarian paprika.

Now, pour the vinegar and Cabernet Sauvignon to deglaze the bottom of the pot. Add the water, beef bouillon granules and reserved beef to the pot.

Stir in the ground bay leaf, onions, celery and carrots and cook an additional 1 hour 15 minutes over medium-low heat.

Add the flaxseed meal to thicken the liquid; stir constantly for 3 minutes. Serve in individual bowls and enjoy!

# 185. Za'atar Strip Steaks with Cabbage

**(Ready in about 20 minutes +marinating time | Servings 4)**

**Per serving: 321 Calories; 14g Fat; 5.3g Carbs; 36.7g Protein;**

## INGREDIENTS

1 pound New York strip steaks, cut into bite-sized pieces
1 tablespoon hoisin sauce
1 tablespoon fresh lemon juice
Sea salt and ground black pepper, to taste
1 teaspoon Za'atar

2 tablespoons sesame oil
1 yellow onion, chopped
2 garlic cloves, chopped
1 cup cabbage, shredded
1 bell pepper, chopped

## DIRECTIONS

Toss the strip steaks with the hoisin sauce, fresh lemon juice, salt, black pepper and Za'atar seasoning. Marinate in the refrigerator for at least 3 hours.
Heat the oil in a skillet that is preheated over a moderately high heat. Now, brown the strip steaks for 3 to 4 minutes, stirring occasionally.
Add the onions to the same skillet and cook until it is translucent. Add the garlic, cabbage and bell pepper and turn the heat to medium-low. Simmer an additional 10 minutes and serve warm. Bon appétit!

# 186. Spicy Winter Sauerkraut with Ground Beef

**(Ready in about 20 minutes | Servings 4)**

**Per serving: 330 Calories; 12.2g Fat; 4.7g Carbs; 44.4g Protein;**

## INGREDIENTS

1 tablespoon tallow, melted
2 onions, chopped
2 garlic cloves, smashed
1 ¼ pounds ground beef
18 ounces sauerkraut, rinsed and well drained

1 teaspoon chili pepper flakes
1 teaspoon mustard powder
1 bay leaf
Sea salt and ground black pepper, to taste

## DIRECTIONS

Heat a saucepan over a moderately high heat. Now, warm the tallow and cook the onions and garlic until aromatic.
Stir in the ground beef and cook until it is slightly browned.
Add the remaining ingredients. Reduce the heat to medium. Cook about 6 minutes or until everything is thoroughly cooked. Bon appétit!

# 187. Winter Cheeseburger Soup

**(Ready in about 20 minutes | Servings 4)**

**Per serving: 326 Calories; 20.5g Fat; 4.5g Carbs; 26.8g Protein;**

## INGREDIENTS

2 tablespoons coconut oil
1/2 pound ground beef
1 cup shallots, chopped
1 celery stalk, chopped
1 tablespoon celery leaves, chopped

1 tablespoon fresh cilantro, chopped
4 cups beef bone broth
1/2 cup full-fat milk
1 cup pepper jack cheese, shredded
1 tablespoon rice vinegar

## DIRECTIONS

Melt the coconut oil in a stock pot that is preheated over a moderate heat. Now, cook the ground beef until it is no longer pink; reserve.
Add the shallots and chopped celery stalk; cook an additional 2 minutes, stirring continuously. Add a splash of broth if needed.
Add the celery leaves, cilantro and broth and bring to a boil; cook another 10 minutes, partially covered.
Gradually add the milk to the soup, stirring often. Reduce the heat and let it simmer an additional 5 minutes. Fold in the cheese and remove from the heat.
Add the vinegar and stir until the cheese is completely melted. Bon appétit!

# 188. Zucchini Spaghetti with Bolognese Sauce

**(Ready in about 1 hour 35 minutes | Servings 4)**

**Per serving: 477 Calories; 25.6g Fat; 6.3g Carbs; 41.8g Protein;**

## INGREDIENTS

**For Bolognese:**
2 tablespoons olive oil
1 onion, finely chopped
2 garlic cloves, thinly sliced
1 celery with leaves, finely chopped
1 carrot, finely chopped
2 slices bacon, chopped
1 pound ground beef
2 tomatoes, pureed

2 tablespoons tomato paste
1/2 cup dry white wine
1/2 cup water
2 rosemary sprigs
1 teaspoon dried oregano
1 teaspoon dried basil
1 teaspoon fresh thyme leaves
Salt and ground black pepper, to taste

**For Zucchini Spaghetti:**
4 zucchinis, peeled
2 tablespoons olive oil
1/4 cup water
Salt, to taste

## DIRECTIONS

Heat the oil in a sauté pan that is preheated over a moderate flame. Now, sauté the onions, garlic, celery and carrots until they are tender. Now, stir in the bacon and ground beef. Cook for 7 more minutes, breaking up lumps with a spatula.

Stir in the other ingredients for the sauce and simmer for 1 hour 15 minutes over medium-low heat. Taste and adjust the seasonings.

Meanwhile, make your zucchini spaghetti. Slice the zucchinis into long strips i.e. noodle-shape strands.

Heat the oil in a pan over medium heat; cook the zucchini for 1 minute or so, stirring continuously. Pour in the water and cook 6 more minutes.

Sprinkle with salt to taste and serve with the prepared Bolognese sauce. Enjoy!

# 189. Filet Mignon with Sour Cream-Mustard Sauce

**(Ready in about 20 minutes | Servings 4)**

**Per serving: 321 Calories; 13.7g Fat; 1g Carbs; 45g Protein;**

## INGREDIENTS

1/3 cup sour cream
1 tablespoon stone-ground mustard
1 ½ tablespoons flat-leaf parsley, finely chopped
4 (1 ½-inch) thick filet mignon steaks
1/2 teaspoon seasoned salt

1/4 teaspoon ground black pepper
2 sprigs thyme, chopped
1 sprig rosemary, chopped
1 tablespoon vegetable oil

## DIRECTIONS

In a mixing bowl, whisk together the sour cream, mustard, and parsley. Keep in your refrigerator until ready to serve.

Then, season the filet mignon steaks with salt, pepper, thyme, and rosemary.

Heat the oil in a pan that is preheated over moderately high heat for 4 minutes on each side. Serve with the prepared mustard sauce and enjoy!

# 190. Saucy Beef Short Loin

**(Ready in about 2 hours | Servings 4)**

**Per serving: 238 Calories; 9.2g Fat; 6.3g Carbs; 27.4g Protein;**

## INGREDIENTS

1 tablespoon olive oil
1 pound beef short loin, thinly sliced
1 leek, sliced
1 parsnip, chopped
3 garlic cloves, thinly sliced
1/2 teaspoon grated nutmeg

1 teaspoon lemon zest
1/2 teaspoon red pepper flakes, crushed
1/3 cup red wine
2 tablespoons Worcestershire sauce
1 ½ cups beef stock

## DIRECTIONS

Heat the oil in a heavy-bottomed skillet that is preheated over a moderate heat. Sear the beef short loin for 10 to 13 minutes; reserve.

Then, in the same skillet, cook the leeks, parsnip and garlic for 3 to 4 minutes, stirring constantly.

Add the remaining ingredients and bring to a rapid boil. Then, turn the heat to a simmer. Cook for 1 ½ to 2 hours. Bon appétit!

# 191. Old-Fashioned Beef Stew

**(Ready in about 40 minutes | Servings 6)**

**Per serving: 259 Calories; 10.1g Fat; 4.1g Carbs; 35.7g Protein;**

## INGREDIENTS

1 tablespoon tallow, at room temperature

1 ½ pounds beef stew meat, cubed

1 cup leeks, thinly sliced

2 garlic cloves, chopped

1 tablespoon cremini mushrooms, thinly sliced

Salt and black pepper, to taste

1 teaspoon dried marjoram

1 teaspoon cayenne pepper

1/4 teaspoon smoked paprika

1 bay leaf

4 cubes beef bouillon, crumbled

4 cups water

1 egg, lightly whisked

## DIRECTIONS

Melt the tallow in your pot that is preheated over a moderate flame.

Now, sear the beef until it's just browned; make sure to stir periodically. Set aside.

In pan drippings, cook the leeks and garlic for 1 minute to 90 seconds or until aromatic. Stir in the mushrooms; cook until they're tender and fragrant.

Add the remaining ingredients, cover and cook for 30 to 40 minutes. Add the whisked egg in the hot soup and stir for 1 minute. Serve in individual bowls and enjoy!

# 192. Filet Mignon Steaks with Wine Sauce

**(Ready in about 30 minutes | Servings 4)**

**Per serving: 451 Calories; 34.4g Fat; 3.6g Carbs; 29.7g Protein;**

## INGREDIENTS

4 (6-ounce) filet mignon steaks

1 tablespoon deli mustard

Celery salt and freshly ground pepper, to taste

2 rosemary sprigs

1 thyme sprigs

2 tablespoons lard, room temperature

1 cup scallions, chopped

2 garlic cloves, minced

1 red bell pepper, deveined and chopped

1/2 cup dry red wine

## DIRECTIONS

Rub filet mignon steaks with the mustard. Sprinkle the filet mignon steaks with the salt, pepper, rosemary and thyme.

Heat the lard in a heavy-bottomed skillet over moderate heat. Cook the filet mignon steaks for 10 minutes on each side or until a thermometer registers 120 degrees F.

Now, cook the scallions, garlic, and pepper in pan drippings about 3 minutes. Pour in the wine to scrape up any browned bits from the bottom of the skillet.

Now, cook until the liquid is reduced by half. Serve immediately.

# 193. Mini Meatloaf Muffins with Cremini Mushrooms

**(Ready in about 40 minutes | Servings 6)**

**Per serving: 404 Calories; 22.8g Fat; 6.2g Carbs; 44g Protein;**

## INGREDIENTS

1 tablespoon olive oil

1 yellow onion, chopped

1/2 pound Cremini mushrooms, chopped

3/4 cup Romano cheese, grated

1/2 cup crushed chicharrones

1/2 teaspoon granulated garlic

2 eggs, lightly beaten

1/4 cup pine nuts, ground

1 ¼ pounds ground beef

1/2 cup tomato puree

Salt and ground black pepper, to taste

1 teaspoon cayenne pepper

## DIRECTIONS

Begin by preheating your oven to 390 degrees F.

Heat the oil in a pan that is preheated over a moderately high heat. Now, sauté the onion until it is translucent and aromatic.

Stir in the mushrooms and cook an additional 4 minutes or until almost all of the liquid has evaporated.

Add the cheese, crushed chicharrones, granulated garlic, eggs, pine nuts and ground beef. Now, mix until everything is well incorporated.

Divide the meatloaf mixture among lightly greased muffin cups. Bake for 25 minutes.

Meanwhile, mix the tomato puree with salt, black pepper and cayenne pepper. Spread the tomato mixture over the meatloaves.

Bake until a thermometer registers 165 degrees F, 5 to 10 minutes more. Allow your meatloaves to cool for a couple of minutes before removing from the pan. Bon appétit!

# 194. Crock Pot Beef Brisket with Blue Cheese

**(Ready in about 8 hours | Servings 6)**

**Per serving: 397 Calories; 31.4g Fat; 3.9g Carbs; 23.5g Protein;**

## INGREDIENTS

2 tablespoons olive oil
1 shallot, chopped
1/2 tablespoon garlic paste
1 ½ pounds corned beef brisket
1/4 teaspoon cloves, ground

1/3 teaspoon ground coriander
1/4 cup soy sauce
1 cup water
6 ounces blue cheese, crumbled

## DIRECTIONS

Heat a sauté pan with the olive oil over medium heat. Cook the shallot until it has softened.
Add the garlic paste and cook an additional minute; transfer to your Crock pot that is previously greased with a nonstick cooking spray.
Sear the brisket until it has a golden-brown crust. Transfer to the Crock pot. Add the remaining ingredient, except for the blue cheese.
Cover and cook on Low heat setting for 6 to 8 hours or until the meat is very tender. Serve topped with the blue cheese. Enjoy!

# 195. Sriracha and Scallion Chuck

**(Ready in about 50 minutes | Servings 4)**

**Per serving: 292 Calories; 14.3g Fat; 3.9g Carbs; 36.9g Protein;**

## INGREDIENTS

2 tablespoons soy sauce
1 teaspoon Sriracha sauce
1 tablespoon garlic paste
Salt and crushed mixed peppercorns, to taste
1 teaspoon mustard seeds
1/2 teaspoon dried marjoram

1 bunch scallions, chopped
1/2 tablespoon tallow
1 ½ pounds chuck pot roast, cubed
1/4 teaspoon cumin
1/4 teaspoon celery seeds
1 tablespoon fresh parsley, roughly chopped

## DIRECTIONS

Whisk the soy sauce, Sriracha sauce and garlic paste in a mixing bowl. Add the salt, crushed peppercorns, mustard seeds, marjoram, and scallions.
Add the cubed beef and let it marinate for 40 minutes in your refrigerator.
Melt the tallow in a frying pan over a moderately high heat. Cook the marinated beef for 5 to 6 minutes, stirring frequently; work in batches to cook the beef cubes through evenly.
Season with cumin and celery seeds. Serve garnished with fresh parsley. Enjoy!

# 196. Beef Casserole with Sour Cream Sauce

**(Ready in about 25 minutes | Servings 4)**

**Per serving: 509 Calories; 29.6g Fat; 6.1g Carbs; 45.2g Protein;**

## INGREDIENTS

1 tablespoon olive oil
1 pound ground beef
2 ripe tomatoes, chopped
2 ounces sun-dried tomatoes, chopped
1/2 tablespoon dill relish
1/2 teaspoon salt
1/4 teaspoon ground black pepper

1/2 teaspoon chili powder
1 teaspoon Italian seasoning
1 cup cheddar cheese
3/4 cup sour cream
1 teaspoon minced garlic
1/2 cup shallots, finely chopped

## DIRECTIONS

Preheat the oven to 400 degrees F.
Then, heat the oil in a nonstick skillet that is preheated over a moderate flame.
Brown the ground beef in butter, crumbling it with a large spatula. Add the tomatoes, dill relish and seasonings.
Place the beef mixture in a baking dish. Top with the cheese and bake for about 18 minutes.
Meanwhile, thoroughly combine the sour cream with the garlic and shallots. Serve with your casserole dish.

# 197. Buttery Roasted Chuck with Horseradish Sauce

**(Ready in about 2 hours | Servings 6)**

**Per serving: 493 Calories; 39.4g Fat; 2.9g Carbs; 27.9g Protein;**

## INGREDIENTS

1 ½ pounds chuck
2 bay leaves
1/4 cup vegetable oil
1 garlic clove, minced
1 tablespoon Italian seasoning mix
1 ½ tablespoons whole grain mustard

1/3 cup dry red wine
1 teaspoon sea salt
1/4 teaspoon black pepper, to taste
1/2 teaspoon cayenne pepper, or more to taste

**For the Sauce:**
2 tablespoons prepared horseradish
1/4 cup sour cream
2 tablespoons mayonnaise

## DIRECTIONS

Toss the chuck with the bay leaves, vegetable oil, garlic, Italian seasoning, mustard, red wine, salt, black pepper and cayenne pepper.
Let it marinate overnight in the refrigerator. Place your chuck in a baking dish that is lined with a piece of foil; pour the marinade over it.
Wrap with the foil. Then, bake at 375 degrees F for 2 hours or until a thermometer registers 125 degrees F.
In the meantime, mix all ingredients for the sauce. Slice your chuck across the grain and serve with the sauce on the side.

# 198. Italian-Style Holiday Meatloaf

**(Ready in about 50 minutes | Servings 6)**

**Per serving: 163 Calories; 8.4g Fat; 5.6g Carbs; 12.2g Protein;**

## INGREDIENTS

Nonstick cooking spray
2 pounds ground chuck
1 egg, slightly beaten
2 shallots, chopped
1 tablespoon garlic paste
1 tablespoon mustard
1 ½ teaspoons coconut aminos

2 tablespoons fresh pureed tomato
1/3 cup full-fat milk
1/3 cup almond flour
2 tablespoons flaxseed meal
1 teaspoon Italian seasonings
Seasoned salt and ground black pepper
1/4 teaspoon ground sage

**For the Tomato Sauce:**
2 ripe tomatoes, crushed
Salt and black pepper, to taste
1 tablespoon cilantro, minced

## DIRECTIONS

Start by preheating your oven 360 degrees F. Lightly grease a loaf pan with a nonstick cooking spray.
In a mixing bowl, thoroughly combine all the meatloaf ingredients.
Now, press the meatloaf mixture into the prepared meatloaf.
Add all ingredients for the sauce to a pan that is preheated over medium-low heat. Simmer for 2 to 3 minutes, stirring periodically.
Spread the sauce over the top of your meatloaf. Bake for 45 minutes. Let it cool down for a couple of minutes before slicing and serving.
Bon appétit!

# 199. Royal Keto Lasagna

**(Ready in about 1 hour 30 minutes | Servings 6)**

**Per serving: 494 Calories; 41g Fat; 3.8g Carbs; 24.1g Protein;**

## INGREDIENTS

**For the Lasagna Sheets:**
3 eggs, whisked
6 ounces mascarpone cheese, at room temperature
1/2 cup Parmesan cheese, grated
1 cup Colby cheese, shredded
1/2 teaspoon dried oregano
1/2 teaspoon onion powder
1/2 teaspoon cumin powder

**For the Filling:**
1 tablespoon olive oil
1 ½ pounds ground chuck
1 onion, chopped
2 garlic cloves, minced
2 slices bacon, chopped

1 cup tomato sauce
1/2 teaspoon oregano
1/2 teaspoon dried basil
2 cups sour cream
1 cup mascarpone cheese
1/4 cup fresh parsley, finely chopped

## DIRECTIONS

Start by preheating your oven to 370 degrees F. Now, coat a baking pan with a sheet of parchment paper or Silpat mat.
Then, thoroughly combine the eggs and 6 ounces of mascarpone cheese with a hand mixer.
Add the other ingredients for the lasagna sheets; mix to combine well.
Press the mixture onto the baking pan, creating an even layer. Bake approximately 20 minutes.
Now, refrigerate the "sheet" for 30 minutes. Cut into lasagna sheets and set aside.
Next, heat the oil in a pan that is preheated over a moderate heat. Brown the ground beef for 3 to 4 minutes.
Add the onion, garlic and bacon and cook an additional 3 minutes, stirring constantly. Now, stir in the tomato sauce, oregano and basil; cook an additional 13 minutes.
Pour 1/4 cup of the sauce into the bottom of a previously greased casserole dish. Top with the first lasagna sheet. Repeat these steps 3 times.
Top with the sour cream and 1 cup of mascarpone cheese. Sprinkle fresh parsley over the top. Bake for 15 to 22 minutes longer. Serve warm and enjoy!

# 200. Cabbage, Beef and Cheese Casserole

**(Ready in about 55 minutes | Servings 6)**

**Per serving: 467 Calories; 37g Fat; 4.9g Carbs; 27.1g Protein;**

## INGREDIENTS

1 head of cabbage, cut into quarters
1/2 pound ground chuck
1/2 pound ground turkey
1 leek, chopped
2 slices bacon, chopped

1 teaspoon dried basil
1 teaspoon dried oregano
1/2 teaspoon dried marjoram
Salt and black pepper, to taste
1 cup salsa, preferably homemade

1 ½ cups cream cheese, crumbled
8 slices American cheese
2 eggs

## DIRECTIONS

Firstly, boil the cabbage approximately 5 minutes; drain. Preheat your oven to 400 degrees F.

Preheat a pan over a moderately high heat; cook the ground beef and turkey, breaking with a spatula, for 4 to 5 minutes.

Now, add the leeks and bacon; cook for a further 3 minutes, stirring frequently.

Stir in the basil, oregano, marjoram, salt, pepper and salsa; bring it to a boil. Turn the heat to medium-low; cook an additional 6 minutes.

Add 1/2 of this mixture to the bottom of a lightly greased baking dish. Add a layer of the boiled cabbage leaves. Repeat the layers one more time.

In a mixing bowl, combine the cream cheese, American cheese, and eggs. Top your casserole with the cheese layer and bake for 30 minutes or until everything is thoroughly cooked.

Allow your casserole to cool down for a couple of minutes before slicing and serving.

# 201. Top Round Steak with Marsala Sauce

**(Ready in about 1 hour 40 minutes | Servings 6)**

**Per serving: 339 Calories; 21.7g Fat; 5.2g Carbs; 35g Protein;**

## INGREDIENTS

1 ½ pounds top round steak, cut into 4 serving-size pieces
2 tablespoons olive oil
1 shallot, chopped
1 garlic clove, pressed
1 ½ cups Brussels sprouts, quartered
1 teaspoon ground bay leaf

1/2 teaspoon dried basil
1 tablespoon dried sage, crushed
1/2 teaspoon sea salt
1/4 teaspoon freshly ground black pepper
1 cup broth

**For the Sauce:**
1/2 cup Marsala wine
1/2 cup chicken broth
1/4 teaspoon freshly grated nutmeg
3/4 teaspoon Dijon mustard
1 cup double cream

## DIRECTIONS

Begin by preheating your oven to 340 degrees F. Flatten each top round steak with a meat tenderizer.

Heat the olive oil in an oven-safe pan over medium-high heat. Now, cook the steak until just browned; reserve.

Next, cook the shallots and garlic in the pan drippings in the same pan until they're softened. After that, cook the Brussels sprouts until tender and smell good.

Add the round steak back to the pan. Season with the ground bay leaf, basil, sage, salt, and pepper. Pour in 1 cup of broth. Wrap with foil and roast for 1 hour 10 minutes.

Add the wine, 1/2 cup chicken cup of broth and nutmeg to the same roasting pan. Let it simmer for 15 to 18 minutes or until the sauce is reduced to half.

Now, stir in the mustard and double cream; cook an additional 15 minutes or until everything is heated through.

Divide the top round steak among four serving plates; ladle the sauce over them and serve warm.

# 202. Skirt Steak and Eggs Skillet

**(Ready in about 30 minutes | Servings 6)**

**Per serving: 429 Calories; 27.8g Fat; 3.2g Carbs; 39.1g Protein;**

## INGREDIENTS

2 tablespoons olive oil
1 ½ pounds skirt steak, cut into cubes
Celery salt and ground black pepper, to taste

1/2 teaspoon red pepper flakes
1/2 cup spring onions onion, chopped
1 teaspoon garlic, minced
1 bell pepper, chopped

1 serrano pepper, chopped
6 eggs

## DIRECTIONS

Heat the oil in a nonstick skillet over a moderately high flame. Cook the beef cubes for 10 minutes or until no longer pink, stirring periodically. Season with salt, black pepper and red pepper flakes and set aside.

In the same skillet, cook the spring onion and garlic until aromatic, 3 to 4 minutes. Stir in the peppers and cook for 3 minutes more.

Now, create six holes in the mixture to reveal the bottom of your pan. Crack an egg into each hole. Now, cook, covered, for 4 to 6 minutes or until the eggs are set. Serve right away!

# FISH & SEAFOOD

## 203. Breakfast Avocado and Tuna Balls

**(Ready in about 5 minutes | Servings 4)**

**Per serving: 316 Calories; 24.4g Fat; 5.9g Carbs; 17.4g Protein;**

### INGREDIENTS

3 ounces sunflower seeds
1 avocado, pitted and peeled
1 can tuna
Salt, to taste

1/2 teaspoon freshly ground black pepper
1/2 teaspoon smoked paprika
1/2 cup onion, chopped
1/2 teaspoon dried dill

### DIRECTIONS

Thoroughly mix all ingredients in a mixing dish. Shape the mixture into 8 balls.
Serve well chilled and enjoy!

## 204. Hot and Spicy Fish Stew

**(Ready in about 25 minutes | Servings 4)**

**Per serving: 296 Calories; 8.6g Fat; 5.5g Carbs; 41.4g Protein;**

### INGREDIENTS

1 tablespoon sesame oil
1 cup onions, chopped
1 teaspoon garlic, smashed
Sea salt, to taste
4 cups water
1 cup fresh tomato, pureed

1 tablespoon chicken bouillon granules
1/2 pound sea bass, cut into 2-inch pieces
1/3 pound halibut, cut into 2-inch pieces
2 rosemary sprigs, chopped
1/2 cup Sauvignon blanc
1/8 teaspoon Tabasco sauce, or more to taste

### DIRECTIONS

Heat the oil in a large stockpot that is preheated over medium heat. Now, sauté the onions and garlic until they're soft and aromatic.
Add the salt, water, tomato and chicken bouillon granules; cook an additional 13 minutes.
Stir in the remaining ingredients and bring to a rolling boil.
After that, turn the heat to medium-low and let it simmer until the fish easily flakes apart, about 4 minutes.
Taste and adjust the seasonings. Ladle the soup into individual bowls and serve hot.

## 205. Easy Oven-Baked Cod Fillets

**(Ready in about 30 minutes | Servings 4)**

**Per serving: 195 Calories; 8.2g Fat; 0.5g Carbs; 28.7g Protein;**

### INGREDIENTS

2 tablespoons olive oil
1/2 tablespoon yellow mustard
1 teaspoon garlic paste
1/2 tablespoon fresh lemon juice
1/2 teaspoon shallot powder

Salt and ground black pepper, to taste
1/2 teaspoon red pepper flakes, crushed
4 cod fillets
1/4 cup fresh cilantro, chopped

### DIRECTIONS

Start by preheating your oven to 420 degrees F. Lightly grease a baking dish with a nonstick cooking spray.
In a small mixing dish, thoroughly combine the oil, mustard, garlic paste, lemon juice, shallot powder, salt, black pepper and red pepper. Rub this mixture on all sides of your fish.
Bake 15 to 22 minutes in the middle of the preheated oven. Serve sprinkled with fresh cilantro.

# 206. Ricotta and Tuna Spread

**(Ready in about 10 minutes | Servings 6)**

**Per serving: 384 Calories; 20.4g Fat; 2.5g Carbs; 45.9g Protein;**

## INGREDIENTS

1 (6-ounce) can tuna in oil, drained
1/2 cup Ricotta cheese
1/2 teaspoon turmeric

2 ounces pecans, ground
1 tablespoon fresh cilantro, chopped

## DIRECTIONS

Blend the tuna, Ricotta cheese, turmeric powder and pecans in your blender.
Transfer to a serving bowl and serve garnished with fresh cilantro.
Serve with veggie sticks. Bon appétit!

# 207. Colorful Scallop Dinner

**(Ready in about 10 minutes | Servings 4)**

**Per serving: 260 Calories; 13.6g Fat; 5.9g Carbs; 28.1g Protein;**

## INGREDIENTS

1 pound sea scallops, halved horizontally
4 spring garlic, roughly chopped
2 plum tomatoes, sliced
1 cucumber, sliced
1 head of Iceberg lettuce, torn into bite-sized pieces
1/2 tablespoon deli mustard

1/4 cup extra-virgin olive oil
2 tablespoons fresh lemon juice
Sea salt and freshly ground pepper, to your liking
1/2 teaspoon dried dill weed
1/2 cup ripe olives, pitted and sliced

## DIRECTIONS

Add the scallops to a pot of a lightly salted water; cook for 1 to 3 minutes or until opaque; rinse under running water and transfer to a salad bowl.
Stir in the spring garlic, tomatoes, cucumber, and lettuce; gently toss to combine.
In a mixing dish, thoroughly combine the mustard, olive oil, lemon, salt, pepper and dill. Drizzle this mixture over the vegetables in the salad bowl.
Serve topped with ripe olives and enjoy!

# 208. Tuna and Cottage Cheese Stuffed Peppers

**(Ready in about 25 minutes | Servings 4)**

**Per serving: 273 Calories; 13.9g Fat; 5.1g Carbs; 28.9g Protein;**

## INGREDIENTS

4 bell peppers
10 ounces canned tuna, drained
1 yellow onion, finely chopped
1 garlic clove, smashed
1/3 cup mayonnaise

1/3 cup Kalamata olives, pitted and chopped
Sea salt and cayenne pepper, to taste
1/2 teaspoon dried parsley
1/2 teaspoon dried oregano
1 cup Cottage cheese

## DIRECTIONS

Start by preheating your oven to broil. Arrange the bell peppers on a baking sheet; broil for 6 minutes, turning the peppers once; make sure to rotate the baking sheet once or twice.
Once the peppers are cool enough to handle, cut them in half; remove the seeds and membranes.
In a mixing bowl, thoroughly combine the tuna, onion, garlic, mayonnaise, olives, salt, cayenne pepper, dried parsley, oregano and Cottage cheese.
Now, fill the peppers with the tuna mixture. Bake the stuffed peppers in the oven for 10 minutes or until thoroughly heated. Serve warm or at room temperature. Enjoy!

## 209. Halibut Steaks with Cheesy Cauliflower

**(Ready in about 25 minutes | Servings 4)**

**Per serving: 508 Calories; 22.9g Fat; 4.7g Carbs; 68.6g Protein;**

### INGREDIENTS

1 head of cauliflower, broken into florets
2 tablespoons olive oil
Sea salt and ground black pepper, to taste

1 cup Colby cheese, shredded
4 halibut steaks
1/2 teaspoon dried sage

1/2 teaspoon dried basil
1 ½ tablespoons fresh parsley, chopped
1 lemon, cut into wedges

### DIRECTIONS

Begin by preheating your oven to 390 degrees F.
Cook the cauliflower in a pot of lightly salted water until just tender.
Transfer to a well-greased casserole dish. Drizzle with 1 tablespoon of olive oil. Season with salt and pepper to taste.
Scatter shredded cheese on top of the cauliflower; bake approximately 17 minutes.
In the meantime, heat the remaining tablespoon of olive oil in a pan that is preheated over a moderately high flame. Fry the halibut steaks until golden and crisp.
Season with sage, basil, salt, and pepper. Serve garnished with fresh parsley and lemon wedges. Bon appétit!

## 210. Smoked Tilapia Pie

**(Ready in about 45 minutes | Servings 6)**

**Per serving: 416 Calories; 34.2g Fat; 5.5g Carbs; 19.5g Protein;**

### INGREDIENTS

**For the Crust:**
1 cup almond flour
3 tablespoons flaxseed meal
2 teaspoons ground psyllium husk powder
1/2 teaspoon baking powder
1/2 teaspoon baking soda
1/2 teaspoon kosher salt
1/2 stick butter
2 eggs
2 tablespoons water

**For the Filling:**
10 ounces smoked tilapia, chopped
1 teaspoon Dijon mustard
1/2 cup sour cream
1/2 cup mayonnaise
2 eggs
1 teaspoon dried rosemary
1/2 teaspoon dried basil
Salt and ground black pepper, to taste
1 ½ cups Cheddar cheese, shredded

### DIRECTIONS

Preheat your oven to 360 degrees F.
Mix all the crust ingredients in your food processor. Press into a baking pan that is lined with parchment paper.
Bake the crust in the middle of the preheated oven approximately 13 minutes.
Then, thoroughly combine all the ingredients for the filling. Spread the mixture over the pie crust. Bake an additional 30 minutes or until the pie is golden at the edges. Bon appétit!

## 211. Spring Shrimp Salad

**(Ready in about 10 minutes + chilling time | Servings 6)**

**Per serving: 209 Calories; 9.5g Fat; 6.8g Carbs; 20.2g Protein;**

### INGREDIENTS

1 medium-sized lime, cut into wedges
2 pounds shrimp
1/2 cup mayonnaise
1/2 cup sour cream
1/2 teaspoon yellow mustard

1 tablespoon Marsala wine
1 tablespoon wine vinegar
1/2 teaspoon freshly ground black pepper
4 spring onions, chopped

2 cucumbers, sliced
1 ½ cups radishes, sliced
1 tablespoon hot sauce

### DIRECTIONS

Add the salt and lime wedges to a large pot; bring to a boil over high heat. Then, peel and devein the shrimp.
Add the shrimp and cook for 2 to 3 minutes, until they are opaque.
Drain and rinse your shrimp under running water. After that, peel your shrimp.
In a mixing dish, thoroughly combine the remaining ingredients. Add the shrimp and gently stir to combine well.
Place in the refrigerator until ready to serve. Enjoy!

## 212. Salmon with Pine Nuts Sauce and Sautéed Brussels Sprouts

**(Ready in about 25 minutes | Servings 4)**

**Per serving: 372 Calories; 27.8g Fat; 5.6g Carbs; 26.5g Protein;**

### INGREDIENTS

1 pound salmon
Sea salt and freshly ground black pepper, to taste
1 teaspoon dried marjoram
1/3 cup fresh cilantro
2 garlic cloves, crushed
1/3 cup pine nuts, chopped

1 tablespoon lime juice
1/4 cup olive oil
1/2 cup chicken broth
1/2 pounds Brussels sprouts
1 medium-sized tomato, cut into slices

### DIRECTIONS

Sprinkle the salmon with salt, black pepper and marjoram on all sides; set aside.

Now, pulse the cilantro, garlic, pine nuts, lemon juice, and olive oil in your food processor until it reaches a paste consistency.

Heat up a nonstick skillet over medium-high heat. Spritz the bottom of the skillet with a nonstick cooking spray and fry the salmon for 2 to 4 minutes on each side; reserve.

In the same skillet, place the chicken broth and Brussels sprouts; sauté for 4 to 6 minutes or until the Brussels sprouts are as tender as you want; reserve.

Now, sear the tomato slices in the same skillet for 2 minutes on each side.

Serve the warm salmon topped with cilantro sauce and tomato slice, garnished with sautéed Brussels sprouts. Bon appétit!

## 213. Aromatic Red Snapper Soup

**(Ready in about 20 minutes | Servings 4)**

**Per serving: 316 Calories; 14.3g Fat; 6.6g Carbs; 32.7g Protein;**

### INGREDIENTS

1/2 stick butter, melted
2 onions, finely chopped
2 garlic cloves, minced
1/4 cup fresh cilantro, chopped
2 tomatoes, pureed

2 cups shellfish stock
1 cup water
1/4 cup dry white wine
1 pound red snapper, chopped
2 rosemary sprigs, chopped

2 thyme sprigs, chopped
1/2 teaspoon dried dill weed
Sea salt and ground black pepper, to taste

### DIRECTIONS

Melt the butter in a stockpot that is preheated over a moderate heat. Sauté the onions and garlic for 3 minutes or until aromatic.

Stir in the fresh cilantro and cook 1 to 2 minutes more. Add the pureed tomatoes, stock, water, wine, and fish; bring to a boil.

Reduce the heat and let it simmer until the fish is thoroughly cooked, about 15 minutes. Add the remaining seasonings and serve warm.

## 214. Easy Fried Tiger Prawns

**(Ready in about 10 minutes + marinating time | Servings 4)**

**Per serving: 294 Calories; 14.3g Fat; 3.6g Carbs; 34.6g Protein;**

### INGREDIENTS

1 teaspoon red pepper flakes, crushed
1 tablespoon garlic paste
1 teaspoon dried rosemary
1/2 teaspoon mustard seeds
1 ½ tablespoons fresh lime juice

2 tablespoons dry sherry
1 ½ pounds tiger prawns, peeled and deveined
1/2 stick butter, at room temperature
Salt and ground black pepper, to taste

### DIRECTIONS

Thoroughly combine the red pepper, flakes, garlic paste, rosemary, mustard seeds, lime juice and dry sherry in a mixing bowl.

Add the prawns to the mixing dish and let them marinate for 1 hour in the refrigerator.

Melt the butter in a skillet that is preheated over medium-high heat. Now, discard the marinade and fry the prawns for 3 to 5 minutes, turning once or twice.

Season with salt and pepper to taste. Serve warm and enjoy!

## 215. Saucy Chilean Sea Bass with Dijon Sauce

**(Ready in about 15 minutes + marinating time | Servings 4)**

**Per serving: 228 Calories; 13g Fat; 6.5g Carbs; 13.7g Protein;**

### INGREDIENTS

1 pound wild Chilean sea bass, cubed
Sea salt, to taste
1/2 teaspoon paprika
1 cup scallions, chopped
2 cloves garlic, minced
2 Poblano pepper, chopped

1/2 cup dry sherry wine
1 tablespoon avocado oil
1 cup double cream
1 teaspoon Dijon mustard
1/4 teaspoon ground black pepper

### DIRECTIONS

Toss the fish, salt, paprika, scallions, garlic, peppers and wine in a mixing bowl. Let it marinate in your refrigerator for 2 hours.
Warm the avocado oil in a cast-iron skillet over a moderate heat. Cook the fish along with the marinade until it is thoroughly cooked, about 5 minutes; reserve the cooked fish.
In the same skillet, place the double cream, Dijon mustard, and ground black pepper. Bring to a boil, and then, lower the heat. Continue to cook until everything is heated through, approximately 3 minutes.
Add the fish back to the skillet, remove from heat and serve immediately.

## 216. Two-Cheese and Smoked Salmon Dip

**(Ready in about 10 minutes | Servings 10)**

**Per serving: 109 Calories; 6.3g Fat; 1.3g Carbs; 11.4g Protein;**

### INGREDIENTS

10 ounces smoked salmon, chopped
5 ounces Cottage cheese
5 ounces Feta cheese
4 hard-boiled egg yolks, finely chopped

Salt and freshly ground black pepper, to your liking
1/2 teaspoon smoked paprika
1/4 cup fresh chives, chopped

### DIRECTIONS

Add all ingredients, except for the chopped chives, to a mixing dish. Stir until everything is well combined.
Put in a mound on a serving plate. Garnish with the freshly chopped chives and serve well-chilled. Bon appétit!

## 217. Halibut Steaks for Two

**(Ready in about 35 minutes | Servings 2)**

**Per serving: 308 Calories; 10.9g Fat; 2g Carbs; 46.5g Protein;**

### INGREDIENTS

1/3 cup fresh lime juice
2 teaspoons olive oil
1/3 teaspoon salt
1/3 teaspoon pepper
1 teaspoon dry dill weed

1 teaspoon dry thyme
1 teaspoon garlic, finely minced
2 halibut steaks
1/3 cup fresh cilantro, chopped

### DIRECTIONS

In a mixing bowl, combine the fresh lime juice with the olive oil, salt, pepper, dill, thyme and garlic. Add the halibut steak and let it marinate about 20 minutes.
Now, grill your fish steaks approximately 13 minutes, turning once or twice; make sure to baste them with the reserved marinade.
Garnish with fresh cilantro leaves. Serve warm with your favorite salad. Enjoy!

# 218. Tuna and Avocado Salad with Mayo Dressing

**(Ready in about 5 minutes | Servings 4)**

**Per serving: 244 Calories; 12.7g Fat; 5.3g Carbs; 23.4g Protein;**

## INGREDIENTS

2 cans tuna chunks in spring water
1 avocado, pitted, peeled and diced
2 bell peppers, deveined and sliced
1 cup cherry tomatoes, halved or quartered
1 head arugula
1 red onion, chopped

1/4 cup mayonnaise
1 teaspoon deli mustard
Salt and ground black pepper, to taste
2 tablespoons fresh lime juice
1/2 cup Kalamata olives, pitted and sliced

## DIRECTIONS

Combine the tuna, avocado, bell peppers, cherry tomato, arugula and onion in a salad bowl.
In a small mixing bowl, whisk the mayonnaise with the mustard, salt, pepper and lime juice. Dress the salad and gently toss to combine.
Top with Kalamata olives and serve well-chilled. Bon appétit!

# 219. Pan-Seared Fish Fillets with Mesclun Salad

**(Ready in about 15 minutes + marinating time | Servings 4)**

**Per serving: 425 Calories; 27.2g Fat; 6.1g Carbs; 38.3g Protein;**

## INGREDIENTS

4 white fish fillets
Salt and ground black pepper, to taste
2 tablespoons fresh lime juice
2 garlic cloves, minced
2 tablespoons fresh chives, chopped
2 tablespoons fresh coriander, chopped

1 tablespoon butter, softened
For Mesclun Salad:
1 head Romaine lettuce
1 cup chicory
1 cup frissee
1 cup arugula

2 tablespoons basil, chiffonade
2 tablespoons dandelion
1/2 cup apple cider
Salt and ground black pepper, to your liking
1/4 cup extra-virgin olive oil

## DIRECTIONS

Toss the white fish fillets with the salt, pepper, lime juice, garlic, chives, and coriander; allow it to marinate at least 1 hour in the refrigerator.
Melt the butter in a pan over moderate heat; sear the fish fillets on each side for 4 minutes. Use the marinade as a basting sauce.
In the meantime, place the Romaine lettuce, chicory, frissee, arugula, basil and dandelion in a salad bowl.
Make the dressing for your salad by whisking the remaining ingredients. Dress the salad and serve with the warm fish fillets. Bon appétit!

# 220. Mediterranean-Style Snapper Salad

**(Ready in about 15 minutes | Servings 4)**

**Per serving: 507 Calories; 42.8g Fat; 6g Carbs; 24.4g Protein;**

## INGREDIENTS

4 snapper fillets
Sea salt and ground black pepper, to taste
1 teaspoon ground sumac
2 tablespoons butter, melted
4 cups baby spinach
12 grape tomatoes, halved
1 carrot, thinly sliced
2 shallots, thinly sliced
6 ounces Halloumi cheese, crumbled
1/2 cup ripe olives, pitted and sliced

For the Vinaigrette:
1 lemon, juiced and zested
1/3 cup extra-virgin olive oil
1/2 tablespoon brown mustard
1 clove garlic, smashed
1 teaspoon dried oregano
2 tablespoons fresh mint, finely chopped
Sea salt and ground black pepper, to taste
1 teaspoon red pepper flakes, crushed

## DIRECTIONS

Lay the fish fillets on a clean board and sprinkle both sides with salt, pepper and sumac.
Warm the butter in a pan that is preheated over a moderate flame. Fry the fish for 5 minutes on each side.
In a nice salad bowl, toss the baby spinach, tomatoes, carrots, shallots, cheese and olives. Top with the chopped fish.
Now, thoroughly combine all ingredients for the vinaigrette in your blender. Dress the salad and serve well-chilled. Bon appétit!

# 221. Cod and Cauliflower Patties

## (Ready in about 20 minutes | Servings 5)

## Per serving: 326 Calories; 21.7g Fat; 5.8g Carbs; 25.6g Protein;

### INGREDIENTS

1 teaspoon ghee
3 cups cauliflower rice
2 ½ cups cod fish, cooked
Sea salt and freshly cracked black peppercorns, to taste
1 teaspoon dried basil
1/2 teaspoon dried oregano

1/2 teaspoon dried rosemary
1/4 cup shallots, chopped
2 eggs, whisked
1/2 cup almond flour
1/2 cup Parmesan cheese
3 tablespoons olive oil

### DIRECTIONS

Melt the ghee in a pan over medium heat. Then, cook the cauli-rice for 6 minutes, until crisp-tender; allow it to cool to room temperature.
Then, mix the cooked and chilled cauli-rice with the cooked fish, salt, pepper, basil, oregano, and rosemary.
After that, stir in the shallots, eggs, almond flour, and parmesan cheese; mix to combine well.
Shape the mixture into 10 patties. Heat the oil in a nonstick skillet that is previously preheated over a moderate flame.
Cook for 5 minutes on each side. Serve with mayo and enjoy!

# 222. Boozy Prawns with Mignonette Sauce

## (Ready in about 15 minutes | Servings 4)

## Per serving: 252 Calories; 7.3g Fat; 5.3g Carbs; 36.6g Protein;

### INGREDIENTS

1 ½ tablespoons olive oil
1 leek, chopped
2 garlic cloves, minced
1 Roma tomato, chopped
1/2 teaspoon seasoned salt
1 ½ pounds prawns, shelled and deveined

2 tablespoons vodka
For Mignonette Sauce:
1/2 cup shallots, chopped
1 teaspoon black pepper, coarsely ground
1/2 cup white wine vinegar

### DIRECTIONS

Heat the oil in a pan over a moderately high heat. Now, sauté the leeks and garlic for 3 minutes or until they are tender and aromatic.
Add the Roma tomato and salt; turn the heat to medium-low and cook the prawns until thoroughly cooked.
Stir in the vodka and remove from heat.
Meanwhile, in a mixing dish, thoroughly combine the shallots, black pepper, and white wine vinegar. Let it stand in the refrigerator until ready to serve.
Serve the warm prawns with the Mignonette sauce on the side. Bon appétit!

# 223. Creole Salmon Fillets

## (Ready in about 40 minutes | Servings 4)

## Per serving: 266 Calories; 11.5g Fat; 5.6g Carbs; 34.9g Protein;

### INGREDIENTS

1/3 cup fresh lime juice
1/3 cup Worcestershire sauce
3 teaspoons avocado oil
1/4 cup fresh chives, chopped

2 garlic cloves, minced
1/4 teaspoon onion powder
1 teaspoon lemon thyme
1/4 teaspoon ground black pepper

1/4 teaspoon white pepper
1 teaspoon dried oregano
4 salmon fillets

### DIRECTIONS

To make the marinade, thoroughly mix the lime juice, Worcestershire sauce, avocado oil, fresh chives, garlic, and onion powder.
Place the salmon fillets in the marinade; place in the refrigerator for 20 to 25 minutes. Season the salmon fillets with lemon thyme, black pepper, white pepper and oregano.
Place the salmon fillets on the preheated grill and reserve the marinade.
Cook your salmon for 10 to 12 minutes, turning once and brushing with the reserved marinade.

## 224. Fish Cutlets with Parsley Mashed Cauliflower

**(Ready in about 35 minutes | Servings 4)**

**Per serving: 404 Calories; 22.2g Fat; 5.7g Carbs; 43.5g Protein;**

### INGREDIENTS

1 pound swordfish cutlets, about 3/4 inch thick
1/2 teaspoon celery salt
1/2 teaspoon mixed peppercorns, freshly ground
1/2 teaspoon dried marjoram
1/2 teaspoon dried basil

1/2 teaspoon dried sage, crushed
1 ½ tablespoons butter, at room temperature
1 tablespoon fresh lime juice
1/2 cup fresh chives, roughly chopped
1 pound cauliflower, broken into florets

1/4 cup heavy cream
2 tablespoons butter
1/4 cup Colby cheese, freshly grated
Salt and pepper, to your liking
1 tablespoon fresh parsley, finely chopped

### DIRECTIONS

Preheat your grill to high. Rub your fish with salt, peppercorns, marjoram, basil, and sage. Whisk the butter with the fresh lime juice and reserve.

Grill the fish cutlets for 8 minutes, coating with the butter/lime mixture. Turn the fish cutlet over and brush the other side with the butter/lime mixture.

Grill another 8 minutes. Transfer to a serving platter and sprinkle with fresh chives.

Next, cook the cauliflower in a microwave-safe bowl with the cream and butter. Microwave on high for 10 to 12 minutes, stirring once.

Then, stir in the Colby cheese, and pulse in your food processor until the mixture is creamy and smooth. Season with salt, pepper and parsley. Serve with the grilled fish cutlets.

## 225. Prawn Cocktail Salad

**(Ready in about 10 minutes | Servings 6)**

**Per serving: 196 Calories; 8.3g Fat; 6.5g Carbs; 21.4g Protein;**

### INGREDIENTS

2 pounds prawns, peeled leaving tails intact
Sea salt and freshly ground black pepper, to taste
1 carrot, sliced

1 cup scallions, chopped
1/2 cup cucumber, chopped
1/2 head Romaine lettuce, torn into pieces
1/4 cup chopped fresh dill

Juice from 1 fresh lemon
1/4 cup capers, drained
1 teaspoon deli mustard
1/2 cup mayonnaise

### DIRECTIONS

Bring a pot of salted water to a boil; cook the prawns for 3 minutes. Drain and transfer to a mixing bowl; allow them to cool completely.

Toss gently with the remaining ingredients. Place in the refrigerator until ready to serve. Bon appétit!

## 226. Halibut en Persillade

**(Ready in about 20 minutes | Servings 4)**

Per serving: 273 Calories; 19.2g Fat; 4.3g Carbs; 22.6g Protein;

### INGREDIENTS

2 tablespoons coconut oil, at room temperature
4 halibut steaks
1/2 cup scallions, sliced
2 cloves garlic, finely minced
1 tablespoon fresh lime juice

1/2 teaspoon fresh ginger, grated
Salt and ground black pepper, to taste
2 tablespoons fresh cilantro, chopped
1 tablespoon oyster sauce
1 tablespoon Worcestershire sauce
3 tablespoons clam juice

1/2 fresh lemon, zested and juiced
1/4 cup fresh parsley, finely chopped
1 teaspoon garlic
1 ½ tablespoons olive oil

### DIRECTIONS

Heat the oil in a cast-iron skillet over high flame until it begins to smoke.

Fry the halibut until golden brown, approximately 7 minutes. Turn and fry on the other side 4 minutes more. Reserve.

Cook the scallions and garlic in the pan drippings until tender. Add the remaining ingredients along with the reserved halibut steaks; cover and cook for 5 minutes more.

Divide among four serving plates.

Then, whisk the remaining ingredients to make the Persillade sauce. Spoon over the halibut steaks on the serving plates and enjoy.

# 227. Hearty Pollock Chowder

**(Ready in about 30 minutes | Servings 4)**

**Per serving: 170 Calories; 5.8g Fat; 5.7g Carbs; 20g Protein;**

## INGREDIENTS

1 ¼ pounds pollock fillets, skin removed
3 teaspoons butter
2 shallots, chopped
1 celery with leaves, chopped
1 parsnip, chopped
2 carrots, chopped

Sea salt and ground black pepper, to taste
1 teaspoon Old Bay seasonings
3 cups boiling water
1/2 cup clam juice
1/4 cup dry white wine
1/2 cup full-fat milk

## DIRECTIONS

Chop the pollock fillets into bite-sized pieces.
Warm the butter in a pan over a moderately high flame. Cook the vegetables until they're softened. Season with salt, pepper and Old Bay seasonings.
Stir in the chopped fish and cook for 12 to 15 minutes more. Add the boiling water and clam juice. Afterwards, pour in the white wine and milk.
Bring to a boil. Reduce the heat and cook for 15 minutes longer. Bon appétit!

# 228. Summer Fish Cakes

**(Ready in about 30 minutes | Servings 6)**

**Per serving: 234 Calories; 10.6g Fat; 2.5g Carbs; 31.2g Protein;**

## INGREDIENTS

1 ½ pounds cod, boned and flaked
2 eggs, lightly beaten
1/3 cup almond flour
2 tablespoons flax meal
1/2 cup Ricotta cheese, at room temperature

2 teaspoons Dijon mustard
Sea salt and freshly ground black pepper, to taste
1 tablespoon fresh chives, chopped
1 tablespoon fresh cilantro, chopped
2 tablespoons peanut oil

## DIRECTIONS

Preheat your oven to 390 degrees F. Pat the fish dry and transfer to a mixing bowl.
Add the eggs; gradually add the flour and flax meal and mix to combine well. Add the remaining ingredients and mix to combine well.
Now, shape the mixture into 12 patties and arrange them on a lightly greased baking pan.
Bake for 20 to 25 minutes, turning once. Enjoy!

# 229. Sardine Salad Pickled Pepper Boats

**(Ready in about 10 minutes | Servings 4)**

**Per serving: 120 Calories; 5.4g Fat; 5.8g Carbs; 12.3g Protein;**

## INGREDIENTS

2 (3.75-ounce) cans sardines, drained
1 teaspoon deli mustard
1 carrot, chopped
1 cup scallions, chopped

2 tablespoons fresh lemon
Salt and freshly ground black pepper, to taste
4 pickled peppers, slice into halves
1 tablespoon fresh parsley, chopped

## DIRECTIONS

In a mixing bowl, thoroughly combine the sardines, mustard, carrot, scallions, lemon juice, salt and black pepper.
Mix until everything is well incorporated.
Fill the pickle boats with the sardine salad. Serve well-chilled garnished with fresh parsley.

# 230. Asian-Inspired Tilapia Chowder

**(Ready in about 30 minutes | Servings 6)**

**Per serving: 165 Calories; 5.5g Fat; 4g Carbs; 25.4g Protein;**

## INGREDIENTS

3 teaspoons sesame oil
1/2 cup scallions, sliced
1 garlic clove, smashed
1 celery stalk, diced
1 bell pepper, deveined and sliced

1 banana chili pepper, deveined and sliced
1 tablespoon fish sauce
2 ½ cups hot water
1 teaspoon Five-spice powder

1 ¼ pounds tilapia fish fillets, cut into small chunks
3/4 cup full-fat milk
1/2 teaspoon paprika
1/4 cup fresh mint, chopped

## DIRECTIONS

Heat the sesame oil in a stockpot that is preheated over a moderately high heat. Cook the scallions and garlic until they are softened.

Now, add the celery, peppers, fish sauce, water, and Five-spice powder. Cover with the lid, turn the heat to medium-low and simmer for 13 minutes longer.

Now, stir in the fish chunks and cook an additional 12 minutes or until the fish is cooked through. Add the milk, stir well, and remove from heat.

Ladle into individual serving plates. Sprinkle with paprika and serve garnished with fresh mint. Bon appétit!

# 231. Smoked Salmon and Cheese Stuffed Tomatoes

**(Ready in about 30 minutes | Servings 6)**

**Per serving: 303 Calories; 22.9g Fat; 6.8g Carbs; 17g Protein;**

## INGREDIENTS

10 ounces smoked salmon, flaked
1 red onion, finely chopped
2 garlic cloves, minced
2 tablespoons cilantro, chopped

1/2 cup aioli
1 teaspoon yellow mustard
1 tablespoon white vinegar
Sea salt and ground black pepper, to

taste
1 ½ cups Monterey Jack cheese, shredded
6 medium-sized tomatoes

## DIRECTIONS

Preheat an oven to 400 degrees F.

In a mixing bowl, thoroughly combine the salmon, onion, garlic, cilantro, aioli, mustard, vinegar, salt, and pepper.

Slice your tomatoes in half horizontally; then, scoop out the pulp and seeds.

Stuff the tomatoes with the filling, and bake until they are thoroughly cooked and tops are golden, about 20 minutes.

Add the shredded cheese and place in the oven for a further 5 minutes. Bon appétit!

# 232. Chilean Sea Bass with Cauliflower and Chutney

**(Ready in about 30 minutes | Servings 4)**

**Per serving: 291 Calories; 9.5g Fat; 3.5g Carbs; 42.5g Protein;**

## INGREDIENTS

2 tablespoons olive oil, for drizzling
1 pound cauliflower, cut into florets
2 bell peppers, thinly sliced
1 onion, thinly sliced
Sea salt and freshly ground black pepper, to taste
1 teaspoon cayenne pepper
1 ½ pounds wild Chilean sea bass

**For Tomato Chutney:**
1 teaspoon vegetable oil
2 garlic cloves, sliced
1 cup ripe on-the-vine plum tomatoes
1 tablespoon small capers
1/2 teaspoon kosher salt
1/4 teaspoon black pepper

## DIRECTIONS

Heat 1 tablespoon of olive oil in a pan that is preheated over a moderate flame.

Now, cook the cauliflower florets, bell peppers, and onion until they are slightly tender; season with salt, black pepper, and cayenne pepper; set aside.

Preheat another tablespoon of olive oil. Sear the sea bass on each side for 5 minutes.

To make the chutney, heat 1 teaspoon of vegetable oil in a pan over a moderately high heat. Sauté the garlic until just browned and aromatic.

Add the plum tomatoes and cook, stirring occasionally, until heated through, or 10 minutes. Season with capers, salt, and pepper.

Divide the seared fish among 4 serving plates. Serve garnished with the sautéed cauliflower mixture and tomato chutney. Enjoy!

## 233. Grilled Halloumi and Tuna Salad

**(Ready in about 15 minutes | Servings 4)**

**Per serving: 199 Calories; 10.6g Fat; 6.1g Carbs; 14.2g Protein;**

### INGREDIENTS

1 cup halloumi cheese
2 cucumbers, thinly sliced
1/2 cup radishes, thinly sliced
2 tablespoons sunflower seeds
1 ½ tablespoons extra-virgin olive oil
1 can light tuna fish in water, rinsed

1/2 head Romaine lettuce
2 medium-sized Roma tomatoes, sliced
1 red onion, thinly sliced
1 tablespoon lime juice
Sea salt and black pepper, to taste
Dried rosemary, to taste

### DIRECTIONS

Grill the halloumi cheese over medium high heat. Cut into cubes.
Toss the grilled halloumi cheese with the remaining ingredients. Bon appétit!

## 234. Colorful Tuna Salad with Bocconcini

**(Ready in about 10 minutes | Servings 4)**

**Per serving: 273 Calories; 11.7g Fat; 6.7g Carbs; 34.2g Protein;**

### INGREDIENTS

1 head Iceberg lettuce
1/2 cup yellow onion, thinly sliced
2 cans tuna in brine, drained
1 teaspoon Pasilla chili pepper, finely chopped
1 green bell pepper, sliced
1 yellow bell pepper, sliced
1 cucumber, sliced
1/2 cup radishes, sliced
1 tomato, diced

1/2 cup Kalamata olives, pitted and sliced
2 teaspoons peanut butter
1 teaspoon olive oil
1 teaspoon champagne vinegar
1 tablespoon oyster sauce
1/4 teaspoon black peppercorns, preferably freshly ground
2 garlic cloves, minced
8 ounces bocconcini

### DIRECTIONS

Mix the Iceberg lettuce, onion, tuna, peppers, cucumbers, radishes, tomatoes and Kalamata olives in a salad bowl.
In a small mixing dish, thoroughly combine the peanut butter, olive oil, champagne vinegar, oyster sauce black peppercorns, and garlic.
Add this vinaigrette to the salad bowl; toss until everything is well coated.
Top with bocconcini and serve well-chilled. Bon appétit!

## 235. Tuna Fillets with Greens

**(Ready in about 20 minutes | Servings 6)**

**Per serving: 444 Calories; 38.2g Fat; 4.7g Carbs; 21.9g Protein;**

### INGREDIENTS

6 tuna fillets
3 tablespoons olive oil, plus more for drizzling
Salt and ground black pepper, to your liking
1 fresh lime, sliced
1 tablespoons apple cider vinegar
2 teaspoons yellow mustard

Salt and red pepper flakes, to taste
2 cups baby spinach
1 cup rocket lettuce
1 yellow onion, thinly sliced
1/2 cup radishes, thinly sliced

### DIRECTIONS

Start by preheating your oven to 450 degrees F. Then, coat a baking dish with parchment paper or Silpat mat.
Now, drizzle each tuna fillet with olive oil; season with salt and pepper.
Transfer the tuna fillets to the baking dish. Top with lime slices and bake 8 to 12 minutes.
In a mixing dish, whisk the vinegar, mustard, salt and red pepper flakes.
Arrange the baby spinach, rocket lettuce, onion and radishes on 6 serving plates. Drizzle with the vinegar/mustard mixture. Top with the tuna fillets. Bon appétit!

## 236. One-Pot Seafood Stew

**(Ready in about 20 minutes | Servings 4)**

**Per serving: 209 Calories; 12.6g Fat; 6.6g Carbs; 15.2g Protein;**

### INGREDIENTS

1/2 stick butter, at room temperature
2 onions, chopped
2 garlic cloves, pressed
2 tomatoes, pureed
1 celery stalk, chopped

2 cups shellfish stock
1 cup hot water
2 tablespoons dry white wine
1/2 teaspoon lemon zest
1/2 pound shrimp

1/2 pound mussels
1 teaspoon Italian seasonings
1 teaspoon saffron threads
Salt and ground black pepper, to taste

### DIRECTIONS

Melt the butter in a stockpot over a moderate heat. Cook the onion and garlic until aromatic.
Now, stir in the pureed tomatoes; cook for 8 minutes or until heated through.
Add the remaining ingredients and bring to a rapid boil. Reduce the heat to a simmer and cook an additional 4 minutes.
Ladle into individual bowls and serve warm.

## 237. Seafood and Andouille Medley

**(Ready in about 25 minutes | Servings 4)**

**Per serving: 481 Calories; 26.9g Fat; 5g Carbs; 46.6g Protein;**

### INGREDIENTS

1/2 stick butter, melted
2 andouille sausages, cut crosswise into 1/2-inch-thick slices
2 garlic cloves, finely minced
1 shallot, chopped
2 tomatoes, pureed
1 tablespoon oyster sauce

3/4 cup clam juice
1/3 cup dry white wine
1/2 pound skinned sole, cut into chunks
20 sea scallops
2 tablespoons fresh cilantro, chopped

### DIRECTIONS

Melt the butter in a heavy-bottomed pot over medium-high heat. Cook the sausages until no longer pink; reserve.
Now, sauté the garlic and shallots in pan drippings until they are softened; reserve.
Add the pureed tomatoes, oyster sauce, clam juice and wine; simmer for another 12 minutes.
Add the skinned sole, scallops and reserved sausages. Let it simmer, partially covered, for 6 minutes.
Serve garnished with fresh cilantro. Bon appétit!

## 238. Quatre Épices Salmon Fillets with Cheese

**(Ready in about 20 minutes | Servings 6)**

**Per serving: 354 Calories; 20.2g Fat; 4.5g Carbs; 39.6g Protein;**

### INGREDIENTS

6 salmon fillets
1 teaspoon seasoned salt
1 teaspoon Quatre épices
1 cup cauliflower
1/2 red onion, thinly sliced
1 garlic clove, finely minced

1 cup Colby cheese, grated
3 tablespoons mayonnaise
1 teaspoon whole grain mustard
1 tablespoon fresh lemon juice
2 tablespoons avocado oil

### DIRECTIONS

Preheat your oven to 400 degrees F. Line a baking dish with aluminum foil.
Sprinkle the salmon fillets with salt and Quatre épices on all sides and place on the piece of foil. Arrange the cauliflower and onions around them.
Wrap the fish and vegetable with the foil. Bake for 10 minutes or until the salmon fillets flake easily with a fork.
In a mixing bowl, thoroughly combine the garlic, cheese, mayo, mustard, lemon juice, and avocado oil.
Pour this mixture over the fish and veggies. Bake for a further 5 to 6 minutes or until the top is golden. Serve warm garnished with fresh chives.

# 239. Easy Parmesan Crusted Tilapia

**(Ready in about 15 minutes | Servings 4)**

**Per serving: 222 Calories; 12.6g Fat; 0.9g Carbs; 27.9g Protein;**

## INGREDIENTS

1 pound tilapia fillets, cut into 4 servings
1/3 teaspoon salt
1/3 teaspoon ground black pepper

1/4 teaspoon red pepper flakes, crushed
2 tablespoons olive oil
3/4 cup grated Parmesan cheese

## DIRECTIONS

Season the fish fillets with salt, black pepper and red pepper flakes.
Brush the tilapia fillets with olive oil; now, press them into the Parmesan cheese.
Place the fish fillets on a foil-lined baking sheet. Bake approximately 10 minutes or until the fish fillets are opaque.

# 240. Creamy Anchovy Salad

**(Ready in about 10 minutes | Servings 4)**

**Per serving: 195 Calories; 14.7g Fat; 6g Carbs; 7.8g Protein;**

## INGREDIENTS

1 head of Romaine lettuce
2 cans anchovies, chopped
1 cup red onions, chopped
1 carrot, thinly sliced
1 cucumber, thinly sliced

Sea salt and ground black pepper, to taste
3/4 cup mayonnaise
1 teaspoon yellow mustard
1/2 teaspoon smoked cayenne pepper
1/4 cup fresh chives, roughly chopped

## DIRECTIONS

Arrange the lettuce leaves in a salad bowl. Add the anchovies, onions, carrot, and cucumber. Season with salt and pepper.
Now, stir in the mayonnaise and mustard. Sprinkle with the cayenne pepper and toss until everything is well combined.
Serve well-chilled and garnished with fresh chives. Bon appétit!

# 241. Moms' Aromatic Fish Curry

**(Ready in about 25 minutes | Servings 6)**

**Per serving: 270 Calories; 16.9g Fat; 5.6g Carbs; 22.3g Protein;**

## INGREDIENTS

2 tablespoons fresh lime juice
2 pounds blue grenadier, cut into large pieces
2 tablespoons olive oil
8 fresh curry leaves
1 cup shallots, chopped
2 green chilies, minced
1/2 tablespoon fresh ginger, grated

2 garlic cloves, finely chopped
2 green cardamom pods
1 teaspoon dried basil
Salt and black pepper, to taste
4 Roma tomatoes, pureed
1 tablespoon ground coriander
1 cup coconut milk

## DIRECTIONS

Drizzle the blue grenadier with lime juice.
Heat the oil in a nonstick skillet over a moderate flame. Cook the curry leaves and shallots until the shallot has softened, about 4 minutes.
After that, add the chilies, ginger and garlic and cook an additional minute or until fragrant. Add the remaining ingredients, except for the coconut milk, and simmer for 10 minutes or until heated through.
Now, stir in the fish; pour in 1 cup of coconut milk and cook, covered, for 6 minutes longer. Serve warm and enjoy!

## 242. Pan-Seared Trout Fillets with Chimichurri

**(Ready in about 15 minutes | Servings 6)**

**Per serving: 265 Calories; 20.9g Fat; 4g Carbs; 17.1g Protein;**

### INGREDIENTS

2 tablespoons ghee
6 trout fillets
Celery salt and ground black pepper,
to taste
1/2 teaspoon turmeric powder
1/2 tablespoon yellow mustard

For Chimichurri Sauce:
1/3 cup wine vinegar
1/2 teaspoon salt
3 garlic cloves, minced
1/2 shallot, finely chopped
1 Fresno chili pepper, finely chopped

1/2 cup fresh flat-leaf parsley, minced
1 tablespoon fresh oregano leaves,
finely chopped
1/3 cup extra-virgin olive oil

### DIRECTIONS

Heat the ghee in a large stainless skillet that is preheated over a moderately high heat. Season the trout fillets with salt, pepper and turmeric powder; brush with the yellow mustard.

Sear the trout fillet for 4 to 5 minutes on each side.

Meanwhile, pulse the wine vinegar, salt, garlic, shallot, Fresno chili pepper, parsley, and oregano in your food processor.

With the food processor running slowly, gradually add the olive oil and blend until uniform and smooth. You can keep the Chimichurri in the refrigerator for up to 2 days.

Serve the warm fish fillets with the Chimichurri sauce on the side. Bon appétit!

## 243. Sunday Amberjack Fillets with Parmesan Sauce

**(Ready in about 20 minutes | Servings 6)**

**Per serving: 285 Calories; 20.4g Fat; 1.2g Carbs; 23.8g Protein;**

### INGREDIENTS

2 tablespoons ghee, at room temperature
6 amberjack fillets
1 teaspoon sea salt
1/2 teaspoon ground black pepper
1/4 teaspoon cayenne pepper, or more to taste
1/4 cup fresh tarragon chopped
1 lemon, cut into wedges

For the Sauce:
3 teaspoons ghee, at room temperature
1 teaspoon garlic, finely minced
1/3 cup beef bone broth
3/4 cup heavy cream
1/3 cup Parmesan cheese, grated
Salt and ground black pepper, to taste

### DIRECTIONS

Melt the ghee in a large bottomed non-stick frying pan.

Then, coat both sides of your fish with the salt, black pepper, cayenne pepper and chopped tarragon.

Fry the fish fillets for about 10 minutes or until the edges are turning opaque and the segments flake apart.

To make the sauce, melt 3 teaspoons of the ghee in a pan over a moderate heat. Then, sauté the garlic until aromatic, about 3 minutes.

Add the broth and cream; continue to cook stirring constantly, about 6 minutes.

Stir in the Parmesan cheese and continue stirring until everything is thoroughly cooked. Season with salt and pepper to taste.

Serve the fish fillets with the sauce garnished with fresh lemon wedges.

## 244. Crabmeat, Prosciutto and Vegetable Delight

**(Ready in about 10 minutes | Servings 4)**

**Per serving: 232 Calories; 15.6g Fat; 6g Carbs; 18.9g Protein;**

### INGREDIENTS

3 tablespoons olive oil
1 tablespoon tahini
1/2 lemon, zested and juiced
Coarse salt and ground black pepper,
to your liking

2 (6-ounce) cans lump crabmeat,
drained
2 ounces thinly sliced prosciutto,
chopped
4 cups baby spinach

10 cherry tomato, halved
10 ripe olives, pitted and halved
1/2 cup fresh Italian parsley, chopped

### DIRECTIONS

In a small-sized mixing dish, whisk the oil, tahini, lemon zest, lemon juice, salt, and pepper.

In a salad bowl, gently toss the crabmeat with the prosciutto, spinach, cherry tomatoes, and olives. Drizzle with the prepared dressing and toss to combine.

Serve garnished with fresh parsley in individual salad bowls.

## 245. Fish with Cremini Mushrooms and Sour Cream Sauce

**(Ready in about 20 minutes | Servings 4)**

**Per serving: 585 Calories; 30.5g Fat; 5.5g Carbs; 66.8g Protein;**

### INGREDIENTS

2 tablespoons vegetable oil
1 onion, chopped
1/2 pound cremini mushrooms, thinly sliced
Coarse salt and freshly ground black pepper, to taste
4 skinless halibut fillets

1 tablespoon ghee
2 garlic cloves, chopped
1 ½ cups clam juice
1 cup sour cream
1/2 cup fresh parsley, chopped

### DIRECTIONS

Heat 1 tablespoon of the vegetable oil in a pan over a moderately high heat. Sauté the onion until it's softened.
Now, stir in the mushrooms, salt, and black pepper; cook for 5 minutes.
Wipe out your pan, and heat the remaining tablespoon of vegetable oil. Now, sear the fish fillets over medium-high heat approximately 4 minutes per side. Transfer to a plate with the mushroom mixture.
Melt the ghee over a moderately high flame. Cook the garlic until slightly browned.
Pour in the clam juice and work it back and forth, stirring continuously over high heat until reduced by half.
Remove the sauce from the heat; let it cool slightly before quickly whisking in the sour cream. Serve with the cremini mushrooms and fish, garnished with fresh parsley. Bon appétit!

## 246. Spring Salad with Harissa Crab Mayo

**(Ready in about 15 minutes | Servings 4)**

**Per serving: 293 Calories; 27.1g Fat; 6.3g Carbs; 9.3g Protein;**

### INGREDIENTS

**For the Crab Mayo:**
2 egg yolks
1/2 tablespoon whole grain mustard
1/2 teaspoon harissa
3/4 cup olive oil
2 tablespoons fresh lemon juice

A pinch of salt
A pinch of freshly ground black pepper
1 clove garlic, crushed
1/2 teaspoon dried dill weed
1 pound white crabmeat

**For the Salad:**
1 head Iceberg lettuce
1/2 cup chervil
A bunch of scallions, chopped
1 cup radishes, sliced
1 bell pepper, julienned

### DIRECTIONS

Whisk the egg yolks and mustard; slowly pour in the oil, in a tiny stream, until you have a thick mixture.
Now, add the lemon juice, salt, black pepper, garlic, dill and crabmeat. Place in your refrigerator until ready to serve.
In a salad bowl, place all salad ingredients. Toss with the prepared crab mayo and serve well-chilled. Bon appétit!

## 247. Grilled Clams with Tomato Sauce

**(Ready in about 25 minutes | Servings 4)**

**Per serving: 134 Calories; 7.8g Fat; 5.9g Carbs; 8.3g Protein;**

### INGREDIENTS

40 littleneck clams
**For the Sauce:**
2 tablespoons olive oil
1 onion, chopped
1 teaspoon crushed garlic

2 tomatoes, pureed
Sea salt and freshly ground black pepper, to taste
1/2 teaspoon cayenne pepper
1/3 cup dry sherry
1 lemon, cut into wedges

### DIRECTIONS

Heat the grill to medium-high. Cook until the clams open, about 6 minutes.
Heat the oil in a sauté pan over moderate heat. Cook the onion and garlic until aromatic.
Add the pureed tomatoes, salt, black pepper and cayenne pepper and cook an additional 10 minutes or until everything is thoroughly cooked.
Remove from the heat and add the dry sherry; stir to combine. Serve with the grilled clams, garnished with fresh lemon wedges.

# 248. Prawn and Avocado Cocktail Salad

**(Ready in about 10 minutes + chilling time | Servings 6)**

**Per serving: 236 Calories; 14.3g Fat; 5.3g Carbs; 16.3g Protein;**

## INGREDIENTS

1 pound large king prawns, peeled leaving tails intact
1/2 cup Lebanese cucumber, chopped
1 small-sized red onion, thinly sliced

1/2 cup mayonnaise
1 tablespoon Worcestershire sauce
2 teaspoons fresh lime juice
A few drops red Tabasco pepper sauce

1/2 head iceberg lettuce leaves
1 avocado, pitted and sliced

## DIRECTIONS

Bring a pot of salted water to a boil; cook the prawns for 3 minutes. Drain and transfer to a mixing bowl.
In the mixing bowl, combine the prawns with the chopped cucumber and red onion. In another bowl, thoroughly combine the mayonnaise with the Worcestershire sauce, lime juice and Tabasco pepper sauce.
Add the mayo mixture to the prawn mixture. Place in your refrigerator until serving time.
To serve, arrange lettuce leaves and avocado slices on a serving platter. Mound the salad onto the lettuce leaves and serve well chilled. Enjoy!

# 249. Chinese-Style Milkfish with Mushroom-Pepper Coulis

**(Ready in about 35 minutes | Servings 4)**

**Per serving: 415 Calories; 28g Fat; 4.4g Carbs; 34.5g Protein;**

## INGREDIENTS

**For the Fish:**
2 tablespoons sesame oil
2 milkfishes, scaled
1/2 teaspoon salt
1/4 teaspoon ground black pepper
1⁄2 teaspoon red pepper flakes, crushed
1/3 cup Rosé wine
2 tablespoons Chinese dark soy sauce

**For the Mushroom/Pepper Coulis:**
1 ½ ounces olive oil
1/2 onion, peeled and chopped
1 bell pepper, deveined and chopped
2 ounces Cremini mushrooms, chopped
3 tablespoons consommé
1/2 tablespoon champagne vinegar
1/2 teaspoon kosher
1/4 teaspoon ground black pepper
1/8 teaspoon freshly grated nutmeg

## DIRECTIONS

Heat the sesame oil in a pan over medium-high heat. Season the milkfish with salt, black pepper, and red pepper flakes.
Fry the milkfish in batches about 5 minutes per side or until golden brown; reserve, keeping warm.
Add the Rosé wine and Chinese dark soy sauce to the same pan. Bring to a rolling boil; reduce the heat to medium-low and let it simmer an additional 5 minutes.
Add the milkfish back to the pan, and continue to cook, basting with the wine sauce, about 3 minutes.
To make your coulis, heat the olive oil in a skillet that is preheated over a moderate heat. Now, cook the onions until translucent.
After that, turn the heat to medium-low and add the peppers and mushrooms along with a splash of consommé; cook, stirring frequently, another 13 minutes or until they have softened.
Now, process the sautéed mixture in your blender until creamy and uniform.
Add the remaining ingredients, stir to combine well and serve with the prepared fish.

# 250. Tuna and Vegetable Kebabs

**(Ready in about 15 minutes | Servings 4)**

**Per serving: 257 Calories; 12.5g Fat; 7g Carbs; 27.5g Protein;**

## INGREDIENTS

1 pound 1 1/4 -inch-thick tuna, cut into bite-sized cubes
Salt and crushed black peppercorns
1/2 teaspoon rosemary

1/2 teaspoon thyme
2 tablespoons sesame oil
2 tablespoons soy sauce
1 onion, cut into wedges

1 zucchini, diced
1 cup grape tomatoes

## DIRECTIONS

Preheat your grill on high. Season the tuna cubes and vegetables with salt, peppercorns, rosemary, and thyme. Drizzle with sesame oil and soy sauce.
Alternate the seasoned tuna cubes, onion, zucchini and tomatoes on each of 8 metal skewers.
Grill 5 minutes for medium-rare, turning frequently. Bon appétit!

# 251. Mackerel Steak Casserole with Cheese and Veggies

**(Ready in about 30 minutes | Servings 4)**

**Per serving: 301 Calories; 14g Fat; 6g Carbs; 33.3g Protein;**

## INGREDIENTS

1/2 stick butter
1 cup carrots, thinly sliced
1 cup parsnip, thinly sliced
2 cloves garlic, thinly sliced
2 onions, thinly sliced
1/4 cup clam juice

3 tomatoes, thinly sliced
1 pound mackerel steaks
1 tablespoon Old Bay seasoning
Salt and black pepper, to your liking
1 cup mozzarella, shredded
1/2 cup fresh chives, chopped

## DIRECTIONS

Preheat your oven to 450 degrees F.
Melt the butter in a pan that is previously preheated over a moderate flame. Cook the carrots, parsnip, garlic, and onions until they are tender.
Add the clam juice and tomatoes and cook 4 minutes more. Transfer this vegetable mixture to a casserole dish.
Lay the fish steaks on top of the vegetable layer. Sprinkle with seasonings. Cover with foil and roast for 10 minutes, until the fish is opaque in the center.
Top with shredded cheese and bake another 5 minutes. Serve warm garnished with freshly chopped chives. Bon appétit!

# 252. Classic Seafood Chowder

**(Ready in about 15 minutes | Servings 5)**

**Per serving: 404 Calories; 30g Fat; 5.3g Carbs; 23.9g Protein;**

## INGREDIENTS

1/2 stick butter
2 tablespoons green onion, chopped
1 teaspoon minced garlic
3/4 pound shrimp, peeled and deveined
1/2 pound crab meat
1/3 cup dry white wine
3 bouillon cubes

1 quart water
2 cups heavy cream
1 tablespoon tomato paste
1 teaspoon dried rosemary
Salt and ground black pepper, to taste
1 egg, lightly beaten

## DIRECTIONS

Melt the butter in a large pot that is preheated over medium-high heat.
Now, cook the onion and garlic until they are tender and aromatic.
Add the shrimp, crab meat, wine, bouillon cubes and water. Now, cook until the seafood is thoroughly warmed, about 5 minutes.
Reduce the heat to low and add the remaining ingredients. Simmer, stirring occasionally, for an additional 2 to 3 minutes. Bon appétit!

# 253. Smoky Cholula Seafood Dip

**(Ready in about 10 minutes + chilling time | Servings 8)**

**Per serving: 108 Calories; 5.4g Fat; 5g Carbs; 8.2g Protein;**

## INGREDIENTS

1/2 cup mayonnaise
2 cloves garlic, finely minced
12 ounces seafood, canned and drained
Sea salt and ground black pepper, to taste
1/4 teaspoon white pepper

1 teaspoon smoked paprika
1/2 teaspoon dried dill weed
1 tablespoon Cholula
A few drops of liquid smoke

## DIRECTIONS

In a mixing bowl, gently stir the mayo, garlic, and canned seafood.
Now, add the remaining ingredients and stir with a wide spatula until everything is well incorporated.
Cover and place in your refrigerator until it is thoroughly chilled. Serve well-chilled with fresh or pickled veggies. Bon appétit!

# FAST SNACKS & APPETIZERS

## 254. Smoked Bacon Fries

**(Ready in about 15 minutes | Servings 6)**

**Per serving: 409 Calories; 31.6g Fat; 1.1g Carbs; 28g Protein;**

### INGREDIENTS

1 pound smoked bacon, cut into small squares
1 teaspoon mustard seeds

1 tablespoon paprika

### DIRECTIONS

Preheat an oven to 360 degrees F.
Bake the smoked bacon for 12 to 15 minutes. Season with mustard seeds and paprika. Enjoy!

## 255. Caramelized Garlic Mushrooms

**(Ready in about 10 minutes | Servings 4)**

**Per serving: 75 Calories; 5.2g Fat; 3.3g Carbs; 2.9g Protein;**

### INGREDIENTS

2 teaspoons olive oil
1 tablespoon butter
2 cloves garlic, minced

1 pound Portobello mushrooms, sliced
1 tablespoon soy sauce
Salt and pepper, to taste

### DIRECTIONS

Heat the oil and butter in a large skillet that is preheated over a moderate heat. Add the garlic and cook until aromatic, 30 seconds or so.
Stir in the mushrooms and cook them for 3 minutes, allowing them to caramelize.
Now, add the soy sauce, salt and pepper; cook for 4 minutes more or to the desired doneness. Enjoy!

## 256. Cilantro and Ricotta Balls

**(Ready in about 10 minutes + chilling time | Servings 6)**

**Per serving: 108 Calories; 9g Fat; 2.2g Carbs; 4.8g Protein;**

### INGREDIENTS

1 cup Ricotta cheese
3 tablespoons butter
1/4 teaspoon red wine vinegar

Salt and pepper, to taste
1/2 cup fresh cilantro, finely chopped

### DIRECTIONS

Blend all ingredients, except for the cilantro, in a food processor.
Place the mixture in the refrigerator for 3 hours.
Shape the mixture into 10 to 12 balls; roll them in the chopped cilantro until evenly coated. Serve with cocktail sticks and enjoy your party!

## 257. Cocktail Meatballs with Romano Cheese

**(Ready in about 40 minutes | Servings 5)**

**Per serving: 244 Calories; 13.3g Fat; 3.7g Carbs; 28.1g Protein;**

### INGREDIENTS

1/3 pound ground turkey
1/3 pound ground pork
1/3 pound ground beef
2 ounces Romano cheese, grated
2 tablespoons buttermilk
2 eggs, whisked

1/2 yellow onion, chopped
2 cloves garlic, minced
1 tablespoon Dijon mustard
1 teaspoon ancho chili powder
Salt and ground black pepper, to taste
1/2 cup ground almonds

### DIRECTIONS

Thoroughly combine all of the above ingredients, except for the ground almonds, in a mixing dish.
Grease your hands with oil and roll the mixture into 20 meatballs. Place the ground almond in a shallow bowl.
Toss your meatballs in the ground almond until they're completely coated.
Heat up a nonstick skillet over a moderately high heat. Now, spritz the bottom and sides of the skillet with a nonstick cooking spray.
Cook your meatballs about 13 minutes, until they're golden brown all around. Serve with toothpicks on a large serving platter. Bon appétit!

## 258. Chicken Wings with Tomato Dip

**(Ready in about 50 minutes | Servings 6)**

**Per serving: 236 Calories; 13.5g Fat; 6g Carbs; 19.4g Protein;**

### INGREDIENTS

12 chicken wings
Salt and pepper, to taste

**For the Tomato Dip:**
4 ripe tomatoes, crushed
1 onion, finely chopped
1 cup mango, peeled and chopped
1 teaspoon chili pepper, deveined and finely minced
2 heaping tablespoons cilantro, finely chopped
2 tablespoons lime juice

### DIRECTIONS

Start by preheating your oven to 400 degrees F. Set a wire rack inside a rimmed baking sheet.
Season the chicken wings with salt and pepper. Bake the wings approximately 45 minutes or until the skin is crispy.
Then, thoroughly combine all ingredients for the tomato dip. Place in your refrigerator until ready to serve.

## 259. Spicy Tuna Deviled Eggs

**(Ready in about 20 minutes | Servings 6)**

**Per serving: 203 Calories; 13.3g Fat; 3.8g Carbs; 17.2g Protein;**

### INGREDIENTS

12 eggs
1/3 cup mayonnaise
1 can tuna in spring water, drained
1/2 teaspoon smoked cayenne pepper

1/4 teaspoon fresh or dried dill weed
2 pickled jalapenos, minced
Salt and black pepper, to taste

### DIRECTIONS

Place the eggs in a wide pot; cover with cold water by 1 inch. Bring to a rapid boil.
Decrease the heat to medium-low; let them simmer an additional 10 minutes.
Peel the eggs and rinse them under running water.
Slice each egg in half lengthwise and remove the yolks. Thoroughly combine the yolks with the remaining ingredients.
Divide the mixture among the egg whites and arrange the deviled eggs on a nice serving platter. Enjoy!

# 260. Broccoli and Goat Cheese Dip

**(Ready in about 10 minutes | Servings 8)**

**Per serving: 134 Calories; 10.2g Fat; 6.5g Carbs; 5.1g Protein;**

## INGREDIENTS

1 pound broccoli, broken into florets
1/2 cup sour cream
1/2 cup goat cheese
1 teaspoon shallot powder
1 teaspoon Italian seasoning mix
1 teaspoon garlic powder
1/3 cup mayonnaise

## DIRECTIONS

Steam the broccoli for 4 to 5 minutes or until crisp-tender. Transfer to a food processor.
Add the remaining ingredients, except for the mayonnaise. Puree in the food processor until well blended.
Stir in the mayonnaise and puree until creamy, uniform and smooth. Serve well-chilled and enjoy!

# 261. Cheese, Mortadella and Salami Roll-Ups

**(Ready in about 10 minutes | Servings 5)**

**Per serving: 381 Calories; 31.2g Fat; 4.8g Carbs; 17.6g Protein;**

## INGREDIENTS

10 slices Provolone cheese
4 ounces mayonnaise
10 slices Mortadella
10 slices Genoa salami
10 olives, pitted

## DIRECTIONS

Spread a thin layer of mayo onto each slice of cheese. Add a slice of Mortadella on top of the mayo.
Top with a slice of Genoa salami. Roll them up; place olives on the top and secure with toothpicks.
Serve immediately.

# 262. Paprika and Mustard Bacon Chips

**(Ready in about 20 minutes | Servings 4)**

**Per serving: 118 Calories; 10g Fat; 1.9g Carbs; 5g Protein;**

## INGREDIENTS

12 bacon strips, cut into small squares
1 tablespoon smoked paprika
1 tablespoon mustard

## DIRECTIONS

Preheat your oven to 360 degrees F
Toss the bacon strips with the paprika and mustard.
Arrange the bacon squares on a parchment lined baking sheet. Bake for 10 to 15 minutes. Enjoy!

## 263. Easy Rutabaga Fries

**(Ready in about 35 minutes | Servings 4)**

**Per serving: 134 Calories; 10.8g Fat; 5.9g Carbs; 1.5g Protein;**

### INGREDIENTS

1 ½ pounds rutabaga, cut into sticks 1/4-inch wide
3 tablespoons olive oil
Salt and ground black pepper, to taste

1/2 teaspoon cayenne pepper
1/2 teaspoon mustard seeds

### DIRECTIONS

Add the rutabaga sticks to a mixing dish. In another small-sized mixing dish, whisk the other ingredients.
Add the oil mixture to the rutabaga sticks and toss to coat well.
Preheat your oven to 440 degrees F. Line a baking sheet with parchment paper.
Place the seasoned rutabaga sticks on the baking sheet. Roast them approximately 30 minutes, turning the baking sheet occasionally. Serve warm and enjoy!

## 264. Dilled Chicken Wingettes with Goat Cheese Dip

**(Ready in about 1 hour 15 minutes | Servings 10)**

**Per serving: 227 Calories; 10.2g Fat; 0.4g Carbs; 31.5g Protein;**

### INGREDIENTS

Nonstick cooking spray
3 pounds chicken wingettes
Salt and black pepper, to taste
1/4 teaspoon smoked paprika
1 teaspoon dried dill weed
For Goat Cheese Dip:
1 cup goat cheese, crumbled

1/3 cup mayonnaise
2 tablespoons Greek-style yogurt
1 teaspoon Dijon mustard
2 cloves garlic, smashed
1 teaspoon onion powder
1/2 teaspoon ground cumin
1/4 cup fresh coriander leaves, finely chopped

### DIRECTIONS

Preheat your oven to 390 degrees F. Set a wire rack inside a rimmed baking sheet. Spritz the rack with a nonstick cooking oil.
Toss the chicken wingettes with the salt, pepper, paprika, and dill.
Place the chicken wingettes skin side up on the rack. Bake in the lower quarter of the oven for 30 to 35 minutes.
Turn the oven up to 420 degrees F. Bake for a further 40 minutes on the higher shelf, rotating the baking sheet once.
In the meantime, combine the goat cheese, mayo, yogurt, mustard, garlic, onion powder and ground cumin. Serve with the warm wingettes, garnished with fresh cilantro.

## 265. Cheese, Ham and Greek Yogurt Dip

**(Ready in about 5 minutes | Servings 6)**

**Per serving: 147 Calories; 10.6g Fat; 2.7g Carbs; 10.2g Protein;**

### INGREDIENTS

5 ounces Greek yogurt
5 ounces Ricotta cheese, at room temperature
1 cup Colby cheese, shredded

1/2 cup ham, crumbled
2 tablespoons fresh parsley, chopped

### DIRECTIONS

Thoroughly combine all of the above ingredients, except for the parsley, in a mixing dish.
Garnish with fresh parsley. Serve with veggie sticks. Bon appétit!

## 266. Cocktail Salad on a Stick

**(Ready in about 10 minutes | Servings 6)**

**Per serving: 249 Calories; 19.3g Fat; 6g Carbs; 9.7g Protein;**

### INGREDIENTS

2 cans of tiny pickled beets, drained and rinsed
2 bell peppers, sliced
4 ounces blue cheese, cubed
1 cup prosciutto, sliced

1/2 cup olives, pitted
1/3 cup champagne vinegar
1/3 cup olive oil
1/2 teaspoon cumin seeds

### DIRECTIONS

Tread the pickled beets, bell peppers, blue cheese, prosciutto, and olives onto cocktail sticks.
Drizzle with champagne vinegar and olive oil; sprinkle with cumin seeds. Bon appétit!

## 267. Greek-Style Meat and Cheese Dip

**(Ready in about 10 minutes | Servings 24)**

**Per serving: 153 Calories; 11.2g Fat; 2.2g Carbs; 10.8g Protein;**

### INGREDIENTS

1 pound ground beef
1/2 pound ground lamb
2 cups sour cream
1 cup cream cheese
1 cup feta cheese

1/2 cup tomato puree
2 garlic cloves, minced
1 sprig dried rosemary, crushed
1 sprig dried thyme, crushed
1 cup Kalamata olives, pitted and sliced

### DIRECTIONS

Brown the ground meat in a pan that is preheated over a medium-high heat. Crumble with a wide spatula and set aside.
In a large bowl, thoroughly combine the remaining ingredients, except for the olives.
Layer the cheese mixture with meat mixture. Top with sliced Kalamata olives and serve with your favorite dippers.

## 268. Celery Root French Fries with Pine Nuts

**(Ready in about 35 minutes | Servings 6)**

Per serving: 96 Calories; 8.5g Fat; 4.1g Carbs; 1.5g Protein;

### INGREDIENTS

1 ½ pounds celery root, cut into sticks
Salt and ground black pepper, to taste
1/2 teaspoon cayenne pepper

2 tablespoons olive oil
1 tablespoon Cajun seasoning
1/4 cup pine nuts, coarsely ground

### DIRECTIONS

Preheat your oven to 390 degrees F. Line a baking sheet with a parchment paper or Silpat mat.
Mix the celery root, salt, black pepper, cayenne pepper, olive oil and Cajun seasoning in a mixing dish.
Arrange the celery stick on the prepared baking sheet and bake for 30 minutes, flipping every 10 minutes to promote even cooking.
Arrange on a serving platter and sprinkle with pine nuts. Serve hot with a homemade mayo or seafood dipping sauce. Bon appétit!

# 269. Cheese-Stuffed Cocktail Meatballs

**(Ready in about 25 minutes | Servings 10)**

**Per serving: 186 Calories; 9.6g Fat; 1.2g Carbs; 23.9g Protein;**

## INGREDIENTS

1/2 pound ground turkey
1 pound ground pork
1/3 cup Parmesan cheese, freshly grated
Sea salt and ground black pepper, to taste
1 teaspoon red pepper flakes, crushed

1 teaspoon oyster sauce
1/2 cup onion, finely chopped
2 cloves garlic, minced
2 eggs
1 cup Monterey Jack cheese, cubed

## DIRECTIONS

Start by preheating your oven to 390 degrees F. Coat a baking pan with parchment paper.
Thoroughly combine all ingredients, except for the Monterey Jack cheese, in a mixing bowl.
Shape this meat mixture into 40 meatballs. Press 1 cheese cube into the middle of each meatball; be sure to seal it inside.
Gently place the meatballs on the prepared baking pan.
Bake about 20 minutes until they are browned and slightly crisp on top. Serve on a serving platter with toothpicks.

# 270. Chorizo and Ricotta Balls

**(Ready in about 15 minutes + chilling time | Servings 5)**

**Per serving: 327 Calories; 25.7g Fat; 6.4g Carbs; 17g Protein;**

## INGREDIENTS

10 ounces chorizo, chopped
10 ounces Ricotta cheese, softened
1/4 cup mayonnaise

1/2 teaspoon deli mustard
2 teaspoons tomato paste
8 Kalamata olives, pitted

## DIRECTIONS

Heat up a skillet over a moderate flame. Now, cook the chorizo until well browned. Transfer it to a mixing bowl.
Add the remaining ingredients and transfer to your refrigerator until it is well chilled. Bon appétit!

# 271. Pork Rinds with Mangold-Ricotta Dip

**(Ready in about 2 hours | Servings 8)**

**Per serving: 163 Calories; 12.8g Fat; 3.9g Carbs; 7.9g Protein;**

## INGREDIENTS

Pork skin
Salt
1 tablespoon butter
2 cups mangold, torn into pieces and steamed
1 rosemary sprig, chopped
1 thyme sprig, chopped

1 teaspoon shallot powder
1 teaspoon garlic powder
1/4 teaspoon cumin powder
Sea salt and ground black pepper, to taste
12 ounces Ricotta cheese
1/2 cup aioli

## DIRECTIONS

Start by preheating your oven to 340 degrees F. Salt pork skin according to your personal preferences.
Arrange the pork skin on a cookie sheet that is lined with a parchment paper.
Bake for 2 hours and then, allow it to cool for a couple of minutes before serving.
In the meantime, steam the mangold leaves until just tender, about 8 minutes. Combine with the remaining ingredients in a large serving bowl.
Serve with the prepared pork rinds and enjoy!

## 272. Cheese Greasy Cucumber Bites

**(Ready in about 10 minutes | Servings 10)**

**Per serving: 63 Calories; 4.3g Fat; 2.7g Carbs; 4g Protein;**

### INGREDIENTS

1 cup blue cheese
2 tablespoons real bacon bits
1/4 cup parsley, chopped

1 teaspoon chili powder
2 cucumbers, cut into thick slices

### DIRECTIONS

Blend the cheese, real bacon bits, parsley and chili powder until everything is well combined.
Spoon the cheese mixture onto the cucumber slices and serve right away!

## 273. Italian-Style Egg and Mortadella Bites

**(Ready in about 5 minutes + chilling time | Servings 6)**

**Per serving: 327 Calories; 25.7g Fat; 6.4g Carbs; 17g Protein;**

### INGREDIENTS

6 hard-boiled eggs, peeled and chopped
1/2 teaspoon Italian seasonings
1/3 cup mayonnaise
Sea salt and ground black pepper, to taste

1/2 teaspoon cayenne pepper
1/2 cup cream cheese, softened
6 slices Mortadella, chopped

### DIRECTIONS

Combine all of the above ingredients in a mixing dish.
Shape the mixture into balls.
Transfer the balls to your refrigerator for 1 hour. Keep in the refrigerator up to 4 days. Bon appétit!

## 274. Sriracha and Parm Chicken Wings

**(Ready in about 1 hour 10 minutes | Servings 6)**

**Per serving: 312 Calories; 23g Fat; 0.9g Carbs; 24.6g Protein;**

### INGREDIENTS

2 pounds chicken wings
Coarse salt and freshly ground black pepper, to taste
1/2 teaspoon smoked cayenne pepper
1 tablespoon balsamic vinegar
2 teaspoons Sriracha chili sauce

2 cloves garlic, smashed
1 stick butter
1 cup Parmesan cheese
2 tablespoons oyster sauce
1/2 cup fresh chives, chopped

### DIRECTIONS

Preheat an oven to 420 degrees F. Set a metal rack on top of a baking sheet.
Season the chicken wings with salt, black pepper, cayenne pepper. Now, roast the wings until the skin is crisp, about 45 minutes.
In the meantime, simmer the vinegar, Sriracha, and garlic until the mixture has reduced slightly, about 12 minutes.
In a shallow bowl, combine the softened butter with the parmesan cheese and oyster sauce.
Next, toss the chicken wings with the Sriracha mixture. After that, dredge the chicken wings in the parmesan mixture until fully coated; then place on the baking sheet.
Bake an additional 10 minutes. Garnish with fresh chopped chives and enjoy!

# 275. Crispy Cheesy Cauliflower Bites

**(Ready in about 40 minutes | Servings 6)**

**Per serving: 167 Calories; 13.4g Fat; 2.4g Carbs; 7.5g Protein;**

## INGREDIENTS

1 head of cauliflower, broken into small florets
1/4 cup olive oil
Sea salt and ground black pepper, to your liking

1 teaspoon lemongrass, grated
1 teaspoon harissa paste
1 cup Romano cheese, freshly grated

## DIRECTIONS

Start by preheating your oven to 450 degrees F. Spritz a baking sheet with a nonstick cooking spray.
Toss the cauliflower florets with the olive oil, salt black pepper, grated lemongrass and harissa paste.
Arrange the cauliflower florets on the prepared baking sheet.
Roast, tossing once or twice, until the cauliflower is tender, about 40 minutes. Serve with aioli or any other ketogenic dip and enjoy!

# 276. Chicharrones with Homemade Guacamole

**(Ready in about 2 hours | Servings 6)**

**Per serving: 199 Calories; 16.1g Fat; 6.5g Carbs; 7.5g Protein;**

## INGREDIENTS

1 whole pork skin from a pork belly
Salt, to taste
**For the Guacamole:**
2 avocados, seeded, peeled and chopped
1/2 fresh lime, juiced
Coarse salt and pepper, to taste

1/4 teaspoon ground cumin
1 small-sized yellow onion, finely chopped
1 teaspoon chili pepper, deveined and finely minced
1 cup tomatoes, chopped
2 tablespoons cilantro, chopped
2 cloves garlic, crushed

## DIRECTIONS

Preheat your oven to 330 degrees F. Line a large baking sheet with parchment paper.
Cut the skin into pieces and bake them for 2 hours.
Meanwhile, make your guacamole by mixing all of the guacamole ingredients in the order listed above.
Serve the chicharrones with the fresh guacamole and enjoy!

# 277. Classic Bacon Deviled Eggs

**(Ready in about 20 minutes | Servings 10)**

**Per serving: 128 Calories; 9.7g Fat; 3.3g Carbs; 6.8g Protein;**

## INGREDIENTS

10 eggs
1/2 cup mayonnaise
1/4 cup cooked bacon, chopped
2 teaspoons lemon juice
1 tablespoon Marsala wine

2 teaspoons country-style Dijon mustard
1/4 teaspoon hot pepper sauce
Salt and red pepper flakes, to taste
Fresh dill weed sprigs, to serve

## DIRECTIONS

Place the eggs in a single layer in a pan; cover with 2 inches of water.
Bring to a boil over a high heat; now, reduce the heat and cook, covered, for 1 minute.
Remove from heat and wait for 15 minutes; rinse.
After that, peel the eggs and halve them lengthwise. Remove the yolks and mash them with a fork. Add the mayonnaise, bacon, lemon juice, wine, mustard, and hot pepper sauce.
Season with salt and crushed red pepper; mix until everything is well combined.
Divide the mayonnaise-bacon mixture among the egg whites. Afterwards, serve garnished with fresh dill weed.

## 278. Cheesy Peppery Bites with Pancetta

**(Ready in about 20 minutes | Servings 4)**

**Per serving: 252 Calories; 13.7g Fat; 5.6g Carbs; 26g Protein;**

### INGREDIENTS

2 tablespoons butter, softened
1 small shallot, peeled and minced
1/2 pound ground beef
6 ounces Cottage cheese, softened
1 teaspoon garlic, smashed

1 tablespoon fresh parsley, finely chopped
Salt and pepper, to taste
4 bell peppers, deveined and quartered
5 slices pancetta, chopped

### DIRECTIONS

Preheat an oven to 380 degrees F.

Melt the butter in a heavy-bottomed skillet that is preheated over a moderately high flame. Now, sauté the shallot until it is slightly tender. Add the ground beef and cook an additional 4 minutes or until slightly browned.

Then, beat the Cottage cheese with hand mixer until softened. Add the meat mixture along with the garlic and parsley; gently stir until everything is well combined; add salt and pepper to taste.

Stuff each pepper slice with the meat/cheese mixture. Scatter chopped pancetta over the top of each pepper.

Bake about 13 minutes or until the stuffing is well browned and the peppers are tender. Bon appétit!

## 279. Mediterranean Cheese Ball

**(Ready in about 10 minutes | Servings 6)**

**Per serving: 182 Calories; 15.5g Fat; 3g Carbs; 7.6g Protein;**

### INGREDIENTS

6 ounces Neufchatel cheese
1/4 cup aioli
1 tablespoon tomato paste
6 slices of Iberian ham, chopped

6 Kalamata olives, pitted and chopped
1 teaspoon dried basil
1 teaspoon dried oregano
1 teaspoon dried rosemary

### DIRECTIONS

Thoroughly combine the Neufchatel cheese, aioli, tomato paste, chopped ham and olives in a mixing bowl; mix until everything is homogeneous.

In a shallow dish, combine the dried basil, oregano, and rosemary.

Shape the mixture into a ball. Roll the ball in the herb mixture. Refrigerate until ready to serve. Serve with veggie sticks. Bon appétit!

## 280. Two-Cheese and Artichoke Dip

**(Ready in about 5 minutes | Servings 8)**

**Per serving: 157 Calories; 11g Fat; 5.9g Carbs; 6.5g Protein;**

### INGREDIENTS

12 ounces canned artichoke hearts, drained
1/2 pound mascarpone cheese
1/2 cup Colby cheese, shredded
1/2 cup mayonnaise
2 garlic cloves, minced

2 tablespoons coriander
2 tablespoons spring onions
Celery salt and ground black pepper, to taste
1 teaspoon dried rosemary
1 teaspoon paprika

### DIRECTIONS

Thoroughly combine all ingredients in a mixing bowl.

Transfer the dipping mixture to a nice serving dish.

Serve and enjoy!

# 281. Shrimp-Stuffed Celery Sticks

**(Ready in about 10 minutes | Servings 16)**

**Per serving: 29 Calories; 1.9g Fat; 0.7g Carbs; 2.5g Protein;**

## INGREDIENTS

6 ounces fully cooked deveined shrimp, chopped
2 tablespoons soy sauce
1/3 cup cream cheese
Salt and crushed red pepper, to your liking

1/2 teaspoon oregano
1 teaspoon yellow mustard
8 celery sticks, cut in halves

## DIRECTIONS

Thoroughly combine the shrimp, soy sauce, cream cheese, salt, pepper, oregano and mustard.
Then, place the celery sticks on a serving plate; divide the shrimp mixture among the celery sticks and serve immediately.

# 282. Oven-Baked Zucchini Bites

**(Ready in about 40 minutes | Servings 4)**

**Per serving: 91 Calories; 6.1g Fat; 6g Carbs; 4.2g Protein;**

## INGREDIENTS

4 zucchinis, cut into thick slices
2 tablespoons butter, melted
2 egg whites

Coarse salt and crushed black peppercorns, to taste
1/2 teaspoon red pepper flakes, crushed
1/2 teaspoon dried dill weed

## DIRECTIONS

Begin by preheating an oven to 420 degrees F. Coat a rimmed baking sheet with parchment paper or Silpat mat.
In a mixing bowl, whisk the butter with two egg whites. Add the seasonings.
Now, toss the zucchini slices with this mixture.
Arrange the coated zucchini slices on the baking sheet; bake for 35 minutes until the slices are golden, turning once.
Check for doneness and bake another 5 minutes if needed. Serve at room temperature and enjoy!

# 283. Cheese and Crab Stuffed Mushrooms

**(Ready in about 25 minutes | Servings 4)**

**Per serving: 221 Calories; 13.5g Fat; 6g Carbs; 19.8g Protein;**

## INGREDIENTS

1 pound medium-sized white mushrooms, stems removed
Salt and pepper, to taste
1/2 teaspoon celery seeds
1/2 teaspoon dried basil
1/2 pound crab meat

1 cup cream cheese
1/4 cup mayonnaise
2 garlic cloves, smashed
1 heaping tablespoon cilantro, minced

## DIRECTIONS

Begin by preheating your oven to 390 degrees F. Spritz a rimmed baking sheet with a nonstick cooking spray.
Season the mushroom caps with salt, pepper, celery seeds and dried basil.
In a mixing dish, thoroughly combine the remaining ingredients. Stuff the mushroom caps and transfer them to the prepared baking sheet.
Bake for 17 to 22 minutes or until tops are golden. Enjoy!

## 284. Prawns on Sticks

**(Ready in about 15 minutes | Servings 4)**

**Per serving: 218 Calories; 11g Fat; 5.1g Carbs; 23.5g Protein;**

### INGREDIENTS

3 tablespoons vegetable oil
1 pound king prawns, peeled and deveined
3 garlic cloves, minced
1 tablespoon fresh sage, minced
1 teaspoon fresh rosemary
Salt and cayenne pepper, to taste

1 tablespoon fresh lime juice
2 tablespoons cilantro, chopped
1 red bell pepper, diced
1 green bell pepper, diced
1 cup cherry tomatoes
Bamboo skewers

### DIRECTIONS

Heat the vegetable oil in a wok over a moderately high heat.
Now, cook the prawns with the garlic until they are fragrant. Stir in the sage, rosemary, salt and cayenne pepper. Cook an additional minute, stirring frequently.
Remove from heat and toss with lime juice and fresh cilantro. Tread the prawns onto skewers, alternating them with peppers and cherry tomatoes.
Serve on a serving platter. Bon appétit!

## 285. Easy and Spicy Shrimp Appetizer

**(Ready in about 15 minutes | Servings 6)**

**Per serving: 107 Calories; 4.9g Fat; 1g Carbs; 15.3g Protein;**

### INGREDIENTS

2 tablespoons coconut oil, room temperature
1 pound shrimp, deveined and shelled, tail on
1 teaspoon garlic, minced
1/2 cup scallions, chopped
1 teaspoon ancho chili powder

2 tablespoons apple cider vinegar
1/4 cup chicken stock
1 teaspoon paprika
Salt and ground black pepper, to taste
Some coriander springs, for garnish

### DIRECTIONS

Heat the coconut oil in a frying pan over a moderately high flame. Now, cook the shrimp together with the garlic and scallions.
Add the chili powder, vinegar, and chicken stock and continue to cook 3 minutes more. Season with paprika, salt, and pepper to taste.
Serve with toothpicks, garnished with coriander sprigs.

## 286. Hot and Spicy Cocktail Meatballs

**(Ready in about 15 minutes | Servings 10)**

**Per serving: 158 Calories; 7.9g Fat; 0.4g Carbs; 20.4g Protein;**

### INGREDIENTS

3/4 pound ground lamb
1/2 pound ground pork
1/4 cup crushed pork rinds
1 large-sized egg, beaten
1/3 cup heavy cream
1/3 cup Parmesan cheese, grated

Sea salt and ground black pepper, to taste
1 teaspoon fresh rosemary, minced
2 garlic cloves, finely minced
1 teaspoon onion powder
1/2 teaspoon cumin, ground
1 teaspoon hot sauce

### DIRECTIONS

Thoroughly combine all ingredients in a bowl by using oiled hands. Shape the mixture into balls.
In a preheated pan, brown the meatballs on one side for 4 minutes; then flip them over and cook another 3 to 5 minutes.
Turn down the heat to low, cover the pan and let them cook an additional 3 minutes or until heated through.
Serve with cocktail sticks.

## 287. Paprika Provolone Crisps

**(Ready in about 15 minutes | Servings 6)**

**Per serving: 268 Calories; 20.4g Fat; 3.4g Carbs; 18.1g Protein;**

### INGREDIENTS

3 cups provolone cheese, shredded
4 tablespoons ground flaxseed meal
1 teaspoon paprika powder

### DIRECTIONS

Begin by preheating your oven to 420 degrees F.
Then, drop a tablespoon of shredded cheese into 12 separate piles. Sprinkle ground flaxseed meal and paprika powder over the top.
Bake in the middle of your oven for roughly 10 to 12 minutes. Store in airtight container. Bon appétit!

## 288. Pepperoni and Cheese Bites

**(Ready in about 10 minutes | Servings 5)**

**Per serving: 341 Calories; 30.6g Fat; 3.4g Carbs; 12.8g Protein;**

### INGREDIENTS

5 ounces Pepperoni, chopped
5 ounces cream cheese
4 large egg yolks, hard-boiled
2 tablespoons mayonnaise

1 teaspoon deli mustard
1/2 teaspoon paprika
2 tablespoons hemp hearts

### DIRECTIONS

Add the Pepperoni, cheese and egg yolks to a mixing dish; stir to combine well.
Now, stir in the mayonnaise, mustard, and paprika; stir again.
Shape the mixture into 10 balls.
Place the hemp hearts on a medium plate; roll each ball through to coat. Arrange these balls on a nice serving platter and serve.

## 289. Roasted Cherry Tomatoes with Cheese-Chive Sauce

**(Ready in about 25 minutes | Servings 6)**

**Per serving: 230 Calories; 21g Fat; 6g Carbs; 5.1g Protein;**

### INGREDIENTS

Nonstick cooking spray
1 ½ pounds cherry tomatoes
1 rosemary sprig, chopped
1 teaspoon dried oregano
1 teaspoon dried sage, crushed
1/4 cup extra-virgin olive oil

Celery salt, to taste
For the Sauce:
1 cup cream cheese
1/2 cup homemade mayonnaise
1/2 cup fresh chives, chopped

### DIRECTIONS

Preheat your oven to 425 degrees F. Spritz a baking sheet with a nonstick cooking spray.
Toss the cherry tomatoes with the rosemary, oregano, sage, oil, and celery salt and arrange on the prepared baking sheet.
Bake about 23 minutes, rotating the baking sheet once or twice.
Meanwhile, make the dipping sauce by whisking all the sauce ingredients in a mixing dish. Serve with the warm roasted tomatoes and enjoy!

## 290. Mini Salami Pizza Cups

**(Ready in about 20 minutes | Servings 6)**

**Per serving: 162 Calories; 13.1g Fat; 2.5g Carbs; 8.7g Protein;**

### INGREDIENTS

1 cup Cheddar cheese, shredded
1/2 cup marinara
1 teaspoon dried oregano

1/2 teaspoon dried basil
1/2 cup green olives, pitted and chopped
12 Genoa salami slices

### DIRECTIONS

Preheat an oven to 360 degrees F; spritz a muffin pan with a nonstick cooking spray.
Divide 1/2 cup of cheddar cheese among the muffin cups. Divide the marinara sauce among the muffin cups.
Sprinkle each cup with oregano, basil, and chopped olives. Add a salami slice to each muffin cup. Top with the remaining 1/2 cup of cheese.
Bake approximately 17 minutes. Allow them to cool slightly before removing from the muffin pan.

## 291. Turkey Tenders with Spicy and Tangy Sauce

**(Ready in about 30 minutes | Servings 8)**

**Per serving: 153 Calories; 6.7g Fat; 4.6g Carbs; 21.8g Protein;**

### INGREDIENTS

1 ¼ pounds turkey tenderloin, cut into 20 pieces
1 teaspoon kosher salt
1/2 teaspoon ground black pepper
1 teaspoon smoked paprika
1/3 cup flax meal
3/4 cup almond flour
2 eggs

**For the Sauce:**
1/3 cup tomato puree
1/2 tablespoon Louisiana hot sauce
1 teaspoon Dijon mustard
1 ½ teaspoons soy sauce
1 teaspoon garlic powder
1 teaspoon paprika
1/3 teaspoon cumin
1/2 teaspoon red pepper flakes, crushed

### DIRECTIONS

Preheat an oven to 370 degrees F. Then, spritz a baking pan with a nonstick cooking spray.
Season the turkey pieces with salt, pepper and paprika. Thoroughly combine the flax meal with the almond flour.
Dip each piece of turkey in the beaten egg. Then, coat them with the almond flour mixture.
Arrange the turkey pieces on the prepared baking pan. Bake approximately 25 minutes.
Meanwhile, make the sauce by whisking all the sauce ingredients. Serve with the hot turkey tenders.

## 292. Muffin Appetizer with Herbes de Provence

**(Ready in about 20 minutes | Servings 6)**

**Per serving: 269 Calories; 20.7g Fat; 5g Carbs; 15.5g Protein;**

### INGREDIENTS

Nonstick cooking spray
1/3 cup flaxseed meal
2/3 cup almond flour
2 tablespoons xylitol
2 teaspoons psyllium
1/8 teaspoon kosher salt

1/8 teaspoon grated nutmeg
1 teaspoon herbes de Provence
1/2 teaspoon baking powder
2 eggs
1/2 cup yogurt
10 slices salami, chopped

### DIRECTIONS

Start by preheating your oven to 360 degrees F. Lightly grease a muffin pan with a nonstick cooking spray.
Thoroughly combine the flaxseed meal with the almond flour, xylitol, psyllium, salt, nutmeg, herbes de Provence and baking powder; stir until well combined.
Now, stir in the eggs, yogurt, and salami. Press the mixture into the prepared muffin pan.
Bake about 15 minutes and transfer to a wire rack to cool slightly before removing from the muffin pan. Bon appétit!

# 293. Mexican-Style Keto Rolls

**(Ready in about 25 minutes | Servings 6)**

**Per serving: 261 Calories; 18.6g Fat; 6.7g Carbs; 17.3g Protein;**

## INGREDIENTS

3 cups Mexican mix cheese, shredded
1 yellow onion, chopped
2 garlic cloves, crushed
1 ½ cups ground beef
Salt and freshly ground black peppercorns, to your liking

1/2 teaspoon ground cumin
2 tomatoes, crushed
1/4 cup sour cream
1/4 cup mayonnaise

## DIRECTIONS

Begin by preheating an oven to 390 degrees F. Line a baking pan with parchment paper or Silpat mat.
Place the shredded cheese to cover the bottom of your baking pan. Bake approximately 13 minutes, or until the cheese is slightly browned on top.
In the meantime, heat up a nonstick skillet over a moderately high flame. Sweat the onion until just tender and fragrant.
Now, cook the garlic until it is slightly browned, about 1 minutes. Stir in the ground beef; cook until it is no longer pink and season with salt, peppercorns and ground cumin.
Top the cheese "crust" with the meat mixture and bake for a further 7 minutes. Top with the tomatoes, sour cream, and mayonnaise.
Cut into 12 slices. Afterwards, roll each slice and serve warm. Bon appétit!

# 294. Crock Pot Little Smokies

**(Ready in about 2 hours 30 minutes | Servings 6)**

**Per serving: 271 Calories; 22.2g Fat; 4.5g Carbs; 12.3g Protein;**

## INGREDIENTS

1 ½ pounds cocktail franks
3 tablespoons wholegrain mustard
1 bottle barbecue sauce

1 tablespoon Swerve
1 teaspoon onion powder

## DIRECTIONS

Heat up a pan over a moderately high heat; now, brown the sausage about 3 minutes.
Treat your Crock pot with a nonstick cooking spray. Add all of the above ingredients and stir well.
Cook on Low heat setting for 2 ½ hours. Serve the little smokies with toothpicks. Bon appétit!

# 295. Adobo Cheese Snack

**(Ready in about 15 minutes | Servings 5)**

**Per serving: 338 Calories; 26.5g Fat; 3.4g Carbs; 21g Protein;**

## INGREDIENTS

10 pieces string cheese
Cooking oil
1/2 cup almond flour
1/3 cup Parmesan cheese powder

1 teaspoon Adobo spice mix
2 eggs
2 tablespoons whole milk

## DIRECTIONS

Cut the string cheese in half lengthwise.
Heat the cooking oil in a deep frying pan that is preheated over a moderately high heat.
Mix the almond flour, parmesan, Adobo spice mix, eggs and milk until everything is well incorporated.
Dip the cheese sticks into the batter and cover on all sides.
Fry the cheese sticks for 4 to 5 minutes, until golden brown; work in batches. Transfer to paper towels to soak up the excess fat. Serve with hot sauce.

# 296. Tortilla Chips with Guacamole

**(Ready in about 20 minutes | Servings 10)**

**Per serving: 109 Calories; 8.4g Fat; 5.3g Carbs; 2.2g Protein;**

## INGREDIENTS

**For the chips:**
1 tablespoon coconut oil
3/4 cup almond flour
2 tablespoons coconut flour
1/4 teaspoon baking powder
1/4 cup psyllium husk powder
1/3 teaspoon xanthan gum
1/3 teaspoon turmeric powder
3/4 cup hot water
2 tablespoons avocado oil

**For the Guacamole:**
2 ripe avocados, seeded and peeled
Fresh juice of 1 fresh lemon
Salt and pepper, to taste
1/3 teaspoon cayenne pepper
1 small-sized onion, chopped
1 serrano chili pepper, stems and seeds removed, minced
1 cup ripe plum tomatoes, seeded and chopped
2 tablespoons fresh cilantro, chopped
2 garlic cloves, finely minced

## DIRECTIONS

Thoroughly combine the coconut oil, almond flour, coconut flour, baking powder, psyllium powder, xanthan gum, and turmeric. Pour in the water and knead into a dough.

Spread the coconut flour on a working surface.

Then, roll out your dough very thin, about 1.2-inch thick. Drizzle with avocado oil.

Cut the dough into triangles; bake the tortilla triangles in the preheated oven at 350 degrees F, on a parchment lined baking sheet for 10 minutes.

Your chips will crisp up as they cool.

Meanwhile, prepare your guacamole by mixing the scooped avocado pulp and fresh lemon juice. Add the remaining ingredients and stir until everything is well blended.

# 297. Saucy Cheesy Baby Carrots

**(Ready in about 35 minutes | Servings 6)**

**Per serving: 216 Calories; 18.7g Fat; 5.4g Carbs; 3.5g Protein;**

## INGREDIENTS

1 ½ pounds baby carrots, florets separated
1 stick butter, melted
1/2 teaspoon coarse salt
1/4 teaspoon ground black pepper
1/4 teaspoon ground cumin
1/4 teaspoon dried dill weed
1/2 cup Asiago cheese, grated

## DIRECTIONS

Begin by preheating your oven to 400 degrees F.

Coat the baby carrots with the melted butter, salt, pepper, cumin and dill weed.

Bake for 30 minutes in the middle of the preheated oven, stirring once or twice.

Top with the shredded Asiago cheese and bake an additional 5 minutes or until cheese is slightly browned. Bon appétit!

# 298. Two-Cheese and Ground Meat Dip

**(Ready in about 15 minutes | Servings 10)**

**Per serving: 195 Calories; 12g Fat; 1.5g Carbs; 19.5g Protein;**

## INGREDIENTS

1 tablespoon olive oil
1/2 pound ground beef
1/2 pound ground pork
Salt and ground black pepper, to taste
1 teaspoon onion powder
1/2 teaspoon garlic powder
1/2 teaspoon red pepper flakes, crushed
8 ounces mascarpone cheese, at room temperature
6 ounces Colby cheese, shredded

## DIRECTIONS

Heat the oil in a large-sized skillet that is preheated over a moderate flame. Now, cook the ground meat until it is well browned, crumbling with a spatula as it cooks.

Add the seasonings and mascarpone cheese. Top with the shredded Colby cheese. Cover and allow the cheese to melt, about 5 minutes. Serve with veggie sticks and enjoy!

# 299. Dippable Cheese Crisps

**(Ready in about 20 minutes | Servings 6)**

**Per serving: 225 Calories; 19.3g Fat; 0.6g Carbs; 12.1g Protein;**

## INGREDIENTS

1 cup Romano cheese, finely shredded
1 cup Pepper Jack cheese, shredded
4 slices bacon, cooked and crumbled
1 jalapeño, finely chopped

1/4 teaspoon red pepper flakes
1/2 teaspoon ground cumin
1/4 teaspoon cardamom
Salt and pepper, to taste

## DIRECTIONS

Begin by preheating your oven to 400 degrees F. Line a baking sheet with a sheet of parchment paper.
Spoon 1 tablespoon of the Romano cheese into a small mound on the parchment paper. Top with about 1 tablespoon of the shredded Pepper Jack cheese.
Add the bacon and chopped jalapeño. Sprinkle with red pepper, cumin, cardamom, salt, and pepper; gently flatten each mound.
Bake approximately 12 minutes. Transfer the baking sheet to a wire rack to cool before serving. Serve with marinara sauce. Bon appétit!

# 300. Cauliflower Balls with Greek Yoghurt Sauce

**(Ready in about 30 minutes | Servings 6)**

**Per serving: 182 Calories; 13.1g Fat; 5.9g Carbs; 11.5g Protein;**

## INGREDIENTS

1 head cauliflower
1/2 cup Parmesan cheese, grated
3 eggs
1 cup Asiago cheese, shredded
1 onion, finely chopped
1 garlic clove, minced
Salt and black pepper, to taste

**For Greek Yoghurt Sauce:**
1 cup Greek yogurt
1 teaspoon lemon juice
1 garlic clove, minced
1 tablespoon mayonnaise
1 tablespoon olive oil
1/2 teaspoon dried dill weed

## DIRECTIONS

Cook the cauliflower in a large pot of salted water until tender, about 6 minutes; cut into florets.
Preheat your oven to 400 degrees F. Coat a baking pan with parchment paper.
Mash the cauliflower with the Parmesan, eggs, cheese, onion, garlic, salt and black pepper; shape the mixture into balls.
Bake for 22 minutes or until they are slightly crisp.
To make the sauce, whisk all remaining ingredients. Serve the cauliflower balls with the Greek yogurt sauce on the side.

# 301. Paprika and Rosemary Crackers

**(Ready in about 30 minutes | Servings 12)**

**Per serving: 119 Calories; 8g Fat; 4.7g Carbs; 2.6g Protein;**

## INGREDIENTS

3/4 cup sesame seeds
2 tablespoons sunflower seeds
2 tablespoons flax seeds
1 tablespoon pecans, ground
1/3 cup sunflower seeds

1/4 cup psyllium husks
Coarse sea salt, to taste
1 teaspoon paprika
1 teaspoon dried rosemary
Warm water

## DIRECTIONS

In a mixing bowl, thoroughly combine all the dry ingredients.
Pour in the warm water and stir to form a dough.
Place the dough in between two large pieces of parchment pepper; roll it out as thin as possible.
Cut the cracker dough into rectangles. Prick with a fork and transfer to a lined baking sheet.
Bake in the preheated oven at 360 degrees F for 8 to 13 minutes or until golden. Flip them over and bake another 10 minutes. Bon appétit!

# 302. Prosciutto-Broccoli Muffins with Tomato Dip

**(Ready in about 30 minutes | Servings 6)**

**Per serving: 375 Calories; 27.6g Fat; 6g Carbs; 24.8g Protein;**

## INGREDIENTS

1 head broccoli, grated
1 cup scallions, chopped
5 ounces prosciutto, chopped
6 eggs, whisked
1 ½ cups Colby cheese, freshly grated
Sea salt and ground black pepper, to taste
1/2 teaspoon black mustard seeds
1/2 teaspoon marjoram
1/2 teaspoon coriander

**For the Dipping Sauce:**
2 ripe tomatoes, chopped
1 garlic clove, chopped
1 roasted pepper, chopped
1 small onion, chopped
2 tablespoons olive oil
1/2 teaspoon oregano
1 teaspoon basil
1 teaspoon rosemary

## DIRECTIONS

Begin by preheating your oven to 390 degrees F. Lightly butter a muffin pan.

Combine the broccoli, scallions and chopped prosciutto in a mixing dish. Now, stir in the eggs and cheese; stir to combine well.

After that, sprinkle with salt, black pepper, black mustard seeds, marjoram, and coriander; stir again to combine thoroughly.

Next, divide the mixture among the prepared muffin cups and bake approximately 30 minutes, or until thoroughly cooked.

In the meantime, make the tomato sauce by whisking the remaining ingredients. Serve with the warm broccoli muffins and enjoy!

# VEGAN

## 303. Spicy Tofu with Vegan Tzatziki

**(Ready in about 40 minutes | Servings 4)**

**Per serving: 162 Calories; 10.9g Fat; 5.8g Carbs; 9.5g Protein;**

### INGREDIENTS

12 ounces tofu, pressed and cut into 1/4-inch thick slices
1 cup scallions, chopped
1 garlic clove, minced
2 tablespoons champagne vinegar
1 tablespoon Sriracha sauce
2 tablespoons sesame oil

**For Vegan Tzatziki:**
2 cloves garlic, pressed
2 tablespoons fresh lemon juice
Sea salt and ground black pepper, to taste
1 teaspoon fresh or dried dill weed
1 cup non-dairy yogurt
1 cucumber, shredded

### DIRECTIONS

Place the tofu slices, scallions, garlic, vinegar, and Sriracha sauce in a bowl; let it stand for 30 minutes.
Heat the oil in a nonstick skillet over medium-high heat. Cook the tofu until it is golden brown, about 5 minutes.
To make the vegan tzatziki, thoroughly combine the garlic, lemon juice, salt, black pepper, dill and yogurt in a mixing bowl.
Stir in the shredded cucumber; stir until everything is well incorporated.
Place the tzatziki in the refrigerator until ready to serve. Divide the tofu among serving plates and serve with a dollop of tzatziki. Enjoy!

## 304. Mushroom Stuffed Avocado

**(Ready in about 10 minutes | Servings 8)**

**Per serving: 245 Calories; 23.2g Fat; 6.2g Carbs; 2.4g Protein;**

### INGREDIENTS

4 avocados, pitted and halved
2 tablespoons olive oil
2 cups button mushrooms, chopped
1 onion, chopped

1 teaspoon garlic, crushed
Salt and black pepper, to taste
1 teaspoon deli mustard
1 tomato, chopped

### DIRECTIONS

Scoop out about 2 teaspoons of the avocado flesh from each half; reserve the scooped avocado flash.
Heat the oil in a sauté pan that is preheated over a moderately high flame. Now, cook the mushrooms, onion, and garlic until the mushrooms are tender and the onion is translucent.
Add the reserved avocado flash to the mushroom mixture and mix to combine. Now, add the salt, black pepper, mustard, and tomato.
Divide the mushroom mixture among the avocado halves and serve immediately.

## 305. Fried Tofu with Peppers

**(Ready in about 40 minutes | Servings 2)**

**Per serving: 223 Calories; 15.9g Fat; 5.1g Carbs; 15.6g Protein;**

### INGREDIENTS

12 ounces extra firm tofu, pressed and cubed
1 ½ tablespoons flaxseed meal
Salt and ground black pepper, to taste
1 teaspoon garlic paste
1/2 teaspoon paprika
1 teaspoon shallot powder

1/2 teaspoon ground bay leaf
1 tablespoon olive oil
1 red bell pepper, deveined and sliced
1 green bell pepper, deveined and sliced
1 serrano pepper, deveined and sliced

### DIRECTIONS

Place the tofu, flaxseed meal, salt, black pepper, garlic paste, paprika, shallot powder, and ground bay leaf in a container.
Cover, toss to coat, and let it marinate at least 30 minutes.
Heat the olive oil in a saucepan over a moderate heat. Cook your tofu along with the peppers for 5 to 7 minutes, gently stirring.
Serve immediately and enjoy!

## 306. Flavorful Tofu Cubes with Pecans

**(Ready in about 13 minutes | Servings 4)**

**Per serving: 232 Calories; 21.6g Fat; 5.3g Carbs; 8.3g Protein;**

### INGREDIENTS

3 teaspoons olive oil
1 cup extra firm tofu, pressed and cubed
1/4 cup pecans, coarsely chopped
1 ½ tablespoons soy sauce
3 tablespoons vegetable broth

1/2 teaspoon granulated garlic
1 teaspoon cayenne pepper
1/2 teaspoon turmeric powder
Sea salt and ground black pepper, to taste
2 teaspoons sunflower seeds

### DIRECTIONS

Heat the oil in a frying pan that is preheated over a moderate heat. Once hot, fry the tofu cubes until golden brown, stirring periodically.
Stir in the pecans; increase the temperature and cook on high for 2 minutes or until fragrant.
Add the remaining ingredients, reduce the heat to medium-low and cook an additional 5 minutes.
Serve drizzled with hot sauce and enjoy!

## 307. Easy Kale Dip with Crudités

**(Ready in about 25 minutes | Servings 6)**

**Per serving: 75 Calories; 3g Fat; 6g Carbs; 2.9g Protein;**

### INGREDIENTS

2 cups kale
1 cup tofu, pressed, drained and crumbled
1/2 cup soy milk
2 teaspoons nutritional yeast
2 garlic cloves, minced
2 teaspoons olive oil

1 teaspoon sea salt
1/4 teaspoon ground black pepper, or more to taste
1/2 teaspoon paprika
1 teaspoon dried basil
1/2 teaspoon dried dill weed

### DIRECTIONS

Start by preheating your oven to 400 degrees F. Lightly oil a casserole dish with a nonstick cooking spray.
Now, parboil the kale leaves until it is just wilted.
Puree the remaining ingredients in your food processor or blender. Stir in the kale; stir until the mixture is homogeneous.
Bake approximately 13 minutes. Now, serve with a crudités platter. Bon appétit!

## 308. Crave-Worthy Stuffed Mushrooms

**(Ready in about 35 minutes | Servings 4)**

**Per serving: 206 Calories; 13.4g Fat; 5.6g Carbs; 12.7g Protein;**

### INGREDIENTS

1/2 head cauliflower
1 pound medium-sized brown cremini mushrooms, cleaned
and stems removed
2 tablespoons vegetable oil
1 onion, finely chopped

1 teaspoon garlic, minced
1 bell pepper, chopped
1 teaspoon Italian seasoning mix
Salt and black pepper, to taste
1 cup vegan parmesan

### DIRECTIONS

Cook the cauliflower in a large pot of salted water until tender, about 6 minutes; cut into florets.
Then, pulse the cauliflower florets in your food processor until they resemble small rice-like granules.
Preheat an oven to 360 degrees F. Now, bake the mushroom caps for 8 to 12 minutes or until they are just tender.
Heat the oil in a heavy-bottomed skillet; sauté the onion, garlic and bell pepper until they have softened.
Add the Italian seasoning mix along with the salt and pepper; taste and adjust seasonings. Fold in the cauliflower rice.
Next, divide the filling mixture among the mushroom caps. Top with the vegan parmesan and bake 17 minutes longer. Serve warm.

# 309. Creamy Avocado and Zucchini Soup

**(Ready in about 45 minutes | Servings 4)**

**Per serving: 165 Calories; 13.4g Fat; 6.7g Carbs; 2.2g Protein;**

## INGREDIENTS

3 teaspoons vegetable oil
1 yellow onion, chopped
1 carrot, sliced
1 parsnip, sliced
3 cups zucchini, peeled and chopped

1/4 teaspoon ground black pepper
4 cups water
1 tablespoon vegetable bouillon powder
1 tomato, pureed
1 avocado pitted, peeled and diced

## DIRECTIONS

Heat the oil in a heavy-bottomed pot that is preheated over a moderate heat. Now, sweat the onions until they are softened.
Add the carrot, parsnip, and zucchini and cook for 7 minutes more; season with black pepper. Reserve the vegetables.
After that, add the water, vegetable bouillon powder, and pureed tomato; bring it to a rapid boil. Turn the heat to medium-low and let it simmer for 18 minutes.
Add reserved vegetables and simmer for a further 18 minutes. Remove from the heat and stir in the avocado.
Blend the soup in batches until smooth and creamy.

# 310. Sunday Stuffed Mushrooms

**(Ready in about 30 minutes | Servings 4)**

**Per serving: 139 Calories; 11.2g Fat; 5.4g Carbs; 4.8g Protein;**

## INGREDIENTS

2 tablespoons sesame oil
1 cup onions, chopped
1 garlic clove, minced
1 pound white mushrooms, stems removed

Salt and black pepper, to taste
1/4 cup raw walnuts, crushed
2 tablespoons cilantro, chopped

## DIRECTIONS

Begin by preheating an oven to 360 degrees F. Lightly grease a large baking sheet with a nonstick cooking spray.
Heat the sesame oil in a frying pan that is preheated over medium-high heat. Now, sauté the onions and garlic until aromatic.
Then, chop the mushroom stems and cook until they are tender. Heat off, season with salt and pepper; stir in the walnuts.
Stuff the mushroom caps with the walnut/mushroom mixture and arrange them on the prepared baking sheet.
Bake for 25 minutes and transfer to a wire rack to cool slightly. Garnish with fresh cilantro and serve. Bon appétit!

# 311. Rich Dark Chocolate Smoothie

**(Ready in about 10 minutes | Servings 2)**

**Per serving: 335 Calories; 31.7g Fat; 5.7g Carbs; 7g Protein;**

## INGREDIENTS

8 walnuts
3/4 cup almond milk
1/4 cup water
1 ½ cups lettuce

2 teaspoons vegan protein powder, zero carbs
1 tablespoon chia seeds
1 tablespoon unsweetened cocoa powder
4 fresh dates, pitted

## DIRECTIONS

Process all ingredients in your blender until everything is uniform and creamy.
Divide between two glasses and serve well-chilled.

# 312. Winter Chanterelle and Leek Stew

**(Ready in about 25 minutes | Servings 4)**

**Per serving: 114 Calories; 7.3g Fat; 5.2g Carbs; 2.1g Protein;**

## INGREDIENTS

2 tablespoons olive oil
1 cup leeks, chopped
2 garlic cloves, pressed
1/2 cup celery with leaves, chopped
2 carrots, chopped

1 cup fresh Chanterelle, sliced
2 tablespoons dry red wine
2 rosemary sprigs, chopped
1 thyme sprig, chopped
3 ½ cups roasted vegetable stock

1/2 teaspoon cayenne pepper
1 teaspoon Hungarian paprika
2 ripe tomatoes, pureed
1 tablespoon flaxseed meal

## DIRECTIONS

Heat the oil in a stockpot over a moderate flame. Now, cook the leeks until they are tender.
Add the garlic, celery, and carrots and cook for a further 4 minutes or until they are softened.
Now, stir in the Chanterelle mushrooms; cook until they lose their liquid; reserve the vegetables.
Pour in the wine to deglaze the bottom of the stockpot. Now, add the rosemary and thyme.
Add the roasted vegetable stock, cayenne pepper, Hungarian paprika, and tomatoes; stir in the reserved vegetables and bring to a boil.
Reduce the heat to a simmer. Let it simmer, covered, an additional 15 minutes. Add the flaxseed meal to thicken the soup. Serve in individual soup bowls with a few sprinkles of Hungarian paprika.

# 313. Parmesan Tomato Chips

**(Ready in about 5 hours | Servings 6)**

**Per serving: 161 Calories; 14g Fat; 6.2g Carbs; 4.6g Protein;**

## INGREDIENTS

1 ½ pounds tomatoes, sliced
1/4 cup extra-virgin olive oil
1 tablespoon Italian seasoning mix

For Vegan Parmesan:
1/2 cup pumpkin seeds
1 tablespoon nutritional yeast

Salt and black pepper, to taste
1 teaspoon garlic powder

## DIRECTIONS

Drizzle the sliced tomatoes with olive oil.
Now, preheat your oven to 200 degrees F. Coat a baking pan with Silpat mat.
Pulse all the parmesan ingredients in your food processor until you reach a Parmesan cheese consistency.
Mix the parmesan with the Italian seasoning mix. Then, toss the seasoned tomato slices with the parmesan mixture until they are well coated.
Arrange the tomato slices on the baking pan and bake for 5 hours. Store in an airtight container.

# 314. Roasted Asparagus with Baba Ghanoush

**(Ready in about 45 minutes | Servings 6)**

**Per serving: 149 Calories; 12.1g Fat; 6.3g Carbs; 3.6g Protein;**

## INGREDIENTS

1 ½ pounds asparagus spears, trim and cut off the woody ends
1/4 cup olive oil
1 teaspoon sea salt
1/2 teaspoon ground black pepper, to taste

1/2 teaspoon paprika
For Baba Ghanoush:
3/4 pound eggplant
2 teaspoons olive oil
1/2 cup scallions, chopped
2 cloves garlic, minced

1 tablespoon tahini
2 tablespoons fresh lemon juice
1/2 teaspoon cayenne pepper
Salt and ground black pepper, to taste
1/4 cup fresh parsley leaves, chopped

## DIRECTIONS

Begin by preheating your oven to 390 degrees F. Line a baking sheet with parchment paper.
Place the asparagus spears on the baking sheet.
Toss the asparagus spears with the oil, salt, pepper, and paprika. Bake about 9 minutes or until thoroughly cooked.
Then, make the Baba Ghanoush. Preheat your oven to 425 degrees F.
Place the eggplants on a lined cookie sheet. Set under the broiler approximately 30 minutes; allow the eggplants to cool. Now, peel the eggplants and remove the stems.
Heat 2 teaspoons of the olive oil in a frying pan over a moderately high flame. Now, sauté the scallions and garlic until tender and aromatic.
Add the roasted eggplant, scallion mixture, tahini, lemon juice, cayenne pepper, salt and black pepper to your food processor. Pulse until the ingredients are evenly mixed.
Garnish with parsley and serve with the roasted asparagus spears. Bon appétit!

# 315. Creamy Broccoli Soup

**(Ready in about 15 minutes | Servings 4)**

**Per serving: 252 Calories; 20.3g Fat; 5.8g Carbs; 8.1g Protein;**

## INGREDIENTS

2 tablespoons coconut oil, at room temperature
2 shallots, finely chopped
1 teaspoon garlic, minced
1 pound broccoli, cut into small florets
8 ounces kale leaves, torn into small pieces

4 cups vegetable broth
1/2 cup almond milk
1/2 teaspoon kosher salt
1/2 teaspoon crushed red pepper flakes
2 tablespoons chives, coarsely chopped

## DIRECTIONS

Heat the coconut oil in a pot that is preheated over a moderate flame. Then, sauté the shallots and garlic until they're fragrant and slightly browned.

Now, add the broccoli, kale and vegetable broth; bring to a boil for 5 minutes.

Pour in the almond milk, salt and pepper; cover and let your soup simmer over a moderate flame.

Afterwards, blend the soup with an immersion blender; serve right away garnished with freshly chopped chives!

# 316. Stuffed Avocado with Pecans

**(Ready in about 10 minutes | Servings 4)**

**Per serving: 263 Calories; 24.8g Fat; 6.5g Carbs; 3.5g Protein;**

## INGREDIENTS

2 avocados, peeled and pitted
5 ounces pecans, ground
2 carrots, chopped
1 garlic clove

1 teaspoon lemon juice
1 tablespoon soy sauce
Salt and freshly ground black pepper, to taste

## DIRECTIONS

In a mixing bowl, thoroughly combine the avocado pulp with the pecans, carrots, garlic, lemon juice, and soy sauce.

Season with salt and black pepper to taste. Divide the mixture among the avocado halves.

You can add some extra pecans for garnish. Bon appétit!

# 317. Roasted Curried Cauliflower with Peppers

**(Ready in about 35 minutes | Servings 4)**

**Per serving: 166 Calories; 13.9g Fat; 5.4g Carbs; 3g Protein;**

## INGREDIENTS

1 pound cauliflower, broken into florets
2 bell peppers, halved
2 pasilla peppers, halved
1/4 cup extra-virgin olive oil
1/2 teaspoon sea salt

1/4 teaspoon freshly ground black pepper, or more to taste
1/2 teaspoon cayenne pepper
1 teaspoon curry powder
1/2 teaspoon nigella seeds

## DIRECTIONS

Preheat your oven to 425 degrees F. Line a large baking sheet with a piece of parchment paper.

Drizzle the cauliflower and peppers with extra-virgin olive oil. Sprinkle with salt, black pepper, cayenne pepper, curry powder and nigella seeds

Next, arrange the vegetables on the prepared baking sheet.

Roast the vegetables, tossing periodically, until they are slightly browned, about 30 minutes.

Serve with homemade tomato dip or mushroom pate. Bon appétit!

# 318. Tofu Stuffed Zucchini with Cashew Nuts

**(Ready in about 50 minutes | Servings 4)**

**Per serving: 148 Calories; 10g Fat; 4.8g Carbs; 7.5g Protein;**

## INGREDIENTS

1 tablespoon olive oil

2 (12-ounce) packages firm tofu, drained and crumbled

2 garlic cloves, pressed

1/2 cup scallions, chopped

2 cups tomato puree

1/4 teaspoon turmeric

1/4 teaspoon chili powder

Sea salt and cayenne pepper, to taste

4 zucchinis, cut into halves lengthwise and scoop out the insides

1 tablespoon nutritional yeast

2 ounces cashew nuts, lightly salted and chopped

## DIRECTIONS

Heat the oil in a pan that is preheated over a moderate heat; now, cook the tofu, garlic, and scallions for 4 to 6 minutes.

Stir in 1 cup of the tomato puree and scooped zucchini flesh; add all seasonings and cook an additional 6 minutes, until the tofu is slightly browned.

Next, preheat your oven to 360 degrees F.

Divide the tofu mixture among the zucchini shells. Place the stuffed zucchini shells in a baking dish that is previously greased with cooking spray. Pour in the remaining 1 cup of tomato puree.

Bake approximately 30 minutes. Sprinkle with the nutritional yeast and cashew nuts; bake an additional 5 to 6 minutes. Enjoy!

# 319. Spinach Chips with Garlic-Avocado Dip

**(Ready in about 20 minutes | Servings 6)**

**Per serving: 269 Calories; 26.7g Fat; 3.4g Carbs; 2.3g Protein;**

## INGREDIENTS

3 ripe avocados, pitted

2 teaspoons lime juice

Salt and black pepper, to taste

2 garlic cloves, finely minced

2 tablespoons extra-virgin olive oil

1/2 teaspoon red pepper flakes

**For Spinach Chips:**

2 cups baby spinach, washed and dried

1 tablespoon olive oil

Sea salt and garlic powder, to taste

## DIRECTIONS

Mash the avocado pulp with a fork. Add the fresh lime juice, salt, pepper, garlic, and 2 tablespoons of olive oil.

Mix until everything is well incorporated. Transfer to a serving bowl and sprinkle with red pepper flakes.

Then, preheat your oven to 300 degrees F. Line a baking sheet with a Silpat mat.

Arrange the spinach leaves on the baking sheet; toss with 1 tablespoon of olive oil, salt, and garlic powder.

Bake for 8 to 12 minutes so the leaves have dried up. Serve with the well-chilled avocado dip. Bon appétit!

# 320. Brussels Sprouts with Tempeh

**(Ready in about 20 minutes | Servings 4)**

**Per serving: 179 Calories; 11.7g Fat; 2.1g Carbs; 10.5g Protein;**

## INGREDIENTS

2 tablespoons olive oil

2 garlic cloves, minced

1/2 cup leeks, chopped

10 ounces tempeh, crumbled

2 tablespoons water

2 tablespoons soy sauce

1 tablespoon tomato puree

1/2 pound Brussels sprouts, quartered

Sea salt and ground black pepper, to taste

## DIRECTIONS

Heat the oil in a saucepan that is preheated over a moderate heat. Now, cook the garlic and leeks until tender and aromatic.

Now, add the tempeh, water and soy sauce. Cook until the tempeh just beginning to brown, about 5 minutes.

Stir in the shredded cabbage; season with salt and pepper; turn the heat to low and cook, stirring often, for about 13 minutes. Serve warm.

# 321. Garam Masala Broccoli Delight

**(Ready in about 15 minutes | Servings 4)**

**Per serving: 100 Calories; 8.2g Fat; 4.7g Carbs; 3.7g Protein;**

### INGREDIENTS

3/4 pound broccoli, broken into florets
1/4 cup extra-virgin olive oil
Seasoned salt and ground black pepper, to taste
1 garlic clove, smashed

1 tablespoon sesame paste
1 tablespoon fresh lime juice
1/2 teaspoon Garam Masala

### DIRECTIONS

Steam the broccoli for 7 minutes, until it is crisp-tender but still vibrant green. Pulse in your blender or a food processor until rice-like consistency is achieved.
Now, add the oil, salt, black paper, garlic, sesame paste, fresh lime juice and Garam Masala.
Blend until everything is well incorporated.
Drizzle with some extra olive oil and serve immediately. Otherwise, keep in your refrigerator until ready to serve.

# 322. Zoodles with Cashew Parmesan

**(Ready in about 15 minutes | Servings 4)**

**Per serving: 145 Calories; 10.6g Fat; 5.9g Carbs; 5.5g Protein;**

### INGREDIENTS

**For Zoodles:**
4 zucchinis, peeled
2 tablespoons olive oil
1/2 cup water
Salt and cayenne pepper, to taste
**For Cashew Parmesan:**

1/2 cup raw cashews
2 tablespoons nutritional yeast
Sea salt and black pepper, to taste
1/4 teaspoon shallot powder
1/2 teaspoon garlic powder

### DIRECTIONS

Slice the zucchinis into long strips i.e. noodle-shape strands.
Heat the oil in a pan over medium heat; cook the zucchini for 1 minute or so, stirring continuously. Pour in the water and cook 6 more minutes. Season with salt and cayenne pepper to taste.
Then, pulse all the parmesan ingredients in your food processor until you reach a Parmesan cheese consistency.
Top the cooked zoodles with the cashew parmesan and enjoy!

# 323. Summer Salad with Sunflower Seed Dressing

**(Ready in about 3 hours 15 minutes | Servings 4)**

**Per serving: 208 Calories; 15.6g Fat; 6.2g Carbs; 7.6g Protein;**

### INGREDIENTS

**For Sunflower Seed Dressing:**
1 cup sunflower seeds, raw and hulled
2 cups water
2 tablespoons scallions, chopped
1 garlic clove, chopped
1 lime, freshly squeezed

Salt and black pepper, to taste
1/2 teaspoon red pepper flakes
crushed
1/4 teaspoon rosemary, minced
2 tablespoons coconut milk

**For the salad:**
1 head fresh lettuce, separated into
leaves
3 tomatoes, diced
3 cucumbers, sliced
2 tablespoons Kalamata olives, pitted

### DIRECTIONS

Soak the sunflower seeds in water for at least 3 hours. Drain the sunflower seeds; transfer them to your blender and add the remaining ingredients for the dressing.
Puree until creamy, smooth and uniform.
Put all the salad ingredients into four serving bowls. Toss with the dressing and serve immediately. Bon appétit!

# 324. Rainbow Vegan Soup

**(Ready in about 25 minutes | Servings 6)**

**Per serving: 142 Calories; 11.4g Fat; 5.6g Carbs; 2.9g Protein;**

## INGREDIENTS

2 teaspoons olive oil
1 shallot, chopped
2 cloves garlic, minced
1 celery stalk, chopped
1 zucchini, chopped
1 carrot, sliced
1 cup kale, torn into pieces
1 cup mustard greens, torn into pieces
Sea salt and ground black pepper, to taste

2 thyme sprigs, chopped
1 rosemary sprig, chopped
2 bay leaves
6 cups vegetable stock
2 ripe tomatoes, chopped
1 cup almond milk, unflavored
1 tablespoon white miso paste
1/2 cup watercress

## DIRECTIONS

Heat the olive oil in a large pot that is preheated over a moderately high heat. Now, sauté the shallots, garlic, celery, zucchini, and carrots until they're softened.

Now, add the kale, mustard greens, salt, ground black pepper, thyme, rosemary, bay leaves, vegetable stock and tomatoes.

Reduce the heat to simmer. Let it simmer another 15 minutes, leaving the lid slightly ajar.

After that, add the almond milk, white miso paste, and watercress. Cook an additional 5 minutes, stirring periodically. Bon appétit!

# 325. Morning Protein Smoothie

**(Ready in about 5 minutes | Servings 4)**

**Per serving: 247 Calories; 21.7g Fat; 4.9g Carbs; 2.6g Protein;**

## INGREDIENTS

1/2 cup water
1 ½ cups almond milk
1 banana, peeled and sliced
1/3 cup frozen cherries

1/3 cup fresh blueberries
1/4 teaspoon vanilla extract
1 tablespoon vegan protein powder, zero carbs

## DIRECTIONS

Mix all ingredients in your blender or a smoothie maker until creamy and uniform.
Serve in individual glasses and enjoy!

# 326. African-Style Carrot Salad

**(Ready in about 10 minutes | Servings 4)**

**Per serving: 196 Calories; 17.2g Fat; 6g Carbs; 1.2g Protein;**

## INGREDIENTS

1 pound carrots, coarsely shredded
1/4 cup fresh cilantro, chopped
For the Vinaigrette:
3 garlic cloves, smashed
Sea salt and ground black pepper, to taste

1/3 cup extra-virgin olive oil
1 lime, freshly squeezed
2 tablespoons balsamic vinegar
1/2 teaspoon ground cumin
1/2 teaspoon harissa

## DIRECTIONS

Place the shredded carrots and fresh, chopped cilantro in a salad bowl.
Combine all ingredients for the vinaigrette; mix until everything is well incorporated.
Add the vinaigrette to the carrot salad and toss to coat well. Bon appétit!

## 327. Roasted Cabbage with Sesame

**(Ready in about 45 minutes | Servings 6)**

**Per serving: 186 Calories; 17g Fat; 5.3g Carbs; 2.1g Protein;**

### INGREDIENTS

Nonstick cooking spray
2 pounds green cabbage, cut into wedges
1/4 cup olive oil

Coarsely salt and freshly ground black pepper, to taste
1 teaspoon sesame seeds
2 tablespoons fresh chives, chopped

### DIRECTIONS

Begin by preheating your oven to 390 degrees F. Brush a rimmed baking sheet with nonstick cooking spray.
Add the cabbage wedges to the baking sheet. Toss with the olive oil, salt, black pepper and sesame seeds.
Roast for 40 to 45 minutes, until the cabbage is softened. Serve garnished with freshly chopped chives. Bon appétit!

## 328. Winter Mushroom Stew

**(Ready in about 50 minutes | Servings 4)**

**Per serving: 65 Calories; 2.7g Fat; 6g Carbs; 2.7g Protein;**

### INGREDIENTS

2 teaspoons olive oil
1 yellow onion, chopped
1 garlic clove, finely minced
1/2 cup celery, chopped
1/2 cup carrot, chopped
1 green bell pepper, chopped
1 jalapeno pepper, chopped
2 ½ cups Chanterelle mushrooms, thinly sliced
1 ½ cups vegetable stock

2 ripe tomatoes, chopped
2 thyme sprigs, chopped
1 rosemary sprig, chopped
2 bay leaves
1/2 teaspoon salt
1/4 teaspoon ground black pepper, or more to taste
1/4 teaspoon grated nutmeg
2 tablespoons apple cider vinegar

### DIRECTIONS

Heat the oil in a pot that is preheated over a moderately high heat. Now, sauté the onions and garlic until tender and fragrant.
Stir in the celery, carrots, pepper, and mushrooms. Cook for 12 minutes more, stirring periodically; add a splash of vegetable stock to prevent sticking.
Add the remaining ingredients, except for the apple cider vinegar.
Turn the heat to medium-low; let it simmer for 25 to 35 minutes or until everything is thoroughly cooked.
Ladle into individual bowls, drizzle each serving with the apple cider vinegar and eat warm.

## 329. Garlicky Savoy Cabbage

**(Ready in about 25 minutes | Servings 4)**

**Per serving: 118 Calories; 7g Fat; 3.4g Carbs; 2.9g Protein;**

### INGREDIENTS

2 pounds Savoy cabbage, torn into pieces
2 tablespoons almond oil
1 teaspoon garlic, minced

1/2 teaspoon dried basil
1/2 teaspoon red pepper flakes, crushed
Salt and ground black pepper, to the taste

### DIRECTIONS

Cook the Savoy cabbage in a pot of a lightly salted water approximately 20 minutes over a moderate heat. Drain and reserve.
Now, heat the oil in a sauté pan over medium-high heat. Now, cook the garlic until just aromatic.
Add the reserved Savoy cabbage, basil, red pepper, salt and black pepper; stir until everything is heated through.
Taste, adjust the seasonings and serve warm over cauliflower rice.

# 330. Voodles with Avocado Sauce

**(Ready in about 15 minutes | Servings 4)**

**Per serving: 233 Calories; 20.2g Fat; 6g Carbs; 1.9g Protein;**

## INGREDIENTS

1/2 pound carrots
1/2 pound bell peppers
1 tablespoon olive oil
1 avocado, peeled and pitted
1 lemon, juiced and zested

2 tablespoons sesame oil
2 tablespoons cilantro, chopped
1 shallot, chopped
1 jalapeno pepper, deveined and minced
Salt and black pepper, to taste

## DIRECTIONS

Spiralize the carrots and bell peppers by using a spiralizer or a julienne peeler.
Heat the olive oil in a wok or a large nonstick skillet. Sauté the carrots and peppers in hot olive oil for about 8 minutes.
Then, mix all remaining ingredients until the creamy. Pour the avocado sauce over the voodles and serve immediately.

# 331. Creamy Cauliflower Soup

**(Ready in about 20 minutes | Servings 4)**

**Per serving: 94 Calories; 7.2g Fat; 7g Carbs; 2.7g Protein;**

## INGREDIENTS

4 cups water
2 heads of cauliflower, broken into florets
1 ½ tablespoons vegetable bouillon granules
1/4 teaspoon ground bay leaves

1/4 teaspoon ground cloves
2 tablespoons extra-virgin olive oil
1/2 teaspoon red pepper flakes

## DIRECTIONS

In a heavy-bottomed pot, bring the water to a boil over a moderately high heat.
Stir in the cauliflower florets; cook for 10 minutes.
Add the bouillon granules, ground bay leaves, and ground cloves. Now, reduce the heat to medium-low; continue to cook for 5 minutes longer.
Puree this mixture by using a food processor or an immersion blender.
Divide among four soup bowl; drizzle each serving with olive oil and sprinkle with red pepper. Eat warm.

# 332. Ethiopian Stuffed Peppers with Cauliflower Rice

**(Ready in about 40 minutes | Servings 4)**

**Per serving: 77 Calories; 4.8g Fat; 5.4g Carbs; 1.6g Protein;**

## INGREDIENTS

1 small head cauliflower
4 bell peppers
1 ½ tablespoons oil
1 onion, chopped
1 garlic cloves, minced

1 teaspoon chipotle powder
1 teaspoon Berbere
2 ripe tomatoes, pureed
Sea salt and pepper, to taste

## DIRECTIONS

To make the cauliflower rice, grate the cauliflower into the size of rice. Place on a kitchen towel to soak up any excess moisture.
Next, preheat your oven to 360 degrees F. Lightly grease a casserole dish.
Cut off the top of the bell peppers. Now, discard the seeds and core.
Roast the peppers in a parchment lined baking pan for 18 minutes until the skin is slightly browned.
In the meantime, heat the oil over medium-high heat. Sauté the onion and garlic until tender and fragrant.
Add the cauliflower rice, chipotle powder, and Berbere spice. Cook until the cauliflower rice is tender, about 6 minutes.
Divide the cauliflower mixture among the bell peppers. Place in the casserole dish.
Mix the tomatoes, salt, and pepper. Pour the tomato mixture over the peppers. Bake about 10 minutes, depending on the desired tenderness. Serve immediately.

# 333. Cream of Almond and Cauliflower Soup

**(Ready in about 25 minutes | Servings 4)**

**Per serving: 114 Calories; 6.5g Fat; 6.4g Carbs; 3.8g Protein;**

## INGREDIENTS

1 tablespoon almond oil
1 cup shallots, chopped
1 celery with leaves, chopped
2 cloves garlic, minced
1 head cauliflower, broken into florets

4 cups water
Salt and white pepper, to taste
1/4 cup ground almonds
1 tablespoon fresh parsley, chopped

## DIRECTIONS

Heat the oil in a stockpot that is preheated over a moderate heat. Now, sauté the shallots, celery and garlic until tender, about 6 minutes.
Add the cauliflower, water, salt, and white pepper. Add the ground almonds.
Bring to a boil; then, reduce the heat to low; continue to simmer for about 17 minutes.
Next, puree the soup with an immersion blender. Serve garnished with fresh parsley. Bon appétit!

# 334. Vegan Tofu Skillet

**(Ready in about 25 minutes | Servings 4)**

**Per serving: 128 Calories; 8.3g Fat; 6.5g Carbs; 5.1g Protein;**

## INGREDIENTS

2 tablespoons olive oil
1 (14-ounce) block tofu, pressed and cubed
1 celery stalk, chopped
1 bunch scallions, chopped
1 teaspoon cayenne pepper
1 teaspoon garlic powder

2 tablespoons Worcestershire sauce
Salt and black pepper, to taste
1 pound Brussels sprouts, trimmed and quartered
1/2 teaspoon turmeric powder
1/2 teaspoon dried sill weed
1/4 teaspoon dried basil

## DIRECTIONS

Heat 1 tablespoon of olive oil in a large-sized skillet over a moderately high flame. Add the tofu cubes and cook, gently stirring, for 8 minutes.
Now, add the celery and scallions; cook until they are softened, about 5 minutes
Add the cayenne pepper, garlic powder, Worcestershire sauce, salt, and pepper; continue to cook for 3 more minutes; reserve.
Heat the remaining 1 tablespoon of oil in the same pan. Cook the Brussels sprouts along with the remaining seasonings for 4 minutes.
Add the tofu mixture to Brussels sprouts and serve warm. Enjoy!

# 335. Chocolate and Blackberry Smoothie

**(Ready in about 5 minutes | Servings 2)**

**Per serving: 103 Calories; 5.9g Fat; 6.1g Carbs; 4.1g Protein;**

## INGREDIENTS

1 cup blackberries
1 cup water
1 tablespoon chia seeds
1 tablespoon cocoa

1/4 teaspoon ground nutmeg
1 tablespoon peanut butter
Liquid Stevia, to taste

## DIRECTIONS

Add all ingredients to your blender or a food processor.
Mix until creamy and uniform. Pour into two tall glasses and serve immediately. Enjoy!

# 336. Rich Breakfast Granola

**(Ready in about 1 hour | Servings 8)**

**Per serving: 262 Calories; 24.3g Fat; 5.2g Carbs; 5.1g Protein;**

## INGREDIENTS

2 tablespoons coconut oil
1/3 cup coconut flakes
1 ½ cups coconut milk
2 tablespoons sugar
1/8 teaspoon Himalayan salt
1 teaspoon orange zest
1/8 teaspoon nutmeg, freshly grated

1/2 teaspoon ground cinnamon
1/2 cup walnuts, chopped
1/2 cup almonds, slivered
2 tablespoons pepitas
2 tablespoons sunflower seeds
1/4 cup flax seed

## DIRECTIONS

Warm the coconut oil in a deep pan that is preheated over a moderately high flame. Toast the coconut flakes for 1 to 2 minutes.
Add the remaining ingredients; stir to combine.
Preheat your oven to 300 degrees F. Spread the mixture out in an even layer onto a parchment lined baking sheet.
Bake for 1 hour, gently tossing every 15 minutes. Serve with some extra coconut milk. Bon appétit!

# 337. Nutty and Yummy Cauliflower Salad

**(Ready in about 15 minutes + chilling time | Servings 4)**

**Per serving: 281 Calories; 26.8g Fat; 5.6g Carbs; 4.2g Protein;**

## INGREDIENTS

1 head fresh cauliflower, cut into florets
1 cup spring onions, chopped
4 ounces bottled roasted peppers, chopped
1/4 cup extra-virgin olive oil
1 tablespoon wine vinegar

1 teaspoon yellow mustard
Coarse salt and black pepper, to your liking
1/2 cup green olives, pitted and chopped
1/2 cup pecans, coarsely chopped

## DIRECTIONS

Steam the cauliflower florets for 4 to 6 minutes; set aside to cool.
In a salad bowl, place the spring onions and roasted peppers.
In a mixing dish, whisk the olive oil, vinegar, mustard, salt and pepper. Drizzle over the veggies in the salad bowl.
Now, add the reserved cauliflower and toss to combine well. Scatter green olives and pecans over the top and serve.

# 338. Overnight "Oats" with Strawberries

**(Ready in about 5 minutes + chilling time | Servings 4)**

**Per serving: 176 Calories; 12.7g Fat; 6g Carbs; 9.7g Protein;**

## INGREDIENTS

1/2 cup water
1/2 cup unsweetened almond milk
3/4 cup hemp hearts
6 drops of liquid stevia

1/4 teaspoon ground cloves
1/4 teaspoon ground cinnamon
1 cup strawberries, halved

## DIRECTIONS

Combine all ingredients, except for the strawberries, in an airtight container.
Cover and place in your refrigerator overnight.
In the morning, top with fresh strawberries and serve immediately.

# 339. Coconut and Hazelnut "Cereals"

**(Ready in about 10 minutes | Servings 4)**

**Per serving: 279 Calories; 23.6g Fat; 5.9g Carbs; 7.2g Protein;**

## INGREDIENTS

2 tablespoons coconut oil
1/3 cup coconut shreds
2 ½ cups coconut milk, full-fat
1/2 cup water
2 tablespoons confectioners' erythritol

1/8 teaspoon salt
1/2 teaspoon vanilla paste
1/2 cup flax seed
16 hazelnuts, roughly chopped

## DIRECTIONS

Melt the coconut oil in a pan over a moderate heat. Then, add the coconut shreds, coconut milk, water, confectioners' erythritol, salt, vanilla paste, and flax seed.
Simmer for 5 minutes, stirring periodically. Allow it to cool down slightly.
Then, ladle into four individual bowls. Serve topped with chopped hazelnuts. Bon appétit!

# 340. The Best Guacamole Ever

**(Ready in about 10 minutes + chilling time | Servings 8)**

**Per serving: 112 Calories; 9.9g Fat; 6.5g Carbs; 1.3g Protein;**

## INGREDIENTS

2 avocados, peeled, pitted, and mashed
2 tablespoons fresh lime juice
Sea salt and ground black pepper, to taste
1/2 teaspoon cumin, ground
1 yellow onion, chopped

2 tablespoons coriander leaves, chopped
1 cup fresh tomatoes, chopped
2 garlic cloves, minced
1 red chili, deseeded and finely chopped

## DIRECTIONS

In a bowl, thoroughly combine the avocados, lime juice, salt and black pepper.
Stir in the onion, cilantro, tomatoes, and garlic; sprinkle with paprika.
Keep in your refrigerator until ready to serve. Bon appétit!

# 341. Rich and Easy Granola

**(Ready in about 1 hour | Servings 6)**

**Per serving: 449 Calories; 44.9g Fat; 6.9g Carbs; 9.3g Protein;**

## INGREDIENTS

1/2 cup pecans, chopped
1 cup walnuts, chopped
1/3 cup flax meal
1/3 cup coconut milk
1/3 cup sesame seeds
1/3 cup pumpkin seeds
8 drops stevia

1/3 cup coconut oil, melted
1 ½ teaspoons vanilla paste
1 teaspoon ground cloves
1 teaspoon freshly grated nutmeg
1 teaspoon orange zest
1/3 cup water

## DIRECTIONS

Begin by preheating your oven to 300 degrees F. Line a baking sheet with parchment paper.
Mix all ingredients until well combined. Now, spread this mixture out in an even layer onto the prepared baking sheet.
Bake about 55 minutes, stirring every 15 minutes. Allow it to cool down at room temperature.
Afterwards, transfer to an airtight container or serve immediately. Bon appétit!

# 342. Smoked Tofu with Asian Tomato Sauce

**(Ready in about 20 minutes | Servings 4)**

**Per serving: 336 Calories; 22.2g Fat; 5.8g Carbs; 27.6g Protein;**

### INGREDIENTS

10 ounces smoked tofu, pressed and drained
2 tablespoons olive oil
1 cup leeks, chopped
1 teaspoon garlic, minced
1/2 cup vegetable broth
1/2 teaspoon turmeric powder
Sea salt and ground black pepper, to taste

For the Sauce:
1/2 tablespoon olive oil
1 cup tomato sauce
2 tablespoons red wine
1 teaspoon fresh rosemary, chopped
1 teaspoon Asian chili garlic sauce

### DIRECTIONS

Pat dry the tofu and cut it into 1-inch cubes. Heat 2 tablespoons of olive oil in a frying pan over medium heat.
Then, fry the tofu cubes until they are slightly browned on all sides. Now, add the leeks, garlic, broth, turmeric powder, salt and pepper. Cook until almost all liquid has evaporated.
Meanwhile, make the sauce. Heat 1/2 tablespoon of olive oil in a pan over a medium heat. Add the tomato sauce and cook until heated through.
Add the remaining ingredients and simmer over a medium-low heat approximately 10 minutes. Serve with the prepared tofu cubes. Enjoy!

# 343. Chia Breakfast Pudding with Plums

**(Ready in about 5 minutes + prep time | Servings 3)**

**Per serving: 153 Calories; 8g Fat; 6.7g Carbs; 6.7g Protein;**

### INGREDIENTS

2 cups almond milk, unsweetened
1/2 cup chia seeds
1/2 teaspoon vanilla extract
1/4 teaspoon cardamom

1/4 teaspoon ground cinnamon
A pinch of salt
2 teaspoons Swerve, powdered
8 plums, pitted and halved

### DIRECTIONS

Place all of the above ingredients, except for the Swerve and plums, in an airtight container.
Allow it to stand, covered, in your refrigerator overnight.
Sweeten with the powdered Swerve and serve well-chilled with fresh plums. Enjoy!

# 344. Sautéed Fennel with Basil-Tomato Sauce

**(Ready in about 20 minutes | Servings 4)**

**Per serving: 135 Calories; 13.6g Fat; 3g Carbs; 0.9g Protein;**

### INGREDIENTS

2 tablespoons olive oil
1 garlic clove, crushed
1 fennel, thinly sliced
1/4 cup vegetable stock
Sea salt and ground black pepper, to taste
For the Sauce:
2 tomatoes, halved

2 tablespoons extra-virgin olive oil
1/2 cup scallions, chopped
1 cloves garlic, minced
1 ancho chili, minced
1 bunch fresh basil, leaves picked
1 tablespoon fresh cilantro, roughly chopped
Sat and pepper, to taste

### DIRECTIONS

Heat the olive oil in a pan over a moderately high heat. Sauté the garlic for 1 to 2 minutes or until aromatic.
Throw the slices of fennel into the pan; add the vegetable stock and continue to cook until the fennel has softened. Season with salt and black pepper to taste. Heat off.
Brush the tomato halves with extra-virgin olive oil. Microwave for 15 minutes on HIGH; be sure to pour off any excess liquid.
Transfer the cooked tomatoes to a food processor; add the remaining ingredients for the sauce. Puree until your desired consistency is reached.
Serve with the sautéed fennel. Bon appétit!

## 345. Autumn Oven-Roasted Vegetables

**(Ready in about 45 minutes | Servings 4)**

**Per serving: 165 Calories; 14.3g Fat; 5.6g Carbs; 2.1g Protein;**

### INGREDIENTS

1 red bell pepper, deveined and sliced
1 green bell pepper, deveined and sliced
1 orange bell pepper, deveined and sliced
1/2 head of cauliflower, broken into large florets
2 zucchinis, cut into thick slices
2 medium-sized leeks, quartered
4 garlic cloves, halved

2 thyme sprigs, chopped
1 teaspoon dried sage, crushed
4 tablespoons olive oil
4 tablespoons tomato puree
1 teaspoon mixed whole peppercorns
Sea salt and cayenne pepper, to taste

### DIRECTIONS

Preheat your oven to 425 degrees F. Sprits a rimmed baking sheet with nonstick cooking spray.
Toss all of the above vegetables with the seasonings, oil and apple cider vinegar.
Roast about 40 minutes. Flip the vegetables halfway through the cook time. Bon appétit!

## 346. Creamed Eggplant and Cashew Soup

**(Ready in about 1 hour 20 minutes | Servings 4)**

**Per serving: 159 Calories; 9.4g Fat; 7.1g Carbs; 4.2g Protein;**

### INGREDIENTS

1 pound eggplant, cut it in half.
2 ripe tomatoes, chopped
2 shallots, chopped
2 garlic cloves, peeled
1 tablespoon olive oil
1/2 teaspoon dried oregano

1/2 teaspoon dried basil
1/2 teaspoon dried marjoram
3 cups water
3 vegan bouillon cubes
1/3 cup raw cashews, soaked
Salt and pepper, to taste

### DIRECTIONS

Start by preheating your oven to 390 degrees F.
Arrange the eggplant on a parchment lined baking sheet. Drizzle olive oil over the eggplant.
Roast about 35 to 40 minutes or until tender. Scoop the eggplant from the skin and transfer to a pot.
Add the remaining ingredient, except for the cashews. Let it simmer, covered, for 40 minutes. Puree the soup with a hand blender.
Drain your cashews and blend them with 1 cup of water in a blender until smooth. Add the cashew cream to the soup; stir well and serve immediately.

## 347. Chocolate and Butternut Squash Smoothie

**(Ready in about 5 minutes | Servings 2)**

**Per serving: 71 Calories; 2.3g Fat; 4.1g Carbs; 4.3g Protein;**

### INGREDIENTS

2 ½ cups almond milk
1/2 cup baby spinach
2 tablespoons cocoa powder
1/2 cup butternut squash, roasted

1/2 teaspoon ground cinnamon
A pinch of grated nutmeg
A pinch of salt

### DIRECTIONS

Mix all ingredients in a blender or a food processor.
Serve well-chilled in tall glasses. Enjoy!

# 348. Raspberry and Peanut Butter Smoothie

**(Ready in about 5 minutes | Servings 1)**

**Per serving: 114 Calories; 8.2g Fat; 5.9g Carbs; 4.2g Protein;**

## INGREDIENTS

1/3 cup raspberries

1/2 cup baby spinach leaves

3/4 cup almond milk, unsweetened

1 tablespoon peanut butter

1 teaspoon Swerve

## DIRECTIONS

Place all ingredients in your blender and puree until creamy, uniform and smooth.

Pour into a tall glass. Serve well-chilled.

# 349. Cremini Mushroom and Broccoli Delight

**(Ready in about 30 minutes | Servings 4)**

**Per serving: 113 Calories; 6.7g Fat; 6.6g Carbs; 5g Protein;**

## INGREDIENTS

Nonstick cooking spray

1 head broccoli, cut into florets

8 ounces cremini mushrooms, halved

2 garlic cloves, smashed

2 ripe tomatoes, pureed

1/4 cup vegan butter, melted

1 teaspoon hot paprika paste

1/4 teaspoon marjoram

1/2 teaspoon curry powder

Coarse salt and black pepper, to taste

## DIRECTIONS

Begin by preheating your oven to 390 degrees F. Brush a baking dish with a nonstick cooking oil.

Next, arrange the broccoli and mushrooms in the baking dish. Scatter the smashed garlic around the vegetables. Add the pureed tomatoes.

Then, drizzle with the melted butter and add the hot paprika paste, marjoram, curry, salt, and black pepper.

Roast for 25 minutes, turning your baking dish once. Serve with a fresh salad of choice. Bon appétit!

# 350. Crunchy-Topped Vegetable Bake

**(Ready in about 40 minutes | Servings 4)**

**Per serving: 242 Calories; 16.3g Fat; 6.7g Carbs; 16.3g Protein;**

## INGREDIENTS

2 tablespoons olive oil

1 cup shallots, chopped

1 celery, chopped

2 carrots, grated

1/2 pound Brussels sprouts, quartered

1 cup roasted vegetable broth

1 teaspoon turmeric

Sea salt and ground black pepper, to taste

1 teaspoon paprika powder

1/2 teaspoon liquid smoke

1 cup vegan parmesan

2 tablespoons fresh chives, roughly chopped

## DIRECTIONS

Start by preheating your oven to 360 degrees F. Brush a baking dish with olive oil.

In a heavy-bottomed skillet, heat the olive oil over a moderately high heat. Now, sweat the shallots until they have softened.

Add the celery, carrots and Brussels sprouts. Cook an additional 4 minutes or until just tender. Transfer the vegetable mixture to the baking dish.

Mix the roasted vegetable broth with the turmeric, salt, black pepper, paprika, and liquid smoke. Pour this mixture over the vegetables.

Top with the vegan parmesan cheese and bake approximately 30 minutes. Serve garnished with fresh chives.

# 351. Artichoke and Tofu Stir Fry

**(Ready in about 30 minutes | Servings 4)**

**Per serving: 138 Calories; 8.9g Fat; 6.8g Carbs; 6.4g Protein;**

## INGREDIENTS

1 pound whole baby artichokes, cut off stems and tough outer leaves

2 tablespoons olive oil

2 blocks tofu, pressed and cubed

2 garlic cloves, minced

1 teaspoon Cajun spice mix

1 teaspoon deli mustard

1 bell pepper, chopped

1/4 cup vegetable broth

Salt and pepper, to your liking

## DIRECTIONS

Cook the artichokes in a large saucepan of lightly salted water for 15 minutes or until they're tender; drain.

Heat the olive oil in a wok that is preheated over medium-high heat; add the tofu cubes and cook about 6 minutes, gently stirring.

Add the garlic and cook until aromatic 30 seconds or so.

Add the remaining ingredients, including the reserved artichokes, and continue to cook 4 more minutes or until heated through. Serve warm on individual plates. Bon appétit!

# EGGS & DAIRY

## 352. Genoa Salami and Vegetable Frittata

**(Ready in about 25 minutes | Servings 4)**

**Per serving: 310 Calories; 26.2g Fat; 3.9g Carbs; 15.4g Protein;**

### INGREDIENTS

1/2 stick butter, at room temperature
1/2 cup scallions, chopped
2 garlic cloves, minced
1 serrano pepper, chopped
1 carrot, chopped

8 Genoa salami slices
8 eggs, whisked
Salt and black pepper, to taste
1/2 teaspoon dried dill weed

### DIRECTIONS

Melt the butter in a pan that is preheated over a moderately high heat. Now, sauté the scallions for 4 minutes, stirring periodically.
Add the garlic and cook for 1 minute or until it is fragrant. Add the serrano pepper and carrot. Cook an additional 4 minutes.
Transfer the mixture to a baking pan that is lightly greased with a nonstick cooking spray. Top with the salami slices.
Pour the eggs over the vegetables and salami; season with salt, pepper, and dill. Bake approximately 18 minutes. Eat warm with a dollop of full-fat Greek yogurt.

## 353. Two Cheese Omelet with Pimenta and Chervil

**(Ready in about 15 minutes | Servings 2)**

**Per serving: 490 Calories; 44.6g Fat; 4.5g Carbs; 22.7g Protein;**

### INGREDIENTS

2 tablespoons avocado oil
4 eggs, beaten
Salt and black pepper, to taste
1/4 teaspoon Pimenta, ground

1/4 teaspoon cayenne pepper
1/2 cup Asiago cheese
1/2 cup Boursin cheese
2 tablespoons fresh chervil, roughly chopped

### DIRECTIONS

Heat the oil in a pan that is preheated over a moderately high heat.
Season the eggs with salt, black pepper, ground Pimenta, and cayenne pepper. Add the seasoned eggs to the pan; tilt the pan to spread the eggs out evenly.
Once set, top your eggs with the cheese. Slice the omelet into two halves.
Serve garnished with fresh chervil. Bon appétit!

## 354. Asiago and Sausage Egg Cups

**(Ready in about 10 minutes | Servings 3)**

**Per serving: 423 Calories; 34.1g Fat; 2.2g Carbs; 26.5g Protein;**

### INGREDIENTS

1 teaspoon butter, melted
6 eggs, separated into yolks and whites
Coarse salt and freshly ground black pepper, to taste
1/2 teaspoon smoked paprika

1/2 teaspoon dried sage
1 cup Asiago cheese, freshly grated
3 beef sausages, chopped

### DIRECTIONS

Begin by preheating your oven to 420 degrees F. Lightly grease a muffin pan with melted butter.
Now, beat the egg whites with an electric mixer until stiff peaks form. Add the seasonings, cheese, and sausage.
Pour into muffin cups and bake for 4 minutes.
Now, add an egg to each cup. Bake for 4 more minutes. Leave the cups to cool down for a few minutes before serving time. Bon appétit!

## 355. Madras and Asparagus Cheesy Frittata

**(Ready in about 20 minutes | Servings 4)**

**Per serving: 248 Calories; 17.1g Fat; 6.2g Carbs; 17.6g Protein;**

### INGREDIENTS

2 tablespoons avocado oil
1/2 cup shallots, chopped
1 cup asparagus tips
8 eggs, beaten
1/2 teaspoon jalapeno pepper, minced

1 teaspoon Madras curry paste
Salt and red pepper, to your liking
3/4 cup Colby cheese, grated
1/4 cup fresh cilantro, to serve

### DIRECTIONS

In an ovenproof frying pan, heat the avocado oil over a medium flame. Now, sauté the shallots until they are caramelized.
Add the asparagus tips and cook until they're just tender.
Stir in the eggs, jalapeno pepper and Madras curry paste; season with salt and pepper. Now, cook until the eggs are nearly set.
Scatter the cheese over the top of your frittata. Cook in the preheated oven at 375 degrees F for about 12 minutes, until your frittata is set in the middle.
Cut into wedges and serve garnished with fresh cilantro.

## 356. Colby Cheese and Sausage Gofres

**(Ready in about 30 minutes | Servings 6)**

**Per serving: 316 Calories; 25g Fat; 1.5g Carbs; 20.2g Protein;**

### INGREDIENTS

6 eggs
6 tablespoons whole milk
1 teaspoon Spanish spice mix
Sea salt and ground black pepper, to taste

3 fully-cooked breakfast sausage links, chopped
1 cup Colby cheese, shredded
Nonstick cooking spray

### DIRECTIONS

In a mixing bowl, beat the eggs, milk, Spanish spice mix, salt, and black pepper.
Now, stir in the chopped sausage and shredded cheese.
Spritz a waffle iron with a nonstick cooking spray.
Cook the egg mixture about 5 minutes, until it is golden. Serve immediately with a homemade sugar-free tomato ketchup. Enjoy!

## 357. Mushroom, Cheese and Tomato Rolls

**(Ready in about 20 minutes | Servings 4)**

**Per serving: 172 Calories; 14g Fat; 3.4g Carbs; 9.5g Protein;**

### INGREDIENTS

**For the Wraps:**
6 eggs, separated into yolks and whites
2 tablespoons full-fat milk
1 tablespoon olive oil
Sea salt, to taste

**For the Filling:**
1 teaspoon olive oil
1 cup button mushrooms, chopped
Salt and black pepper, to taste
1/2 teaspoon cayenne pepper
6-8 fresh lettuce leaves
4 slices of Swiss cheese
2 small-sized Roma tomatoes, thinly sliced

### DIRECTIONS

Thoroughly combine all ingredients for the wraps.
Preheat a frying pan. Pour 1/4 of the mixture into the pan; cook over medium-low heat until thoroughly heated, 4 minutes per side.
Repeat three more times and set your wraps aside, keeping them warm.
In another pan, heat 1 teaspoon of olive oil over a moderately high flame. Now, cook the mushrooms until they have softened, about 5 minutes; season with salt, black pepper and cayenne pepper.
Lay 1-2 lettuce leaves onto each wrap. Divide the mushrooms among the prepared wraps. Top with cheese and tomatoes. Enjoy!

# 358. Eggs with Crabmeat and Sour Cream Sauce

**(Ready in about 15 minutes | Servings 3)**

**Per serving: 334 Calories; 26.2g Fat; 4.4g Carbs; 21.1g Protein;**

## INGREDIENTS

1 tablespoon olive oil
6 eggs, whisked
1 can crabmeat, flaked
1 teaspoon Montreal seasoning

**For the Sauce:**
3/4 cup sour cream
1/2 cup scallions, white and green parts, chopped
1/2 teaspoon garlic powder
Salt and black pepper to the taste
1/2 teaspoon fresh dill, chopped

## DIRECTIONS

Heat the olive oil in a sauté pan that is preheated over a moderate flame. Now, add the eggs and scramble them.
Add the crabmeat and cook, stirring frequently, until everything is thoroughly cooked; sprinkle with Montreal seasoning.
In a mixing dish, gently whisk all the sauce ingredients.
Divide the egg/crabmeat mixture among 4 plates; serve with the scallion/sour cream sauce on the side. Bon appétit!

# 359. Easy Breakfast Muffins

**(Ready in about 20 minutes | Servings 6)**

**Per serving: 81 Calories; 3.5g Fat; 6.7g Carbs; 5.5g Protein;**

## INGREDIENTS

3/4 cream cheese
1/4 cup Greek-style yogurt
3 eggs, beaten
2 tablespoons hazelnuts, ground

4 tablespoons erythritol
1/2 teaspoon vanilla essence
1/3 teaspoon ground cinnamon
1 apple, cored and sliced

## DIRECTIONS

Preheat your oven to 360 degrees F. Treat a muffin pan with a nonstick cooking spray.
Then, thoroughly combine all of the above ingredients. Divide the batter among the muffin cups.
Bake for 12 to 15 minutes. Transfer to a wire rack to cool slightly before serving. Serve garnished with apples and enjoy!

# 360. Dill Pickle, Cheese, and Cauliflower Balls

**(Ready in about 3 hours 15 minutes | Servings 6)**

**Per serving: 407 Calories; 26.8g Fat; 5.8g Carbs; 33.4g Protein;**

## INGREDIENTS

4 cups cauliflower rice
1/2 pound pancetta, chopped
6 ounces Cottage cheese, curds, 2% fat
6 ounces Ricotta cheese
1 cup Colby cheese
1/2 cup dill pickles, chopped and thoroughly squeezed
2 cloves garlic, crushed

1 cup grated Parmesan cheese
1/2 teaspoon caraway seeds
1/4 teaspoon dried dill weed
1/2 teaspoon shallot powder
Salt and black pepper, to taste
1 cup crushed pork rinds
Cooking oil

## DIRECTIONS

Thoroughly combine the cauliflower rice, pancetta, Cottage cheese, Ricotta cheese, Colby cheese, dill pickles, garlic, and 1/2 cup of grated Parmesan.
Stir until everything is well mixed and shape the cauliflower mixture into even balls. Now, transfer to your refrigerator for 3 hours.
Now, in a mixing bowl, thoroughly combine the remaining 1/2 cup of Parmesan cheese, caraway seeds, dill, shallot powder, salt, black pepper and crushed pork rinds.
Roll the cheese balls in Parmesan mixture until they are completely coated.
Then, heat about 1-inch of oil in a skillet over a moderately high flame. Fry the cheeseballs until they are golden brown on all sides.
Transfer to a paper towel to soak up the excess oil. Serve immediately or at room temperature. Enjoy!

# 361. Easy Two-Cheese Omelet

**(Ready in about 15 minutes | Servings 2)**

**Per serving: 307 Calories; 25g Fat; 2.5g Carbs; 18.5g Protein;**

## INGREDIENTS

4 eggs
Salt, to taste
1/4 teaspoon black peppercorns, crushed
1 tablespoon sesame oil

1/4 cup Blue Cheese, crumbled
1/4 cup Appenzeller cheese, shredded
1 tomato, thinly sliced

## DIRECTIONS

Whisk the eggs in a mixing bowl; season with salt and crushed peppercorns.
Heat the oil in a sauté pan over medium-low heat. Now, pour in the eggs and cook, using a spatula to swirl the eggs around the pan.
Cook the eggs until partially set. Top with the cheese; fold your omelet in half to enclose the filling.
Serve warm, garnished with the tomato slices. Bon appétit!

# 362. Spicy Cheese Crisps

**(Ready in about 10 minutes | Servings 4)**

**Per serving: 205 Calories; 15g Fat; 2.9g Carbs; 14.5g Protein;**

## INGREDIENTS

2 cups Swiss cheese, shredded
1/2 teaspoon garlic powder
1/4 teaspoon shallot powder

1 rosemary sprig, minced
1/2 teaspoon chili powder

## DIRECTIONS

Preheat an oven to 400 degrees F. Coat two baking sheets with parchment paper or Silpat mat.
Then, thoroughly combine the Swiss cheese with the seasonings.
Then, form 1 tablespoons of the cheese mixture into small mounds on the baking sheets.
Bake for 6 minutes and let them cool before serving. Enjoy!

# 363. Three-Cheese Party Balls

**(Ready in about 10 minutes | Servings 10)**

**Per serving: 105 Calories; 7.2g Fat; 2.8g Carbs; 7.5g Protein;**

## INGREDIENTS

1 ½ cups Ricotta cheese, at room temperature
3/4 cup Monterey Jack cheese, shredded
3/4 cup goat cheese, shredded
1/3 cup black olives, pitted and chopped

1 ½ tablespoons tomato paste
1 teaspoon cayenne pepper
Salt and freshly ground black pepper
20 fresh basil leaves

## DIRECTIONS

In a bowl, thoroughly combine the cheese, olives, tomato paste, cayenne pepper, salt and black pepper. Then, shape the mixture into 20 balls.
Place 1 basil leaf on top of each ball and secure with a toothpick. Serve and enjoy!

## 364. Sriracha Egg Salad with Scallions

**(Ready in about 15 minutes | Servings 8)**

**Per serving: 174 Calories; 13g Fat; 5.7g Carbs; 7.4g Protein;**

### INGREDIENTS

10 eggs
3/4 cup mayonnaise
1 teaspoon Sriracha
1 tablespoon whole grain mustard
1/2 cup scallions

1/2 stalk of celery, minced
1/2 teaspoon fresh lime juice
1/2 teaspoon sea salt
1/2 teaspoon ground black pepper, to taste
1 head Romaine lettuce, torn into pieces

### DIRECTIONS

Place the eggs in a pan and cover them with at least 1-inch of water; bring to a boil. Then, remove from the heat, cover, and let them sit approximately 10 minutes.
Chop the eggs coarsely and add them to a salad bowl.
Add the remaining ingredients and gently stir until everything is well incorporated. Place in the refrigerator until ready to serve. Bon appétit!

## 365. Easy Vegetarian Cheese Tacos

**(Ready in about 10 minutes | Servings 6)**

**Per serving: 370 Calories; 30g Fat; 4.9g Carbs; 19.5g Protein;**

### INGREDIENTS

1/2 pound Cheddar cheese, grated
1/2 pound Colby cheese, grated
1 teaspoon taco seasoning mix

1 ½ cups guacamole
1 cup sour cream
A small-sized head of lettuce

### DIRECTIONS

Combine both types of cheese with the taco seasoning mix.
Then, preheat a pan over a moderate flame.
Scatter the shredded cheese mixture all over the pan, covering the bottom. Fry for 4 to 5 minutes, turning once.
Top with the guacamole, sour cream and lettuce, roll them up and serve immediately. Bon appétit!

## 366. Sopressata and Blue Cheese Waffles

**(Ready in about 20 minutes | Servings 2)**

**Per serving: 470 Calories; 40.3g Fat; 2.9g Carbs; 24.4g Protein;**

### INGREDIENTS

2 tablespoons butter, melted
Salt and black pepper, to your liking
1/2 teaspoon parsley flakes
1/2 teaspoon chili pepper flakes

4 eggs
1/2 cup blue cheese, crumbled
4 slices Sopressata, chopped
2 tablespoons fresh chives, chopped

### DIRECTIONS

Combine all ingredients, except for the fresh chives, in a mixing bowl. Preheat your waffle iron and grease with cooking spray.
Add the omelet mixture and close the lid.
Fry about 5 minutes or until the desired consistency is reached. Repeat with the remaining batter. Serve garnished with fresh chives and eat warm.

## 367. Festive Eggs with Cheese and Aioli

**(Ready in about 20 minutes | Servings 8)**

**Per serving: 285 Calories; 22.5g Fat; 1.8g Carbs; 19.5g Protein;**

### INGREDIENTS

8 eggs, hard-boiled
2 cans tuna in brine, drained
1/2 cup Bibb lettuces, torn into pieces
1/2 cup red onions, finely chopped
1/2 goat cheese, crumbled
1/3 cup sour cream
1/2 tablespoon yellow mustard

For Aioli:
1 egg
2 medium cloves garlic, minced
1 tablespoon lemon juice
1/2 cup olive oil
Salt and black pepper, to taste

### DIRECTIONS

Peel and chop the eggs; transfer them to a serving bowl. Add the tuna, lettuce, onion, cheese, sour cream and yellow mustard.
To make the aioli, beat the egg, garlic, and lemon juice with an immersion blender. Add the oil, salt and pepper, and blend again until everything is well mixed.
Add the prepared aioli to the bowl and gently stir until everything is well incorporated.
Serve with pickles or bell peppers. Bon appétit!

## 368. Kid-Friendly Avocado Boats

**(Ready in about 20 minutes | Servings 4)**

**Per serving: 342 Calories; 30.4g Fat; 6.5g Carbs; 11.1g Protein;**

### INGREDIENTS

2 avocados, halved and pitted, skin on
2 ounces blue cheese, crumbled
2 ounces Colby cheese, grated

2 eggs, beaten
Salt and pepper, to taste
1 tablespoon fresh cilantro, chopped

### DIRECTIONS

Preheat your oven to 360 degrees F.
Arrange the avocado halves in an ovenproof dish.
In a mixing dish, combine both types of cheeses, eggs, salt and pepper. Divide the mixture among the avocado halves.
Bake for 15 to 17 minutes or until everything is thoroughly baked. Serve garnished with fresh cilantro. Enjoy!

## 369. Cheesy Cauliflower Fritters

**(Ready in about 35 minutes | Servings 6)**

**Per serving: 199 Calories; 13.8g Fat; 6.8g Carbs; 13g Protein;**

### INGREDIENTS

1 ½ tablespoons olive oil
1 shallot, chopped
1 garlic clove, minced
1 pound cauliflower, grated
6 tablespoons almond flour

1/2 cup Swiss cheese, shredded
1 cup parmesan cheese
2 eggs, beaten
1/2 teaspoon dried dill weed
Sea salt and ground black pepper, to taste

### DIRECTIONS

Heat the oil in a cast iron skillet over medium heat. Cook the shallots and garlic until they are aromatic.
Add the grated cauliflower and stir with a spatula for another minute or so; set aside to cool to room temperature so you can handle it easily.
Add the remaining ingredients; shape the mixture into balls, then, press each ball to form burger patties.
Bake in the preheated oven at 400 degrees F for 20 minutes. Flip and bake for another 10 minutes or until golden brown on top. Bon appétit!

# 370. Parmesan and Mushroom Burger Patties

**(Ready in about 20 minutes | Servings 4)**

**Per serving: 370 Calories; 30g Fat; 4.7g Carbs; 16.8g Protein;**

## INGREDIENTS

1/2 stick butter, softened
2 garlic cloves, minced
2 cups brown mushrooms, chopped
4 tablespoons blanched almond flour
4 tablespoons ground flax seeds
4 tablespoons hemp seeds

4 tablespoons sunflower seeds
1 tablespoon Cajun seasonings
1 teaspoon deli mustard
2 eggs, whisked
1/2 cup parmesan cheese

## DIRECTIONS

Melt 1 tablespoon of butter in a pan that is preheated over medium-high heat. Now, sauté the garlic and mushrooms until the mushrooms lose their water.

Add the almond flour, flax seeds, hemp seeds, sunflower seeds, Cajun seasonings, mustard, eggs and Parmesan cheese.

Form the mixture into 4 burger patties with lightly oiled hands.

Melt the remaining butter in a pan; fry your patties for 6 to 7 minutes. Then, carefully flip them over with a wide spatula. Cook another 6 minutes. Serve warm.

# 371. Tinga and Queso Manchego Frittata

**(Ready in about 25 minutes | Servings 6)**

**Per serving: 225 Calories; 17g Fat; 5.1g Carbs; 13.2g Protein;**

## INGREDIENTS

10 eggs
1 teaspoon seasoned salt
1/4 teaspoon ground black pepper, or more to taste
1/3 cup chive & onion cream cheese, room temperature
1 heaping tablespoon lard, room temperature
1 leek, chopped

1 teaspoon garlic paste
1 red bell pepper, chopped
1/2 green bell pepper, chopped
1 teaspoon Mexican Tinga paste
1 ½ cups baby spinach
1/2 cup Queso Manchego, shredded

## DIRECTIONS

Begin by preheating the oven to 370 degrees F.

Whisk the eggs with salt, pepper and cream cheese.

Melt the lard in an oven-safe skillet over a moderately high heat. Sauté the leeks until they are aromatic.

Now, stir in the garlic paste, bell peppers, and Tinga paste, and continue sautéing an additional 3 to 4 minute or until they have softened

Add the baby spinach and cook for 1 to 2 minutes more. Stir in the egg/cheese mixture. Shake your skillet to distribute the mixture evenly and transfer to the oven.

Bake about 8 minutes or until your frittata is golden brown on top but still slightly wobbly in the middle.

Top with the shredded Queso Manchego and bake an additional 3 minutes or until the cheese melts completely

Cut into 6 wedges and serve warm. Enjoy!

# 372. Two-Minute Eggs in a Mug

**(Ready in about 5 minutes | Servings 2)**

**Per serving: 197 Calories; 13.8g Fat; 2.7g Carbs; 15.7g Protein;**

## INGREDIENTS

4 eggs
1/4 cup full-fat milk
1/4 cup Asiago cheese, freshly grated
1 garlic clove, minced

1/4 teaspoon dried basil
1/4 teaspoon turmeric powder
Sea salt and red pepper flakes, to taste

## DIRECTIONS

In a mixing bowl, thoroughly combine the eggs, milk, cheese, garlic, salt and pepper.

Spritz 2 microwave-safe mugs with a nonstick spray. Pour in the egg mixture.

Now, microwave for 30 to 40 seconds. Stir with a spoon and microwave for 60 to 70 seconds more or until they're set.

## 373. Scrambled Eggs with Kale Pesto

**(Ready in about 15 minutes | Servings 4)**

**Per serving: 495 Calories; 45g Fat; 6.3g Carbs; 19.5g Protein;**

### INGREDIENTS

2 tablespoons ghee
8 eggs, well beaten
1/4 cup full-fat milk
Salt and ground black pepper, to your liking

**For the Kale Pesto:**
2 cups kale
1 cup parmesan cheese, grated
2 garlic cloves, minced
1/2 cup olive oil
2 tablespoons fresh lemon juice

### DIRECTIONS

Melt the ghee in a heavy-bottomed sauté pan over moderately high heat. Whisk the eggs with the milk, salt, and pepper.
Now, cook this egg mixture, gently stirring, until the eggs are set but still moist and tender.
Put all the ingredients for the pesto, except for the olive oil, in your food processor or blender.
Pulse until roughly chopped. With the machine running, slowly pour in the olive oil until you get the desired consistency.
Serve over the warm scrambled eggs. Bon appétit!

## 374. Spicy Sausage with Eggs

**(Ready in about 20 minutes | Servings 2)**

**Per serving: 462 Calories; 40.6g Fat; 7.1g Carbs; 16.9g Protein;**

### INGREDIENTS

2 tablespoons olive oil
1/2 cup leeks, chopped
1 teaspoon smashed garlic
1 teaspoon habanero pepper, deveined and minced
Salt and black pepper to the taste

6 ounces sausage, crumbled
4 eggs, whisked
1 thyme sprig, chopped
1/2 teaspoon dried marjoram, chopped
1/2 cup ripe olives, pitted and sliced

### DIRECTIONS

Heat the oil in a nonstick skillet over medium heat; now, sauté the leeks until they are just tender, about 4 minutes.
Add the garlic, habanero pepper, salt, black pepper, and sausage; cook, stirring frequently, for 8 minutes longer.
Now, pour in the eggs and sprinkle with thyme and marjoram; cook an additional 4 minutes, stirring with a spoon. Serve with sliced olives and enjoy!

## 375. Three-Cheese and Salami Stuffed Avocado

**(Ready in about 15 minutes | Servings 6)**

**Per serving: 308 Calories; 27g Fat; 6.4g Carbs; 8.8g Protein;**

### INGREDIENTS

3 avocados, cut into halves and pitted
1/3 cup Cottage cheese
1/3 cup Neufchatel cheese
1/3 cup Queso Fresco, crumbled
1 cup salami, chopped

1 teaspoon Dijon mustard
Salt and ground black pepper, to your liking
1/2 teaspoon paprika
1/4 teaspoon hot sauce

### DIRECTIONS

Scoop out the avocados and place the avocado flesh in a mixing bowl.
Add the remaining ingredients and stir until everything is well combined.
Divide the mixture between the avocado halves. Taste, adjust the seasonings and serve. Bon appétit!

## 376. Baked Cheese Balls Salad

**(Ready in about 20 minutes | Servings 6)**

**Per serving: 234 Calories; 16.7g Fat; 5.9g Carbs; 12.4g Protein;**

### INGREDIENTS

**For the Cheese Balls:**
3 eggs
1 cup goat cheese, crumbled
1/2 cup Parmesan, shredded
1 cup almond flour
1 tablespoon flax meal
1 teaspoon baking powder
Salt and ground black pepper, to taste

**For the Salad:**
1 head Romaine lettuce
1/2 cup cucumber, thinly sliced
2 small Roma tomatoes, seeded and chopped
1/2 cup red onion, thinly sliced
1/2 cup radishes, thinly sliced
1/3 cup mayonnaise
1 teaspoon brown mustard
1 teaspoon paprika
1 teaspoon oregano
Salt, to taste

### DIRECTIONS

Start by preheating your oven to 390 degrees F. Line a baking sheet with a piece of parchment paper.
In a mixing dish, thoroughly combine all ingredients for the cheese balls. Then, shape the mixture into balls.
Arrange the balls on the prepared baking sheet. Bake until crisp, approximately 10 minutes.
In a large-sized salad bowl, arrange the lettuce leaves. Now, add the cucumbers, tomatoes, red onion and radishes.
In a small mixing bowl, whisk the mayonnaise, mustard, paprika, oregano and salt to taste. Drizzle this mixture over the vegetables.
Top with the baked cheese balls and serve immediately.

## 377. Two-Cheese and Roasted Pepper Dip

**(Ready in about 35 minutes | Servings 10)**

**Per serving: 228 Calories; 17.2g Fat; 5.7g Carbs; 10.2g Protein;**

### INGREDIENTS

10 ounces mascarpone cheese, room temperature
1 cup mayonnaise
1 jar (17-ounce) roasted red peppers, drained and chopped

2 pickled poblano peppers, drained and finely chopped
1 ¼ cups Asiago cheese, grated
Salt and black pepper, to taste

### DIRECTIONS

Begin by preheating your oven to 360 degrees F. Spritz a baking dish with a nonstick cooking spray.
Thoroughly combine all ingredients and transfer to the prepared baking dish.
Bake for 25 to 35 minutes, turning the dish once or twice. Bon appétit!

## 378. Greek-Style Cheese Balls

**(Ready in about 5 minutes | Servings 6)**

**Per serving: 217 Calories; 18.7g Fat; 2.1g Carbs; 9.9g Protein;**

### INGREDIENTS

4 ounces pancetta, chopped
4 ounces Feta cheese, crumbled
1/4 cup aioli

1/2 cup green olives, pitted and chopped
1/2 teaspoon red pepper flakes
2 tablespoons parsley, finely chopped

### DIRECTIONS

Thoroughly combine the pancetta with the feta cheese and aioli in a mixing dish. Now, add the green olives, red pepper flakes and fresh parsley.
Taste and adjust the seasonings. Shape the mixture into 10 balls.
Serve right away or keep in your refrigerator up to 3 days. Bon appétit!

## 379. Egg Mug Muffins

**(Ready in about 5 minutes | Servings 2)**

**Per serving: 244 Calories; 17.5g Fat; 2.9g Carbs; 19.2g Protein;**

### INGREDIENTS

4 eggs
4 tablespoons milk
1/4 cup Asiago cheese, shredded

1/2 teaspoon cayenne pepper
Kosher salt and black pepper, to taste
2 tablespoons scallions, chopped

### DIRECTIONS

Thoroughly combine all of the above ingredients, except for the scallions.
Spritz two microwave-safe mugs with a nonstick cooking spray. Spoon the egg mixture into the mugs.
Place in the microwave and cook for 1 minute. Serve garnished with fresh scallions. Bon appétit!

## 380. Ham, Cheese and Eggs Balls

**(Ready in about 5 minutes | Servings 6)**

**Per serving: 156 Calories; 12.2g Fat; 1.6g Carbs; 9.7g Protein;**

### INGREDIENTS

6 ounces smoked ham, chopped
6 ounces Chive & onion cream cheese
A pinch of salt

1/4 teaspoon ground black pepper, or more to taste
1 ½ tablespoons fresh parsley, chopped
2 hard-boiled eggs, chopped

### DIRECTIONS

Mix all of the above ingredients until everything is well incorporated. Shape into 12 balls.
Arrange on a serving platter and serve well-chilled. Enjoy!

## 381. Colby and Tuna Stuffed Avocado

**(Ready in about 25 minutes | Servings 4)**

**Per serving: 286 Calories; 23.9g Fat; 6g Carbs; 11.2g Protein;**

### INGREDIENTS

2 large-sized avocados, halved and pitted
4 ounces Colby cheese, freshly grated
2 ounces canned tuna, flaked
2 tablespoons scallions, chopped

Salt and freshly ground black pepper, to taste
2 tablespoons fresh cilantro, chopped
1/2 cup radicchios, sliced

### DIRECTIONS

Begin by preheating your oven to 360 degrees F. Place the avocado halves in an ovenproof dish.
Now, thoroughly combine the Colby cheese, tuna, scallions, salt and pepper in a mixing bowl. Stuff the avocado halves with cheese/tuna mixture.
Divide the mixture among the avocado halves. Bake approximately 18 minutes and top with fresh cilantro. Garnish with radicchio and serve immediately. Bon appétit!

# 382. Cheese and Scallion Stuffed Tomatoes

## (Ready in about 45 minutes | Servings 5)

### Per serving: 306 Calories; 27.5g Fat; 4.4g Carbs; 11.3g Protein;

**INGREDIENTS**

Nonstick cooking spray
5 vine-ripened tomatoes
1 cup cream cheese, at room temperature

1 ½ cups Monterey-Jack cheese, shredded
1/4 cup sour cream
1 egg, whisked

1 clove garlic, minced
4 tablespoons fresh scallions, chopped
Salt and ground black pepper, to taste
2 teaspoons butter

**DIRECTIONS**

Preheat your oven to 360 degrees F. Lightly grease a rimmed baking sheet with a nonstick cooking spray.
Slice the tomatoes into halves horizontally and discard the hard cores; scoop out the pulp and seeds.
In a mixing bowl, thoroughly combine the cheese, sour cream, egg, garlic, scallions, salt, pepper, and butter.
Divide the filling between the tomatoes and bake in the preheated oven for 30 to 35 minutes. Allow them to cool on a wire rack for 5 minutes; serve with fresh rocket leaves. Bon appétit!

# 383. Cheese Sticks with Roasted Red Pepper Dip

## (Ready in about 40 minutes | Servings 8)

### Per serving: 200 Calories; 16.9g Fat; 3.7g Carbs; 9.4g Protein;

**INGREDIENTS**

2 (8-ounce) packages Monterey Jack cheese with jalapeno peppers
3/4 cup Parmigiano-Reggiano cheese, grated
2 tablespoons almond flour
1 tablespoon flax meal

1 teaspoon baking powder
Salt and red pepper flakes, to serve
1/3 teaspoon cumin powder
1/2 teaspoon dried oregano
1/3 teaspoon dried rosemary
2 eggs

**For Roasted Red Pepper Dip:**
1 cup cream cheese
1/3 cup Greek yogurt
3/4 cup jarred fire-roasted red peppers, drained and chopped
1 tablespoon Dijon mustard
1 chili pepper, deveined and minced
2 garlic cloves, chopped
Sea salt and pepper to taste

**DIRECTIONS**

Cut the cheese crosswise into sticks.
In a shallow bowl, combine the dry ingredients. In another bowl, whisk the eggs.
Dip each stick into the eggs, and then roll in the dry mixture. Place the cheese sticks on a wax paper-lined baking sheet; place in your freezer for about 30 minutes.
Deep fry the cheese sticks until the coating is golden brown and crisp about 5 minutes. Transfer to pepper towels to drain the excess oil.
Then, make the dipping sauce by mixing all ingredients for the roasted red pepper dip. Bon appétit!

# 384. Curried Pickled Eggs

## (Ready in about 20 minutes | Servings 5)

### Per serving: 145 Calories; 9g Fat; 2.8g Carbs; 11.4g Protein;

**INGREDIENTS**

10 eggs
1/2 cup onions, sliced
3 cardamom pods
1 tablespoon yellow curry powder
1 teaspoon yellow mustard seeds

2 clove garlic, sliced
1 cup cider vinegar
1 ¼ cups water
1 tablespoon salt

**DIRECTIONS**

Boil the eggs until hard-cooked; peel them and rinse under cold, running water. Add the peeled eggs to a large-sized jar.
Add all remaining ingredients to a pan that is preheated over a moderately high heat; bring to a rapid boil.
Now, turn the heat to medium-low; let it simmer for 6 minutes. Spoon this mixture into the jar.
Keep in your refrigerator for 2 to 3 weeks. Bon appétit!

## 385. Easy and Yummy Scotch Eggs

**(Ready in about 20 minutes | Servings 8)**

**Per serving: 247 Calories; 11.4g Fat; 0.6g Carbs; 33.7g Protein;**

### INGREDIENTS

8 eggs
1 ½ pounds ground beef
1/2 cup parmesan cheese, freshly grated
1 teaspoon granulated garlic

1/2 teaspoon shallot powder
1/2 teaspoon cayenne pepper
1 teaspoon dried rosemary, chopped
Salt and pepper to taste

### DIRECTIONS

Boil the eggs until hard-cooked; peel them and rinse under cold, running water. Set aside.
In a mixing bowl, thoroughly combine the other ingredients. Divide the meat mixture among 8 balls; flatten each ball and place a boiled egg on it.
Shape the meat mixture around the eggs by using your fingers.
Add the balls to a baking pan that is previously greased with a nonstick cooking spray.
Bake in the preheated oven, at 360 degrees F for 18 minutes, until crisp and golden. Bon appétit!

## 386. Traditional Egg Soup with Tofu

**(Ready in about 15 minutes | Servings 3)**

**Per serving: 153 Calories; 9.8g Fat; 2.7g Carbs; 15g Protein;**

### INGREDIENTS

2 cups homemade chicken stock
1 tablespoon tamari sauce
1 teaspoon coconut oil, softened
2 eggs, beaten
1/2 teaspoon turmeric powder

1-inch knob of ginger, grated
Salt and ground black ground, to taste
1/4 teaspoon paprika
1/2 pound extra-firm tofu, cubed

### DIRECTIONS

In a pan that is preheated over a moderately high heat, whisk the stock, tamari sauce and coconut oil; bring to a rolling boil.
Stir in the eggs, whisking constantly, until it is well incorporated.
Now, turn the heat to medium-low and season with the turmeric, ginger, salt, black pepper and paprika.
Add the tofu and let it simmer another 1 to 2 minutes
Ladle into individual soup bowls and eat warm. Bon appétit!

## 387. Zucchini Boats with Sausage and Eggs

**(Ready in about 35 minutes | Servings 3)**

**Per serving: 506 Calories; 41g Fat; 4.5g Carbs; 27.5g Protein;**

### INGREDIENTS

3 medium-sized zucchinis, cut into halves
1 tablespoon deli mustard
2 sausages, cooked and crumbled
6 eggs

Salt, to taste
1/4 teaspoon black pepper, or more to taste
1/4 teaspoon dried dill weed

### DIRECTIONS

Scoop the flesh from each zucchini halve to make the shells; place the zucchini boats on a baking pan.
Spread the mustard on the bottom of each zucchini halve. Divide the crumbled sausage among the zucchini boats.
Crack an egg in each zucchini halve, sprinkle with salt, pepper, and dill.
Bake in the preheated oven at 400 degrees F for 30 minutes or until zucchini boats are tender. Bon appétit!

# 388. Creamy Gruyère Egg Bites

**(Ready in about 20 minutes | Servings 5)**

**Per serving: 177 Calories; 12.7g Fat; 4.6g Carbs; 11.4g Protein;**

## INGREDIENTS

10 eggs

1/4 cup mayonnaise

1 tablespoon tomato paste

2 tablespoons celery, finely chopped

2 tablespoons carrot, finely chopped

2 tablespoons scallion, minced

2 tablespoons Gruyère cheese, grated

1/2 teaspoon paprika

Salt and black pepper, to taste

## DIRECTIONS

Place the eggs in a wide pot; cover with cold water by 1 inch. Bring to a rapid boil. Now, turn the heat to medium-low; let the eggs simmer for a further 10 minutes.

Peel the eggs and rinse them under running water.

Slice each egg in half lengthwise and remove the yolks. Thoroughly combine the yolks with the remaining ingredients.

Divide the mixture among the egg whites and arrange the deviled eggs on a nice serving platter. Bon appétit!

# 389. Classic Egg Salad

**(Ready in about 20 minutes | Servings 4)**

**Per serving: 284 Calories; 21.3g Fat; 6.8g Carbs; 16.7g Protein;**

## INGREDIENTS

8 eggs

1/3 cup mayonnaise

1 tablespoon minced shallot

1/2 teaspoon brown mustard

1 ½ teaspoons lime juice

Salt and black pepper, to taste

10 lettuce leaves

1/2 cup bacon crumbs

## DIRECTIONS

Place the eggs in a single layer in a pan; cover with 2 inches of water.

Bring to a boil over a high heat; now, reduce the heat and cook, covered, for 1 minute.

Remove from the heat and leave your eggs for 15 minutes; rinse. Peel and chop the eggs.

Transfer them to a mixing bowl along with the mayonnaise, shallots, mustard, lime juice, salt and black pepper.

Mound on fresh lettuce leaves; sprinkle with bacon crumbs and serve.

# 390. Mom's Pepper Jack Cheese Soup

**(Ready in about 20 minutes | Servings 4)**

**Per serving: 296 Calories; 14.1g Fat; 6.4g Carbs; 14.2g Protein;**

## INGREDIENTS

2 tablespoons ghee

1/2 cup scallions, chopped

1 celery stalk, chopped

1 jalapeno pepper, finely chopped

1 teaspoon garlic paste

1 ½ tablespoons flaxseed meal

2 cups water

1 ½ cups milk

6 ounces Pepper Jack cheese, shredded

Salt and black pepper, to taste

A pinch of paprika, to garnish

## DIRECTIONS

Warm the ghee in a deep pan over a moderately high heat.

Now, sauté the scallions, celery and jalapeno until they are softened and aromatic.

Add the garlic paste, flaxseed meal, water, and milk and reduce the heat to medium-low. Let it simmer, partially covered, 10 minutes more or until thoroughly cooked.

Afterwards, fold in the shredded cheese, heat off and stir until the cheese has melted and everything is homogenous. Season with salt and pepper to taste.

Taste and adjust the seasonings. Ladle into individual bowls, sprinkle with paprika and serve. Eat warm.

# 391. Alfredo, Kale and Cheese Dip

**(Ready in about 30 minutes | Servings 12)**

**Per serving: 154 Calories; 13g Fat; 3.3g Carbs; 6.2g Protein;**

## INGREDIENTS

2 tablespoons butter
6 ounces heavy cream
Salt and ground black pepper, to taste
2 egg yolks
2 cloves garlic, chopped

1 ½ cups kale, chopped
3/4 cup sour cream
1/2 cup Swiss cheese, grated
1 cup Cottage cheese, softened
1/2 cup smoked ham, roughly chopped

## DIRECTIONS

To make an Alfredo-style sauce, melt the butter in a pan over medium heat. Now, cook the heavy cream, stirring constantly. Add the salt and pepper; whisk in the egg yolks.
Turn the heat to medium-low; cook for a further 4 minutes, stirring continuously. Transfer to a casserole dish.
Add the remaining ingredients and stir to combine well.
Bake in the preheated oven at 360 degrees F, approximately 25 minutes. Bon appétit!

# 392. Italian Salami and Cheese Casserole

**(Ready in about 1 hour | Servings 4)**

**Per serving: 334 Calories; 23g Fat; 6.2g Carbs; 25.5g Protein;**

## INGREDIENTS

Nonstick cooking spray
8 eggs
Coarse salt, to taste
1 cup Mozzarella cheese, grated

1/2 cup Ricotta cheese
1 bell pepper, chopped
1 poblano pepper, deveined and chopped

1/2 teaspoon dried dill weed
1 teaspoon Dijon mustard
4 slices pepperoni, chopped
4 slices pancetta, chopped

## DIRECTIONS

Begin by preheating your oven to 360 degrees F. Generously grease a casserole dish with a nonstick cooking spray.
Beat the eggs, salt and cheese on medium-high speed until everything is well incorporated. Spoon the mixture into the casserole dish.
Add the remaining ingredients; gently stir with a spoon. Place a roasting pan with 6 cups of hot water in the middle of the preheated oven. Lower the casserole dish into the roasting pan.
Bake about 1 hour. Allow it to cool down for a couple of minutes before cutting it into squares. Serve warm and enjoy!

# 393. Panna Cotta with Roasted Cartos and Basil

**(Ready in about 40 minutes | Servings 8)**

**Per serving: 155 Calories; 12.7g Fat; 6.2g Carbs; 4.6g Protein;**

## INGREDIENTS

4 large carrots, sliced
1 tablespoon coconut oil, melted
1/4 cup fresh basil, chopped
1 cup heavy cream
1/2 cup creme fraiche
1 cup Ricotta cheese
2 teaspoons powdered unflavored gelatin

2-inch section of fresh rosemary stem, chopped
Celery salt, to taste
1/4 teaspoon onion flakes
1/2 teaspoon fennel seeds
1/2 teaspoon mixed peppercorns, crushed
1/2 teaspoon cayenne pepper

## DIRECTIONS

Drizzle the carrot slices with the melted coconut oil. Roast the carrots in the preheated oven approximately 30 minutes, stirring once.
Transfer the carrots to a blender. Pulse until creamy and smooth.
Meanwhile, heat a saucepan over low heat; cook the fresh basil with the cream for 4 minutes. Add the remaining ingredients and cook until completely melted, 4 to 6 minutes longer.
Fold in the pureed carrots and stir to combine well. Spoon mixture into 8 ramekins. Transfer to your refrigerator and let it sit overnight or until set.
Run a thin knife around the edge of each panna cotta; flip the ramekin onto serving plate. Bon appétit!

# 394. Stuffed Peppers with Cheese and Pork Rinds

**(Ready in about 45 minutes | Servings 4)**

**Per serving: 359 Calories; 29.7g Fat; 6.7g Carbs; 17.7g Protein;**

## INGREDIENTS

4 bell peppers
6 ounces cream cheese, room temperature
6 ounces blue cheese, crumbled
1/2 cup pork rinds, crushed
2 cloves garlic, smashed

1 ½ cups pureed tomatoes
1/2 teaspoon dried oregano
1 teaspoon dried basil
Salt and ground black pepper, to taste
1/2 teaspoon cayenne pepper

## DIRECTIONS

Parboil the peppers in salted water for 4 to 6 minutes.
Preheat the oven to 360 degrees F. Lightly grease the sides and bottom of a casserole dish with a nonstick cooking spray.
In a mixing bowl, thoroughly combine the cream cheese, blue cheese, pork rinds, and garlic.
Stuff the peppers and transfer to the prepared casserole dish.
Then, mix the pureed tomatoes with the oregano, basil, salt, black pepper and cayenne pepper. Pour the tomato mixture over the stuffed pepper; cover the dish with foil.
Bake for 40 minutes and serve warm. Bon appétit!

# 395. Flavored Asiago Cheese Chips

**(Ready in about 18 minutes | Servings 2)**

**Per serving: 100 Calories; 8g Fat; 0g Carbs; 7g Protein;**

## INGREDIENTS

3 cups Asiago cheese, freshly grated
1/3 teaspoon salt
1/2 teaspoon garlic powder

1/2 teaspoon cayenne pepper
½ teaspoon dried rosemary
1/3 teaspoon chili powder

## DIRECTIONS

Preheat your oven to 420 degrees F. Now, line a baking sheet with parchment paper.
Then, thoroughly combine the grated Asiago cheese with the spices.
Then, form 2 tablespoons of the cheese mixture into small mounds on the baking sheet.
Bake approximately 15 minutes; your chips will start to get hard as they cool.

# 396. Keto Mac and Cheese

**(Ready in about 15 minutes | Servings 4)**

**Per serving: 357 Calories; 32.5g Fat; 6.9g Carbs; 8.4g Protein;**

## INGREDIENTS

1 large-sized head cauliflower, broken into florets
2 tablespoons butter
Salt and pepper, to taste
1/2 cup milk
1/2 cup heavy whipping cream

1 cup cream cheese
1/2 teaspoon turmeric powder
1 teaspoon garlic paste
1/2 teaspoon onion flakes

## DIRECTIONS

Begin by preheating your oven to 450 degrees F. Brush a baking sheet with a nonstick cooking spray.
Toss the cauliflower florets with the melted butter, salt, and pepper. Place the cauliflower florets on the prepared baking sheet; roast about 13 minutes.
Heat the remaining ingredients in a heavy-bottomed saucepan, stirring frequently. Simmer over medium-low heat until cooked through.
Toss the cauliflower with the creamy cheese sauce and eat warm.

# 397. Vegetable and Cheeseburger Quiche

**(Ready in about 45 minutes | Servings 6)**

**Per serving: 310 Calories; 18.3g Fat; 3.8g Carbs; 30.7g Protein;**

## INGREDIENTS

1 pound ground beef
1 onion, chopped
1 garlic clove, chopped
1 bell pepper, chopped
1/2 teaspoon coarse salt
1/4 teaspoon black pepper, or more to taste

2 zucchinis, thinly sliced
2 tomatoes, thinly sliced
1/4 cup whipping cream
8 eggs
1/2 cup Cheddar cheese, grated

## DIRECTIONS

Preheat an oven to 360 degrees F. Brush a baking dish with a nonstick cooking spray.
Then, in a heavy-bottomed skillet, brown the ground beef along with the onion, garlic and bell pepper. Season with salt and pepper.
Spread the meat layer on the bottom of the baking dish. Layer the zucchini slices on top. Top with tomato slices.
After that, whisk the whipping cream, eggs and cheese in a mixing bowl. Spoon this creamy mixture on the top of the vegetables.
Bake for 40 to 45 minutes, until it is browned around the edges. Bon appétit!

# 398. French-Style Eggs with Appenzeller Cheese

**(Ready in about 20 minutes | Servings 5)**

**Per serving: 444 Calories; 35.3g Fat; 2.7g Carbs; 29.8g Protein;**

## INGREDIENTS

1 tablespoon olive oil
4 slices Jambon de Bayonne, chopped
1/2 cup scallions, chopped
1/2 cup broccoli, chopped
1 clove garlic, minced

1 teaspoon fines herbes
1/4 cup chicken broth
5 eggs
1 ½ cups Appenzeller cheese, shredded

## DIRECTIONS

Heat the oil in a nonstick frying pan; cook the Jambon de Bayonne about 4 minutes, until browned and crisp; set it aside.
In the same pan, cook the scallions in the pan drippings. Add the broccoli and garlic and continue to cook, stirring periodically, until they are softened. Add the fines herbes and chicken broth and cook an additional 6 minutes.
Now, make 5 holes in the vegetable mixture to reveal the bottom of your pan. Crack an egg into each hole.
Scatter the shredded cheese over the top and cook an additional 6 minutes. Remove from the heat and top with the reserved Jambon de Bayonne.

# 399. Two-Cheese and Walnut Logs

**(Ready in about 10 minutes + chilling time | Servings 15)**

**Per serving: 209 Calories; 18.9g Fat; 3.7g Carbs; 6.6g Protein;**

## INGREDIENTS

14 ounces cream cheese, at room temperature
14 ounces sharp American cheese
1/2 cup full-fat mayonnaise

1 (1-ounce) package ranch dressing mix
1 teaspoon lime juice
1/2 cup walnuts, finely chopped

## DIRECTIONS

Combine the cream cheese and sharp cheese with an electric mixer.
Stir in the mayonnaise, ranch dressing mix, and lime juice; mix well. Place in your refrigerator for 3 to 4 hours or until solid and firm.
When firm, shape the mixture into two logs; roll in walnuts. Serve well-chilled.

# 400. Omelet with Bacon and Blue Cheese

**(Ready in about 10 minutes | Servings 2)**

**Per serving: 431 Calories; 33.1g Fat; 2.7g Carbs; 30.3g Protein;**

## INGREDIENTS

4 slices cooked bacon, crumbled

4 eggs, beaten

1 teaspoon rosemary, chopped

1 teaspoon parsley, chopped

Sea salt and black pepper

4 ounces blue cheese

## DIRECTIONS

Add the bacon to the frying pan; cook until sizzling.

Then, mix in the eggs, rosemary, parsley, salt, and black pepper.

Crumble the cheese over the eggs; fold in half. Cook an additional 1 to 2 minutes or until everything is heated through.

# 401. Mini Ham Frittatas with Swiss cheese

**(Ready in about 40 minutes | Servings 5)**

**Per serving: 261 Calories; 16g Fat; 6.6g Carbs; 21.1g Protein;**

## INGREDIENTS

1 tablespoon avocado oil

1 red onion, chopped

1 bell pepper, chopped

1 cup mustard greens

6 slices ham, chopped

8 eggs, whisked

1 cup Swiss cheese, shredded

Salt and pepper, to taste

1/4 teaspoon tarragon

1/2 teaspoon ancho powder

1/2 teaspoon Korean red pepper flakes

1 tablespoon fresh parsley, chopped

## DIRECTIONS

Start by preheating your oven to 390 degrees F. Add cupcake liners to your muffin pan.

Heat the avocado oil in nonstick skillet and sweat the onions for 5 to 6 minutes. Add the bell pepper and mustard greens, and continue to cook an additional 4 minutes, stirring frequently.

Add the ham and cook an additional 3 minutes. Stir in the remaining ingredients; stir until everything is well incorporated.

Transfer the mixture to the lined muffin pan and bake for 23 minutes or until set. Allow the muffins to cool for a couple of minutes before removing them from the cups. Enjoy!

# 402. Salami and Cheese Balls

**(Ready in about 15 minutes | Servings 8)**

**Per serving: 168 Calories; 13g Fat; 2.5g Carbs; 10.3g Protein;**

## INGREDIENTS

1 egg

6 slices Genoa salami, chopped

6 ounces Ricotta cheese

6 ounces Colby cheese

Salt and ground black pepper, to taste

1/4 cup almond flour

1 teaspoon baking powder

1 teaspoon garlic powder

1 teaspoon Italian seasoning

## DIRECTIONS

Begin by preheating an oven to 420 degrees F.

Whisk the eggs vigorously; add the remaining ingredients and mix to combine well.

Divide the mixture into 16 balls; arrange the balls on a baking sheet lined with parchment paper or a silicone mat.

Bake approximately 13 minutes or until they are crisp and golden brown.

# DESSERTS

## 403. Frozen Cocoa and Almond Dessert

**(Ready in about 10 minutes + chilling time | Servings 6)**

**Per serving: 84 Calories; 8.9g Fat; 1.5g Carbs; 0.8g Protein;**

### INGREDIENTS

1/2 stick butter, melted
1/2 teaspoon vanilla paste
10 drops liquid stevia

2 tablespoons cocoa powder
2 tablespoons almonds, chopped

### DIRECTIONS

Melt the butter, vanilla paste, and liquid stevia in a pan that is preheated over a moderate heat.
Stir in the cocoa powder and stir well to combine.
Spoon the mixture into 12 molds of a silicone candy mold tray. Scatter the chopped almonds on top. Freeze until set. Enjoy!

## 404. Chocolate and Coconut Truffles

**(Ready in about 15 minutes + chilling time | Servings 16)**

**Per serving: 90 Calories; 6.3g Fat; 4.9g Carbs; 3.7g Protein;**

### INGREDIENTS

1 ½ cups bittersweet chocolate, sugar-free, broken into chunks
4 tablespoons coconut, desiccated
1/2 stick butter
1 cup double cream
3 tablespoons xylitol
1/2 teaspoon pure almond extract

1 teaspoon vanilla paste
A pinch of salt
A pinch of freshly grated nutmeg
1 tablespoon cognac
1/4 cup unsweetened Dutch-processed cocoa powder

### DIRECTIONS

Thoroughly combine the chocolate, coconut, butter, double cream, xylitol, almond extract, vanilla, salt, and grated nutmeg.
Microwave for 1 minute on medium-high; let it cool slightly. Now, stir in the cognac and vanilla.
Place in your refrigerator for 2 hours. Shape the mixture into balls; roll each ball in the cocoa powder and enjoy!

## 405. Almond Dessert Bars

**(Ready in about 30 minutes | Servings 8)**

**Per serving: 241 Calories; 23.6g Fat; 3.7g Carbs; 5.2g Protein;**

### INGREDIENTS

2 cups almond flour
3/4 teaspoon baking powder
1/2 cup Swerve
1/2 teaspoon ground cinnamon
A pinch of sea salt
A pinch of grated nutmeg

1 stick butter, melted
3 eggs
1/2 cup Swerve
1 teaspoon vanilla paste
3/4 cup heavy whipping cream
1/2 cup almonds, chopped

### DIRECTIONS

Preheat your oven to 360 degrees F. Then, line a baking pan with parchment paper.
In a mixing bowl, thoroughly combine the almond flour, baking powder, Swerve, cinnamon, salt, and nutmeg.
Now, stir in the melted butter, eggs, Swerve, and vanilla paste. Next, stir in the heavy cream to create a soft texture.
Fold in the chopped almonds and gently stir until everything is well incorporated. Spoon the batter into the baking pan.
Bake approximately 27 minutes. Allow it to cool completely before serving. Bon appétit!

# 406. Espresso and Coconut Delight

**(Ready in about 10 minutes + chilling time | Servings 6)**

**Per serving: 218 Calories; 24.7g Fat; 1.1g Carbs; 0.4g Protein;**

### INGREDIENTS

4 ounces coconut oil
4 ounces coconut cream
2 teaspoons butter, softened
1 teaspoon instant espresso powder

3 tablespoons confectioners Swerve
A pinch of salt
1 teaspoon pure vanilla extract

### DIRECTIONS

Melt the coconut oil in a double boiler over medium-low heat.
Add the remaining ingredients. Remove from the heat; stir until everything is well combined.
Pour into a silicone mold and freeze overnight. Bon appétit!

# 407. Chocolate and Orange Mousse

**(Ready in about 15 minutes | Servings 4)**

**Per serving: 154 Calories; 13g Fat; 6.3g Carbs; 5.3g Protein;**

### INGREDIENTS

2 egg yolks
3/4 cup heavy cream
3 ounces Ricotta cheese, at room temperature
1 tablespoon freshly squeezed orange juice

1 ½ teaspoons orange zest
1/2 teaspoon ground cinnamon
1/4 cup granulated stevia erythritol blend
1/4 cup unsweetened cocoa powder

### DIRECTIONS

Beat the egg yolks with your electric mixer until thick and pale.
Heat the cream in a pan over medium heat. Gradually stir the hot cream into the egg yolk mixture.
Turn the heat to low and cook for about 5 minutes, stirring constantly, until your mixture is thickened.
Now, beat the remaining ingredients with your electric mixer until everything is creamy.
Fold this mixture into cream mixture and serve well chilled.

# 408. Melt-in-Your-Mouth Chocolate Squares

**(Ready in about 25 minutes + chilling time | Servings 10)**

**Per serving: 119 Calories; 11.7g Fat; 5.2g Carbs; 1.1g Protein;**

### INGREDIENTS

1/2 cup coconut flour
1 cup almond flour
2 packets stevia
1/4 teaspoon cardamom
1/2 teaspoon star anise, ground
1/2 teaspoon coconut extract

1 teaspoon pure vanilla extract
1 tablespoon rum
A pinch of table salt
1/2 stick butter, cold
1 ½ cups double cream
8 ounces bittersweet chocolate chips, sugar-free

### DIRECTIONS

Preheat an oven to 330 degrees F. Now, line a baking dish with parchment paper.
Add the flour, stevia, cardamom, anise, coconut extract, vanilla extract, rum and salt to your food processor. Blitz until everything is well combined.
Cut in the cold butter and process to combine again.
Press the batter into the bottom of the prepared baking dish. Bake about 13 minutes; transfer to a wire rack to cool slightly.
To make the filling, bring the double cream to a simmer in a pan. Add the chocolate and whisk until uniform. Spread over the crust; cut into squares and serve well-chilled. Enjoy!

# 409. Cheesy Coconut Cake

**(Ready in about 30 minutes | Servings 12)**

**Per serving: 246 Calories; 22.2g Fat; 5.7g Carbs; 8.1g Protein;**

## INGREDIENTS

10 ounces almond meal
1 ounce coconut, shredded
1 teaspoon baking powder
1/8 teaspoon salt
4 eggs, lightly beaten

3 ounces stevia
1/2 stick butter
5 ounces coconut yogurt
5 ounces cream cheese

## DIRECTIONS

Start by preheating your oven to 350 degrees F. Spritz 2 spring form pans with a nonstick cooking spray.
In a mixing bowl, thoroughly combine the almond meal, coconut and baking powder. Stir in the salt, eggs and 2 ounces of stevia.
Combine the 2 mixtures and stir until everything is well incorporated.
Transfer the mixture into 2 spring form pans, introduce in the oven at 350 degrees F; bake for 20 to 25 minutes.
Transfer to a wire rack to cool completely. In the meantime, mix the other ingredients, including the remaining 1 ounce of stevia.
Place one cake layer on a plate; spread half of the cream cheese filling over it. Now, top with another cake layer; spread the rest of the cream cheese filling over the top. Bon appétit!

# 410. Coconut Apple Cobbler

**(Ready in about 30 minutes | Servings 8)**

**Per serving: 152 Calories; 11.8g Fat; 6.2g Carbs; 2.5g Protein;**

## INGREDIENTS

2 ½ cups apples, cored and sliced
1/2 tablespoon fresh lemon juice
1/3 teaspoon xanthan gum
1 cup almond flour

1/4 cup coconut flour
3/4 cup xylitol
2 eggs, whisked
5 tablespoons coconut oil, melted

## DIRECTIONS

Start by preheating your oven to 360 degrees F. Lightly grease a baking dish with a nonstick cooking spray.
Arrange the apples on the bottom of the baking dish. Drizzle with lemon juice and xanthan gum.
Then, in a mixing bowl, mix the flour with xylitol and eggs until the mixture resembles coarse meal. Spread this mixture over the apples.
Drizzle coconut oil over topping. Bake for 25 minutes or until dough rises. Bon appétit!

# 411. Summer Keto Frappe Dessert

**(Ready in about 2 hours | Servings 2)**

**Per serving: 371 Calories; 37.8g Fat; 7.1g Carbs; 3.4g Protein;**

## INGREDIENTS

2 teaspoons instant coffee
4 drops liquid Stevia
1 tablespoon cacao butter
1/4 cup cold water

16 raspberries, frozen
1 cup almond milk
2 tablespoons coconut whipped cream

## DIRECTIONS

Combine the instant coffee, Stevia, cacao butter and cold water. Shake with a drink mixer for 20 seconds.
Place the frozen raspberries in dessert glasses. Pour the coffee mixture over it. Add the almond milk and ice cubes, if desired.
Now, freeze for at least 2 hours or until firm. Serve topped with coconut whipped cream. Enjoy!

# 412. Cheesecake Cupcakes with Vanilla Frosting

**(Ready in about 30 minutes + chilling time | Servings 8)**

**Per serving: 165 Calories; 15.6g Fat; 5.4g Carbs; 5.2g Protein;**

## INGREDIENTS

For the Muffins:
3 tablespoons coconut oil
10 ounces Ricotta cheese, at room temperature
1 tablespoon rum
2 eggs
2 packets stevia
1/8 teaspoon ground cloves

1/4 teaspoon ground cinnamon
1/8 teaspoon nutmeg, preferably freshly grated
For the Frosting:
1/2 cup confectioners' Swerve
1/2 stick butter, softened
1 teaspoon vanilla
1 ½ tablespoons full-fat milk

## DIRECTIONS

Preheat your oven to 360 degrees F; coat the muffin cups with cupcake liners.
Thoroughly combine the coconut oil, Ricotta cheese, rum, eggs, stevia, cloves, cinnamon and nutmeg in your food processor.
Scrape the batter into the muffin tin; bake for 13 to 16 minutes. Now, place in the freezer for 2 hours.
In the meantime, combine the confectioners' Swerve with the butter and vanilla with an electric mixer.
Slowly pour in the milk in order to make a spreadable mixture. Frost the chilled cheesecake cupcakes. Bon appétit!

# 413. Easy Almond Fudge

**(Ready in about 3 hours | Servings 8)**

**Per serving: 180 Calories; 18.3g Fat; 4.5g Carbs; 1g Protein;**

## INGREDIENTS

3/4 cup almond butter, sugar-free, preferably homemade
1 stick butter
1/3 cup coconut milk
1/4 cup xylitol
1/8 teaspoon salt

1/8 teaspoon grated nutmeg
3 tablespoons xylitol
3 tablespoons butter, melted
1 teaspoon vanilla essence
3 tablespoons cocoa powder

## DIRECTIONS

Microwave the almond butter and regular butter until they melt.
Add the coconut milk, 1/4 cup xylitol, salt, and nutmeg; stir to combine well and press into a well-greased glass baking dish.
Refrigerate for 2 to 3 hours or until set.
In a mixing bowl, make the sauce by whisking 3 tablespoons xylitol, 3 tablespoons of butter melted, vanilla essence and cocoa powder.
Spread the sauce over your fudge. Cut into squares and store in an airtight container.

# 414. Peanut Ice Cream

**(Ready in about 10 minutes + chilling time | Servings 4)**

**Per serving: 305 Calories; 18.3g Fat; 4.5g Carbs; 1g Protein;**

## INGREDIENTS

1 ¼ cups almond milk
1/3 cup whipped cream
17 drops liquid stevia
1/2 cup peanuts, chopped
1/2 teaspoon xanthan gum

## DIRECTIONS

Combine all of the above ingredients, except for the xanthan gum, with an electric mixer.
Now, stir in the xanthan gum, whisking constantly, until the mixture is thick.
Then, prepare your ice cream in a machine following the manufacturer's instructions.
Serve directly from the machine or store in your freezer.

# 415. Coconut Chia Pudding

**(Ready in about 30 minutes | Servings 4)**

**Per serving: 270 Calories; 24.7g Fat; 6.5g Carbs; 4.6g Protein;**

## INGREDIENTS

1/3 cup chia seeds
1/2 cup water
1 cup coconut cream
1/2 cup sour cream

1/3 teaspoon vanilla extract
1 teaspoon key lime zest
1/4 teaspoon ground cinnamon
2 tablespoons granular Swerve

## DIRECTIONS

In a bowl, place all ingredients and stir well; let it sit at least 30 minutes.
Divide among individual bowls to serve.
Can be stored in the refrigerator up to 3 days.

# 416. Festive Cake with Cream Cheese Frosting

**(Ready in about 40 minutes + chilling time | Servings 10)**

**Per serving: 241 Calories; 22.6g Fat; 4.2g Carbs; 6.6g Protein;**

## INGREDIENTS

2/3 cup coconut flour
1 ½ cups almond flour
1/2 teaspoon baking soda
1/2 teaspoon baking powder
A pinch of salt
A pinch of grated nutmeg
1/2 teaspoon Konjac root fiber
1 cup Swerve
1 teaspoon fresh ginger, grated
2 ½ tablespoons ghee

4 eggs
1 cup coconut milk, sugar-free
1 teaspoon rum extract
1 teaspoon vanilla extract
For the Cream Cheese Frosting:
10 ounces cream cheese, cold
1/3 cup powdered granular sweetener
3 ounces butter, at room temperature
1 teaspoon vanilla
A few drops chocolate flavor

## DIRECTIONS

Start by preheating your oven to 360 degrees F. Line a baking pan with parchment paper.
In a mixing bowl, combine the coconut flour, almond flour, baking soda, baking powder, salt, nutmeg, Konjac root fiber, Swerve, and ginger.
Microwave the ghee until melted and add to the dry mixture in the mixing bowl. Fold in the eggs, one at a time, and stir until combined.
Lastly, pour in the coconut milk, rum extract, and vanilla extract until your batter is light and fluffy.
Press the mixture into the prepared baking pan. Bake for 28 to 33 minutes or until a cake tester inserted in center comes out clean and dry.
Let it cool to room temperature.
Meanwhile, beat the cream cheese with an electric mixer until smooth. Stir in the powdered granular sweetener and beat again. Beat in the vanilla until it is completely incorporated.
Add the butter, vanilla, and chocolate flavor; whip until light, fluffy and uniform. Frost the cake and serve well-chilled. Bon appétit!

# 417. Sinfully Delicious Whiskey Chocolate Bites

**(Ready in about 10 minutes + chilling time | Servings 8)**

**Per serving: 70 Calories; 3.4g Fat; 5.1g Carbs; 2.4g Protein;**

## INGREDIENTS

1 cup chocolate chunks, sugar-free
3 tablespoons cocoa powder
3/4 cup buttermilk
1/2 cup milk
2 tablespoons whiskey

1/4 teaspoon grated nutmeg
1/8 teaspoon ground cloves
1/8 teaspoon cinnamon powder
1/2 teaspoon vanilla paste

## DIRECTIONS

Melt the chocolate, along with the cocoa and buttermilk in a microwave-safe bowl, on high for 70 seconds.
Stir in the other ingredients. Pour the mixture into silicone molds.
Refrigerate at least 1 hour 30 minutes. Bon appétit!

# 418. Vanilla Walnut Cheesecake

**(Ready in about 1 hour | Servings 14)**

**Per serving: 393 Calories; 38g Fat; 4.1g Carbs; 9.8g Protein;**

## INGREDIENTS

8 ounces walnuts, chopped
8 packets stevia
1/4 teaspoon grated nutmeg
A pinch of salt
1/2 cup butter, melted

**For the Filling:**
22 ounces cream cheese, at room temperature
30 packets stevia
4 eggs
1 teaspoon vanilla essence
1 teaspoon pure almond extract
14 ounces sour cream

## DIRECTIONS

Combine all ingredients for the crust until well mixed; press the crust mixture into a springform pan. Set aside
Now, beat the cream cheese on low speed until creamy and fluffy.
Add the stevia and eggs, one at a time; mix on low speed. Add the remaining ingredients until well mixed.
Bake in the preheated oven at 300 degrees F for 55 minutes. Let it cool on a wire rack. Serve well chilled.

# 419. Chocolate Cream Cheese Muffins

**(Ready in about 25 minutes | Servings 12)**

**Per serving: 134 Calories; 12.5g Fat; 3.3g Carbs; 4.6g Protein;**

## INGREDIENTS

7 tablespoons butter, melted
5 eggs
2 ounces cocoa powder
1 teaspoon pure vanilla extract

1 teaspoon maple flavor
1/3 teaspoon baking powder
6 ounces Neufchatel cheese, at room temperature
1/4 cup xylitol

## DIRECTIONS

Beat all ingredients with an electric mixer.
Place a paper baking cup in each of 12 muffin cups. Fill each cup 2/3 full.
Bake at 360 degrees F about 23 minutes. Allow your muffins to cool completely; frost as desired and serve.

# 420. Chocolate and Orange Mousse

**(Ready in about 15 minutes + chilling time | Servings 6)**

**Per serving: 158 Calories; 15.7g Fat; 7.2g Carbs; 2.2g Protein;**

## INGREDIENTS

2 cups heavy cream
3 tablespoons confectioners Swerve
3 1/3 tablespoons cocoa powder, unsweetened
Fresh juice and zest of 1/2 orange
1/4 teaspoon sea salt

A pinch of grated nutmeg
1/4 teaspoon ground cloves
1/4 teaspoon ground cinnamon
6 ounces sugar-free chocolate chunks

## DIRECTIONS

Whip the heavy cream and Swerve with an electric mixer.
Add the cocoa powder and beat again. Now, add the remaining ingredients and beat again until everything is well combined.
Place in your refrigerator until ready to serve. Bon appétit!

# 421. Cashew Butter Fat Bombs

**(Ready in about 40 minutes | Servings 12)**

**Per serving: 114 Calories; 10.6g Fat; 3.4g Carbs; 3.1g Protein;**

## INGREDIENTS

1/2 cup almonds
1/3 cup walnuts
1/2 cup cashew butter
1/2 stick butter

2 tablespoons cocoa powder, unsweetened
10 drops liquid stevia
1 teaspoon vanilla extract
1/4 cup unsweetened peanut flour

## DIRECTIONS

Chop the almonds and walnuts in your food processor.
Transfer to a mixing bowl; add the other ingredients.
Scoop out tablespoons of batter onto a cookie sheet lined with a wax paper.
Place in your freezer approximately 30 minutes. Store in your refrigerator up to 1 week.

# 422. Vanilla Keto Pudding

**(Ready in about 1 hour | Servings 6)**

**Per serving: 248 Calories; 20.8g Fat; 7g Carbs; 4.6g Protein;**

## INGREDIENTS

3 avocados, pitted, peeled and mashed
1 tablespoon vanilla extract
1 cup xylitol
1/8 teaspoon xanthan gum

1 teaspoon lemon juice
1 cup buttermilk
1 cup full-fat milk

## DIRECTIONS

Mix all ingredients in your blender or a food processor.
Refrigerate for 1 hour before serving. Enjoy!

# 423. Brownie Pecan Cupcakes

**(Ready in about 25 minutes | Servings 12)**

**Per serving: 251 Calories; 21.5g Fat; 4.6g Carbs; 6.4g Protein;**

## INGREDIENTS

3/4 cup butter, melted
5 eggs
4 ounces cocoa powder
1/2 cup pecans, ground
1 teaspoon vanilla paste

3/4 teaspoon baking powder
1/4 teaspoon ground cloves
3 ounces cream cheese
3 ounces sour cream
2 tablespoons stevia powder

## DIRECTIONS

Preheat your oven to 360 degrees F. Place a baking cup in each of 12 regular-size muffin cups.
Thoroughly combine all ingredients in your food processor. Spoon the batter into the muffin cups.
Bake for 18 to 22 minutes. Transfer to a wire rack to cool completely before serving. Bon appétit!

## 424. Nutty Mother's Day Cake

**(Ready in about 30 minutes + chilling time | Servings 10)**

**Per serving: 211 Calories; 19g Fat; 4.4g Carbs; 7g Protein;**

### INGREDIENTS

**For the Crust:**
4 tablespoons peanut butter, room temperature
1 cup almond meal
2 tablespoons almonds, toasted and chopped

**For the Filling:**
10 ounces cream cheese, room temperature
2 eggs
1/2 teaspoon Stevia
1/2 teaspoon vanilla essence
1/2 teaspoon sugar-free caramel flavored syrup
1 teaspoon fresh ginger, grated
A pinch of salt
A pinch of grated nutmeg

### DIRECTIONS

Begin by preheating your oven to 360 degrees F. Line a baking pan with parchment paper.
Thoroughly combine the peanut butter with almond meal. Then, press the crust mixture into your baking pan and bake for 7 minutes.
Then, make the filling, by mixing all the filling ingredients with an electric mixer.
Spread the filling onto the prepared crusts; bake for a further 18 minutes.
Transfer it to the refrigerator to chill. Garnish with chopped, toasted almonds; cut into squares and serve well-chilled. Bon appétit!

## 425. Luscious Key Lime Curd

**(Ready in about 10 minutes + chilling time | Servings 6)**

**Per serving: 180 Calories; 17.6g Fat; 5.2g Carbs; 2.8g Protein;**

2 eggs, well whisked
1 egg yolk, well whisked
10 ounces fresh key lime juice
1 heaping tablespoon key lime zest

1 ½ cups Swerve
A pinch of salt
1 stick butter, softened

### DIRECTIONS

Whisk the eggs in a pan that is preheated over a moderate flame.
Stir in the remaining ingredients and cook for 6 minutes more, whisking constantly.
Turn the heat to low and continue whisking 2 minutes longer. Remove from heat.
Cover with a plastic wrap and chill overnight. Serve chilled and enjoy!

## 426. The Best Walnut Truffles Ever

**(Ready in about 1 hour | Servings 10)**

**Per serving: 162 Calories; 14.6g Fat; 5.9g Carbs; 2.3g Protein;**

### INGREDIENTS

1/2 stick butter
4 ounces heavy cream
1/4 cup Sukrin Icing
1 tablespoon brandy

1/2 teaspoon pure almond extract
1/2 cup chopped toasted walnuts
1/2 cup chocolate chips, sugar-free
4 tablespoons walnuts, coarsely chopped

### DIRECTIONS

Melt the butter in a double boiler, stirring constantly.
Then, stir in the cream and Sukrin icing; stir to combine well. Remove from heat and add the brandy, almond extract and chopped walnuts.
Now, allow it to cool at room temperature. Shape into 20 balls and chill for 40 to 50 minutes.
In a double boiler, melt the chocolate chips over medium-low heat. Dip each ball into the chocolate coating.
Afterwards, roll your truffles in chopped walnuts. Keep in an airtight container in your refrigerator. Enjoy!

# 427. Avocado and Peanut Butter Pudding

**(Ready in about 15 minutes | Servings 4)**

**Per serving: 288 Calories; 27.3g Fat; 6.9g Carbs; 6.2g Protein;**

## INGREDIENTS

1 ½ cups avocado, peeled, pitted, and diced
1/2 cup crunchy peanut butter
50 drops liquid stevia
1/2 cup canned coconut milk

1 teaspoon pure vanilla extract
1/4 teaspoon ground cloves
1 tablespoon lime juice
1/2 cup coconut whipped cream

## DIRECTIONS

Process the avocados, peanut butter, stevia and coconut milk in a blender.
Now, add the vanilla extract, cloves, and lime juice.
Refrigerate until ready serve. Garnish with coconut whipped cream and enjoy!

# 428. Caramel Macchiato Candies

**(Ready in about 10 minutes + chilling time | Servings 8)**

**Per serving: 145 Calories; 12.8g Fat; 6.2g Carbs; 0.9g Protein;**

## INGREDIENTS

3 tablespoons cocoa butter
3 tablespoons butter
3 ounces dark chocolate, sugar-free

1 teaspoon cold brew coffee concentrate
1 teaspoon sugar-free caramel flavored syrup
6 drops liquid stevia

## DIRECTIONS

Microwave the cocoa butter, butter, and chocolate for 1 minute or so.
Stir in the remaining ingredients. Pour into candy-safe molds. Refrigerate until hard. Enjoy!

# 429. Blueberry and Chocolate Holiday Candy

**(Ready in about 15 minutes + chilling time | Servings 10)**

**Per serving: 334 Calories; 37g Fat; 5.3g Carbs; 1.6g Protein;**

## INGREDIENTS

1 cup freeze-dried blueberries
1 stick butter
1 cup coconut oil

4 ounces unsweetened chocolate, roughly chopped
1 teaspoon vanilla crème stevia

## DIRECTIONS

Crush the dried blueberries with a pestle and mortar until you get a powder consistency; reserve.
Heat a pan over a moderate heat; melt butter, coconut oil, chocolate and vanilla crème stevia, stirring continuously.
Now, transfer the chocolate mixture to a parchment-lined baking sheet.
Sprinkle the blueberries and gently press them down into the melted chocolate. Swirl with a knife and transfer to your freezer.
Let them cool and harden completely before breaking into pieces.

## 430. Peanut Butter Cup Cookies

**(Ready in about 40 minutes | Servings 10)**

**Per serving: 266 Calories; 28.1g Fat; 2.6g Carbs; 3.3g Protein;**

### INGREDIENTS

1/2 cup coconut oil
1/2 cup butter
1/2 cup crunchy peanut butter

3 tablespoons heavy cream
1 tablespoon granular Swerve

### DIRECTIONS

Simmer all of the above ingredients in a pan over medium-low heat; stir continuously until everything is well incorporated.
Divide the batter among muffin cups lined with cupcake wrappers.
Allow them to harden at least 30 minutes in your freezer. Bon appétit!

## 431. Homemade Hazelnut Chocolate

**(Ready in about 15 minutes + chilling time | Servings 8)**

**Per serving: 184 Calories; 16.9g Fat; 7.2g Carbs; 1.8g Protein;**

### INGREDIENTS

1 stick butter, room temperature
1/4 cup cocoa powder, unsweetened
1/4 cup granulated Swerve

1/2 cup hazelnuts, finely chopped
A pinch of salt
A pinch of ground cloves

### DIRECTIONS

Melt the butter in a pan over a moderate heat. Now, stir in the cocoa powder and Swerve. Heat off and mix well.
Add the hazelnuts, salt and ground cloves; stir until everything is incorporated.
Line a baking dish with a piece of aluminum foil. Spoon the mixture into the baking dish and let it sit in your refrigerator until completely set.
Broken into pieces and serve. Keep in the refrigerator.

## 432. Orange-Star Anise Custard Pudding

**(Ready in about 1 hour | Servings 5)**

**Per serving: 205 Calories; 16.4g Fat; 6.5g Carbs; 7.4g Protein;**

### INGREDIENTS

3/4 cup Swerve
1 ½ cups whipping cream
3/4 cup water
6 eggs
1 teaspoon orange rind, grated

1/4 teaspoon orange essence
1/2 teaspoon vanilla essence
1/4 teaspoon ground cloves
1 teaspoon star anise star ground

### DIRECTIONS

Melt the Swerve in a pan on medium-low until it is richly browned.
Spoon the caramelized Swerve into the bottom of a baking dish; set aside.
Then heat the cream and water in a pan, bringing to a boil.
In a mixing bowl, whisk the remaining ingredients until everything is well combined. Stir the warm cream mixture into this egg mixture.
Cook, stirring frequently, for a further 3 minutes.
Spread this mixture over the Swerve layer. Place the baking dish in a larger baking pan that is filled with boiling water.
Bake at 330 degrees F for 1 hour. Invert your pudding onto a serving plate and serve. Bon appétit!

## 433. Melt-in-Your-Mouth Hazelnut Chocolate

**(Ready in about 25 minutes | Servings 8)**

**Per serving: 140 Calories; 14g Fat; 5.9g Carbs; 2g Protein;**

### INGREDIENTS

4 ounces cacao butter
1 tablespoon extra-virgin coconut oil
8 tablespoons cocoa powder
1/4 cup Swerve
1/4 teaspoon hazelnut extract

1 teaspoon pure vanilla extract
1/8 teaspoon coarse salt
1/4 teaspoon grated nutmeg
1/2 cup roasted hazelnuts, chopped

### DIRECTIONS

Melt the cacao butter and coconut oil in a microwave for 1 minute or so.
Now, stir in the cocoa powder, Swerve, hazelnut extract, vanilla extract, salt and nutmeg.
Pour the mixture into an ice cube mold. Add the roasted hazelnuts and place in your freezer for 20 minutes or until solid. Enjoy!

## 434. Chocolate Lover's Dream Fudge

**(Ready in about 15 minutes + chilling time | Servings 8)**

**Per serving: 220 Calories; 20g Fat; 7g Carbs; 1.7g Protein;**

### INGREDIENTS

1 cup condensed milk, sugar-free
3/4 Sukrin chocolate, broken into pieces
1 stick butter

2 tablespoons coconut oil
4-5 drops Stevia
1/2 cup heavy cream

### DIRECTIONS

Microwave the condensed milk and Sukrin chocolate for 70 seconds; spoon into a baking dish and freeze until firm.
Melt the butter in a small-sized pan; stir in the melted coconut oil, Stevia, and heavy cream; whisk to combine well or beat with a hand mixer.
Spread the cream mixture over the fudge layer in the baking dish. Transfer to the refrigerator or freezer until solid. Bon appétit!

## 435. Creamy Mint Jello

**(Ready in about 45 minutes | Servings 10)**

**Per serving: 56 Calories; 5.5g Fat; 0.4g Carbs; 1.5g Protein;**

### INGREDIENTS

2 envelopes unflavored gelatin
5 tablespoons Swerve
1 teaspoon peppermint oil

1 teaspoon pure vanilla essence
3/4 cup boiling water
1 ¼ cups heavy cream

### DIRECTIONS

Combine the gelatin, Swerve, peppermint oil, and vanilla extract in a heatproof dish.
Pour in the boiling water and stir well until the gelatin is dissolved.
Stir in the heavy cream; whisk to combine well. Pour the mixture into paper cups sprayed with a nonstick cooking spray.
Place in your refrigerator for 30 minutes or until they are firm. Unmold before serving and enjoy!

## 436. Butterscotch Ice Cream

**(Ready in about 15 minutes + chilling time | Servings 8)**

**Per serving: 89 Calories; 9.3g Fat; 1.5g Carbs; 0.8g Protein;**

### INGREDIENTS

3/4 cup heavy cream
1/2 cup coconut milk
1 tablespoon butterscotch flavoring
25 drops liquid stevia

1/3 teaspoon pure vanilla extract
A pinch of salt
1/4 cup sour cream

### DIRECTIONS

Cook the heavy cream and coconut milk in a pan that is preheated over a medium-low flame. Let it simmer, stirring constantly, until there are no lumps.
Allow it to cool at room temperature; mix in the remaining ingredients.
Blend with an electric mixer until your desired consistency is reached. Transfer to your freezer for about 5 hours. Enjoy!

## 437. Silky Peanut and Coconut Bark

**(Ready in about 10 minutes + chilling time | Servings 12)**

**Per serving: 316 Calories; 31.6g Fat; 4.6g Carbs; 6.6g Protein;**

### INGREDIENTS

3/4 cup peanut butter
3/4 cup coconut oil
1 cup Swerve

1 teaspoon pure vanilla extract
1/2 teaspoon pure almond extract
1/2 cup coconut flakes

### DIRECTIONS

Combine all ingredients in a pan over a moderate heat; cook, stirring continuously, for 4 to 5 minutes.
Spoon the mixture into a parchment-lined baking sheet. Refrigerate overnight and break your bark into pieces. Serve.

## 438. Decadent Pistachio Truffles

**(Ready in about 25 minutes + chilling time | Servings 6)**

**Per serving: 113 Calories; 8.5g Fat; 5.9g Carbs; 1.7g Protein;**

### INGREDIENTS

3 bars sugar-free chocolate spread
1/2 cup heavy cream
1 teaspoon vanilla essence

1/4 teaspoon ground cinnamon
1/2 cup toasted pistachios, finely chopped

### DIRECTIONS

Melt the chocolate spread with heavy cream in your microwave for 1 minute or so.
Add the vanilla and ground cinnamon; transfer to your refrigerator for 8 hours or until firm enough to shape.
Shape the chocolate mixture into balls. Freeze for 20 minutes.
Afterwards, roll the balls into the chopped pistachios. Keep refrigerated until ready to serve.

# 439. Walnut and White Chocolate Fudge

**(Ready in about 15 minutes + chilling time | Servings 12)**

**Per serving: 202 Calories; 21.3g Fat; 2.3g Carbs; 2.4g Protein;**

## INGREDIENTS

3/4 cup butter, softened
1 ¼ cups walnut butter, sugar-free
3 ounces sugar-free white chocolate
1/3 cup coconut milk, unsweetened
2 tablespoons xylitol

1/8 teaspoon coarse sea salt
1/4 teaspoon grated nutmeg
1/4 teaspoon ground star anise
1/4 teaspoon lemon peel zest

## DIRECTIONS

Microwave the butter, walnut butter, and white chocolate until they are melted. Add the butter mixture to your food processor.
Now, add the other ingredients and mix again until everything is well incorporated. Scrape the mixture into a parchment lined baking pan.
Place in the refrigerator for 3 hours. Cut into squares and serve. Bon appétit!

# 440. Cappuccino Ice Candy

**(Ready in about 10 minutes + chilling time | Servings 8)**

**Per serving: 117 Calories; 11.2g Fat; 5g Carbs; 1.3g Protein;**

## INGREDIENTS

1 ½ cups avocado, pitted, peeled and mashed
1 cup brewed espresso
2 tablespoons cocoa powder
1 cup heavy whipping cream

3 tablespoons erythritol
1/2 teaspoon cappuccino flavor extract
A pinch of salt
A pinch of grated nutmeg

## DIRECTIONS

Throw all of the above ingredients into your food processor; mix until everything is well combined.
Pour the mixture into an ice cube tray. Freeze overnight, at least 6 hours. Serve well-chilled.

# 441. Orange Panna Cotta

**(Ready in about 10 minutes + chilling time | Servings 10)**

**Per serving: 221 Calories; 21.5g Fat; 3.8g Carbs; 4.3g Protein;**

## INGREDIENTS

1 ½ teaspoons gelatin, unflavored
1 ½ cups coconut milk
1/4 cup erythritol

1 teaspoon Blood orange juice
1 teaspoon blood orange zest

## DIRECTIONS

Place the gelatin and coconut milk in a pan; let it sit for 2 minutes. Add the remaining ingredients.
Simmer the mixture over low heat until the gelatin is dissolved, about 3 minutes.
Pour the mixture into 4 molds. Place in your refrigerator until set, at least 6 hours.
To serve invert over a small plate. Enjoy!

# 442. Christmas Walnut Penuche

**(Ready in about 2 hours | Servings 8)**

**Per serving: 167 Calories; 17.1g Fat; 6.8g Carbs; 2.4g Protein;**

## INGREDIENTS

1 cup xylitol
1 cup condensed milk, unsweetened
1 stick butter
1/2 teaspoon vanilla paste

2 ounces toasted walnuts, chopped
1/4 teaspoon orange rind, grated
A pinch of salt

## DIRECTIONS

Combine the xylitol and milk in a pan that is preheated over a moderate heat. Simmer, stirring often, for 5 to 6 minutes.
Stir in the butter and vanilla. Cream with an electric mixer at low speed; beat until very creamy.
Fold in the chopped walnuts, orange rind, and salt; stir again. Afterwards, spoon into a baking dish and freeze until firm, about 2 hours.
Bon appétit!

# 443. Coconut and Peanut Butter Flan

**(Ready in about 40 minutes + chilling time | Servings 4)**

**Per serving: 304 Calories; 27.7g Fat; 6.6g Carbs; 11.6g Protein;**

## INGREDIENTS

1 cup coconut cream, unsweetened
4 eggs
1/2 cup peanut butter
1/2 cup granulated Swerve

1/4 teaspoon ground mace
1/2 teaspoon pure vanilla extract
1/2 teaspoon pure almond extract

## DIRECTIONS

Begin by preheating your oven to 340 degrees F. Place 4 ramekins in a deep baking pan. Pour boiling water to a depth of about 1 inch.
In a saucepan, bring the coconut cream to a simmer. In a mixing dish, whisk the remaining ingredients until the eggs are foamy.
Slowly and gradually pour the egg mixture into the warm coconut cream, whisking constantly.
Spoon the mixture into the prepared ramekins and bake for 35 minutes, or until a tester comes out dry.
Allow it to cool about 4 hours. Can be stored in the refrigerator up to 3 days. Bon appétit!

# 444. Berry and Coconut Cup Smoothie

**(Ready in about 10 minutes | Servings 4)**

**Per serving: 274 Calories; 26.8g Fat; 7.5g Carbs; 3.9g Protein;**

## INGREDIENTS

1/2 cup raspberries, frozen
1 cup coconut milk
2 tablespoons almond butter
1/4 cup coconut shreds

1 teaspoon vanilla paste
4 drops liquid stevia
2 tablespoons hemp seeds

## DIRECTIONS

Pulse the frozen berries in your food processor to the desired consistency.
Add the coconut milk, almond butter, coconut, vanilla and stevia. Blend until everything is well incorporated.
Dived between 4 individual bowls; top with hemp seeds and serve immediately.

# 445. Quick Chocolate and Walnut Cookies

**(Ready in about 30 minutes | Servings 10)**

**Per serving: 157 Calories; 14.8g Fat; 3.5g Carbs; 4.5g Protein;**

## INGREDIENTS

1 stick butter
1/2 teaspoon pure almond extract
2 eggs
15 drops liquid stevia
1/8 teaspoon kosher salt

1 ¾ cups almond flour
1/2 teaspoon baking powder
1/4 teaspoon ground cinnamon
1/2 cup walnuts, chopped
1/3 cup sugar-free baker's chocolate, cut into chunks

## DIRECTIONS

Heat the butter in a pan that is preheated over a moderate flame; stir and cook until it is browned.
In a mixing bowl, beat the pure almond extract with the eggs, stevia, and salt.
Add the melted butter, along with the other ingredients.
Preheat your oven to 350 degrees F. Line a cookie sheet with a parchment paper. Spritz with a nonstick cooking spray.
Bake for 25 minutes and transfer to a wire rack to cool before serving.

# 446. Coconut Creamsicle Chia Pudding

**(Ready in about 20 minutes | Servings 4)**

**Per serving: 226 Calories; 17.9g Fat; 7g Carbs; 5.9g Protein;**

## INGREDIENTS

1 cup water
1 cup heavy cream
1 cup coconut milk, unsweetened
1 teaspoon vanilla extract
1 cup chia seeds

1/4 cup coconut shreds, unsweetened
2 tablespoons erythritol
1/4 teaspoon ground cloves
1/2 teaspoon ground anise star

## DIRECTIONS

Thoroughly combine all of the above ingredients in a mixing dish.
Allow it to stand at least 20 minutes, stirring periodically.
Divide among four individual cups to serve. Enjoy!

# 447. Cheesecake Bars with Raspberry Topping

**(Ready in about 30 minutes | Servings 6)**

**Per serving: 333 Calories; 28.4g Fat; 6.3g Carbs; 11.7g Protein;**

## INGREDIENTS

**For the Cheesecake Bars:**
1 stick butter, melted
4 eggs
1 cup mascarpone cheese
1 teaspoon vanilla paste
1/4 teaspoon star anise, ground
3 tablespoons Swerve
1/3 teaspoon baking powder

**For the Raspberry Topping:**
3/4 cup, frozen raspberries
1 ½ tablespoons erythritol
1/2 teaspoon lemon juice
A pinch of salt
1 ½ tablespoons water

## DIRECTIONS

Thoroughly combine all ingredients for the cheesecakes with a hand mixer. Line a baking pan with parchment paper or Silpat mat.
Bake in the preheated oven at 330 degrees F, approximately 25 minutes. Transfer to a wire rack to cool completely.
Meanwhile, place all of the ingredients for the topping in a pan that is preheated over a moderate heat; bring the mixture to a boil.
Now, reduce the heat and let it simmer until the sauce has thickened.
Cut the cheesecake into squares. Spoon about 2 tablespoons of the raspberry sauce over each cheesecake square. Enjoy!

# 448. Simple Strawberries Scones

**(Ready in about 25 minutes | Servings 10)**

**Per serving: 245 Calories; 21.6g Fat; 7.4g Carbs; 3.8g Protein;**

## INGREDIENTS

1 cup coconut flour
1 cup almond flour
1 teaspoon baking powder
A pinch of salt

1 cup strawberries
2 eggs
1 ½ sticks butter
1 cup heavy cream

10 tablespoons liquid stevia
1 teaspoon vanilla extract

## DIRECTIONS

Start by preheating your oven to 350 degrees F.

In a mixing bowl, thoroughly combine the flour with the baking powder, salt and strawberries.

In another mixing bowl, beat the eggs with the butter and cream. Stir in the liquid stevia and vanilla extract; stir to combine well.

Combine the 2 mixtures and stir until you obtain a soft dough. Knead gently and avoid overworking your dough.

Shape into 16 triangles and arrange on a lined baking sheet. Bake for 18 minutes and serve your scones cold.

# 449. Coconut and Avocado Mousse

**(Ready in about 15 minutes+ chilling time | Servings 6)**

**Per serving: 303 Calories; 30g Fat; 3.1g Carbs; 3.5g Protein;**

## INGREDIENTS

1 cup coconut milk
1 ½ cups avocado, pitted, peeled and mashed

A pinch of salt
A pinch of grated nutmeg
1 cup heavy cream

1/2 cup softened cream cheese
2 tablespoons confectioners Swerve

## DIRECTIONS

In a deep pan, warm the coconut milk over medium heat.

Stir in the avocado, salt, and nutmeg and cook, stirring continuously, about 5 minutes or until the mixture bubbles up.

Then, beat the heavy cream, cheese, and Swerve with an electric mixer on medium-high speed. Reserve roughly 4 tablespoons of this cream mixture to top mousse before serving.

Afterwards, place in your refrigerator to set for a couple of hours.

Serve with a dollop of cream mixture on top. Bon appétit!

# 450. Chocolate Cake with Almond-Choc Ganache

**(Ready in about 50 minutes + chilling time | Servings 10)**

**Per serving: 313 Calories; 30.7g Fat; 7.5g Carbs; 7.3g Protein;**

## INGREDIENTS

1/2 cup water
3/4 cup granulated Swerve
14 ounces unsweetened chocolate chunks
2 sticks butter, cold
5 eggs
1/2 teaspoon pure almond extract
1/4 teaspoon ground nutmeg
1/4 teaspoon ground cardamom
A pinch of salt

**For Almond-Choc Ganache:**

3/4 cups double cream
9 ounces sugar-free dark chocolate, broken into chunks
1/4 cup smooth almond butter
A pinch of salt
1/2 teaspoon ginger powder
1/2 teaspoon cardamom powder

## DIRECTIONS

Begin by preheating your oven to 360 degrees F. Line a baking pan with parchment paper.

Now bring the water to a rolling boil in a deep pan; add the Swerve and cook until it is dissolved.

Microwave the chocolate until it has melted. Add the butter to the melted chocolate and beat with an electric mixer.

Add the chocolate mixture to the hot water mixture. Now, add the eggs, one at a time, whipping continuously.

Add the almond extract, nutmeg, cardamom, and salt; stir well. Spoon the mixture into the prepared baking pan; wrap with foil.

Lower the baking pan into a larger pan; add boiling water about 1 inch deep.

Bake for 40 to 45 minutes. Allow it to cool completely before removing from the pan.

Meanwhile, place the double cream in a pan over a moderately high heat and bring to a boil. Pour the hot cream over the dark chocolate; whisk until the chocolate is melted.

Add the remaining ingredients for the ganache and whip until it is uniform and smooth. Finally, glaze a cooled cake and serve well-chilled. Enjoy!

# 451. Melt-in-the-Mouth Blueberry Meringues

**(Ready in about 2 hours | Servings 10)**

**Per serving: 51 Calories; 0g Fat; 4g Carbs; 12g Protein;**

## INGREDIENTS

3 large egg whites, at room temperature
1/2 teaspoon vanilla paste
A pinch of salt
1 teaspoon finely grated lemon zest

1/3 cup Swerve
3 tablespoons freeze-dried blueberry, crushed with a pestle and mortar

## DIRECTIONS

Preheat an oven to 200 degrees F.

Now, beat the egg whites, vanilla, salt, and lemon zest with an electric mixer on medium-high speed. Add the Swerve and continue mixing on high until stiff and glossy.

Add crushed blueberries and mix until everything is well incorporated.

Drop the meringue, about 2 inches apart, on the parchment-lined baking sheets; you can use a pastry tube here.

Bake about 2 hours. Leave the meringues in the turned-off oven for several hours.

# KETO FAVORITES

## 452. Mediterranean-Style Garlic Aioli

**(Ready in about 10 minutes | Servings 8)**

**Per serving: 116 Calories; 13.2g Fat; 0.2g Carbs; 0.4g Protein;**

### INGREDIENTS

1 tablespoon balsamic vinegar
1 egg yolk, at room temperature
1 clove garlic, crushed
1/2 teaspoon sea salt

1/2 cup olive oil
1/4 teaspoon ground black pepper
1/4 cup fresh dill, chopped

### DIRECTIONS

Add the vinegar, egg yolk, garlic and salt to a blender; pulse until creamy and smooth. Turn to low setting.
Slowly drizzle in the olive oil and mix until the oil is well incorporated.
Add the ground black pepper and dill; gently stir to combine. Store in the refrigerator and garnish with fresh snipped chives to serve.

## 453. Juicy & Flavorful Lamb Cheeseburgers

**(Ready in about 20 minutes | Servings 6)**

**Per serving: 252 Calories; 15.5g Fat; 1.2g Carbs; 26g Protein;**

### INGREDIENTS

1 pound ground lamb
1/2 cup scallions, chopped
2 garlic cloves, finely chopped
1/4 teaspoon ground black pepper, or more to taste

Sea salt and cayenne pepper, to taste
2 ounces mascarpone cheese
3 ounces Asiago cheese, grated
2 tablespoons olive oil

### DIRECTIONS

In a mixing bowl, combine the ground meat, scallions, garlic, black pepper, salt and cayenne pepper.
Shape the meat mixture into 6 balls; flatten to make 6 patties.
In another mixing bowl, combine the mascarpone with the grated Asiago cheese.
Divide the cheese mixture among the prepared patties. Wrap the meat mixture around the cheese until the filling is sealed inside.
Heat the oil in a heavy-bottomed skillet over a moderately high heat. Cook your burgers 5 to 6 minutes per side, until thoroughly cooked.
Serve with fresh or pickled salad. Bon appétit!

## 454. Chocolate and Cashew Chia Pudding

**(Ready in about 35 minutes | Servings 4)**

**Per serving: 93 Calories; 5.1g Fat; 7.2g Carbs; 4.4g Protein;**

### INGREDIENTS

3/4 cup cashew milk, preferably homemade
1/4 cup water
2 tablespoons almond butter
1/2 cup chia seeds

20 drops liquid stevia
1/2 teaspoon maple extract
3 tablespoons orange flower water
2 tablespoons cocoa powder, unsweetened

### DIRECTIONS

Place the cashew milk, almond butter, chia seeds, stevia, maple extract, orange flower water, and cocoa powder in a mixing bowl.
Allow it to stand for 30 minutes, stirring periodically.
Divide among 4 serving bowls and garnish with hemp seeds.

# 455. Prosciutto, Egg and Brie Cups

**(Ready in about 20 minutes | Servings 6)**

**Per serving: 268 Calories; 18.3g Fat; 0.7g Carbs; 26.2g Protein;**

## INGREDIENTS

24 small and thin slices of prosciutto
6 eggs, beaten
Coarse salt and freshly ground black pepper, to taste

1/4 cup fresh cilantro, coarsely chopped
2 ounces cream cheese
2 ounces Brie, chopped

## DIRECTIONS

Start by preheating your oven to 390 degrees F.
Line each muffin cup with 2 slices of prosciutto so that they circle each mold.
In a mixing dish, thoroughly combine the remaining ingredients. Fill each prosciutto lined muffin cup 3/4 of the way with the egg/cheese mixture.
Bake for 15 minutes or until your cups don't jiggle. Serve immediately and enjoy!

# 456. Colby and Carrot Meatballs

**(Ready in about 35 minutes | Servings 5)**

**Per serving: 342 Calories; 23.7g Fat; 4.3g Carbs; 31.7g Protein;**

## INGREDIENTS

1 egg, beaten
1 pound ground turkey
1 carrot, grated
2 garlic cloves, minced
1 onion, chopped

1 tablespoon Italian mixed herbs
Salt and freshly ground black pepper, to taste
2 tablespoons olive oil
1 cup Colby cheese, shredded

## DIRECTIONS

Preheat your oven to 360 degrees F.
Mix all of the above ingredients, except for the cheese, until everything is well incorporated.
Then, shape this mixture into 20 meatballs; arrange on a parchment-lined baking sheet.
Bake for 25 minutes, turning once. Scatter the cheese over the balls and bake an additional 7 minutes or until it melts completely. Bon appétit!

# 457. Italian-Style Prosciutto and Mascarpone Balls

**(Ready in about 15 minutes | Servings 4)**

**Per serving: 88 Calories; 6.5g Fat; 0.7g Carbs; 6.5g Protein;**

## INGREDIENTS

4 prosciutto slice
1/2 cup mascarpone cheese
1/2 teaspoon smoke flavor
1/2 teaspoon maple flavor

1/4 teaspoon apple cider vinegar
1 teaspoon shallot powder
1/2 teaspoon garlic powder
1 teaspoon red pepper flakes

## DIRECTIONS

In a mixing bowl, thoroughly combine the prosciutto, mascarpone cheese, smoke flavor, maple flavor and apple cider vinegar.
After that, add the remaining ingredients and stir to combine well.
Form into 4 balls with a spoon.
Serve right away or refrigerate up to 3 days. Bon appétit!

# 458. Apple Pie Granola

**(Ready in about 35 minutes | Servings 8)**

**Per serving: 281 Calories; 26.6g Fat; 7.7g Carbs; 5.4g Protein;**

## INGREDIENTS

3 tablespoons coconut oil
1/4 cup stevia
1 cup shredded coconut, unsweetened
3/4 cup pecans, chopped
1/2 cup cashews, chopped

1/2 cup pumpkin seeds
1/3 cup sunflower seeds
1 teaspoon apple pie spice mix
A pinch of salt

## DIRECTIONS

Start by preheating your oven to 300 degrees F.
Heat the coconut oil in a pan over moderate heat, add the stevia and stir until everything is well combined.
In a large bowl, combine the remaining ingredients. Add the mixture to the pan; stir to combine.
Spread this mixture on a lined baking sheet. Bake for 30 minutes, stirring once or twice. Leave your granola to cool down before serving.
Enjoy!

# 459. Spicy and Savory Tuna Mousse

**(Ready in about 20 minutes + chilling time | Servings 5)**

**Per serving: 100 Calories; 5.8g Fat; 4.1g Carbs; 8g Protein;**

## INGREDIENTS

1 ½ teaspoons gelatin, powdered
3 tablespoons water
2 ounces mascarpone cheese
3 tablespoons mayonnaise
1 teaspoon Dijon mustard
3 ounces canned tuna, flaked

1/4 cup shallots, finely chopped
1 garlic clove, minced
1 teaspoon jalapeno, minced
1/2 teaspoon celery salt
1/4 teaspoon black pepper, preferably freshly ground
1/3 teaspoon fresh ginger, grated

## DIRECTIONS

Dissolve the gelatin in water; allow it to stand for 10 minutes.
Now, melt the mascarpone in a pan over moderate heat; stir in the gelatin and whisk vigorously until well blended.
Allow this mixture to cool to room temperature. Add the other ingredients and mix again until everything is well incorporated.
Divide the mixture among 5 mousse molds and place in your refrigerator overnight. To serve, invert the mold over a plate and enjoy!

# 460. Cheese and Garlicky Chicken Fillets

**(Ready in about 20 minutes | Servings 4)**

**Per serving: 416 Calories; 26g Fat; 3.2g Carbs; 40.7g Protein;**

## INGREDIENTS

1 tablespoon butter
1 pound chicken fillets, sliced
2 garlic cloves, minced
1/2 cup heavy cream

1/3 cup vegetable broth
2 tablespoon tomato paste
1 cup Colby cheese, shredded

## DIRECTIONS

Heat the butter in a pan that is preheated over moderate heat; fry the chicken with the garlic for 4 minutes, stirring periodically; reserve.
Now, whisk in the heavy cream, vegetable broth, and tomato paste; cook until it has thickened.
Add the reserved chicken back to the pan; scatter the shredded cheese over it. Cover and let it sit for 5 to 10 minutes or until the cheese has melted. Bon appétit!

## 461. Camembert, Gruyere and Provolone Fondue

**(Ready in about 15 minutes | Servings 10)**

**Per serving: 148 Calories; 10.2g Fat; 1.5g Carbs; 9.3g Protein;**

### INGREDIENTS

1/3 pound camembert cheese, chopped
1/3 pound Gruyere cheese, shredded
1/2 cup Provolone, freshly grated
1 tablespoon xanthan gum
1/2 teaspoon granulated garlic

1 teaspoon onion powder
3/4 cup Sauvignon blanc
1/2 tablespoon lemon juice
Ground black pepper, to taste
1 Roma tomato, chopped

### DIRECTIONS

Preheat the broiler.
In a cast-iron skillet, combine the cheese with the xanthan gum, granulated garlic, and onion powder; stir to combine well.
Now, add the wine and lemon juice. Season with black pepper to taste and stir again.
Then, place the skillet under the broiler for 6 to 7 minutes, until the cheese begins to brown.
Garnish with chopped tomatoes and serve hot. Bon appétit!

## 462. Grilled Feta Cheese and Eggs Plate

**(Ready in about 20 minutes | Servings 4)**

**Per serving: 542 Calories; 46.4g Fat; 6.2g Carbs; 23.7g Protein;**

### INGREDIENTS

1 (12-ounce) piece of Feta cheese
3 teaspoons olive oil
1 teaspoon dried Greek seasoning blend
1 tablespoon butter
6 eggs

1/2 teaspoon sea salt
1/4 teaspoon crushed red pepper flakes, or more to taste
1 ½ cups avocado, pitted and sliced
1 cup grape tomatoes, halved
4 tablespoons walnuts, coarsely chopped

### DIRECTIONS

Heat your grill to a medium-low. Place the Feta in the center of a piece of heavy-duty foil. Now, drizzle with the oil and season with the Greek seasoning blend.
Seal the foil to form a packet. Grill for 15 minutes; after that, slice into four pieces.
Meanwhile, melt 1 tablespoon of butter in a frying pan; then, cook the eggs over a medium-high heat. Gently stir with a spatula to form large, soft curds.
Season with salt and pepper.
To serve, place the eggs and grilled cheese on a plate. Serve with the avocado and tomatoes, garnished with chopped walnuts.

## 463. Family Short Ribs with Bell Peppers

**(Ready in about 15 minutes | Servings 4)**

**Per serving: 490 Calories; 44g Fat; 5.5g Carbs; 16.9g Protein;**

### INGREDIENTS

1 pound boneless short ribs, cut into serving pieces
1/4 teaspoon ground black pepper
1 teaspoon paprika
Garlic salt, to taste

1 tablespoon tallow, at room temperature
2 garlic cloves, smashed
2 bell peppers, deveined and thinly sliced
2 tablespoons chives, chopped

### DIRECTIONS

Season the short ribs with black pepper, paprika and garlic salt. Melt the tallow in a pan that is preheated over a moderately high heat.
Then, brown the short ribs for 3 minutes per side or until no longer pink; reserve. Cook the garlic and peppers in the pan drippings until tender and fragrant.
Serve with the reserved short ribs, garnished with fresh chives.

# 464. Mascarpone and Caramel Balls

**(Ready in about 5 minutes | Servings 4)**

**Per serving: 180 Calories; 17.3g Fat; 3.4g Carbs; 5.3g Protein;**

### INGREDIENTS

3 ounces mascarpone

3 ounces pine nuts, chopped

1/2 teaspoon caramel flavor

1/4 teaspoon allspice

### DIRECTIONS

Mix all ingredients in a food processor until uniform and smooth.

Form the mixture into 8 balls and serve well chilled.

# 465. Extraordinary Pizza Dip

**(Ready in about 20 minutes | Servings 10)**

**Per serving: 160 Calories; 12.7g Fat; 2.4g Carbs; 8.9g Protein;**

### INGREDIENTS

8 ounces salami, chopped, a few slices reserved

8 ounces Ricotta cheese, room temperature

2 ounces Colby cheese, shredded

1 cup ripe tomato, pureed

1 teaspoon garlic paste

1/4 teaspoon chipotle powder

1/2 teaspoon red pepper flakes, crushed

1 teaspoon shallot powder

1 teaspoon porcini powder

1/2 teaspoon dried oregano

1/2 teaspoon dried basil

Flaky sea salt and freshly ground black pepper, to taste

1/2 cup Kalamata olives, to garnish

### DIRECTIONS

Preheat an oven to 360 degrees F.

Place all ingredients, except for the Kalamata olives, in a casserole dish. Mix until everything is well combined.

Top with the reserved salami slices and Kalamata olives. Bake for 15 minutes or until it is done to your liking. Serve warm and enjoy!

# 466. Spring Sour Cream Omelet

**(Ready in about 15 minutes | Servings 2)**

**Per serving: 319 Calories; 25g Fat; 7.4g Carbs; 14.9g Protein;**

### INGREDIENTS

2 teaspoons butter

2 spring onions, chopped

2 spring garlic, chopped

4 eggs, beaten

1 (8-ounce) carton sour cream, divided

2 medium-sized tomatoes, sliced

1 piquillo pepper, minced

2 tablespoons chervil, chopped

Kosher salt and freshly ground black pepper, to taste

### DIRECTIONS

Melt the butter in a pan that is preheated over a moderate flame. Sauté the spring onion and garlic until they are just tender and fragrant. Then, whisk the eggs with the sour cream. Add the egg mixture to the pan and gently smooth the surface with a wide spatula; cook until the eggs are puffy and lightly browned on the bottom.

Place the tomatoes, piquillo pepper and chervil on one side of the omelet. Season with salt and pepper.

Fold your omelet in half. Slide the omelet onto a warm serving plate and cut into wedges. Bon appétit!

# 467. Baked Chicken Skin Chips with Cheesy Sauce

**(Ready in about 15 minutes | Servings 4)**

**Per serving: 119 Calories; 10.5g Fat; 1.1g Carbs; 5.1g Protein;**

## INGREDIENTS

Skin from 4 chicken thighs
1/4 cup Cottage cheese
2 tablespoons sour cream
1 tablespoon ghee, at room temperature

1/2 teaspoon ground cumin
2 tablespoons green onions, finely chopped
Sea salt and ground black pepper, to taste

## DIRECTIONS

Start by preheating your oven to 360 degrees F. Then, bake the skins for 10 to 12 minutes until they are browned and crispy. Allow the chicken skins to cool slightly; then, cut them into bite-sized pieces.
In a mixing bowl, thoroughly combine the remaining ingredients to make the spread. Serve with the prepared chicken skins.

# 468. Must Make Cheese Sauce

**(Ready in about 15 minutes | Servings 6)**

**Per serving: 110 Calories; 10.5g Fat; 0.7g Carbs; 3.4g Protein;**

## INGREDIENTS

1/3 cup heavy cream
1 ½ tablespoons ghee
1/2 cup Neufchatel cheese
1/3 cup Gouda, grated

3 tablespoons water
1 teaspoon shallot powder
1/3 teaspoon hot paprika

## DIRECTIONS

Heat the cream with the ghee in a sauté pan over a moderate flame. Once it is heated, add the Neufchatel to the pan.
Then, stir in the other ingredients. Cook approximately 4 minutes, stirring continuously. Serve right away!

# 469. Creamy Walnut Bars

**(Ready in about 20 minutes | Servings 4)**

**Per serving: 278 Calories; 30.1g Fat; 2.2g Carbs; 2.2g Protein;**

## INGREDIENTS

1 cup double cream
1/4 teaspoon cardamom
2 tablespoons coconut oil
2 tablespoons walnut butter

A pinch of coarse salt
A pinch of grated nutmeg
1/2 cup walnuts, coarsely chopped

## DIRECTIONS

Line a baking pan with foil.
In a mixing bowl, thoroughly combine the double cream and cardamom. Scrape the mixture into the prepared pan.
In a separate bowl, whisk together the coconut oil, walnut butter, salt, and nutmeg. Spread this glaze over the creamed mixture.
Scatter the chopped walnuts over the top. Place it in the freezer for 15 minutes.
Cut into squares and enjoy!

## 470. Creole Crawfish Frittata

**(Ready in about 25 minutes | Servings 3)**

**Per serving: 265 Calories; 15.8g Fat; 7.1g Carbs; 22.9g Protein;**

### INGREDIENTS

1 tablespoon olive oil
1 red onion, chopped
4 ounces crawfish tail meat, chopped

1 teaspoon Creole seasoning blend
6 large eggs, slightly beaten
1/2 cup yogurt

### DIRECTIONS

Preheat your oven to 350 degrees F.

Heat the oil in a large oven-proof non-stick skillet that is preheated over medium-high heat.

Sauté the onions until they are softened; add the crawfish and cook for 2 minutes longer. Sprinkle with Creole seasoning.

Make sure your ingredients are evenly distributed across the bottom of the skillet.

Now, whisk the eggs with the yogurt. Pour the egg mixture into the skillet.

Transfer the skillet to the preheated oven and bake approximately 18 minutes or until the eggs are thoroughly cooked. Cut into wedges and serve warm. Bon appétit!

## 471. Reblochon and Bacon Party Balls

**(Ready in about 15 minutes | Servings 5)**

**Per serving: 206 Calories; 16.5g Fat; 0.6g Carbs; 13.4g Protein;**

### INGREDIENTS

3 ounces bacon
6 ounces Reblochon
1 jalapeño pepper, seeded and finely chopped

1/4 teaspoon parsley flakes
1/2 teaspoon paprika

### DIRECTIONS

Cook the bacon in a frying pan over a moderately high flame. Cook until it is well browned; then, finely chop the bacon into small pieces.

In your food processor, blend the other ingredients until everything is well incorporated. Allow the mixture to chill in your refrigerator.

Shape the well-chilled mixture into 10 balls.

Place the crushed bacon in a shallow plate. Roll your balls around to coat all sides.

Serve immediately or refrigerate up to 3 days. Bon appétit!

## 472. Pimiento-Cheese Bites with Carrot Pepper Chips

**(Ready in about 25 minutes | Servings 8)**

**Per serving: 177 Calories; 12.9g Fat; 6.8g Carbs; 8.8g Protein;**

### INGREDIENTS

1 cup Pepper-Jack cheese, shredded
1/2 cup Greek yogurt
1 cup Romano cheese, freshly grated
2 tablespoons tomato paste
1/2 teaspoon dried rosemary leaves, crushed
1 teaspoon dried thyme leaves, crushed
2 tablespoons pimientos, chopped
Coarse salt and freshly ground black pepper, to taste

**For Carrot Pepper Chips:**
1 pound carrots, cut into sticks
2 tablespoons sesame oil
1 teaspoon black pepper, preferably freshly cracked
Coarse salt, to taste

### DIRECTIONS

Thoroughly combine the cheese, yogurt, tomato paste, rosemary, thyme, pimientos, salt, and black pepper in a mixing bowl.

Place in foil liners - candy cups and keep in the refrigerator until ready to serve.

Now, preheat your oven to 430 degrees F.

Toss the carrots with the sesame oil, pepper, and salt. Place them in a single layer on a cookie sheet.

Bake about 20 minutes, tossing once or twice. Dip the carrot pepper chips in pimiento-cheese cups. Bon appétit!

## 473. Mushroom Panna Cotta

**(Ready in about 15 minutes + chilling time | Servings 6)**

**Per serving: 489 Calories; 47.4g Fat; 6.9g Carbs; 12.7g Protein;**

### INGREDIENTS

1 tablespoon butter

2 ounces fresh mushrooms, chopped

2 teaspoons powdered unflavored gelatin

1 1/3 cups heavy cream

1 cup sour cream

8 ounces blue cheese

1 teaspoon Herbes de Provence

1/4 cup pecan halves

### DIRECTIONS

Melt the butter in a pan over high heat; now sauté the mushrooms for 4 minutes, stirring continuously.

Add the gelatin and heavy cream and cook, bringing to a boil.

Remove from heat; add the sour cream, cheese, and Herbes de Provence. Pour this mixture evenly into 6 glasses. Refrigerate at least 6 hours or overnight.

Serve garnished with pecan halves.

## 474. Fajita Beef Sausage with Vegetables

**(Ready in about 25 minutes | Servings 4)**

**Per serving: 227 Calories; 18g Fat; 7g Carbs; 7.1g Protein;**

### INGREDIENTS

1 tablespoon lard

2 smoked beef sausage links, sliced

1 teaspoon crushed garlic

2 zucchinis, sliced

1 carrot, sliced

1 teaspoon fajita seasoning

1 piquillo pepper, minced

2 bell peppers, sliced

1/2 teaspoon saffron

### DIRECTIONS

Warm the lard in a wok that is preheated over a moderate flame.

Now, brown the chicken sausage along with the garlic approximately 8 minutes.

Add the other ingredients and cook, stirring periodically, for 13 minutes more. Eat warm.

## 475. Three-Cheese Fried Pizza with Peppers

**(Ready in about 15 minutes | Servings 4)**

**Per serving: 266 Calories; 23.6g Fat; 6.6g Carbs; 9g Protein;**

### INGREDIENTS

2 tablespoons olive oil

1/2 cup Pepper Jack cheese, shredded

1 ¼ cups mozzarella cheese, shredded

1/2 cup cream cheese

2 tablespoons sour cream

2 garlic cloves, chopped

1 red bell pepper, sliced

1 green bell pepper, sliced

10 cherry tomatoes, halved

1 teaspoon oregano

Salt and black pepper, to taste

### DIRECTIONS

Heat the olive oil in a pan that is preheated over a moderate flame.

Add the cheese and make sure to cover the bottom; cook about 5 minutes until it is golden brown and crispy.

Spread the sour cream and garlic over the crust. Add the bell peppers and tomatoes; cook for a further 2 minutes.

Sprinkle with oregano, salt, and pepper and serve warm.

# 476. Easy Pumpkin and Cheese Mousse

**(Ready in about 15 minutes + chilling time | Servings 6)**

**Per serving: 368 Calories; 33.7g Fat; 5.6g Carbs; 13.8g Protein;**

## INGREDIENTS

1 ½ cups heavy cream
1/2 cup cream cheese
1/2 cup erythritol
3 eggs
1 ¼ cups canned pumpkin

1/2 teaspoon ground cloves
1/2 teaspoon ground cinnamon
1/4 teaspoon grated nutmeg
A pinch of coarse salt

## DIRECTIONS

In a pan, combine the heavy cream, cream cheese, and erythritol, and bring it to a boil; whisk frequently.
Whisk the eggs; slowly add 1/2 of the hot heavy cream mixture to the beaten eggs. Add the mixture back to the pan. Cook another 2 to 4 minutes, or until the mixture has thickened.
Heat off; stir in the pumpkin, cloves, cinnamon, nutmeg, and salt. Divide the mixture among serving bowls and place in the refrigerator. Serve well-chilled. Bon appétit!

# 477. 5-Minute Egg and Salami Breakfast

**(Ready in about 5 minutes | Servings 3)**

**Per serving: 303 Calories; 22.4g Fat; 3.6g Carbs; 21.6g Protein;**

## INGREDIENTS

3 teaspoons butter, melted
6 eggs
1/2 cup American yellow cheese, shredded
1/2 cup cottage cheese

3 slices Genoa salami, chopped
Coarse salt and ground black pepper, to taste
1 teaspoon yellow mustard

## DIRECTIONS

Grease 3 mason jars with melted butter.
Crack two eggs into each jar. Divide the other ingredients among the two jars.
Cover and shake until everything is well incorporated.
Remove the lids and microwave for 2 minutes on high. Eat warm and enjoy!

# 478. Turkey and Bacon Meatloaf Cups

**(Ready in about 30 minutes | Servings 6)**

**Per serving: 276 Calories; 18.3g Fat; 1.2g Carbs; 29.2g Protein;**

## INGREDIENTS

2 tablespoons shallot, chopped
1 teaspoon garlic, minced
1 pound ground turkey
2 ounces cooked bacon, chopped
1 egg, beaten
1 teaspoon brown mustard

Coarse salt and ground black pepper, to taste
1/2 teaspoon crushed red pepper flakes
1 teaspoon dried basil
1/2 teaspoon dried oregano
4 ounces Brie cheese, cubed

## DIRECTIONS

Thoroughly combine the shallot, garlic, ground turkey, bacon, egg and mustard in a mixing bowl.
Season with salt, black pepper, red pepper, basil and oregano.
Mix until everything is well incorporated. Divide the mixture among muffin cups. Insert one cube of Brie into each meatloaf cup. Seal the top to cover the Brie by using your fingers.
Bake at 350 degrees F for about 20 minutes, or until the meatloaf cups are golden brown. Allow them to cool for 10 minutes before removing from the muffin pan.

# 479. French-Style Strawberry Omelet

**(Ready in about 10 minutes | Servings 1)**

**Per serving: 488 Calories; 42g Fat; 8g Carbs; 15.3g Protein;**

## INGREDIENTS

2 eggs, beaten
2 tablespoons heavy cream
1/2 teaspoon ground cloves
1 tablespoon coconut oil

2 tablespoons cream cheese
6 fresh strawberries, sliced
1 tablespoon Cognac (optional

## DIRECTIONS

Whisk the eggs with the heavy cream and ground cloves.
Next, melt the coconut oil in a pan that is preheated over medium-high heat. When hot, add the egg mixture; cook for about 3 minutes until the base is thoroughly cooked.
Tip the omelet out onto a plate; top with cheese and strawberries.
Add warmed Cognac over your omelet and flambé. (optional)
Bon appétit!

# 480. Crêpes with Butter-Rum Syrup

**(Ready in about 25 minutes | Servings 6)**

**Per serving: 243 Calories; 19.6g Fat; 5.5g Carbs; 11g Protein;**

## INGREDIENTS

**For Crêpes:**
6 ounces cream cheese, softened
6 eggs
1 ½ tablespoons granulated Swerve
1/4 cup almond flour
1 teaspoon baking soda
1 teaspoon baking powder
1/2 teaspoon apple pie spice mix

**For the Syrup:**
3/4 cup water
1 tablespoon butter
3/4 cup Swerve, powdered
1 tablespoon rum extract
1/2 teaspoon xanthan gum

## DIRECTIONS

Combine all ingredients for the crepes using an electric mixer. Mix until everything is well incorporated.
Grease a frying pan with melted butter; fry your crepes over a moderate heat until the edges begin to brown.
Flip and fry on the other side until it is slightly browned.
Whisk the water, butter, and Swerve in a pan over medium heat; simmer about 6 minutes, stirring continuously.
Add the mixture to a blender along with the rum extract and 1/4 teaspoon of xanthan gum; mix to combine.
Add the remaining 1/4 teaspoon of xanthan gum and let it stand until the syrup has thickened. Serve with the warm crepes and enjoy!

# 481. Mustard Rolled Turkey with Prosciutto

**(Ready in about 50 minutes | Servings 6)**

**Per serving: 275 Calories; 9.5g Fat; 1.3g Carbs; 44.5g Protein;**

## INGREDIENTS

6 (4-ounce) turkey fillets
1 tablespoon herb-infused olive oil
3 tablespoons whole grain mustard

2 tablespoons fresh parsley, roughly chopped
3 garlic cloves, chopped
1 jalapeno pepper, chopped

1 teaspoon tarragon
Salt and ground black pepper, to taste
1 teaspoon hot paprika
6 slices prosciutto

## DIRECTIONS

Preheat your oven to 390 degrees F. Flatten the turkey fillets with a meat mallet.
Rub the herb-infused olive oil and mustard all over the turkey breasts.
Place the fresh parsley on each fillet. Divide the chopped garlic, jalapeno pepper, tarragon, salt, black pepper and paprika among fillets.
Roll the fillets in the prosciutto. Place in a glass baking dish and transfer to the preheated oven.
Bake for 35 to 45 minutes (until the internal temperature reaches 180 degrees F). Bon appétit!

# 482. Pancetta, Cheese and Egg Muffins

**(Ready in about 30 minutes | Servings 9)**

**Per serving: 294 Calories; 21.4g Fat; 3.5g Carbs; 21g Protein;**

## INGREDIENTS

9 slices pancetta
9 eggs
A bunch of scallions, chopped
1/2 cup Monterey Jack cheese, shredded

1/4 teaspoon garlic powder
1/2 teaspoon dried dill weed
Sea salt and ground black pepper, to taste

## DIRECTIONS

Start by preheating your oven to 390 degrees F.
Then, brush a 9-cup muffin pan with oil; line each cup with one slice of pancetta.
In a mixing bowl, thoroughly combine the remaining ingredients.
Divide the egg mixture among the muffin cups. Bake in the preheated oven for 20 minutes. Bon appétit!

# 483. Perfect Tuna Pâté

**(Ready in about 10 minutes + chilling time | Servings 12)**

**Per serving: 64 Calories; 2.9g Fat; 1.3g Carbs; 7.9g Protein;**

## INGREDIENTS

1 (14-ounce) tuna in brine, drained
1/2 cup Ricotta cheese
1/4 cup sour cream
2 tablespoons mayonnaise
1/2 teaspoon country Dijon mustard

2 ounces cilantro, finely chopped
Coarse salt and freshly cracked mixed peppercorns, to your liking
1/2 teaspoon smoked paprika

## DIRECTIONS

Add all ingredients to a mixing bowl.
Mix with a wide spatula until everything is well incorporated.
Pour into a greased mold; chill for 6 hours or overnight. Unmold onto a serving platter and enjoy.

# 484. Hemp Heart Porridge with Brazil Nuts

**(Ready in about 20 minutes | Servings 4)**

**Per serving: 405 Calories; 37g Fat; 6.6g Carbs; 14.8g Protein;**

## INGREDIENTS

2 tablespoons coconut oil, room temperature
4 eggs, lightly whisked
1/4 cup hemp hearts
1/4 cup flax seed, freshly ground
20 drops liquid stevia

1/4 teaspoon pinch psyllium husk powder
1 teaspoon pure vanilla extract
1/4 teaspoon coarse salt
A dash of ground cinnamon
16 Brazil nuts

## DIRECTIONS

Preheat a sauté pan over medium-low heat. Add the coconut oil, eggs, hemp, flaxseed, stevia, and psyllium husk powder.
Stir, uncovered, until the mixture is well combined; raise the heat to medium and stir in the vanilla, salt, and cinnamon. Cook until the porridge starts to boil lightly.
Divide the warm porridge among four serving bowls. Top each serving with 4 Brazil nuts and eat warm.

# 485. Pancetta and Asiago Waffles

**(Ready in about 20 minutes | Servings 3)**

**Per serving: 453 Calories; 37g Fat; 4.5g Carbs; 25.6g Protein;**

## INGREDIENTS

6 large-sized eggs, separate the egg whites and egg yolks
1/2 teaspoon baking powder
1/2 teaspoon baking soda

4 tablespoons ghee
Kosher salt, to taste
1/2 teaspoon dried oregano
3 tablespoons tomato paste

3 ounces pancetta, chopped
3 ounces Asiago cheese, shredded

## DIRECTIONS

Thoroughly combine the egg yolks, baking powder, baking soda, ghee, salt, and oregano in a mixing bowl.
Now, beat the egg whites with an electric mixer until pale. Gently mix the egg whites into the egg yolk mixture.
Generously grease a waffle iron. Heat you waffle iron and pour in 1/4 cup of the batter. Cook until golden, about 3 minutes. Repeat until you run out of batter; you will have 6 thin waffles.
Add one waffle back to the waffle iron; spread 1 tablespoon of tomato paste onto your waffle; top with 1 ounce of pancetta and 1 ounce of shredded cheese.
Top with another waffle; cook until the cheese is melted. Repeat with the remaining ingredients. Serve right away!

# 486. Greek-Style Berry Pancakes

**(Ready in about 20 minutes | Servings 4)**

**Per serving: 237 Calories; 16.3g Fat; 5.5g Carbs; 14.5g Protein;**

## INGREDIENTS

**For the Batter:**
5 eggs
6 ounces Ricotta cheese, room temperature
1 teaspoon baking powder§
A pinch of salt

**For the Topping:**
2 tablespoons coconut oil
1 cup fresh mixed berries
1/4 teaspoon freshly grated nutmeg
2 tablespoons Swerve
1/2 cup Greek yogurt

## DIRECTIONS

Thoroughly combine all the batter ingredients with an electric mixer.
Heat up a small amount of the coconut oil in a frying pan over medium heat.
Spoon some of the batter into the pan and cook approximately 3 minutes on each side.
Divide the fresh berries among the prepared pancakes; sprinkle with grated nutmeg and Swerve, and top with a dollop of Greek yogurt. Serve immediately!

# 487. Mexican-Style Pan Pizza

**(Ready in about 15 minutes | Servings 2)**

**Per serving: 397 Calories; 31g Fat; 6.1g Carbs; 22g Protein;**

## INGREDIENTS

**For the Crust:**
4 eggs, beaten
1/4 cup sour cream
2 tablespoons flax seed meal
1 teaspoon chipotle pepper

1/4 teaspoon cumin seeds, ground
1/2 teaspoon dried coriander leaves
Salt, to taste
1 tablespoon garlic-infused olive oil

**For the Toppings:**
2 tablespoons tomato paste
2 ounces 4-cheese Mexican blend, shredded

## DIRECTIONS

Thoroughly combine all ingredients for the crust, except for the oil.
Heat 1/2 tablespoon of the garlic-infused oil in a pan over moderately high heat. Now, spoon 1/2 of the crust mixture into the pan and spread out evenly.
Cook until the edges are set; then, flip the pizza crust and cook on the other side. Turn the broiler on high.
Heat the remaining 1/2 tablespoon of oil in the pan. Repeat with another pizza crust. Spread the tomato paste over the top of each of the prepared pizza crusts.
Divide the Mexican cheese blend among these two pizza crusts.
Broil them on high until the cheese is completely melted. Eat warm and enjoy!

# 488. Homemade Bread with Herbs and Seeds

**(Ready in about 40 minutes | Servings 6)**

**Per serving: 109 Calories; 10.2g Fat; 1g Carbs; 3.9g Protein;**

## INGREDIENTS

5 eggs, separated
1/2 teaspoon cream of tartar
2 cups almond flour
1/2 stick butter, melted
3 teaspoons baking powder

1 teaspoon sea salt
1 teaspoon dried basil
1/2 teaspoon dried oregano
1 tablespoon poppy seeds
2 tablespoons sesame seeds

## DIRECTIONS

Preheat your oven to 360 degrees F. Lightly oil a loaf pan with a nonstick cooking spray.
Mix the eggs with the cream of tartar on medium-high speed until stiff peaks form.
Add the flour, butter, baking powder and salt to your food processor; blitz until everything is well mixed.
Now, stir in the egg white mixture; gently stir to combine well. Spoon the batter into the prepared loaf pan.
Sprinkle dried basil, oregano, poppy seeds and sesame seeds on the loaf and bake for 35 minutes. Serve with butter and enjoy!

# 489. Blue Cheese and Cauliflower Purée

**(Ready in about 15 minutes | Servings 4)**

**Per serving: 230 Calories; 17.7g Fat; 7.2g Carbs; 11.9g Protein;**

## INGREDIENTS

1 ½ pounds cauliflower, broken into florets
2 tablespoons olive oil, divided
1 teaspoon crushed garlic
1 rosemary sprig, chopped

1 thyme sprig, chopped
2 cups blue cheese, crumbled
1/2 teaspoon paprika
Freshly ground black pepper, to taste

## DIRECTIONS

Boil the cauliflower in a deep pan of salted water over moderately high heat about 8 minutes.
Transfer the cooked cauliflower florets to a casserole dish.
Pulse 1/2 of the cauliflower in your food processor. Add 1 cup of the cooking liquid and 1 tablespoon of oil to the food processor.
Repeat with the remaining cauliflower, water and 1 tablespoon of olive oil.
Afterwards, add the remaining ingredients and stir to combine well.

# 490. Ham and Broccoli with Queso Quesadilla

**(Ready in about 15 minutes | Servings 4)**

**Per serving: 323 Calories; 24g Fat; 7.4g Carbs; 18.8g Protein;**

## INGREDIENTS

1 tablespoon lard
1/2 pound ham, cut into strips
1 pound broccoli, broken into florets
1/4 cup sour cream

3/4 cup heavy whipping cream
1 teaspoon smashed garlic
2 tablespoons apple cider vinegar
1/2 cup Queso Quesadilla, shredded

## DIRECTIONS

Warm the lard in a frying pan over moderate heat; brown the ham, stirring frequently, about 3 minutes. Set it aside.
Now, cook the broccoli in pan drippings until the broccoli florets are tender.
Pour the sour cream and whipping cream into the frying pan. Add the garlic and vinegar; cook until it is thoroughly warmed.
Add the reserved ham back to the pan. Fold in the shredded Queso Quesadilla and cook for a further 2 minutes, or until the cheese is completely melted. Bon appétit!

# 491. Keto Iced Coffee

**(Ready in about 10 minutes | Servings 4)**

**Per serving: 161 Calories; 13.7g Fat; 4.4g Carbs; 0.7g Protein;**

### INGREDIENTS

4 cups strong brewed coffee, cooled
4 teaspoons coconut oil
1/4 cup coconut milk

4 teaspoons granular Swerve
1/4 teaspoon ground cinnamon
4 tablespoons heavy cream

### DIRECTIONS

Pour the coffee into a large bowl and mix with the remaining ingredients, except for the cream.
Place ice cubes in 4 tall glasses. Divide the coffee among these glasses.
Add the cream on top of each glass without stirring. Serve right away.

# 492. Cheese Flat Bread with Salami

**(Ready in about 30 minutes | Servings 6)**

**Per serving: 464 Calories; 33.6g Fat; 5.1g Carbs; 31.1g Protein;**

### INGREDIENTS

10 ounces Mascarpone cheese, melted
2 ½ cups Provolone cheese, shredded
4 large eggs, beaten
3 tablespoons Romano cheese, grated
1/2 cup pork rinds, crushed

2 ½ teaspoons baking powder
A pinch of sea salt
A pinch of grated nutmeg
1/2 cup tomato puree, preferably homemade
12 large slices of salami

### DIRECTIONS

Mix the Mascarpone cheese and Provolone cheese with the eggs. Stir in the grated Romano cheese, pork rinds, and baking powder.
Season with salt and nutmeg; stir until everything is well combined.
Preheat a nonstick pan over a moderately high heat. Cook each flatbread about 2 minutes per side. Spread the tomato puree over each flatbread; top with 2 slices of salami and serve warm.

# 493. Baked Avocado Stuffed with Grapes and Cheese

**(Ready in about 25 minutes | Servings 4)**

**Per serving: 264 Calories; 24.4g Fat; 6g Carbs; 3.7g Protein;**

### INGREDIENTS

1 teaspoon grapeseed oil
1/2 cup red grapes, seedless
2 avocados, halved and pitted

3 ounces cream cheese
8 almonds, slivered

### DIRECTIONS

Start by preheating your oven to 425 degrees F.
Arrange the seedless grapes on a baking pan that is previously greased with grapeseed oil.
Roast approximately 15 minutes or until they are caramelized on the outside; sprinkle with a pinch of salt and reserve.
Decrease the oven temperature to 360 degrees F.
Add the cream cheese and slivered almonds to the avocado halves and bake approximately 18 minutes. Top with the roasted grapes and serve at room temperature.

# 494. Smoked Bacon and Gorgonzola Muffins

**(Ready in about 25 minutes | Servings 5)**

**Per serving: 240 Calories; 15.3g Fat; 7g Carbs; 16.1g Protein;**

## INGREDIENTS

4 slices smoked back bacon
4 eggs, beaten
1/2 cup coconut flour
1 teaspoon baking powder

1 cup gorgonzola cheese, diced
A pinch of kosher salt
A pinch of grated nutmeg

## DIRECTIONS

Preheat a frying pan over a moderately high heat. Now, cook the bacon, turning with tongs, until it is crisp and browned on both sides; drain your bacon on paper towels.

Chop the bacon and combine it with the other ingredients; stir to combine well.

Grease the muffin molds. Fill the prepared molds with batter (3/4 full). Bake in the preheated oven at 390 degrees F for 15 minutes. Bon appétit!

# 495. Almond Coconut Cream Pie

**(Ready in about 30 minutes | Servings 6)**

**Per serving: 305 Calories; 30.6g Fat; 4.7g Carbs; 4.6g Protein;**

## INGREDIENTS

**For the Crust:**
1/2 stick butter
1/3 cup erythritol
3/4 cup almond flour
1/3 cup coconut shreds, unsweetened

**For the Custard**
1 ¼ cups double cream
3 egg yolks
1/3 cup almond flour
3/4 cup water
1/2 teaspoon ground cinnamon
1/2 teaspoon star anise, ground
1/2 teaspoon vanilla paste
1/2 teaspoon pure almond extract
1/3 cup erythritol

**For the Topping**
1 cup double cream
2 tablespoons almonds, toasted and chopped

## DIRECTIONS

Melt your butter in a pan that is preheated over medium-low. Add the erythritol and cook, stirring frequently, until it has dissolved completely.

Stir in the almond flour and coconut shreds and cook 2 minutes longer. Scrape the crust mixture into the bottom of a baking dish. Transfer to your refrigerator.

Now, heat up the pan; add 1 ¼ cups of the double cream and cook over medium-low heat. Fold in the egg yolks and whisk until well combined. Whisk in the almond flour and water until it has thickened. Add the cinnamon, anise star, vanilla, pure almond extract, and erythritol. Cook until the mixture has thickened. Allow it to cool about 10 minutes; spread over the crust. Refrigerate for a couple of hours.

Beat 1 cup of the cream just until the cream reaches stiff peaks. Top the cake with the cream. Scatter toasted almonds on top and serve well chilled.

# 496. Queso Oaxaca and Avocado Fat Bombs

**(Ready in about 20 minutes + chilling time | Servings 8)**

**Per serving: 145 Calories; 12.6g Fat; 3.7g Carbs; 5.5g Protein;**

## INGREDIENTS

6 ounces avocado pulp
6 ounces Queso Oaxaca, softened
2 ounces smoked bacon, cooked and crumbled

1/2 teaspoon chipotle powder
1/4 teaspoon ground bay leaf
1 tablespoon red pepper flakes

## DIRECTIONS

Stir all ingredients, except for the red pepper flakes, in a mixing bowl; whisk until everything is well combined.

Shape the mixture into 8 balls. Place in the refrigerator until they are solid.

Roll each ball into red pepper flakes. Serve well-chilled. Bon appétit!

## 497. Chia Egg Balls

**(Ready in about 35 minutes | Servings 6)**

**Per serving: 174 Calories; 15.2g Fat; 4.3g Carbs; 5.9g Protein;**

### INGREDIENTS

3 eggs
1/2 stick butter, at room temperature
8 black olives, pitted and coarsely chopped
3 tablespoons mayonnaise

Salt and crushed red pepper flakes, to taste
3 slices cooked ham, chopped
2 tablespoons chia seeds

### DIRECTIONS

Place the eggs, butter, olives, mayonnaise, salt and pepper in your food processor. Pulse until everything is well combined but not over blended. Add the chopped ham; stir again.

Transfer to your refrigerator approximately 30 minutes. Shape the mixture into balls.

Place the chia seeds on a plate; roll your balls through to coat evenly. Refrigerate in an airtight container up to 4 days. Bon appétit!

## 498. Star Anise and Pecan Porridge

**(Ready in about 25 minutes | Servings 2)**

**Per serving: 430 Calories; 41.1g Fat; 5.8g Carbs; 11.4g Protein;**

### INGREDIENTS

3 eggs
3 tablespoons Swerve
1/2 cup double cream
1 ½ tablespoons coconut oil

1/2 teaspoon star anise
1/4 teaspoon turmeric powder
1/4 cup pecans, chopped

### DIRECTIONS

Thoroughly combine the eggs with the Swerve and double cream in a mixing bowl.

Melt the coconut oil in a pot over moderately high heat; stir in the egg/cream mixture and cook until they are warmed through.

Take off the heat and stir in the star anise and turmeric.

Divide the porridge among individual bowls, scatter chopped pecans on top and serve.

## 499. Sour Cream and Chocolate Donuts

**(Ready in about 25 minutes | Servings 6)**

**Per serving: 218 Calories; 20g Fat; 6g Carbs; 4.8g Protein;**

### INGREDIENTS

2/3 cup coconut flour
1/4 cup xylitol
1 teaspoon baking powder
1/2 teaspoon baking soda
1 teaspoon cinnamon, ground
A pinch of salt
A pinch of ground cloves
1/2 stick butter, melted
1/2 cup sour cream
1 eggs
1 teaspoon pure vanilla extract

**For the Frosting:**
1 cup double cream
1 cup sugar-free chocolate, broken into chunks

### DIRECTIONS

Begin by preheating your oven to 360 degrees F. Generously spritz a donut pan with a nonstick cooking spray.

In a mixing bowl, thoroughly combine the coconut flour, xylitol, baking powder, baking soda, cinnamon, sea salt and cloves.

In another mixing bowl, mix together the butter, sour cream, egg, and vanilla extract. Add the wet mixture to the dry mixture.

Spoon the batter evenly into the donut pan. Bake approximately 17 minutes or until done.

In the meantime, heat the double cream in a pan over a moderate flame; let it simmer for 2 minutes.

Fold in the chocolate chunks; mix until all the chocolate is melted. Frost your donuts and serve. Bon appétit!

# 500. Chèvre Custard with Sautéed Morels

**(Ready in about 45 minutes | Servings 6)**

**Per serving: 263 Calories; 22.4g Fat; 6.1g Carbs; 10g Protein;**

## INGREDIENTS

1 ½ cups double cream

4 ounces Chèvre cheese, crumbled

3 eggs, beaten

Salt and ground black pepper, to taste

1 tablespoon butter, softened

4 ounces morels, chopped

1 garlic clove, smashed

## DIRECTIONS

Preheat your oven to 320 degrees F. Lower 6 ramekins into a large pan. Pour boiling water into the pan to a depth of about 1-inch.

Heat the double cream over a moderately high heat. Turn the heat to a simmer; add the Chèvre cheese and stir until it is completely melted.

Place the beaten eggs in a bowl and add 3 tablespoons of the hot cream mixture; mix well. Add the mixture back to the pan with the hot cream/cheese mixture.

Season with salt and ground black pepper to taste. Spoon the mixture into ramekins. Bake for 40 minutes or until the center is set. The custard should wiggle like firm jello.

Meanwhile, warm the butter in a sauté pan that is preheated over a moderately high heat. Now, sauté the morels along with the garlic until they are tender and fragrant.

Top each custard with morels and serve immediately. Bon appétit!

# MORE KETO RECIPES

## 501. Buttery Mixed Greens with Cheese

**(Ready in about 25 minutes | Servings 5)**

**Per serving: 160 Calories; 10g Fat; 7.1g Carbs; 11g Protein;**

### INGREDIENTS

1 tablespoon butter
2 garlic cloves, chopped
1 bunch of scallions
2 pounds mixed greens, trimmed and torn into pieces
1/4 cup chicken broth

1 tablespoon apple cider vinegar
1 teaspoon cayenne pepper
1/2 teaspoon salt
1/4 teaspoon black pepper
1 cup Colby cheese, shredded

### DIRECTIONS

Melt the butter in a large pan over a moderately high heat. Sauté the garlic and scallions about 2 minutes or until tender and aromatic.
Stir in the mixed greens and chicken broth; continue to cook until the leaves are wilted and all liquid has evaporated, about 13 minutes.
Now, add the apple cider vinegar, cayenne pepper, salt and black pepper. Remove from the heat.
Sprinkle with the shredded cheese and serve immediately. Bon appétit!

## 502. Cheesy Broccoli Casserole

**(Ready in about 25 minutes | Servings 3)**

**Per serving: 195 Calories; 12.7g Fat; 6.7g Carbs; 11.6g Protein;**

### INGREDIENTS

3 tablespoons avocado oil
1 shallot, minced
1/2 teaspoon garlic, minced
1 head broccoli, cut into small florets
3 eggs, well-beaten

1/2 cup half-and-half
1/2 teaspoon dried basil
1/2 teaspoon turmeric powder
Kosher salt and cayenne pepper, to taste
2 ounces Monterey Jack cheese, shredded

### DIRECTIONS

Preheat your oven to 310 degrees F.
Melt the avocado oil in a pan over moderate heat. Now, sauté the shallots and garlic for a few minutes. Stir in the broccoli florets and cook until they're tender. Transfer the mixture to a lightly greased casserole dish.
In a separate mixing bowl, combine the eggs with the half-and-half, basil, turmeric, salt and cayenne pepper.
Pour the egg mixture over the broccoli mixture. Bake for 20 minutes or until set. Check the temperature with an instant-read food thermometer. Serve warm topped with cheese.

## 503. Family Vegetable Bake

**(Ready in about 1 hour | Servings 4)**

**Per serving: 159 Calories; 10.4g Fat; 7.7g Carbs; 6.4g Protein;**

### INGREDIENTS

1 large eggplant, cut into thick slices
1 tomato, diced
1/2 garlic head, crushed
1 medium-sized leek, sliced
1 celery, peeled and diced

1 Habanero pepper, minced
1 teaspoon Taco seasoning mix
2 tablespoons extra-virgin olive oil
1 tablespoon fresh sage leaves, chopped
1/3 cup Parmigiano-Reggiano cheese, shredded

### DIRECTIONS

Place the eggplant in a medium-sized bowl; sprinkle with salt and let it stand for 30 minutes; now, drain and rinse the eggplant slices.
Meanwhile, preheat your oven to 345 degrees F. Spritz a casserole dish with a nonstick cooking spray.
Mix the vegetables along with the seasoning, olive oil, and sage in the prepared casserole dish.
Roast the vegetables approximately 20 minutes. Scatter the shredded cheese over the top and bake an additional 10 minutes. Serve right away!

## 504. Easy and Yummy Cabbage with Bacon

**(Ready in about 20 minutes | Servings 6)**

**Per serving: 259 Calories; 18.1g Fat; 6.6g Carbs; 15.5g Protein;**

### INGREDIENTS

1 tablespoon lard
1 large-sized head of red cabbage, shredded
1 carrot, finely chopped
1/2 pound bacon, chopped

1 bouillon cube
1/2 cup water
1/2 teaspoon cayenne pepper

### DIRECTIONS

Melt the lard in a pan that is preheated over a moderate heat. Now, cook the cabbage and carrot until they are tender,
Add the remaining ingredients, reduce the heat to a medium-low and cover the pan. Let it simmer for 10 minutes more.
Taste, adjust the seasonings, and serve right away!

## 505. Ground Turkey and Cheese Stuffed Tomatoes

**(Ready in about 25 minutes | Servings 4)**

**Per serving: 413 Calories; 28.2g Fat; 7.8g Carbs; 35.2g Protein;**

### INGREDIENTS

4 tomatoes
1 tablespoon olive oil
1/2 pound ground turkey
1/2 cup scallions, chopped
1 garlic clove, smashed
1 tablespoon fresh parsley, chopped

1 teaspoon fresh rosemary, chopped
Seasoned salt and ground black pepper, to taste
1 cup Monterey Jack cheese, shredded
1 cup Romano cheese, freshly grated
1/2 cup chicken stock

### DIRECTIONS

Slice the top off of each tomato. Discard the hard cores and scoop out the pulp from the tomatoes with a small metal spoon.
Now, heat the oil in a cast-iron skillet that is preheated over a moderately high heat. Brown the turkey meat for 3 to 4 minutes; reserve.
In the same skillet, sauté the scallions and garlic until they are just tender, about 4 minutes. Add the reserved beef and tomato pulp; sprinkle
with fresh parsley, rosemary, salt, and pepper.
Arrange the tomatoes in a casserole dish. Divide the stuffing among the tomatoes and top with the cheese.
Pour the chicken stock around the tomatoes and bake in the middle of the preheated oven at 360 degrees F, approximately 18 minutes. Bon
appétit!

## 506. Refreshing and Nutty Spring Salad

**(Ready in about 5 minutes | Servings 4)**

**Per serving: 184 Calories; 16.8g Fat; 5g Carbs; 2.1g Protein;**

### INGREDIENTS

1 medium-sized head lettuce, torn into bite-sized pieces
1/2 pound cucumber, thinly sliced
1 large-sized carrot, grated
1 cup radishes, thinly sliced
2 spring onions, sliced
1 ounce macadamia nuts, chopped

1/2 lime, freshly squeezed
3 tablespoons peanut oil
1 teaspoon chili sauce, sugar-free
1/2 teaspoon red pepper flakes, crushed
Coarse salt, to taste
1 tablespoon sesame seeds, lightly toasted

### DIRECTIONS

Add the vegetables along with the macadamia nuts to a large salad bowl. Toss to combine.
In a small mixing dish, thoroughly whisk the lime juice, peanut oil, chili sauce, red pepper and salt.
Dress the salad and serve sprinkled with toasted sesame seeds.

# 507. Spicy Cremini Mushroom Stew

**(Ready in about 30 minutes | Servings 4)**

**Per serving: 133 Calories; 3.7g Fat; 6.7g Carbs; 14g Protein;**

## INGREDIENTS

1 tablespoon olive oil
1 cup shallots, chopped
1 teaspoon chili pepper, finely minced
1 teaspoon garlic, minced
1 celery, chopped
2 carrots, chopped

1/2 pound Cremini mushrooms, chopped
2 ½ cups bone broth, low-sodium
1/4 cup dry white wine
1/2 cup water
2 ripe tomatoes, crushed

Salt and ground black pepper, to taste
1/4 teaspoon ground ginger
1/2 teaspoon ground allspice
1/4 teaspoon ground cinnamon
2 bay leaves
1/2 cup fresh basil, chopped

## DIRECTIONS

Heat the oil in a large heavy pot that is preheated over a moderate flame. Now, sweat the shallots, peppers, garlic, celery, carrots, and mushrooms approximately 8 minutes.
Add the broth, tomatoes, and seasonings, except for the basil; bring to a boil. Now, turn the heat to a medium and let it simmer for 18 minutes, stirring periodically.
Serve in individual bowls, garnished with fresh basil leaves. Bon appétit!

# 508. Absolutely Incredible Turkey Kebabs

**(Ready in about 30 minutes | Servings 6)**

**Per serving: 293 Calories; 13.8g Fat; 5.7g Carbs; 34.5g Protein;**

## INGREDIENTS

1 ½ pounds British turkey diced thigh
2 tablespoons butter, at room temperature
1 tablespoon dry ranch seasoning
2 orange bell peppers, sliced

1 red bell peppers, sliced
1 green bell peppers, sliced
1 zucchini, cut into thick slices
1 red onion, cut into wedges
1 cucumber, sliced

1 cup radishes, sliced
2 tablespoons red wine vinegar
1 tablespoon fresh parsley, roughly chopped

## DIRECTIONS

Rub the turkey with the softened butter and toss with the dry ranch seasoning. Thread the turkey pieces onto skewers.
Alternate with bell peppers, zucchini, and onion until all the ingredients are used up. Now, place your skewers in the refrigerator while you're lighting the grill.
Grill your kebabs, turning periodically, for 9 minutes or until they are cooked through.
In the meantime, toss the cucumbers and radishes with red wine vinegar and fresh parsley.
Serve the kebabs immediately with the cucumber-radicchio salad on the side. Bon appétit!

# 509. Easy Grilled Chicken Salad

**(Ready in about 20 minutes | Servings 4)**

**Per serving: 408 Calories; 34.2g Fat; 4.8g Carbs; 22.7g Protein;**

## INGREDIENTS

2 chicken breasts
1/2 teaspoon sea salt
1/3 teaspoon red pepper flakes, crushed

1/4 teaspoon dried thyme, or more to taste
1 large-sized avocado, pitted and sliced
2 egg yolks
1 tablespoon lime juice

1/2 teaspoon mustard powder
1/3 teaspoon sea salt
1/3 cup olive oil
1 tablespoon Worcestershire sauce

## DIRECTIONS

Preheat your grill on high. Season the chicken breasts with salt, pepper and thyme. Now, grill the chicken for 3 to 5 minutes on each side.
Cut the grilled chicken into the strips.
Divide the avocado slices among four serving plates.
Then, prepare the dressing. In a mixing dish or a measuring cup, thoroughly combine the remaining ingredients.
Place the chicken strips on the serving plates and drizzle with the prepared dressing. Enjoy!

# 510. Spicy Chicken Strips with Hemp Seeds

**(Ready in about 55 minutes | Servings 6)**

**Per serving: 420 Calories; 28.2g Fat; 5g Carbs; 35.3g Protein;**

## INGREDIENTS

3 chicken breasts, cut into strips
1/2 stick butter
Salt and pepper, to taste
2 tablespoons soy sauce
3 teaspoons apple cider vinegar

1/2 teaspoon hot chili sauce, sugar-free
2 tablespoons tomato paste
2 cloves garlic, minced
2 eggs
1/4 cup hemp seeds

## DIRECTIONS

Preheat your oven to 410 degrees F. Lightly grease a baking dish with a nonstick cooking spray.
Now, rub the chicken wings with the butter, salt, and pepper.
Drizzle with the soy sauce, vinegar, chili sauce, tomato sauce and garlic. Let it marinate at least 30 minutes in your refrigerator.
In a mixing dish, whisk the eggs with the hemp seeds. Dip each chicken strip in the hemp mixture. Transfer your chicken to the baking dish.
Bake for 20 to 25 minutes, turning once. You can broil these chicken strips to make them crispy, if desired.
Serve garnished with fresh chives.

# 511. Chicken Fillets with Cream-Mustard Sauce

**(Ready in about 25 minutes | Servings 4)**

**Per serving: 311 Calories; 16.9g Fat; 2.1g Carbs; 33.6g Protein;**

## INGREDIENTS

1 pound chicken fillets
Salt and pepper, to taste
1 tablespoon butter, melted
1/2 cup scallions, chopped
1 teaspoon garlic paste

1/4 cup dry white wine
1/4 cup low-sodium chicken broth
1/2 cup double cream
2 tablespoons whole grain mustard
1/2 cup fresh cilantro, roughly chopped

## DIRECTIONS

Rub the chicken fillets with salt and pepper to your liking.
Melt the butter in a saucepan that is preheated over a moderate flame. Now, cook the chicken fillets until they are just barely done. Transfer the chicken to a plate and set it aside.
Add the scallions and garlic paste to the saucepan; cook, stirring often, until it is aromatic or about 4 minutes.
Raise the heat to medium-high; pour in the wine and scrape the bits that may be stuck to the bottom of your saucepan.
Next, pour in the broth; allow the liquid to reduce by about half. Stir in the double cream and mustard.
Pour the sauce over the reserved chicken fillets and serve garnished with fresh cilantro. Enjoy!

# 512. Easy and Yummy Chicken Drumettes

**(Ready in about 30 minutes | Servings 4)**

**Per serving: 165 Calories; 9.8g Fat; 7.7g Carbs; 12.4g Protein;**

## INGREDIENTS

2 tablespoons tallow
4 chicken drumettes
Salt, to taste
1/2 cup leeks, chopped
1 carrot, sliced

2 cloves garlic, minced
1 teaspoon cayenne pepper
1 teaspoon dried marjoram
1/2 teaspoon mustard seeds
1 cup turkey stock

2 tomatoes, crushed
1 tablespoon Worcestershire sauce
1 teaspoon mixed peppercorns
1 thyme sprig
1 rosemary sprig

## DIRECTIONS

Melt the tallow in a saucepan over medium-high heat. Sprinkle the chicken drumettes with the salt.
Then, fry the chicken drumettes until they are no longer pink and lightly browned on all sides; reserve.
Now, cook the leeks, carrots and garlic in pan drippings over medium heat for 4 to 6 minutes.
Reduce the heat to simmer, and add the remaining ingredients along with the reserved chicken. Simmer, partially covered, for 15 to 20 minutes. Serve warm.

## 513. Chicken Sausage with Salsa

**(Ready in about 15 minutes | Servings 4)**

**Per serving: 156 Calories; 4.2g Fat; 5.1g Carbs; 16.2g Protein;**

### INGREDIENTS

2 teaspoons lard, room temperature
4 chicken sausage, sliced
1/4 cup Sauvignon Blanc
1 cup pureed tomatoes
1 teaspoon granulated garlic

2 bell peppers, deveined and chopped
1 minced jalapeno, chopped
1 cup onion, diced
2 tablespoons fresh cilantro, minced
3 teaspoons lime juice

### DIRECTIONS

Warm the lard in a heavy-bottomed skillet over moderately high heat.
Sauté the sausage until well browned; pour in the wine and cook an additional 3 minutes. Reserve.
Then, make the salsa by mixing the pureed tomatoes, garlic, bell pepper, jalapeno pepper, onions, cilantro and lime juice.
Serve the sausage with the salsa on the side. Bon appétit!

## 514. Turkey Sausage with Bok Choy

**(Ready in about 50 minutes | Servings 4)**

**Per serving: 189 Calories; 12g Fat; 6.6g Carbs; 9.4g Protein;**

### INGREDIENTS

1 tablespoon butter
4 mild turkey sausages, breakfast links, sliced
2 shallots, chopped
Coarse salt and ground black pepper, to taste
1 pound Bok choy, tough stem ends trimmed

1 cup chicken stock
1/2 cup full-fat milk
1/8 teaspoon freshly grated nutmeg
6 ounces Gruyère, coarsely grated

### DIRECTIONS

Start by preheating an oven to 360 degrees F. Melt the butter in a pan; now, brown the sausage for a couple of minutes, stirring periodically; reserve.
Add the shallots, salt, pepper, and Bok choy. Add the chicken stock and cook until just tender, 2 to 3 minutes.
Spread the Bok choy mixture in a lightly greased baking dish. Top with the reserved sausage.
In a mixing bowl, thoroughly combine the chicken stock, milk, and nutmeg. Pour the mixture over the sausage.
Cover with a piece of foil and bake for 40 minutes. Remove the foil and scatter the grated cheese over the top.
Bake in upper third of oven an additional 4 minutes or until bubbly.

## 515. Easy Herby Turkey Drumsticks

**(Ready in about 1 hour | Servings 2)**

**Per serving: 488 Calories; 24.5g Fat; 2.1g Carbs; 33.6g Protein;**

### INGREDIENTS

2 tablespoons apple cider vinegar
2 thyme sprigs, chopped
2 rosemary sprigs, chopped
1 teaspoon dried marjoram
1 teaspoon dried basil

1 teaspoon granulated garlic
2 tablespoons olive oil
2 turkey drumsticks
Salt and black pepper, to taste
1/2 cup Taco bell sauce

### DIRECTIONS

To make the marinade, thoroughly combine the apple cider vinegar, thyme, rosemary, marjoram, basil, granulated garlic, and olive oil in a mixing bowl.
Now, marinate the turkey at least 3 hours in the refrigerator.
Cook the turkey drumsticks on a preheated grill for 45 minutes to 1 hour or until a meat thermometer has reached the temperature of 180 degrees F. Season with salt and pepper to taste.
Serve with Taco bell sauce on the side. Bon appétit!

# 516. Mediterranean Chicken Drumsticks with Aioli

**(Ready in about 35 minutes | Servings 4)**

**Per serving: 562 Calories; 43.8g Fat; 2.1g Carbs; 40.8g Protein;**

## INGREDIENTS

1 ½ tablespoons ghee
4 chicken drumsticks
Sea salt and crushed mixed peppercorns, to taste

1 tablespoon fresh parsley, chopped
6 Kalamata olives, pitted and halved
1 cup Halloumi cheese, cubed
1 hard-boiled egg yolk

1 tablespoon garlic, finely minced
1 tablespoon lemon juice
1/2 cup extra-virgin olive oil
1/4 teaspoon sea salt

## DIRECTIONS

Preheat your oven to 395 degrees F.

Melt the ghee in a nonstick skillet.

Season the chicken drumsticks with salt and crushed peppercorns; brown the chicken drumsticks in the hot skillet for 3 to 4 minutes.

Arrange the fried chicken on a baking sheet; scatter fresh parsley and olives over the top.

In the meantime, make the Aioli by mixing the remaining ingredients, except for the cheese, with an immersion blender. Mix until it comes together.

Now, spread the Aioli over the fried chicken. Bake in the preheated oven approximately 25 minutes. Add the Halloumi on top and bake an additional 3 to 4 minutes. Serve warm.

# 517. Dinner Party Pork Gumbo

**(Ready in about 35 minutes | Servings 6)**

**Per serving: 427 Calories; 26.2g Fat; 7.6g Carbs; 35.2g Protein;**

## INGREDIENTS

2 tablespoons olive oil
1 pound pork shoulder, cubed
8 ounces pork sausage, sliced
2 shallots, toughly chopped
1 teaspoon beef bouillon granules

Sea salt and freshly cracked black
pepper
1 teaspoon gumbo file
1 teaspoon crushed red pepper
1 tablespoon Cajun spice
4 cups bone broth

1 cup water
2 bell peppers, deveined and thinly
sliced
2 celery stalks, chopped
1/4 cup flaxseed meal
3/4 pound okra

## DIRECTIONS

Heat the oil in a heavy-bottomed pot that is preheated over a moderately high flame. Now, cook the pork until it is just browned; reserve. Add the sausage and cook in the pan drippings approximately 5 minutes; reserve.

Stir in the shallots and cook until they have softened. Add the beef bouillon granules, salt, pepper, gumbo file, red pepper, Cajun spice and bone broth. Bring it to a boil.

Add the water, bell pepper and celery, and reduce the heat to medium-low. Cook an additional 15 to 23 minutes.

Afterwards, stir in the flax seed meal and okra; cook for a further 5 minutes or until heated through.

# 518. Pork Meatloaf with Homemade Tomato Sauce

**(Ready in about 45 minutes | Servings 6)**

**Per serving: 251 Calories; 7.9g Fat; 6.5g Carbs; 34.6g Protein;**

## INGREDIENTS

Nonstick cooking spray
1 ½ pounds ground pork
1/4 cup pork rinds, crushed
1/3 cup flaxseed meal
2 shallots, chopped

3 cloves garlic, finely minced
1 large egg
Sea salt and ground black pepper
1 teaspoon mustard powder

**For the Sauce:**
2 ripe plum tomatoes, pureed
2 tablespoons ketchup
1 ½ tablespoons Swerve
1 tablespoon cider vinegar
1/2 teaspoon dried thyme
1 teaspoon fresh parsley

## DIRECTIONS

Start by preheating your oven to 360 degrees F. Lightly spray a loaf pan with a nonstick cooking oil or line with foil.

Add the pork mince, pork rinds, flaxseed meal, shallot, garlic, egg, salt, pepper, and mustard powder to a mixing dish. Thoroughly combine the ingredients until everything is well mixed.

Press the meatloaf mixture into the pan.

Next, cook the sauce ingredients over moderate heat. Pour the sauce evenly over the meatloaf. Bake for 40 minutes or until a meat ther-mometer registers 165 degrees F.

Allow it to cool down for a couple of minutes before slicing. Cut into 3/4-inch thick slices and serve immediately.

# 519. Pork Shoulder with Blue Cheese Sauce

**(Ready in about 30 minutes | Servings 6)**

**Per serving: 495 Calories; 36.9g Fat; 3.6g Carbs; 33.4g Protein;**

## INGREDIENTS

1 ½ pounds pork shoulder, boneless and cut into 6 pieces
Salt and freshly cracked black peppercorns, to taste
1 teaspoon dried thyme
1 tablespoon butter
1 onion, chopped
2 garlic cloves, chopped

1/3 cup dry sherry wine
1/3 cup broth, preferably homemade
1 teaspoon dried hot chile flakes
1 tablespoon soy sauce
6 ounces blue cheese
1/3 cup double cream

## DIRECTIONS

Rub each piece of the pork shoulder with salt, black peppercorns, and thyme.
Now, warn the butter in a sauté pan over moderately high heat. Then, brown the pork on all sides about 18 minutes; reserve.
Next, sauté the onions and garlic until the onions are caramelized. Add the wine and broth and stir, scraping up any brown bits from the bottom.
Turn the heat to medium and add the other ingredients; continue to simmer until the desired thickness is reached by evaporation.
Serve the reserved pork with the sauce on the side. Bon appétit!

# 520. Carrot and Meat Loaf Muffins

**(Ready in about 35 minutes | Servings 6)**

**Per serving: 220 Calories; 6.3g Fat; 5.4g Carbs; 33.8g Protein;**

## INGREDIENTS

1 pound pork, ground
1/2 pound turkey, ground
1 cup carrots, shredded
2 ripe tomatoes, pureed
1 ounce envelope onion soup mix
1 tablespoon Worcestershire sauce
1 tablespoon Dijon mustard

1/2 teaspoon dry basil
1 teaspoon dry oregano
Kosher salt and ground black pepper, to taste
2 cloves of garlic, minced
1 eggs, whisked
1 cup mozzarella cheese, shredded

## DIRECTIONS

Start by preheating your oven to 350 degrees F.
Then, thoroughly combine all ingredients until everything is blended.
Spoon the mixture into a muffin tin that is previously coated with a nonstick cooking spray.
Bake for 30 minutes; allow them to cool slightly before removing from the tin. Bon appétit!

# 521. Hearty Pork Soup with Avocado

**(Ready in about 20 minutes | Servings 6)**

**Per serving: 423 Calories; 31.8g Fat; 6.5g Carbs; 25.9g Protein;**

## INGREDIENTS

2 tablespoons lard
1 medium-sized yellow onion, peeled and chopped
2 cloves garlic, peeled and minced
1 teaspoon Mezzeta pepper, seeded and minced
1 celery, chopped
1 ¼ pounds pork shoulder, cut into chunks

3 cups beef broth, less-sodium
Sea salt and ground black pepper, to taste
A pinch of dried basil
2 ripe tomatoes, undrained
1/4 cup fresh parsley, roughly chopped
1 medium-sized avocado, pitted and sliced

## DIRECTIONS

Melt the lard in a large-sized stock pot over a moderate flame. Next, sauté the onion, garlic, Mezzeta pepper and celery for 2 to 3 minutes or until the onion is translucent.
Stir in the pork chunks and continue cooking for 4 minutes more, stirring continuously. Add the other ingredients.
Now, lower the heat and simmer for 10 minutes, partially covered; make sure to stir periodically.
Serve topped with fresh parsley leaves and sliced avocado.

## 522. Greek Souvlaki with Tzatziki Sauce

**(Ready in about 20 minutes + marinating time | Servings 6)**

**Per serving: 147 Calories; 4.8g Fat; 5.8g Carbs; 17.3g Protein;**

### INGREDIENTS

1/3 cup red wine vinegar

2 tablespoons cilantro, chopped

2 tablespoons fresh lemon juice

3 cloves garlic, smashed

Sea salt and ground black pepper, to taste

1 teaspoon Greek oregano

2 pounds pork loin, trimmed of silver skin and excess fat, cut into 1-inch cubes

Wooden skewers, soaked in cold water for 30 minutes before use

**For Tzatziki Sauce:**

1 small-sized cucumber, shredded and drained

1 cup full-fat Greek yogurt

1 teaspoon garlic, smashed

3 teaspoons olive oil

Sea salt, to taste

2 teaspoons fresh dill, finely minced

### DIRECTIONS

To make the marinade, thoroughly combine the vinegar, cilantro, lemon juice, garlic, salt, black pepper and Greek oregano.

Add the pork loin to the marinade. Let it marinate in your refrigerator for 3 hours. Now, thread the pork cubes onto the skewers.

Grill your souvlaki until they are browned on all sides, about 8 to 12 minutes in total.

Mix all ingredients for the Tzatziki sauce. Serve with the souvlaki skewers. Bon appétit!

## 523. Kansas City-Style Meatloaf

**(Ready in about 1 hour 10 minutes | Servings 8)**

**Per serving: 318 Calories; 14.7g Fat; 6.2g Carbs; 39.3g Protein;**

### INGREDIENTS

2 pounds ground pork

2 eggs, beaten

1/2 cup shallots, chopped

1/2 cup chipotle salsa, bottled

8 ounces sharp Cheddar cheese, shredded

1 teaspoon garlic powder

1 teaspoon paprika

Sea salt and freshly ground black pepper, to taste

1 teaspoon lime zest

1 tablespoon whole grain mustard

1/2 cup tomato paste

1 tablespoon Swerve

### DIRECTIONS

Start by preheating your oven to 360 degrees F.

In a mixing bowl, thoroughly combine the ground pork with the eggs, shallots, chipotle salsa, cheddar cheese, garlic powder, paprika, salt, pepper, lime zest, and mustard.

Mix until everything is well incorporated. Press the mixture into a loaf pan that is previously greased with a nonstick cooking spray.

Then, whisk the tomato paste with the Swerve; pour the mixture over the top of your meatloaf.

Bake about 65 minutes, rotating the pan once or twice. Place under the broiler during the last 5 minutes if desired.

Let your meatloaf stand 5 to 10 minutes before slicing and serving.

## 524. Asian Saucy Pork

**(Ready in about 1 hour 15 minutes | Servings 8)**

**Per serving: 369 Calories; 20.2g Fat; 2.9g Carbs; 41.3g Protein;**

### INGREDIENTS

1 tablespoon olive oil

2 pounds pork belly, cubed

Salt and freshly ground pepper

1/2 teaspoon ground coriander

A bunch of scallions, chopped

2 garlic cloves, minced

1/2 tablespoon curry powder

1/2 tablespoon ground cloves

2 tomatoes, pureed

1 bell pepper, deveined and chopped

1 Thai chile, deveined and minced

1/2 teaspoon fennel seeds

1/2 cup unsweetened coconut milk

2 cups bone broth

### DIRECTIONS

Heat the oil in a saucepan over a moderate heat. Sprinkle the pork belly with salt, pepper and ground coriander.

Cook the pork about 10 minutes, stirring frequently.

Next, cook the scallions, garlic, curry, and cloves in the pan drippings. Scrape the mixture into the slow cooker. Add the remaining ingredients. Cook, covered, for 1 hour over low heat. Serve warm.

## 525. Pork Rib Chops with Spinach

**(Ready in about 25 minutes + marinating time | Servings 6)**

**Per serving: 234 Calories; 11g Fat; 2g Carbs; 29.8g Protein;**

### INGREDIENTS

1 ½ pounds pork rib chops
Sea salt and ground black pepper, to taste
2 tablespoons oyster sauce
1 tablespoon cider vinegar

1 tablespoon fresh lime juice
1/4 cup Champagne wine
1 tablespoon garlic paste
2 teaspoons olive oil
1 red onion, sliced

1 celery stalk, sliced
1 bell pepper, chopped
2 cups spinach

### DIRECTIONS

Season the pork rib chops with salt and pepper. In another small dish, make the marinade by whisking the oyster sauce, vinegar, lime juice, Champagne and garlic paste.

Add the pork to the marinade; let it stand for at least 2 hours.

Next, heat 1 teaspoon of the olive oil in a large-sized pan that is preheated over a moderate flame; cook the onion, celery and bell pepper about 5 minutes, stirring frequently; reserve.

Heat another teaspoon of the olive oil in the same pan. Add the pork, along with the marinade, to the pan. Now, brown the pork for 3 to 5 minutes per side.

Add the reserved vegetables to the pan along with the spinach. Cook until the spinach leaves are wilted, about 6 minutes. Serve warm. Bon appétit!

## 526. Breakfast Pork in a Mug

**(Ready in about 10 minutes | Servings 2)**

**Per serving: 327 Calories; 16.6g Fat; 5.8g Carbs; 40g Protein;**

### INGREDIENTS

1/2 pound ground pork
1/2 cup Asiago cheese, shredded
1/2 cup tomato sauce

Salt and ground black pepper, to taste
1 teaspoon garlic paste
1/2 teaspoon onion powder

1/2 teaspoon cayenne pepper

### DIRECTIONS

Thoroughly combine all ingredients in a mixing bowl.

Divide the mixture among 2 microwave-safe mugs.

Microwave for 7 minutes and serve warm with pickles. Bon appétit!

## 527. Bacon-Wrapped Meatballs with Parsley Sauce

**(Ready in about 30 minutes | Servings 6)**

**Per serving: 399 Calories; 27g Fat; 1.8g Carbs; 37.7g Protein;**

### INGREDIENTS

1 pound ground beef
1 egg, beaten
1 ½ tablespoons olive oil
1/2 cup crushed pork rinds
1/4 cup fresh cilantro, chopped
2 cloves garlic, smashed

Sea salt and ground black pepper, to your liking
1/2 teaspoon cayenne pepper
1/2 pound bacon slices
Toothpicks

**For the Parsley Sauce:**
1 cup fresh parsley
1 tablespoon almonds, toasted
1 tablespoon sunflower seeds, soaked
1/2 tablespoon olive oil
Sea salt and black pepper, to taste

### DIRECTIONS

Preheat your oven to 390 degrees F.

Then, in a mixing bowl, thoroughly combine the ground beef, egg, olive oil, crushed pork rinds, cilantro, garlic, salt, black pepper, and cayenne pepper.

Shape the mixture into 1.5-inch meatballs. Wrap each ball with a slice of bacon; secure with a toothpick.

Arrange the meatballs on a baking sheet; bake in the preheated oven for 25 to 30 minutes.

In the meantime, make the parsley sauce. Pulse all ingredients in a food processor until uniform and smooth.

Serve the warm meatballs with the parsley sauce on the side and enjoy!

## 528. Sunday Flank Steak

**(Ready in about 20 minutes + marinating time | Servings 6)**

**Per serving: 350 Calories; 17.3g Fat; 2.1g Carbs; 42.7g Protein;**

### INGREDIENTS

2 tablespoons olive oil

2 tablespoons soy sauce

1 teaspoon garlic paste

A bunch of scallions, chopped

1 tablespoon lime lemon juice

1/4 cup dry red wine

2 pounds flank steak

Salt and cayenne pepper, to taste

1/2 teaspoon black peppercorns, crushed

### DIRECTIONS

In a mixing bowl, thoroughly combine the oil, soy sauce, garlic paste, scallions, lemon juice, and red wine.

Now, season the flank steak with the salt, cayenne pepper and black peppercorns. Place the meat in a marinade; cover and refrigerate for 6 hours.

Preheat a nonstick skillet over a moderately high flame. Fry your steaks about 10 minutes, turning once. Bon appétit!

## 529. Father's Day Stuffed Avocado

**(Ready in about 20 minutes | Servings 6)**

**Per serving: 407 Calories; 28.8g Fat; 6.4g Carbs; 23.4g Protein;**

### INGREDIENTS

1 tablespoon avocado oil

3/4 pound beef, ground

1/3 cup beef broth

1/2 cup shallots, sliced

Salt and black pepper, to taste

3 ripe avocados, pitted and halved

2 small-sized tomatoes, chopped

3/4 cup Colby cheese, shredded

3 tablespoons Kalamata olives, pitted and sliced

1/2 cup mayonnaise

### DIRECTIONS

Preheat an oven to 340 degrees F.

Heat the avocado oil in a pan over moderate heat; now, brown the ground beef for 2 to 3 minutes, crumbling it with a wooden spatula.

Add the broth and shallots. Cook until the shallots turn translucent. Season with salt and pepper.

Then, scoop out some of the middle of each avocado. Mash the avocado flash that you scooped out along with the chopped tomatoes.

Add the reserved beef mixture and stuff your avocado. Afterward, top with the shredded cheese and sliced olives.

Place the stuffed avocado on a roasting pan. Bake for 8 to 10 minutes in the preheated oven. Serve with mayonnaise and enjoy!

## 530. Beef Sausage and Vegetable Skillet

**(Ready in about 40 minutes | Servings 4)**

**Per serving: 250 Calories; 17.5g Fat; 5.4g Carbs; 6.8g Protein;**

### INGREDIENTS

2 tablespoons canola oil

4 beef sausages, sliced

2 shallots, chopped

2 spring garlic, minced

2 bell peppers, deveined and chopped

1 parsnip, chopped

Salt and pepper, to taste

2 ripe tomatoes, pureed

2 tablespoons ketchup, sugar-free

1 ½ cups beef bone broth

1/4 cup dry red wine

2 thyme sprigs

2 rosemary sprigs

### DIRECTIONS

Heat the oil in a deep skillet over a moderate heat. Cook the sausage for 2 to 3 minutes, stirring periodically.

Stir in the shallots, garlic, bell peppers, and parsnip; season with salt and pepper. Cook approximately 7 minutes.

Add the remaining ingredients and bring it to a boil. Reduce the heat to medium-low. Let it simmer for 25 minutes. Serve warm.

# 531. Spicy Sausage and Vegetable Casserole

**(Ready in about 30 minutes | Servings 4)**

**Per serving: 424 Calories; 32.4g Fat; 6.8g Carbs; 23.7g Protein;**

## INGREDIENTS

1 tablespoon tallow, softened
4 beef sausages
1 banana shallot, sliced
1 cup broccoli, broken into small florets
1 carrot, sliced

1 celery stalk, chopped
1 bell pepper, sliced
1 dried Poblano pepper, crushed
2 garlic cloves, finely chopped
Salt, to taste

1 teaspoon black peppercorns, freshly crushed
1/2 teaspoon smoked cayenne pepper
1 ¼ cups beef stock, preferably home-made

## DIRECTIONS

Melt the tallow in a nonstick skillet over a moderately high heat. Cook the sausages until they are browned on all sides; reserve.
Now, cook the shallot, broccoli, carrots, celery, peppers, and garlic in the same skillet; cook for 6 to 9 minutes or until the vegetables are tender.
Season with salt, peppercorns and smoked cayenne pepper. Transfer the sautéed vegetables to a lightly greased casserole dish. Nestle the reserved sausages within the sautéed vegetables.
Pour in the stock and bake in the preheated oven at 350 degrees F for about 10 minutes. Serve warm garnished with fresh chives if desired.

# 532. Hamburger Soup with Cabbage

**(Ready in about 35 minutes | Servings 4)**

**Per serving: 307 Calories; 23.6g Fat; 6.4g Carbs; 14.8g Protein;**

## INGREDIENTS

2 tablespoons lard, melted
3/4 pound ground chuck
1/2 cup scallions, chopped
2 cloves garlic, minced
1 carrot, diced

1 cup cabbage, shredded
1 celery with leaves, diced
1 tomato, pureed
6 cups chicken broth
1 bay leaf

Seasoned salt and ground black pepper, to taste
1 cup sour cream

## DIRECTIONS

Melt the lard in a stockpot. Cook the chuck until it is no longer pink; reserve.
Then, cook the scallions, garlic, carrot, cabbage, and celery in the pan drippings, stirring constantly.
Stir in the other ingredients along with the reserved chuck, bringing to a rapid boil. Turn the heat to a simmer. Cook another 27 minutes, partially covered.
Taste and adjust the seasonings. Ladle into individual bowls; serve dolloped with full-fat sour cream.

# 533. Ultimate Thai Beef Salad

**(Ready in about 15 minutes | Servings 4)**

**Per serving: 404 Calories; 32.9g Fat; 8g Carbs; 12.8g Protein;**

## INGREDIENTS

1/2 pound beef rump steak, cut into strips
1/2 teaspoon sea salt
1/3 teaspoon freshly cracked black pepper
1 teaspoon soy sauce

2 tablespoons sesame oil
1 red onion, peeled and sliced
1 garlic clove, minced
1 bunch fresh mint
2 avocados, pitted, peeled and sliced
2 cucumbers, sliced

1 bunch fresh Thai basil, leaves picked
1 teaspoon minced Thai chili
2 tablespoons rice vinegar
1 tablespoon fresh lime juice
1/4 cup pumpkin seeds

## DIRECTIONS

Combine the beef with the salt, pepper and soy sauce.
Preheat the oil in a nonstick skillet over medium-low heat. Then, sauté the onion and garlic until tender and aromatic, about 4 minutes.
Cook the beef on a grill pan for 5 minutes or until cooked to your liking.
Arrange the fresh mint, avocado slices, cucumber, Thai basil, and Thai chili in a nice salad bowl. Top with the beef slices. Add the onion-garlic mixture.
Drizzle with rice vinegar and lime juice. Sprinkle with pumpkin seeds and serve.

## 534. Hungarian Beef Stew

**(Ready in about 1 hour 25 minutes | Servings 4)**

**Per serving: 357 Calories; 15.8g Fat; 7g Carbs; 40.2g Protein;**

### INGREDIENTS

2 tablespoons olive oil

1 ¼ pounds chuck-eye roast, diced

Celery salt and ground black pepper, to taste

1 tablespoon Hungarian paprika

1 tablespoon pear cider vinegar

1/2 cup Cabernet Sauvignon

4 cups water

2 tablespoons beef bouillon granules

1/4 teaspoon ground bay leaf

2 onions, peeled and chopped

1 celery with leaves, chopped

2 carrots, peeled and cut into 1/4-inch rounds

1 tablespoon flaxseed meal

### DIRECTIONS

Heat the oil in a heavy-bottomed pot. Then, cook the meat until no longer pink, for 3 to 4 minutes; work in batches and set aside. Season with celery salt, pepper, and Hungarian paprika.

Now, pour the vinegar and Cabernet Sauvignon to deglaze the bottom of the pot. Add the water, beef bouillon granules and reserved beef to the pot.

Stir in the ground bay leaf, onions, celery and carrots and cook an additional 1 hour 15 minutes over medium-low heat.

Add the flaxseed meal to thicken the liquid; stir constantly for 3 minutes. Serve in individual bowls and enjoy!

## 535. Za'atar Strip Steaks with Cabbage

**(Ready in about 20 minutes +marinating time | Servings 4)**

**Per serving: 321 Calories; 14g Fat; 7.3g Carbs; 36.7g Protein;**

### INGREDIENTS

1 pound New York strip steaks, cut into bite-sized pieces

1 tablespoon hoisin sauce

1 tablespoon fresh lemon juice

Sea salt and ground black pepper, to taste

1 teaspoon Za'atar

2 tablespoons sesame oil

1 yellow onion, chopped

2 garlic cloves, chopped

1 cup cabbage, shredded

1 bell pepper, chopped

### DIRECTIONS

Toss the strip steaks with the hoisin sauce, fresh lemon juice, salt, black pepper and Za'atar seasoning. Marinate in the refrigerator for at least 3 hours.

Heat the oil in a skillet that is preheated over a moderately high heat. Now, brown the strip steaks for 3 to 4 minutes, stirring occasionally.

Add the onions to the same skillet and cook until it is translucent. Add the garlic, cabbage and bell pepper and turn the heat to medium-low. Simmer an additional 10 minutes and serve warm. Bon appétit!

## 536. Spicy Winter Sauerkraut with Ground Beef

**(Ready in about 20 minutes | Servings 4)**

**Per serving: 330 Calories; 12.2g Fat; 6.7g Carbs; 44.4g Protein;**

### INGREDIENTS

1 tablespoon tallow, melted

2 onions, chopped

2 garlic cloves, smashed

1 ¼ pounds ground beef

18 ounces sauerkraut, rinsed and well drained

1 teaspoon chili pepper flakes

1 teaspoon mustard powder

1 bay leaf

Sea salt and ground black pepper, to taste

### DIRECTIONS

Heat a saucepan over a moderately high heat. Now, warm the tallow and cook the onions and garlic until aromatic.

Stir in the ground beef and cook until it is slightly browned.

Add the remaining ingredients. Reduce the heat to medium. Cook about 6 minutes or until everything is thoroughly cooked. Bon appétit!

## 537. Hearty Pollock Chowder

**(Ready in about 30 minutes | Servings 4)**

**Per serving: 170 Calories; 5.8g Fat; 6.2g Carbs; 20g Protein;**

### INGREDIENTS

1 ¼ pounds pollock fillets, skin removed
3 teaspoons butter
2 shallots, chopped
1 celery with leaves, chopped
1 parsnip, chopped
2 carrots, chopped

Sea salt and ground black pepper, to taste
1 teaspoon Old Bay seasonings
3 cups boiling water
1/2 cup clam juice
1/4 cup dry white wine
1/2 cup full-fat milk

### DIRECTIONS

Chop the pollock fillets into bite-sized pieces.
Warm the butter in a pan over a moderately high flame. Cook the vegetables until they're softened. Season with salt, pepper and Old Bay seasonings.
Stir in the chopped fish and cook for 12 to 15 minutes more. Add the boiling water and clam juice. Afterwards, pour in the white wine and milk.
Bring to a boil. Reduce the heat and cook for 15 minutes longer. Bon appétit!

## 538. Summer Fish Cakes

**(Ready in about 30 minutes | Servings 6)**

**Per serving: 234 Calories; 10.6g Fat; 2.5g Carbs; 31.2g Protein;**

### INGREDIENTS

1 ½ pounds cod, boned and flaked
2 eggs, lightly beaten
1/3 cup almond flour
2 tablespoons flax meal
1/2 cup Ricotta cheese, at room temperature

2 teaspoons Dijon mustard
Sea salt and freshly ground black pepper, to taste
1 tablespoon fresh chives, chopped
1 tablespoon fresh cilantro, chopped
2 tablespoons peanut oil

### DIRECTIONS

Preheat your oven to 390 degrees F. Pat the fish dry and transfer to a mixing bowl.
Add the eggs; gradually add the flour and flax meal and mix to combine well. Add the remaining ingredients and mix to combine well.
Now, shape the mixture into 12 patties and arrange them on a lightly greased baking pan.
Bake for 20 to 25 minutes, turning once. Enjoy!

## 539. Sardine Salad Pickled Pepper Boats

**(Ready in about 10 minutes | Servings 4)**

**Per serving: 120 Calories; 5.4g Fat; 5.8g Carbs; 12.3g Protein;**

### INGREDIENTS

2 (3.75-ounce) cans sardines, drained
1 teaspoon deli mustard
1 carrot, chopped
1 cup scallions, chopped

2 tablespoons fresh lemon
Salt and freshly ground black pepper, to taste
4 pickled peppers, slice into halves
1 tablespoon fresh parsley, chopped

### DIRECTIONS

In a mixing bowl, thoroughly combine the sardines, mustard, carrot, scallions, lemon juice, salt and black pepper.
Mix until everything is well incorporated.
Fill the pickle boats with the sardine salad. Serve well-chilled garnished with fresh parsley.

## 540. Asian-Inspired Tilapia Chowder

**(Ready in about 30 minutes | Servings 6)**

**Per serving: 165 Calories; 5.5g Fat; 4g Carbs; 25.4g Protein;**

### INGREDIENTS

3 teaspoons sesame oil
1/2 cup scallions, sliced
1 garlic clove, smashed
1 celery stalk, diced
1 bell pepper, deveined and sliced

1 banana chili pepper, deveined and sliced
1 tablespoon fish sauce
2 ½ cups hot water
1 teaspoon Five-spice powder

1 ¼ pounds tilapia fish fillets, cut into small chunks
3/4 cup full-fat milk
1/2 teaspoon paprika
1/4 cup fresh mint, chopped

### DIRECTIONS

Heat the sesame oil in a stockpot that is preheated over a moderately high heat. Cook the scallions and garlic until they are softened.

Now, add the celery, peppers, fish sauce, water, and Five-spice powder. Cover with the lid, turn the heat to medium-low and simmer for 13 minutes longer.

Now, stir in the fish chunks and cook an additional 12 minutes or until the fish is cooked through. Add the milk, stir well, and remove from heat.

Ladle into individual serving plates. Sprinkle with paprika and serve garnished with fresh mint. Bon appétit!

## 541. Smoked Sal.mon and Cheese Stuffed Tomatoes

**(Ready in about 30 minutes | Servings 6)**

**Per serving: 303 Calories; 22.9g Fat; 5.8g Carbs; 17g Protein;**

### INGREDIENTS

10 ounces smoked salmon, flaked
1 red onion, finely chopped
2 garlic cloves, minced
2 tablespoons cilantro, chopped
1/2 cup aioli

1 teaspoon yellow mustard
1 tablespoon white vinegar
Sea salt and ground black pepper, to taste

1 ½ cups Monterey Jack cheese, shredded
6 medium-sized tomatoes

### DIRECTIONS

Preheat an oven to 400 degrees F.

In a mixing bowl, thoroughly combine the salmon, onion, garlic, cilantro, aioli, mustard, vinegar, salt, and pepper.

Slice your tomatoes in half horizontally; then, scoop out the pulp and seeds.

Stuff the tomatoes with the filling, and bake until they are thoroughly cooked and tops are golden, about 20 minutes.

Add the shredded cheese and place in the oven for a further 5 minutes. Bon appétit!

## 542. Chilean Sea Bass with Cauliflower and Chutney

**(Ready in about 30 minutes | Servings 4)**

**Per serving: 291 Calories; 9.5g Fat; 5.6g Carbs; 42.5g Protein;**

### INGREDIENTS

2 tablespoons olive oil, for drizzling
1 pound cauliflower, cut into florets
2 bell peppers, thinly sliced
1 onion, thinly sliced
Sea salt and freshly ground black pepper, to taste
1 teaspoon cayenne pepper
1 ½ pounds wild Chilean sea bass

**For Tomato Chutney:**
1 teaspoon vegetable oil
2 garlic cloves, sliced
1 cup ripe on-the-vine plum tomatoes
1 tablespoon small capers
1/2 teaspoon kosher salt
1/4 teaspoon black pepper

### DIRECTIONS

Heat 1 tablespoon of the olive oil in a pan that is preheated over a moderate flame.

Now, cook the cauliflower florets, bell peppers, and onion until they are slightly tender; season with salt, black pepper, and cayenne pepper; set aside.

Preheat another tablespoon of the olive oil. Sear the sea bass on each side for 5 minutes.

To make the chutney, heat 1 teaspoon of vegetable oil in a pan over a moderately high heat. Sauté the garlic until just browned and aromatic.

Add the plum tomatoes and cook, stirring occasionally, until heated through, or 10 minutes. Season with capers, salt, and pepper.

Divide the seared fish among 4 serving plates. Serve garnished with the sautéed cauliflower mixture and tomato chutney. Enjoy!

## 543. Grilled Halloumi and Tuna Salad

**(Ready in about 15 minutes | Servings 4)**

**Per serving: 199 Calories; 10.6g Fat; 3.1g Carbs; 14.2g Protein;**

### INGREDIENTS

1 cup halloumi cheese
2 cucumbers, thinly sliced
1/2 cup radishes, thinly sliced
2 tablespoons sunflower seeds
1 ½ tablespoons extra-virgin olive oil
1 can light tuna fish in water, rinsed

1/2 head Romaine lettuce
2 medium-sized Roma tomatoes, sliced
1 red onion, thinly sliced
1 tablespoon lime juice
Sea salt and black pepper, to taste
Dried rosemary, to taste

### DIRECTIONS

Grill the halloumi cheese over medium high heat. Cut into cubes.
Toss the grilled halloumi cheese with the remaining ingredients. Bon appétit!

## 544. Sriracha Egg Salad with Scallions

**(Ready in about 15 minutes | Servings 8)**

**Per serving: 174 Calories; 13g Fat; 2.7g Carbs; 7.4g Protein;**

### INGREDIENTS

10 eggs
3/4 cup mayonnaise
1 teaspoon Sriracha
1 tablespoon whole grain mustard
1/2 cup scallions

1/2 stalk of celery, minced
1/2 teaspoon fresh lime juice
1/2 teaspoon sea salt
1/2 teaspoon ground black pepper, to taste
1 head Romaine lettuce, torn into pieces

### DIRECTIONS

Place the eggs in a pan and cover them with at least 1-inch of water; bring to a boil. Then, remove from the heat, cover, and let them sit approximately 10 minutes.
Chop the eggs coarsely and add them to a salad bowl.
Add the remaining ingredients and gently stir until everything is well incorporated. Place in the refrigerator until ready to serve. Bon appétit!

## 545. Easy Vegetarian Cheese Tacos

**(Ready in about 10 minutes | Servings 6)**

**Per serving: 370 Calories; 30g Fat; 4.9g Carbs; 19.5g Protein;**

### INGREDIENTS

1/2 pound Cheddar cheese, grated
1/2 pound Colby cheese, grated
1 teaspoon taco seasoning mix

1 ½ cups guacamole
1 cup sour cream
A small-sized head of lettuce

### DIRECTIONS

Combine both types of cheese with the taco seasoning mix.
Then, preheat a pan over a moderate flame.
Scatter the shredded cheese mixture all over the pan, covering the bottom. Fry for 4 to 5 minutes, turning once.
Top with the guacamole, sour cream and lettuce, roll them up and serve immediately. Bon appétit!

# 546. Sopressata and Blue Cheese Waffles

**(Ready in about 20 minutes | Servings 2)**

**Per serving: 470 Calories; 40.3g Fat; 2.9g Carbs; 24.4g Protein;**

## INGREDIENTS

2 tablespoons butter, melted
Salt and black pepper, to your liking
1/2 teaspoon parsley flakes
1/2 teaspoon chili pepper flakes

4 eggs
1/2 cup blue cheese, crumbled
4 slices Sopressata, chopped
2 tablespoons fresh chives, chopped

## DIRECTIONS

Combine all ingredients, except for the fresh chives, in a mixing bowl. Preheat your waffle iron and grease with a cooking spray.
Add the omelet mixture and close the lid.
Fry about 5 minutes or until desired consistency is reached. Repeat with the remaining batter. Serve garnished with fresh chives and eat warm.

# 547. Festive Eggs with Cheese and Aioli

**(Ready in about 20 minutes | Servings 8)**

**Per serving: 285 Calories; 22.5g Fat; 1.8g Carbs; 19.5g Protein;**

## INGREDIENTS

8 eggs, hard-boiled
2 cans tuna in brine, drained
1/2 cup Bibb lettuces, torn into pieces
1/2 cup red onions, finely chopped
1/2 goat cheese, crumbled
1/3 cup sour cream
1/2 tablespoon yellow mustard

**For Aioli:**

1 egg
2 medium cloves garlic, minced
1 tablespoon lemon juice
1/2 cup olive oil
Salt and black pepper, to taste

## DIRECTIONS

Peel and chop the eggs; transfer them to a serving bowl. Add the tuna, lettuce, onion, cheese, sour cream and yellow mustard.
To make the aioli, beat the egg, garlic, and lemon juice with an immersion blender. Add the oil, salt and pepper, and blend again until everything is well mixed.
Add the prepared aioli to the bowl and gently stir until everything is well incorporated.
Serve with pickles or bell peppers. Bon appétit!

# 548. Kid-Friendly Avocado Boats

**(Ready in about 20 minutes | Servings 4)**

**Per serving: 342 Calories; 30.4g Fat; 6.5g Carbs; 11.1g Protein;**

## INGREDIENTS

2 avocados, halved and pitted, skin on
2 ounces blue cheese, crumbled
2 ounces Colby cheese, grated

2 eggs, beaten
Salt and pepper, to taste
1 tablespoon fresh cilantro, chopped

## DIRECTIONS

Preheat your oven to 360 degrees F.
Arrange the avocado halves in an ovenproof dish.
In a mixing dish, combine both types of cheeses, eggs, salt and pepper. Divide the mixture among the avocado halves.
Bake for 15 to 17 minutes or until everything is thoroughly baked. Serve garnished with fresh cilantro. Enjoy!

## 549. Cheesy Cauliflower Fritters

**(Ready in about 35 minutes | Servings 6)**

**Per serving: 199 Calories; 13.8g Fat; 6.8g Carbs; 13g Protein;**

### INGREDIENTS

1 ½ tablespoons olive oil
1 shallot, chopped
1 garlic clove, minced
1 pound cauliflower, grated
6 tablespoons almond flour

1/2 cup Swiss cheese, shredded
1 cup parmesan cheese
2 eggs, beaten
1/2 teaspoon dried dill weed
Sea salt and ground black pepper, to taste

### DIRECTIONS

Heat the oil in a cast iron skillet over medium heat. Cook the shallots and garlic until they are aromatic.
Add the grated cauliflower and stir with a spatula for another minute or so; set aside to cool to room temperature so you can handle it easily.
Add the remaining ingredients; shape the mixture into balls, then, press each ball to form burger patties.
Bake in the preheated oven at 400 degrees F for 20 minutes. Flip and bake for another 10 minutes or until golden brown on top. Bon appétit!

## 550. Espresso and Coconut Delight

**(Ready in about 10 minutes + chilling time | Servings 6)**

**Per serving: 218 Calories; 24.7g Fat; 1.1g Carbs; 0.4g Protein;**

### INGREDIENTS

4 ounces coconut oil
4 ounces coconut cream
2 teaspoons butter, softened
1 teaspoon instant espresso powder

3 tablespoons confectioners Swerve
A pinch of salt
1 teaspoon pure vanilla extract

### DIRECTIONS

Melt the coconut oil in a double boiler over medium-low heat.
Add the remaining ingredients. Remove from the heat; stir until everything is well combined.
Pour into a silicone mold and freeze overnight. Bon appétit!

## 551. Fall Cabbage Soup

**(Ready in about 25 minutes | Servings 4)**

**Per serving: 185 Calories; 16.6g Fat; 2.4g Carbs; 2.9g Protein;**

### INGREDIENTS

1 ½ tablespoons butter, melted
1 leek, chopped
2 garlic cloves, minced
2 carrots, chopped
1 cup cabbage, shredded

1 green pepper, chopped
4 cups water
2 bouillon cubes
1 cup sour cream
Fresh tarragon sprigs, for garnish

### DIRECTIONS

Warm the butter in a large pot over a medium flame. Sauté the leeks until just tender and fragrant. Now, add the remaining vegetables and cook for 5 to 7 minutes, stirring periodically.
Add the water and bouillon cubes; cover partially and cook an additional 13 minutes.
Blend the mixture until creamy, uniform and smooth. Stir in the sour cream; gently heat, stirring continuously, until your soup is hot.
Ladle into individual bowls and serve garnished with fresh tarragon. Bon appétit!

# 552. French Style Vegetables

**(Ready in about 15 minutes | Servings 4)**

**Per serving: 318 Calories; 24.3g Fat; 5.1g Carbs; 15.4g Protein;**

## INGREDIENTS

2 tablespoons olive oil
2 garlic cloves, minced
1/2 cup red onion, chopped
1/2 pound button mushrooms, chopped
1 cup cauliflower, cut into small florets
1 medium-sized eggplant, chopped
1 teaspoon dried basil

1 teaspoon dried oregano
1 rosemary sprig, leaves picked
1 thyme sprig, leaves picked
1/2 cup tomato sauce
1/4 cup dry white wine
8 ounces Halloumi cheese, cubed

## DIRECTIONS

Heat the olive oil in a saucepan over a moderately high heat. Now, sauté the garlic for 1 to 1½ minutes.
Now, stir in the onion, mushrooms, cauliflower, and eggplant; cook an additional 5 minutes, stirring periodically.
Add the seasonings, tomato sauce, and wine; continue to cook for 4 more minutes. Remove from the heat and divide among individual plates.
Serve topped with Halloumi cheese and enjoy!

# 553. Asparagus with Feta Cheese

**(Ready in about 15 minutes | Servings 6)**

**Per serving: 128 Calories; 9.4g Fat; 2.9g Carbs; 6.4g Protein;**

## INGREDIENTS

1 ½ pounds asparagus spears
2 tablespoons butter, melted
2 green onions, chopped
2 garlic cloves, minced

Salt and black pepper, to the taste
1 cup feta cheese, crumbled
1/2 cup fresh parsley, roughly chopped

## DIRECTIONS

Preheat an oven to 420 degrees F.
Drizzle the asparagus with the melted butter. Toss with the green onions, garlic, salt, and black pepper.
Place the asparagus on a lightly-greased baking pan in a single layer. Roast for about 14 minutes.
Scatter the crumbled feta over the warm asparagus spears. Serve garnished with fresh parsley.

# 554. Yummy Greek Salad

**(Ready in about 15 minutes + chilling time | Servings 4)**

**Per serving: 318 Calories; 24.3g Fat; 4.1g Carbs; 15.4g Protein;**

## INGREDIENTS

1 cup Greek-style yogurt
1 teaspoon garlic, minced
1 tablespoon fresh lime juice
1 teaspoon fresh or dried rosemary, minced
2 green onions, thinly sliced

4 cucumbers, sliced
6 radishes, sliced
Sea salt and ground black pepper, to taste
4 Boston lettuce leaves

## DIRECTIONS

In a mixing bowl, thoroughly whisk the Greek-style yogurt, garlic, lime juice and rosemary.
Toss the green onions, cucumbers, and radishes with prepared yogurt dressing; season with salt and pepper to taste and toss to coat well.
Divide the Boston lettuce leaves among four serving plates. Mound well-chilled salad onto each lettuce leaf and serve. Bon appétit!

# 555. Nutty Coleslaw

**(Ready in about 10 minutes + chilling time | Servings 4)**

**Per serving: 242 Calories; 20.5g Fat; 6.2g Carbs; 1g Protein;**

## INGREDIENTS

3/4 pound Napa cabbage, cored and shredded
1 large-sized carrot, shredded
1 cup mayonnaise
1 teaspoon coarse ground mustard

1/2 cup fresh parsley leaves, loosely packed and coarsely chopped
1 teaspoon celery seeds
Salt and ground pepper, to taste
2 tablespoons sunflower seeds

## DIRECTIONS

Add the cabbage and carrots to your salad bowl. Now, stir in the mayonnaise, mustard, parsley, celery seeds, salt, and pepper. Gently stir to combine all ingredients. Allow it to sit for 3 hours in the refrigerator. Serve sprinkled with sunflower seeds.

# 556. Hot Vegetarian Delight

**(Ready in about 15 minutes | Servings 4)**

**Per serving: 290 Calories; 21.7g Fat; 6.5g Carbs; 10.6g Protein;**

## INGREDIENTS

2 tablespoons olive oil
2 small-sized shallots, chopped
1 garlic clove, minced
1 pound cremini mushroom, sliced
1/2 teaspoon salt

1/2 teaspoon ground black pepper
1 cup tomatillo, chopped
4 eggs
1/4 cup enchilada sauce
1 medium-sized avocado, pitted and mashed

## DIRECTIONS

Heat the olive oil in a saucepan over a moderate flame. Now, cook the shallot and garlic until just tender and fragrant.
Now, add the mushrooms and stir until they're tender. Season with salt and pepper; stir in the chopped tomatillo.
Stir in the eggs and scramble them well. Top with the enchilada sauce; serve warm with avocado slices.

# 557. Cheese Balls with Fresh Cucumber

**(Ready in about 25 minutes | Servings 2)**

**Per serving: 133 Calories; 9.9g Fat; 6.8g Carbs; 6g Protein;**

## INGREDIENTS

1 ounce blue cheese
1 ounce Neufchatel
1 medium-sized cucumber, chopped

1 tablespoon fresh parsley, chopped
2 tablespoons walnuts, chopped

## DIRECTIONS

Drop the chopped cucumbers into a colander; sprinkle with a pinch of salt. Let it stand for 20 minutes in the sink; press your cucumber firmly to drain away the excess liquid.
Thoroughly mix the cheese, cucumber, and parsley in a bowl.
Shape into 4 balls and roll them in chopped walnuts. Refrigerate until ready to serve.

## 558. Tasty Oven-Roasted Asparagus

**(Ready in about 20 minutes | Servings 4)**

**Per serving: 48 Calories; 1.6g Fat; 4.4g Carbs; 5.5g Protein;**

### INGREDIENTS

1 pound asparagus spears
Salt and freshly ground black pepper, to your liking
1 teaspoon onion powder

1/4 teaspoon cumin powder
1/2 teaspoon dried thyme
4 tablespoons bacon bits

### DIRECTIONS

Start by preheating your oven to 460 degrees F.
Toss the asparagus spears with the salt, black pepper, onion powder, cumin powder, and thyme. Arrange them on a baking sheet.
Spritz with a nonstick cooking spray. Bake for 8 to 10 minutes; turn them over and bake an additional 8 minutes.
Serve garnished with bacon bits and enjoy!

## 559. Yummy Vegetables with Hot Dip

**(Ready in about 45 minutes | Servings 4)**

**Per serving: 357 Calories; 35.8g Fat; 5.2g Carbs; 3.4g Protein;**

### INGREDIENTS

2 carrots, cut into sticks
1 celery stalk, cut into sticks
1 red bell pepper, sliced
1 green bell pepper, sliced
1 red onion, sliced into rings
1/4 cup olive oil
1 garlic clove, minced
1 tablespoon fresh parsley, minced
1/2 teaspoon paprika

For the Spicy Sour Cream Dip:
1 ½ cups sour cream
2 tablespoons mayonnaise
3/4 teaspoon Dijon mustard
1 jalapeño pepper, finely minced
1 tablespoon lime juice
Salt and black pepper, to taste
2 tablespoons sage leaves, chopped

### DIRECTIONS

Preheat your oven to 390 degrees F. Line a baking sheet with parchment paper.
In a mixing dish, toss the carrots, celery, bell pepper, onion, olive oil, garlic, parsley, and paprika.
Arrange the vegetables on the baking sheet and roast about 40 minutes; be sure to stir halfway through.
Combine all ingredients for the sour cream dip; whisk until everything is well incorporated. Serve with the roasted vegetables and enjoy!

## 560. Stuffed Chanterelles with Prosciutto

**(Ready in about 25 minutes | Servings 6)**

**Per serving: 98 Calories; 5.8g Fat; 3.9g Carbs; 8.4g Protein;**

### INGREDIENTS

6 medium-sized Chanterelles, stems removed
3 teaspoons sesame oil
1 tablespoon Worcestershire sauce
Coarse salt and ground black pepper, to your liking

3 slices of prosciutto, finely chopped
2 tablespoons fresh cilantro, minced
1 teaspoon fresh rosemary, minced
2 ounces Asiago cheese, grated

### DIRECTIONS

Start by preheating your oven to 355 degrees F. Line a baking sheet with a piece of parchment paper.
Rub the sesame oil and Worcestershire sauce on the mushroom caps. Season them with salt and pepper.
Now, combine the prosciutto, cilantro, rosemary and cheese; mix well. Stuff the mushroom caps and bake for 18 to 22 minutes.
Adjust the seasonings and serve immediately. Bon appétit!

# 561. Green Beans with Tapenade

**(Ready in about 15 minutes | Servings 4)**

**Per serving: 183 Calories; 16.1g Fat; 4.4g Carbs; 3.2g Protein;**

## INGREDIENTS

1 pound green beans
1 tablespoon sesame oil
1 celery stalk, shredded
1 garlic clove, smashed
1/2 teaspoon smoked paprika
Flaky sea salt and ground black pepper, to taste

**For Tapenade:**
1/2 cup Kalamata olives
1 ½ tablespoons capers
2 anchovy fillets
1 tablespoon fresh lemon juice
3 tablespoons extra-virgin olive oil

## DIRECTIONS

Put the green beans in a steamer basket over boiling water; steam approximately 4 minutes or until crisp-tender.
Heat the sesame oil in a sauté pan over a moderate flame. Add the celery and garlic; sauté an additional 4 minutes, stirring periodically.
Season with paprika, salt, and black pepper.
Puree all the ingredients for the tapenade in your food processor. Serve immediately with the sautéed green beans. Bon appétit!

# 562. Spinach with Cottage Cheese

**(Ready in about 10 minutes | Servings 4)**

**Per serving: 208 Calories; 13.5g Fat; 6g Carbs; 14.5g Protein;**

## INGREDIENTS

1/2 stick butter
2 garlic cloves, minced
2 pounds spinach leaves, rinsed and torn into pieces
1 teaspoon salt

1/2 teaspoon cayenne pepper
1/4 teaspoon turmeric powder
1 cup cottage cheese

## DIRECTIONS

Melt the butter in a Dutch oven and sauté the garlic until it's just browned.
Add the spinach leaves, salt, cayenne pepper, and turmeric powder; cook another 2 to 3 minutes over a moderate heat, adding a splash of warm water if needed.
Next, turn the heat on high, and cook for 1 to 2 minutes more, stirring often. Taste and adjust the seasonings.
Serve topped with cottage cheese.

# 563. Family Vegetable Patties

**(Ready in about 15 minutes | Servings 6)**

**Per serving: 153 Calories; 11.8g Fat; 6.6g Carbs; 6.4g Protein;**

## INGREDIENTS

2 medium-sized zucchinis, shredded
2 carrots, shredded
1 small-sized celery stalk, shredded
2 tablespoons parsley, chopped
1 white onion, finely chopped
1 garlic clove, finely minced

1 cup cheddar cheese, grated
2 tablespoons olive oil
1 egg yolk
Salt and black pepper, to taste
Lemon wedges, to serve

## DIRECTIONS

Start by preheating your oven to 360 degrees F. Line a baking sheet with parchment paper.
Now, press the shredded vegetables firmly to drain away the excess liquid. Then, thoroughly combine all ingredients, except for the lemon wedges, in a mixing bowl.
Shape the mixture into 12 patties and bake for 5 minutes per side. Serve with fresh lemon wedges and enjoy!

# 564. Pork and Cheese Sausage Balls

**(Ready in about 15 minutes + chilling time | Servings 6)**

**Per serving: 353 Calories; 30.7g Fat; 3g Carbs; 16.1g Protein;**

## INGREDIENTS

1 tablespoon olive oil
1/2 pound pork sausage, ground
1 tomato, pureed
1 teaspoon garlic paste
2 tablespoons onion, minced
4 ounces Neufchatel cheese, room temperature

1/4 teaspoon kosher salt
1/4 teaspoon ground black pepper
4 ounces chive & onion cream cheese
4 ounces fontina cheese, crumbled
2 tablespoons flaxseed meal

## DIRECTIONS

Heat the oil in a skillet that is preheated over moderate heat. Now, brown the sausage for 3 to 4 minutes, stirring periodically.
Add the tomatoes, garlic paste, and onion; cook for a further 5 minutes. Add the other ingredients and mix well to combine.
Place the mixture in your refrigerator to harden. Shape the mixture into bite-sized balls. Serve well-chilled.

# 565. Brie-Stuffed Meatballs

**(Ready in about 25 minutes | Servings 5)**

**Per serving: 302 Calories; 17.3g Fat; 1.9g Carbs; 33.4g Protein;**

## INGREDIENTS

1 pound ground pork
1/3 cup heavy cream
2 eggs, beaten
1 tablespoon fresh cilantro
2 tablespoons shallots, minced

2 cloves garlic, minced
1 teaspoon kosher salt
1/2 teaspoon ground black pepper
1 teaspoon dried thyme
10 (1-inch) cubes of brie

## DIRECTIONS

Combine all ingredients, except for the cubes of brie, in a mixing bowl.
Then, shape the mixture into 10 patties by using oiled hands. Now, place a piece of brie in the center of each patty and roll into a ball.
Preheat your oven to 390 degrees F. Arrange the meatballs on a foil-lined baking pan. Bake for 20 to 22 minutes.
Serve with mustard or low-carb salsa. Enjoy!

# 566. Yummy Muffins with Ground Pork

**(Ready in about 25 minutes | Servings 6)**

**Per serving: 479 Calories; 42g Fat; 5.8g Carbs; 17.9g Protein;**

## INGREDIENTS

1 tablespoon canola oil
1 ½ cups ground pork
Salt and cayenne pepper, to your liking
1 stick butter
3 ½ cups almond flour
1/2 teaspoon baking powder

1/2 teaspoon baking soda
3 large eggs, lightly beaten
2 tablespoons full-fat milk
1/2 teaspoon ground cloves
1/2 teaspoon dried oregano

## DIRECTIONS

Heat the oil in a frying pan over medium heat. Now, cook the ground pork until the juices run clear, about 4 to 5 minutes.
Then, preheat your oven to 360 degrees F.
Add the remaining ingredients to a mixing dish, in the order listed above. Thoroughly combine until everything is well incorporated.
Divide the mixture among 12 muffin cups. Bake in the preheated oven for 15 to 18 minutes.
Allow your muffins to cool down before removing from the baking tin. Serve with full-fat sour cream. Bon appétit!

## 567. Pork Shoulder with Blue Cheese Sauce

**(Ready in about 30 minutes | Servings 6)**

**Per serving: 495 Calories; 36.9g Fat; 3.6g Carbs; 33.4g Protein;**

### INGREDIENTS

1 ½ pounds pork shoulder, boneless and cut into 6 pieces
Salt and freshly cracked black peppercorns, to taste
1 teaspoon dried thyme
1 tablespoon butter
1 onion, chopped
2 garlic cloves, chopped

1/3 cup dry sherry wine
1/3 cup broth, preferably homemade
1 teaspoon dried hot chile flakes
1 tablespoon soy sauce
6 ounces blue cheese
1/3 cup double cream

### DIRECTIONS

Rub each piece of the pork shoulder with salt, black peppercorns, and thyme.
Now, warn the butter in a sauté pan over a moderately high heat. Then, brown the pork on all sides about 18 minutes; reserve.
Next, sauté the onions and garlic until the onions are caramelized. Add the wine and broth and stir, scraping up any brown bits from the bottom.
Turn the heat to medium and add the other ingredients; continue to simmer until the desired thickness is reached by evaporation.
Serve the reserved pork with the sauce on the side. Bon appétit!

## 568. Meat Loaf and Carrot Muffins

**(Ready in about 35 minutes | Servings 6)**

**Per serving: 220 Calories; 6.3g Fat; 5.4g Carbs; 33.8g Protein;**

### INGREDIENTS

1 pound pork, ground
1/2 pound turkey, ground
1 cup carrots, shredded
2 ripe tomatoes, pureed
1 ounce envelope onion soup mix
1 tablespoon Worcestershire sauce
1 tablespoon Dijon mustard

1/2 teaspoon dry basil
1 teaspoon dry oregano
Kosher salt and ground black pepper, to taste
2 cloves of garlic, minced
1 eggs, whisked
1 cup mozzarella cheese, shredded

### DIRECTIONS

Start by preheating your oven to 350 degrees F.
Then, thoroughly combine all ingredients until everything is blended.
Spoon the mixture into a muffin tin that is previously coated with a nonstick cooking spray.
Bake for 30 minutes; allow them to cool slightly before removing from the tin. Bon appétit!

## 569. Pork Soup with Avocado

**(Ready in about 20 minutes | Servings 6)**

**Per serving: 423 Calories; 31.8g Fat; 6g Carbs; 25.9g Protein;**

### INGREDIENTS

2 tablespoons lard
1 medium-sized yellow onion, peeled and chopped
2 cloves garlic, peeled and minced
1 teaspoon Mezzeta pepper, seeded and minced
1 celery, chopped
1 ¼ pounds pork shoulder, cut into chunks

3 cups beef broth, less-sodium
Sea salt and ground black pepper, to taste
A pinch of dried basil
2 ripe tomatoes, undrained
1/4 cup fresh parsley, roughly chopped
1 medium-sized avocado, pitted and sliced

### DIRECTIONS

Melt the lard in a large-sized stock pot over a moderate flame. Next, sauté the onion, garlic, Mezzeta pepper and celery for 2 to 3 minutes or until the onion is translucent.
Stir in the pork chunks and continue cooking for 4 minutes more, stirring continuously. Add the other ingredients.
Now, lower the heat and simmer for 10 minutes, partially covered; make sure to stir periodically.
Serve topped with fresh parsley leaves and sliced avocado.

# 570. Hot Sauerkraut with Beef

**(Ready in about 20 minutes | Servings 4)**

**Per serving: 330 Calories; 12.2g Fat; 4.7g Carbs; 44.4g Protein;**

## INGREDIENTS

1 tablespoon tallow, melted
2 onions, chopped
2 garlic cloves, smashed
1 ¼ pounds ground beef
18 ounces sauerkraut, rinsed and well drained

1 teaspoon chili pepper flakes
1 teaspoon mustard powder
1 bay leaf
Sea salt and ground black pepper, to taste

## DIRECTIONS

Heat a saucepan over a moderately high heat. Now, warm the tallow and cook the onions and garlic until aromatic.
Stir in the ground beef and cook until it is slightly browned.
Add the remaining ingredients. Reduce the heat to medium. Cook about 6 minutes or until everything is thoroughly cooked. Bon appétit!

# 571. Yummy Cheeseburger Soup

**(Ready in about 20 minutes | Servings 4)**

**Per serving: 326 Calories; 20.5g Fat; 4.5g Carbs; 26.8g Protein;**

## INGREDIENTS

2 tablespoons coconut oil
1/2 pound ground beef
1 cup shallots, chopped
1 celery stalk, chopped
1 tablespoon celery leaves, chopped

1 tablespoon fresh cilantro, chopped
4 cups beef bone broth
1/2 cup full-fat milk
1 cup pepper jack cheese, shredded
1 tablespoon rice vinegar

## DIRECTIONS

Melt the coconut oil in a stock pot that is preheated over a moderate heat. Now, cook the ground beef until it is no longer pink; reserve.
Add the shallots and chopped celery stalk; cook an additional 2 minutes, stirring continuously. Add a splash of broth if needed.
Add the celery leaves, cilantro and broth and bring to a boil; cook another 10 minutes, partially covered.
Gradually add the milk to the soup, stirring often. Reduce the heat and let it simmer an additional 5 minutes. Fold in the cheese and remove from the heat.
Add the vinegar and stir until the cheese is completely melted. Bon appétit!

# 572. Beef Steaks with Sour Cream-Mustard Sauce

**(Ready in about 20 minutes | Servings 4)**

**Per serving: 321 Calories; 13.7g Fat; 1g Carbs; 45g Protein;**

## INGREDIENTS

1/3 cup sour cream
1 tablespoon stone-ground mustard
1 ½ tablespoons flat-leaf parsley, finely chopped
4 (1 ½-inch) thick filet mignon steaks
1/2 teaspoon seasoned salt

1/4 teaspoon ground black pepper
2 sprigs thyme, chopped
1 sprig rosemary, chopped
1 tablespoon vegetable oil

## DIRECTIONS

In a mixing bowl, whisk together the sour cream, mustard, and parsley. Keep in your refrigerator until ready to serve.
Then, season the filet mignon steaks with salt, pepper, thyme, and rosemary.
Heat the oil in a pan that is preheated over moderately high heat for 4 minutes on each side. Serve with the prepared mustard sauce and enjoy!

# 573. Juicy Beef Short Loin

**(Ready in about 2 hours | Servings 4)**

**Per serving: 238 Calories; 9.2g Fat; 6.3g Carbs; 27.4g Protein;**

## INGREDIENTS

1 tablespoon olive oil
1 pound beef short loin, thinly sliced
1 leek, sliced
1 parsnip, chopped
3 garlic cloves, thinly sliced
1/2 teaspoon grated nutmeg

1 teaspoon lemon zest
1/2 teaspoon red pepper flakes, crushed
1/3 cup red wine
2 tablespoons Worcestershire sauce
1 ½ cups beef stock

## DIRECTIONS

Heat the oil in a heavy-bottomed skillet that is preheated over a moderate heat. Sear the beef short loin for 10 to 13 minutes; reserve.

Then, in the same skillet, cook the leeks, parsnip and garlic for 3 to 4 minutes, stirring constantly.

Add the remaining ingredients and bring to a rapid boil. Then, turn the heat to a simmer. Cook for 1 ½ to 2 hours. Bon appétit!

# 574. Traditional Beef Stew

**(Ready in about 40 minutes | Servings 6)**

**Per serving: 259 Calories; 10.1g Fat; 4.1g Carbs; 35.7g Protein;**

## INGREDIENTS

1 tablespoon tallow, at room temperature
1 ½ pounds beef stew meat, cubed
1 cup leeks, thinly sliced
2 garlic cloves, chopped
1 tablespoon cremini mushrooms, thinly sliced
Salt and black pepper, to taste
1 teaspoon dried marjoram

1 teaspoon cayenne pepper
1/4 teaspoon smoked paprika
1 bay leaf
4 cubes beef bouillon, crumbled
4 cups water
1 egg, lightly whisked

## DIRECTIONS

Melt the tallow in your pot that is preheated over a moderate flame.

Now, sear the beef until it's just browned; make sure to stir periodically. Set aside.

In pan drippings, cook the leeks and garlic for 1 minute to 90 seconds or until aromatic. Stir in the mushrooms; cook until they're tender and fragrant.

Add the remaining ingredients, cover and cook for 30 to 40 minutes. Add the whisked egg in the hot soup and stir for 1 minute. Serve in individual bowls and enjoy!

# 575. Yummy Steaks with Wine Sauce

**(Ready in about 30 minutes | Servings 4)**

**Per serving: 451 Calories; 34.4g Fat; 3.6g Carbs; 29.7g Protein;**

## INGREDIENTS

4 (6-ounce) filet mignon steaks
1 tablespoon deli mustard
Celery salt and freshly ground pepper, to taste
2 rosemary sprigs
1 thyme sprigs

2 tablespoons lard, room temperature
1 cup scallions, chopped
2 garlic cloves, minced
1 red bell pepper, deveined and chopped
1/2 cup dry red wine

## DIRECTIONS

Rub filet mignon steaks with the mustard. Sprinkle the filet mignon steaks with the salt, pepper, rosemary and thyme.

Heat the lard in a heavy-bottomed skillet over moderate heat. Cook the filet mignon steaks for 10 minutes on each side or until a thermometer registers 120 degrees F.

Now, cook the scallions, garlic, and pepper in pan drippings about 3 minutes. Pour in the wine to scrape up any browned bits from the bottom of the skillet.

Now, cook until the liquid is reduced by half. Serve immediately.

# 576. Slow Cooker Beef Brisket with Blue Cheese

**(Ready in about 8 hours | Servings 6)**

**Per serving: 397 Calories; 31.4g Fat; 3.9g Carbs; 23.5g Protein;**

## INGREDIENTS

2 tablespoons olive oil
1 shallot, chopped
1/2 tablespoon garlic paste
1 ½ pounds corned beef brisket
1/4 teaspoon cloves, ground

1/3 teaspoon ground coriander
1/4 cup soy sauce
1 cup water
6 ounces blue cheese, crumbled

## DIRECTIONS

Heat a sauté pan with the olive oil over medium heat. Cook the shallot until it has softened.
Add the garlic paste and cook an additional minute; transfer to your slow cooker that is previously greased with a nonstick cooking spray.
Sear the brisket until it has a golden-brown crust. Transfer to the slow cooker. Add the remaining ingredient, except for the blue cheese.
Cover and cook on Low heat setting for 6 to 8 hours or until the meat is very tender. Serve topped with the blue cheese. Enjoy!

# 577. Scallion and Sriracha Chuck

**(Ready in about 50 minutes | Servings 4)**

**Per serving: 292 Calories; 14.3g Fat; 3.9g Carbs; 36.9g Protein;**

## INGREDIENTS

2 tablespoons soy sauce
1 teaspoon Sriracha sauce
1 tablespoon garlic paste
Salt and crushed mixed peppercorns, to taste
1 teaspoon mustard seeds
1/2 teaspoon dried marjoram

1 bunch scallions, chopped
1/2 tablespoon tallow
1 ½ pounds chuck pot roast, cubed
1/4 teaspoon cumin
1/4 teaspoon celery seeds
1 tablespoon fresh parsley, roughly chopped

## DIRECTIONS

Whisk the soy sauce, Sriracha sauce and garlic paste in a mixing bowl. Add the salt, crushed peppercorns, mustard seeds, marjoram, and scallions.
Add the cubed beef and let it marinate for 40 minutes in your refrigerator.
Melt the tallow in a frying pan over a moderately high heat. Cook the marinated beef for 5 to 6 minutes, stirring frequently; work in batches to cook the beef cubes through evenly.
Season with cumin and celery seeds. Serve garnished with fresh parsley. Enjoy!

# 578. Beef Casserole with Creamy Sauce

**(Ready in about 25 minutes | Servings 4)**

**Per serving: 509 Calories; 29.6g Fat; 6.1g Carbs; 45.2g Protein;**

## INGREDIENTS

1 tablespoon olive oil
1 pound ground beef
2 ripe tomatoes, chopped
2 ounces sun-dried tomatoes, chopped
1/2 tablespoon dill relish
1/2 teaspoon salt
1/4 teaspoon ground black pepper

1/2 teaspoon chili powder
1 teaspoon Italian seasoning
1 cup cheddar cheese
3/4 cup sour cream
1 teaspoon minced garlic
1/2 cup shallots, finely chopped

## DIRECTIONS

Preheat the oven to 400 degrees F.
Then, heat the oil in a nonstick skillet that is preheated over a moderate flame.
Brown the ground beef in butter, crumbling it with a large spatula. Add the tomatoes, dill relish and seasonings.
Place the beef mixture in a baking dish. Top with the cheese and bake for about 18 minutes.
Meanwhile, thoroughly combine the sour cream with the garlic and shallots. Serve with your casserole dish.

## 579. Tasty Skirt Steak and Eggs Skillet

**(Ready in about 30 minutes | Servings 6)**

**Per serving: 429 Calories; 27.8g Fat; 3.2g Carbs; 39.1g Protein;**

### INGREDIENTS

2 tablespoons olive oil
1 ½ pounds skirt steak, cut into cubes
Celery salt and ground black pepper, to taste
1/2 teaspoon red pepper flakes
1/2 cup spring onions onion, chopped

1 teaspoon garlic, minced
1 bell pepper, chopped
1 serrano pepper, chopped
6 eggs

### DIRECTIONS

Heat the oil in a nonstick skillet over a moderately high flame. Cook the beef cubes for 10 minutes or until no longer pink, stirring periodically. Season with salt, black pepper and red pepper flakes and set aside.
In the same skillet, cook the spring onion and garlic until aromatic, 3 to 4 minutes. Stir in the peppers and cook for 3 minutes more.
Now, create six holes in the mixture to reveal the bottom of your pan. Crack an egg into each hole. Now, cook, covered, for 4 to 6 minutes or until the eggs are set. Serve right away!

## 580. Avocado and Tuna Balls

**(Ready in about 5 minutes | Servings 4)**

**Per serving: 316 Calories; 24.4g Fat; 5.9g Carbs; 17.4g Protein;**

### INGREDIENTS

3 ounces sunflower seeds
1 avocado, pitted and peeled
1 can tuna
Salt, to taste

1/2 teaspoon freshly ground black pepper
1/2 teaspoon smoked paprika
1/2 cup onion, chopped
1/2 teaspoon dried dill

### DIRECTIONS

Thoroughly mix all ingredients in a mixing dish. Shape the mixture into 8 balls.
Serve well chilled and enjoy!

## 581. Oven-Baked Cod Fillets

**(Ready in about 30 minutes | Servings 4)**

**Per serving: 195 Calories; 8.2g Fat; 0.5g Carbs; 28.7g Protein;**

### INGREDIENTS

2 tablespoons olive oil
1/2 tablespoon yellow mustard
1 teaspoon garlic paste
1/2 tablespoon fresh lemon juice
1/2 teaspoon shallot powder

Salt and ground black pepper, to taste
1/2 teaspoon red pepper flakes, crushed
4 cod fillets
1/4 cup fresh cilantro, chopped

### DIRECTIONS

Start by preheating your oven to 420 degrees F. Lightly grease a baking dish with a nonstick cooking spray.
In a small mixing dish, thoroughly combine the oil, mustard, garlic paste, lemon juice, shallot powder, salt, black pepper and red pepper. Rub this mixture on all sides of your fish.
Bake 15 to 22 minutes in the middle of the preheated oven. Serve sprinkled with fresh cilantro.

# 582. Yummy Ricotta and Tuna Spread

**(Ready in about 10 minutes | Servings 6)**

**Per serving: 384 Calories; 20.4g Fat; 2.5g Carbs; 45.9g Protein;**

## INGREDIENTS

1 (6-ounce) can tuna in oil, drained
1/2 cup Ricotta cheese
1/2 teaspoon turmeric

2 ounces pecans, ground
1 tablespoon fresh cilantro, chopped

## DIRECTIONS

Blend the tuna, Ricotta cheese, turmeric powder and pecans in your blender.
Transfer to a serving bowl and serve garnished with fresh cilantro.
Serve with veggie sticks. Bon appétit!

# 583. Yummy Scallop Dinner

**(Ready in about 10 minutes | Servings 4)**

**Per serving: 260 Calories; 13.6g Fat; 5.9g Carbs; 28.1g Protein;**

## INGREDIENTS

1 pound sea scallops, halved horizontally
4 spring garlic, roughly chopped
2 plum tomatoes, sliced
1 cucumber, sliced
1 head of Iceberg lettuce, torn into bite-sized pieces
1/2 tablespoon deli mustard

1/4 cup extra-virgin olive oil
2 tablespoons fresh lemon juice
Sea salt and freshly ground pepper, to your liking
1/2 teaspoon dried dill weed
1/2 cup ripe olives, pitted and sliced

## DIRECTIONS

Add the scallops to a pot of a lightly salted water; cook for 1 to 3 minutes or until opaque; rinse under running water and transfer to a salad bowl.
Stir in the spring garlic, tomatoes, cucumber, and lettuce; gently toss to combine.
In a mixing dish, thoroughly combine the mustard, olive oil, lemon, salt, pepper and dill. Drizzle this mixture over the vegetables in the salad bowl.
Serve topped with ripe olives and enjoy!

# 584. Stuffed Peppers with Tuna and Cottage Cheese

**(Ready in about 25 minutes | Servings 4)**

**Per serving: 273 Calories; 13.9g Fat; 5.1g Carbs; 28.9g Protein;**

## INGREDIENTS

4 bell peppers
10 ounces canned tuna, drained
1 yellow onion, finely chopped
1 garlic clove, smashed
1/3 cup mayonnaise

1/3 cup Kalamata olives, pitted and chopped
Sea salt and cayenne pepper, to taste
1/2 teaspoon dried parsley
1/2 teaspoon dried oregano
1 cup Cottage cheese

## DIRECTIONS

Start by preheating your oven to broil. Arrange the bell peppers on a baking sheet; broil for 6 minutes, turning the peppers once; make sure to rotate the baking sheet once or twice.
Once the peppers are cool enough to handle, cut them in half; remove the seeds and membranes.
In a mixing bowl, thoroughly combine the tuna, onion, garlic, mayonnaise, olives, salt, cayenne pepper, dried parsley, oregano and Cottage cheese.
Now, fill the peppers with the tuna mixture. Bake the stuffed peppers in the oven for 10 minutes or until thoroughly heated. Serve warm or at room temperature. Enjoy!

## 585. Fish Steaks with Cauliflower

**(Ready in about 25 minutes | Servings 4)**

**Per serving: 508 Calories; 22.9g Fat; 4.7g Carbs; 68.6g Protein;**

### INGREDIENTS

1 head of cauliflower, broken into florets
2 tablespoons olive oil
Sea salt and ground black pepper, to taste
1 cup Colby cheese, shredded
4 halibut steaks

1/2 teaspoon dried sage
1/2 teaspoon dried basil
1 ½ tablespoons fresh parsley, chopped
1 lemon, cut into wedges

### DIRECTIONS

Begin by preheating your oven to 390 degrees F.
Cook the cauliflower in a pot of lightly salted water until just tender.
Transfer to a well-greased casserole dish. Drizzle with 1 tablespoon of olive oil. Season with salt and pepper to taste.
Scatter shredded cheese on top of the cauliflower; bake approximately 17 minutes.
In the meantime, heat the remaining tablespoon of olive oil in a pan that is preheated over a moderately high flame. Fry the halibut steaks until golden and crisp.
Season with sage, basil, salt, and pepper. Serve garnished with fresh parsley and lemon wedges. Bon appétit!

## 586. Smoked Bacon Fries

**(Ready in about 15 minutes | Servings 6)**

**Per serving: 409 Calories; 31.6g Fat; 1.1g Carbs; 28g Protein;**

### INGREDIENTS

1 pound smoked bacon, cut into small squares
1 teaspoon mustard seeds

1 tablespoon paprika

### DIRECTIONS

Preheat an oven to 360 degrees F.
Bake the smoked bacon for 12 to 15 minutes. Season with mustard seeds and paprika. Enjoy!

## 587. Yummy Sunday Mushrooms

**(Ready in about 10 minutes | Servings 4)**

**Per serving: 75 Calories; 5.2g Fat; 3.3g Carbs; 2.9g Protein;**

### INGREDIENTS

2 teaspoons olive oil
1 tablespoon butter
2 cloves garlic, minced

1 pound Portobello mushrooms, sliced
1 tablespoon soy sauce
Salt and pepper, to taste

### DIRECTIONS

Heat the oil and butter in a large skillet that is preheated over a moderate heat. Add the garlic and cook until aromatic, 30 seconds or so.
Stir in the mushrooms and cook them for 3 minutes, allowing them to caramelize.
Now, add the soy sauce, salt and pepper; cook for 4 minutes more or to the desired doneness. Enjoy!

# 588. Ricotta and Cilantro Balls

**(Ready in about 10 minutes + chilling time | Servings 6)**

**Per serving: 108 Calories; 9g Fat; 2.2g Carbs; 4.8g Protein;**

## INGREDIENTS

1 cup Ricotta cheese
3 tablespoons butter
1/4 teaspoon red wine vinegar

Salt and pepper, to taste
1/2 cup fresh cilantro, finely chopped

## DIRECTIONS

Blend all ingredients, except for the cilantro, in a food processor.
Place the mixture in the refrigerator for 3 hours.
Shape the mixture into 10 to 12 balls; roll them in the chopped cilantro until evenly coated. Serve with cocktail sticks and enjoy your party!

# 589. Chicken Wings with Salsa Roja

**(Ready in about 50 minutes | Servings 6)**

**Per serving: 236 Calories; 13.5g Fat; 6g Carbs; 19.4g Protein;**

## INGREDIENTS

12 chicken wings
Salt and pepper, to taste
For the Tomato Dip:
4 ripe tomatoes, crushed
1 onion, finely chopped

1 cup mango, peeled and chopped
1 teaspoon chili pepper, deveined and finely minced
2 heaping tablespoons cilantro, finely chopped
2 tablespoons lime juice

## DIRECTIONS

Start by preheating your oven to 400 degrees F. Set a wire rack inside a rimmed baking sheet.
Season the chicken wings with salt and pepper. Bake the wings approximately 45 minutes or until the skin is crispy.
Then, thoroughly combine all ingredients for the tomato dip. Place in your refrigerator until ready to serve.

# 590. Hot Tuna Eggs

**(Ready in about 20 minutes | Servings 6)**

**Per serving: 203 Calories; 13.3g Fat; 3.8g Carbs; 17.2g Protein;**

## INGREDIENTS

12 eggs
1/3 cup mayonnaise
1 can tuna in spring water, drained
1/2 teaspoon smoked cayenne pepper

1/4 teaspoon fresh or dried dill weed
2 pickled jalapenos, minced
Salt and black pepper, to taste

## DIRECTIONS

Place the eggs in a wide pot; cover with cold water by 1 inch. Bring to a rapid boil.
Decrease the heat to medium-low; let them simmer an additional 10 minutes.
Peel the eggs and rinse them under running water.
Slice each egg in half lengthwise and remove the yolks. Thoroughly combine the yolks with the remaining ingredients.
Divide the mixture among the egg whites and arrange the deviled eggs on a nice serving platter. Enjoy!

## 591. Ricotta and Chorizo Balls

**(Ready in about 15 minutes + chilling time | Servings 5)**

**Per serving: 327 Calories; 25.7g Fat; 6.4g Carbs; 17g Protein;**

### INGREDIENTS

10 ounces chorizo, chopped
10 ounces Ricotta cheese, softened
1/4 cup mayonnaise

1/2 teaspoon deli mustard
2 teaspoons tomato paste
8 Kalamata olives, pitted

### DIRECTIONS

Heat up a skillet over a moderate flame. Now, cook the chorizo until well browned. Transfer it to a mixing bowl.
Add the remaining ingredients and transfer to your refrigerator until it is well chilled. Bon appétit!

## 592. Icy Almond and Cocoa Dessert

**(Ready in about 10 minutes + chilling time | Servings 6)**

**Per serving: 84 Calories; 8.9g Fat; 1.5g Carbs; 0.8g Protein;**

### INGREDIENTS

1/2 stick butter, melted
1/2 teaspoon vanilla paste
10 drops liquid stevia

2 tablespoons cocoa powder
2 tablespoons almonds, chopped

### DIRECTIONS

Melt the butter, vanilla paste, and liquid stevia in a pan that is preheated over a moderate heat.
Stir in the cocoa powder and stir well to combine.
Spoon the mixture into 12 molds of a silicone candy mold tray. Scatter the chopped almonds on top. Freeze until set. Enjoy!

## 593. Coconut and Chocolate Truffles

**(Ready in about 15 minutes + chilling time | Servings 16)**

**Per serving: 90 Calories; 6.3g Fat; 4.9g Carbs; 3.7g Protein;**

### INGREDIENTS

1 ½ cups bittersweet chocolate, sugar-free, broken into chunks
4 tablespoons coconut, desiccated
1/2 stick butter
1 cup double cream
3 tablespoons xylitol
1/2 teaspoon pure almond extract

1 teaspoon vanilla paste
A pinch of salt
A pinch of freshly grated nutmeg
1 tablespoon cognac
1/4 cup unsweetened Dutch-processed cocoa powder

### DIRECTIONS

Thoroughly combine the chocolate, coconut, butter, double cream, xylitol, almond extract, vanilla, salt, and grated nutmeg.
Microwave for 1 minute on medium-high; let it cool slightly. Now, stir in the cognac and vanilla.
Place in your refrigerator for 2 hours. Shape the mixture into balls; roll each ball in the cocoa powder and enjoy!

## 594. Coconut and Espresso Delight

**(Ready in about 10 minutes + chilling time | Servings 6)**

**Per serving: 218 Calories; 24.7g Fat; 1.1g Carbs; 0.4g Protein;**

### INGREDIENTS

4 ounces coconut oil
4 ounces coconut cream
2 teaspoons butter, softened
1 teaspoon instant espresso powder

3 tablespoons confectioners Swerve
A pinch of salt
1 teaspoon pure vanilla extract

### DIRECTIONS

Melt the coconut oil in a double boiler over medium-low heat.
Add the remaining ingredients. Remove from the heat; stir until everything is well combined.
Pour into a silicone mold and freeze overnight. Bon appétit!

## 595. Orange and Chocolate Mousse

**(Ready in about 15 minutes | Servings 4)**

**Per serving: 154 Calories; 13g Fat; 6.3g Carbs; 5.3g Protein;**

### INGREDIENTS

2 egg yolks
3/4 cup heavy cream
3 ounces Ricotta cheese, at room temperature
1 tablespoon freshly squeezed orange juice

1 ½ teaspoons orange zest
1/2 teaspoon ground cinnamon
1/4 cup granulated stevia erythritol blend
1/4 cup unsweetened cocoa powder

### DIRECTIONS

Beat the egg yolks with your electric mixer until thick and pale.
Heat the cream in a pan over medium heat. Gradually stir the hot cream into the egg yolk mixture.
Turn the heat to low and cook for about 5 minutes, stirring constantly, until your mixture is thickened.
Now, beat the remaining ingredients with your electric mixer until everything is creamy.
Fold this mixture into cream mixture and serve well chilled.

## 596. Yummy Chocolate Cubes

**(Ready in about 25 minutes + chilling time | Servings 10)**

**Per serving: 119 Calories; 11.7g Fat; 5.2g Carbs; 1.1g Protein;**

### INGREDIENTS

1/2 cup coconut flour
1 cup almond flour
2 packets stevia
1/4 teaspoon cardamom
1/2 teaspoon star anise, ground
1/2 teaspoon coconut extract

1 teaspoon pure vanilla extract
1 tablespoon rum
A pinch of table salt
1/2 stick butter, cold
1 ½ cups double cream
8 ounces bittersweet chocolate chips, sugar-free

### DIRECTIONS

Preheat an oven to 330 degrees F. Now, line a baking dish with parchment paper.
Add the flour, stevia, cardamom, anise, coconut extract, vanilla extract, rum and salt to your food processor. Blitz until everything is well combined.
Cut in the cold butter and process to combine again.
Press the batter into the bottom of the prepared baking dish. Bake about 13 minutes; transfer to a wire rack to cool slightly.
To make the filling, bring the double cream to a simmer in a pan. Add the chocolate and whisk until uniform. Spread over the crust; cut into squares and serve well-chilled. Enjoy!

# 597. Coconut Apple Cobbler

**(Ready in about 30 minutes | Servings 8)**

**Per serving: 152 Calories; 11.8g Fat; 6.2g Carbs; 2.5g Protein;**

## INGREDIENTS

2 ½ cups apples, cored and sliced
1/2 tablespoon fresh lemon juice
1/3 teaspoon xanthan gum
1 cup almond flour

1/4 cup coconut flour
3/4 cup xylitol
2 eggs, whisked
5 tablespoons coconut oil, melted

## DIRECTIONS

Start by preheating your oven to 360 degrees F. Lightly grease a baking dish with a nonstick cooking spray.
Arrange the apples on the bottom of the baking dish. Drizzle with lemon juice and xanthan gum.
Then, in a mixing bowl, mix the flour with xylitol and eggs until the mixture resembles coarse meal. Spread this mixture over the apples.
Drizzle coconut oil over topping. Bake for 25 minutes or until dough rises. Bon appétit!

# 598. Refreshing Keto Frappe Dessert

**(Ready in about 2 hours | Servings 2)**

**Per serving: 371 Calories; 37.8g Fat; 7.1g Carbs; 3.4g Protein;**

## INGREDIENTS

2 teaspoons instant coffee
4 drops liquid Stevia
1 tablespoon cacao butter
1/4 cup cold water

16 raspberries, frozen
1 cup almond milk
2 tablespoons coconut whipped cream

## DIRECTIONS

Combine the instant coffee, Stevia, cacao butter and cold water. Shake with a drink mixer for 20 seconds.
Place the frozen raspberries in dessert glasses. Pour the coffee mixture over it. Add the almond milk and ice cubes, if desired.
Now, freeze for at least 2 hours or until firm. Serve topped with coconut whipped cream. Enjoy!

# 599. Simple Almond Fudge

**(Ready in about 3 hours | Servings 8)**

**Per serving: 180 Calories; 18.3g Fat; 4.5g Carbs; 1g Protein;**

## INGREDIENTS

3/4 cup almond butter, sugar-free, preferably homemade
1 stick butter
1/3 cup coconut milk
1/4 cup xylitol
1/8 teaspoon salt

1/8 teaspoon grated nutmeg
3 tablespoons xylitol
3 tablespoons butter, melted
1 teaspoon vanilla essence
3 tablespoons cocoa powder

## DIRECTIONS

Microwave the almond butter and regular butter until they melt.
Add the coconut milk, 1/4 cup xylitol, salt, and nutmeg; stir to combine well and press into a well-greased glass baking dish.
Refrigerate for 2 to 3 hours or until set.
In a mixing bowl, make the sauce by whisking 3 tablespoons xylitol, 3 tablespoons of butter melted, vanilla essence and cocoa powder.
Spread the sauce over your fudge. Cut into squares and store in an airtight container.

# 600. Easy Peanut Ice Cream

**(Ready in about 10 minutes + chilling time | Servings 4)**

**Per serving: 305 Calories; 18.3g Fat; 4.5g Carbs; 1g Protein;**

## INGREDIENTS

1 ¼ cups almond milk

1/3 cup whipped cream

17 drops liquid stevia

1/2 cup peanuts, chopped

1/2 teaspoon xanthan gum

## DIRECTIONS

Combine all of the above ingredients, except for the xanthan gum, with an electric mixer.

Now, stir in the xanthan gum, whisking constantly, until the mixture is thick.

Then, prepare your ice cream in a machine following the manufacturer's instructions.

Serve directly from the machine or store in your freezer.

Made in the USA
San Bernardino, CA
21 July 2019